The Nashville Way

THE NASHVILLE WAY

Racial Etiquette and the Struggle
for Social Justice in a Southern City

BENJAMIN HOUSTON

The University of Georgia Press   *Athens and London*

© 2012 by the University of Georgia Press
Athens, Georgia 30602
www.ugapress.org
All rights reserved
Set in Minion Pro by
   Graphic Composition, Inc., Bogart, Georgia
Manufactured by Thomson-Shore

The paper in this book meets the guidelines for
permanence and durability of the Committee on
Production Guidelines for Book Longevity of the
Council on Library Resources.

Printed in the United States of America
16 15 14 13 12 P 5 4 3 2 1

Library of Congress Cataloging-in-Publication Data

Houston, Benjamin.
The Nashville way : racial etiquette and the struggle
for social justice in a southern city /
Benjamin Houston.
p. cm. — (Politics and culture in the twentieth-century South)
Includes bibliographical references and index.
ISBN-13: 978-0-8203-4326-6 (hardcover : alk. paper)
ISBN-10: 0-8203-4326-9 (hardcover : alk. paper)
ISBN-13: 978-0-8203-4327-3 (pbk. : alk. paper)
ISBN-10: 0-8203-4327-7 (pbk. : alk. paper)
1. Nashville (Tenn.)—Race relations. 2. African Americans—
Tennessee—Nashville. I. Title.
F444.N29N44 2012
305.896'076855—dc23   2012008404

British Library Cataloging-in-Publication Data available

TO

ROBERT J. HOUSTON

AND

EVELYN YURCISIN HOUSTON

CONTENTS

ACKNOWLEDGMENTS

This book has been with me for a long time and through a lot of changes. There are tons of people to thank, personally and professionally.

I gratefully acknowledge the financial support that underwrote major parts of the research and writing of this book. The McLaughlin Grant from the College of Liberal Arts and Sciences, University of Florida, was absolutely critical in providing a summer of intensive research in Nashville. A Dissertation Writing Fellowship from the Louisville Institute was similarly significant in allowing concentrated energy and attention to completing the first draft. Smaller but valuable grants from the Southern Baptist Library and Archives, Emory University, and Georgia State University, plus the John F. Kennedy and Lyndon B. Johnson presidential libraries, permitted me to explore important research angles. The Center for Africanamerican Urban Studies and the Economy (CAUSE) at Carnegie Mellon University generously supported my ongoing research agenda, as has Newcastle University. I also thank folks at Edinburgh, Sunderland, and Cambridge Universities for chances to present my work and talk through my findings. Similarly, I'm grateful to the staff and fellows at Harvard University's W. E. B. Du Bois Institute, sponsor of the National Endowment for the Humanities' Summer Institute on civil rights, for a month of intensive thinking and study. All created tremendous opportunities for me.

I would also like to acknowledge those in Nashville who were incredibly supportive. George Barrett welcomed me with dozens of stories and insights, and I thank him for his boundless generosity (and for the cigars). Don Doyle and Marjorie Spruill graciously opened their home during a summer of research, making an immense difference during my Nashville jaunt. Pete Kuryla and Bob Hutton were especially fantastic in welcoming me to the city, talking shop and hilarious nonsense in equally entertaining measure. And I am most appreciative of those who were agreeable to being interviewed or pointed me in new directions. Similarly, I cannot thank enough all the fantastic archivists who rolled up their sleeves and helped a rookie researcher immerse myself in Nashville's documentation. I particularly am grateful to Kathy Smith and Teresa Gray at Vanderbilt, Beth Howse at Fisk, Ken Fieth at the Nashville Metro Archives, Kathy Bennett and Sue Loper at the Nashville Public Library, and Chris Harter at Amistad Research Center. Beth Odle at the Nashville Public Library was particularly patient in helping me find the right photos for this book.

In direct and indirect ways, the driving interest in this book first stirred at Rhodes College. Tim Huebner saw something and worked indefatigably for my sake more than his, and I thank him for the belief. Russ Wigginton gave me a first peek at the civil rights movement; he and Doug Hatfield gave sage advice freely. Even before that, I carried a bit of Paul Hammock's and Doreen Uhas-Sauer's influence on me wherever I went, and still do—thank you for what you did. As a dissertation, this project was birthed at the History Department at the University of Florida, where I had the great fortune of working with great people and scholar-teachers. Julian Pleasants is a good man and had my back in a number of ways. Roberta Peacock looked after me in many different ways. Bert Wyatt-Brown, Fitz Brundage, and Jack Davis were very good role models for me in various ways, and I thank them for their energy and support. And special thanks especially to mate and tireless mentor, Brian Ward.

I'm also grateful for all the UF gang: Jenny, Jace and Shannon, Craig and Amanda, Sonya and Barclay, Carmen, Bud and Theodora, Jason, Mike, Tim, Kristin, Randall, Kim, Bryan, Dave, and Chris—good times and fine people all the way around. Alan and Lynn were exceptional for their wisdom, caring, and hilarity, and triple thanks to Barclay for enduring all those damn e-mails. Professionally, I would also like to mention Wesley Hogan, Tony Badger, Ray Arsenault, Jane Dailey, Mike Foley, Bill Link, Ellie Shermer, Mike Ezra, Clive Webb, George Lewis and Liz Gritter for advice and good sense in varied capacities, as well as the good folks at the University of Georgia Press.

Working at the Carnegie Mellon's Center for Africanamerican Urban Studies and the Economy was a tremendous first job. Thanks go to Joe Trotter, a fine man and consummate professional who taught me a lot. I'm also grateful to Tera Hunter, Johanna Fernandez, Edda Fields-Black, John Soluri, Nancy Aronson, Allen Hahn, and Jared Day for welcoming me to the school and the profession. Similar thanks go to Kevin, Russell, Lisa, and the rest of the graduate students for their cheerful energy, with special appreciation to Kate Chilton and Alex Bennett for able research assistance. Lisa Hazirjian and Derek Musgrove were especially splendid comrades/colleagues/friends and, in the case of "Gee, Derek," a sorry excuse for a beer drinker but a very fine voicemail leaver.

Shifting across the pond to teach in England has landed me among a lot of amazing people. Hot-water bottles were just the start from Martin Dusinberre, but now that I've thanked him in print, I can stop checking my phone and he can stop killing me in squash. Saying thank you is simply inadequate for Joe Street, Martin F., Felix, Xavier, Asuka, Susan-Mary, Carolyn, Lorenzo, Matt, Monica, Alex, Sam, Claudia, Joan, Tim, Samiksha, Di, Kate, Mike, David, and Scott, but I hope they know that I mean it. Thanks also to the Friday footy crew for enduring my sad attempts at being a striker and for the ales afterward. Now that the book is done, I can safely exhort: "Long live Big W"!

On a more personal note: thanks to Melanie Sylvan, Heather Sebring, Andrew Vlahutin, Christine Leong, B.J. and Andrea Yurcisin, and Brandon and Trudy Barr for letting me crash on sofas during various research trips and always being there, in so many rich and amazing ways. Thanks for reminding me where I came from and where I could go. Much love to Nikolai and Ellen, who more than anyone can keep me balanced (and I'm sorry about the printer), and to Lori for the e-mails, laughter, and moral support. This book is dedicated to Robert J. Houston and Evelyn Yurcisin Houston, my parents. Both of them taught me about history in very different but hugely important ways. Their sustenance and love was manifested every day in a thousand large and small examples.

And finally: Michelle. It's not just any person who on any given day can and will proofread my chapters, give me a yoga lesson, help me thrash out ideas over a pint, or bring me countless cups of coffee as I furiously pound away on a keyboard. That's just a fraction of what she does. Yet, who she is, and what she has brought to my life, is even more luminous.

The Nashville Way

These aberrations are kept going more by unwritten and un-writable laws than by the written law affecting the races: by an immense and elaborate code of etiquette that governs their daily relations; by an exquisite and intuitive tact on the part of both whites and Negroes; by adherence to a labyrinthine code of manners, taboos and conventions. There is therefore a sense of strain in the air, of a delicately poised equilibrium of forces held in leash. Here men toss uneasily at night, and awake fatigued in the morning.
—David L. Cohn, "How the South Feels," 1944

Among all the vivid examples of Jim Crow–style segregation in the South, some of the ugliest were the stark WHITE and COLORED signs paired with shiny or shabby restrooms and water fountains. As powerful symbols of the racial divide, these markers were all the more chilling for being so casual. And yet, for someone strolling through downtown Nashville in the 1940s, those signs were not always there, forcing the visitor to chart a far more bewildering path. No WHITE or COLORED designations adorned the restrooms in the state capitol, for example. Nor were there any in the post office, where both races waited in line together—although the watchful eye would note that black postal employees always worked in the back room under white supervision but never at the service window.[1]

Walking through the city-county building downtown, however, yielded mixed messages. The upper floor did have segregated restrooms, but no one bothered to ensure that people obeyed the mandate. The first floor instead had what used to be a COLORED sign, painted over because of a lack of white facilities, alongside a water fountain used by both races. Similarly, in one railway station where some whites worked side by side with blacks, the restrooms were segregated but "similarly equipped" and a common water fountain served both races. At the customs house, the COLORED restroom for black employees was considered well-appointed despite being segregated—but the *public* restrooms and water fountains were used by both races. For audiences at the city auditorium, the color line switched invisibly depending on the crowd: sometimes blacks were relegated to balconies, but other times both floors were divided, with the poorer of both races up in the cheaper seats. And while Nashville courtrooms did not have racially designated seating, "Negroes always discreetly leave a foot or more of space between themselves and whites."[2]

In myriad ways, an important aspect of race's legacy in modern U.S. history is how space and place were preserved or rearranged by whites and African Americans in large and small dimensions. As both races went about their lives, the South's social dynamics loomed conspicuously in even the most routine interracial interaction. In a Nashville courtroom, the quiet use of gaps between people seated on a bench had far deeper meaning as an expression of social distance. But, on a vaster scale, the molding of various spaces into black and white neighborhoods told equally important stories about how economic and political clout constructed laws and public policies that shaped and reflected the social dynamics of Nashville.

This book is an account of how two races in one city, with a shared history yet divergent paths, utilized and fought over social and physical space in diverse ways. Within that story is a bigger tale about the urban South most immediately, U.S. history more generally, and particularly how racial legacies remain in the present. Even as the turbulent years of the modern civil-rights era altered laws and customs, the patterns of segregation, in reforming, retained resonance with the past.

It may seem surprising that Nashville's story is at least somewhat analogous with other southern—and, indeed, U.S.—places given that Nashville boosters relentlessly conveyed a sense of the city's uniqueness, often in cheery nicknames. For example, "The Rock City" derived from its perch atop graceful limestone cliffs with the Cumberland River meandering through the gentle hilly landscape of middle Tennessee below. "The Protestant Vatican" invokes Nashville's religiosity, as the city to this day has numerous churches and headquarters several major denominational institutions. Similarly, "The Athens of the South" refers to the city's seventeen colleges and universities, many of them religiously affiliated, and locals even built a full-scale replica of the Parthenon in homage to this appellation. "The Wall Street of the South" tips a hat to the banks and insurance companies responsible for Nashville's prosperity. Taken together, these appellations epitomized Nashville's religious, educated, and white-collar character. More recently, "Music City, U.S.A." acknowledges Nashville's heritage in fostering and capitalizing on the rich tradition of country music.

Because Nashville's elite had such fervent pride in the city's image, it was startling when someone tried to puncture these affectations. This happened in July 1945 when white Nashville educator J. E. Windrow addressed the Kiwanis Club and lauded Nashville as "the ideal city" and the "queen city of culture," with "all the ingredients of civilized society," where "at last is found man at his best." But Windrow immediately deflated these glowing plaudits with a lengthy list of Nashville's problems: the smoke smothering the city skyline, the "civil lethargy" represented by voter apathy, the "staggering death rate" of tuberculosis victims, and assorted social ills such as high venereal disease rates, infestations of flea-ridden rats, inadequate garbage collection, juvenile delinquency, and poor housing, sanitation, and sewage. Disgusted with the inaction of Nashville's professors and civic clubs in confronting such problems, Windrow chided those who "buried their heads in the sands of the magnolia-scented past."[3]

Windrow's critique suggested that Nashville's slogans give only superficial glimpses into the city's character. Many stress instead that understanding Nashville requires grasping the city's inherent paradoxes. One observer, traveling through Tennessee in 1962, noted that "It is difficult to believe one state can have such different 'moods.'" Nashville personified this as the capital city in the middle of a state adjoining eight others. The city stood geographically at a crossroads roughly equidistant between border and Deep South, and likewise between the cool rugged mountains around Chattanooga and the flat scorching Delta surrounding Memphis. One historian and resident of the city used the same term in writing that Nashville is "as much a mood as it is a place," as it commingled remnants of a self-professed "genteel Old South" and "reminders of a Confederate heritage" with the "bustle of a New South commercial town," the bawdiness of a river city and the fundamentalist roots of a religious center, an urban lifestyle and the homespun country values of rural people tied to the land. As the city's elites built the trappings of a major urban center (sophisticated political leadership, art galleries, a symphony, renowned institutions of higher education, reputable newspapers), rural migrants of both races from surrounding counties in Middle Tennessee, South Kentucky, and North Alabama flocked to Nashville, searching for more lucrative work or more fun in hardscrabble lives. Even Nashville's fledgling country music scene grew from uncertain parenthood, mixing sharecropper's blues migrating east from Memphis with Appalachian folk music filtering west. Never mind that Nashville's best citizens sniffed haughtily at the unwashed crowds who littered outside fine churches before cramming into the pews of a hillbilly show called the Grand Ole Opry. The city housed all these paradoxes and more; anyone looking to comprehend Nashville's history must hold these tensions in place—rural and urban, polished elites and gritty common folk, a backward-looking past and a forward-looking gaze—to discern the city's character.[4]

When Windrow spoke in 1945, he addressed changing political shifts in the city. But the internal contradictions he identified were especially apparent as Nashville grappled with tumultuous racial issues during the post–World War II era. Here, too, another slogan, "The Nashville Way," captured the self-professed style of Tennessee's capital city, where pride, provincialism, and paternalism melded in powerful ways. Nashville's boosters trumpeted amicable race relations as a city virtue and recourse to catch-phrase characterization was tempting. "In Nashville, we don't have race relations, we have human relations!" Mayor Ben West crowed in the 1950s. "Nashville's segregation," remembered local white journalist David Halberstam, "was largely of a soft kind, administered, it sometimes seemed, not with the passion of angry racist officials, but more as a cultural leftover from the past."[5]

In the vernacular of the time, Nashville was a *moderate* city. Even those casually familiar with the dynamics of southern race relations will recognize this word and its synonyms *civil, progressive, genteel,* and *respectable,* all used widely throughout the South. Traditionally, these words were all different hues of the same color; they corresponded to an upper-class emphasis on manners, decorum, and a hypersensitive avoidance of civic unrest. Moderation meant a more or less genuine sympathy for black advancement undergirded by deeply felt assumptions of black inferiority and white superiority. This combination, taken for granted by white southerners in the mid-twentieth century, remained so deeply ingrained that it barely needed conscious consideration or even acknowledgment. As historian William Chafe puts it precisely, it was "a paternalism so unconscious it would never be called such by whites." *Moderation* was used frequently to depict a racial stance that positioned itself between sweeping declarations of vicious racism and the sanctioning of racial equality, defining itself against extremism rather than for a particular racial philosophy. Thus the moderate philosophy had no internal cohesion in steering between two powerful poles of racial thinking: avoiding the vituperative racism of hard-core segregationists, but often equally skeptical about southern racial progressives. Essentially, moderates *were* segregationists—segregation was, after all, what they had been raised on, taught, and acculturated to, and the prospect of an integrated society confounded their imagination—but the style with which they professed their racial superiority differed from other whites.[6]

For black southerners, who knew more about the agonies of segregation than whites ever could, moderation was empty and self-serving rhetoric, and black Nashvillians especially knew better than to accept local platitudes about race. Local observers dismissed the collective back-patting of white moderates as superficial, noting that "[Nashville's white] citizens are constantly under the temptation to glory in the past when present problems seem too much for them." They saw moderate discussions, even those under the auspices of interracial cooperation, as rarely yielding concrete or significant change. Instead, "the tendency is to talk over local problems so much that we think we talk them out of existence." The irony was that Nashville's black community, despite segregated realities, were fundamental to the qualities that white Nashville took such pride in: the prominent African American colleges and universities in Nashville were part of the "Athens of the South," black banks and businesses were a small but notable component of the "Wall Street of the South," and black religious institutions part of the "Protestant Vatican." These black institutions cultivated resultant values among African Americans in Nashville in much the same way that white Nashville did.[7]

It is significant, then, that there was an identifiable black "Nashville Way" that looms prominently in civil rights movement history—as movement veteran John Lewis later recalled, "something happened in Nashville that did not happen any other place in America." In 1960, as lunch-counter sit-ins swept the South, Nashvillians found their city home to a unique cohort of demonstrators, most from elsewhere but uniquely incubated in this environment. Perhaps more than any other cluster of civil rights activists, this Nashville-based group fused African American religious tradition with a number of different intellectual influences in absorbing the philosophy and meaning behind nonviolent direct action and adopting it as a way of life rather than as a mere tactic. Thus emboldened, these Nashvillians later played crucial roles in founding the Student Nonviolent Coordinating Committee (SNCC), rescuing the 1961 Freedom Rides, and participating in virtually every major subsequent southern battle of the movement, including those in Jackson, Birmingham, and Selma. Although the absolute quality inherent in this conception of the movement's possibilities frequently jarred with more pragmatically inclined civil rights veterans, the Nashvillians comprised, in many ways, both the literal and figurative soul of this phase of the black freedom struggle. The 1960 sit-ins began in other states, argues activist C. T. Vivian, "but the Movement began here in Nashville."[8]

Thus more paradoxes: the carefully mannered representative politeness of the white Nashville Way and the uniquely daring, radical, and transformative possibilities of the black Nashville Way both sprang from the same city. This book attempts to explore both Nashville Ways, their origins and trajectories, and the results when the two clashed. Both ways were styles of belief and action that shed light on southern urban racial dynamics during the civil rights era. All the self-clichés about white Nashville's culture and pretensions of mannered graciousness, the self-image as a city that retained the finest aspects of the Old South's "magnolia-scented past" while adapting to the best elements of progress and change, signaled the unspoken belief that race relations could be managed, that the Southern Way of Life could adapt without sacrificing core elements. The laid-back political and business climate in white Nashville made for a functional approach to race relations that begrudgingly dealt with immediate conflicts while resisting structural, functional, and comprehensive change. And, by claiming Nashville as a good city for black people, white Nashvillians were able to downplay and deemphasize civic issues that had profound racial implications for the city. Conversely, the unusual example of nonviolence in Nashville highlights longer trends within black Nashville, as African Americans sought refuge in the same virtues of civic pride and personal respectability while still challenging white Nashvillians to match moderate rhetoric with substantive action. That internal tensions within the black community, much like the white, dictated the course of racial activism was another critical part of the story. Thus some shared values smoothed over what was a deeper racial reality of constant contentiousness between and within the races. This tension between Nashville's rhetoric and Nashville's actions—and how integration did or did not occur across the city—is the core theme of this book.

The Nashville Way argues that both civil rights activism and white responses to battles over jobs and public accommodations sprang from the elaborate racial etiquette of the Jim Crow past and were updated according to new circumstances decades later. This etiquette simultaneously provided whites with self-justification for their racial beliefs while channeling black resistance. But a combination of legal and political maneuvers in the mid-1950s, responding to movement endeavors and accelerating throughout the 1960s, changed the rules. Whether by explicit design or benign indifference, this maneuvering remapped the spatial layout of the city so that race and class remained deeply encoded in the physical layout of the city. To be sure, this had happened consistently throughout the twentieth century as neighborhoods around the city changed racial demographics according to the demands of white businesses and politicians. It was not only a case of white flight to suburbs, although that happened in droves, but a combination of city policies that directly targeted black neighborhoods and institutions where movement activism had flourished. As the racial etiquette of the first half of the century was meant to preserve social hierarchies in the spaces where the races interacted, so did the second half of the century see whites dictating the same in terms of the city's physical design to preclude that sort of interaction. Both were meant to reinforce black economic dependence on whites. Whites reshaped urban space as the blacks, however fitfully, began to break out of their "place"; despite the change in etiquette, the structural dimensions of segregation were reinforced in analogous ways.

These conflicts between rhetoric and action, racial law and racial custom, space and place, were just some of the tensions embedded in the Jim Crow racial order before this book begins. Nashville's racial culture drew directly from the wider socioeconomic makeup of the city, but this was part of an ongoing reality that most urban U.S. locales during the twentieth century were struggling between traditional and progressive impulses more broadly in negotiating shifting economic contexts. By 1945, Nashville was a major city regionally, although less so nationally, lagging behind Atlanta and Birmingham in attracting industry. Instead, the local economy depended on shipping and distribution businesses plus local banking and insurance companies that were regional powerhouses. Conservative mentalities governed white businessmen in these years, especially with a distinctive laggardly attitude toward interfering in political and social affairs, and racial matters in particular.[9]

While white Nashville was happy to make its peace with the New South in economic terms, its conservatism aligned naturally with a cultural harkening back to the Old South. If Atlanta was "the city too busy to hate," Nashville may well have termed itself "the city too well-bred to hate." Like Atlanta's motto, that was Nashville's white lie, even though it spoke to a certain attitude that was historically rooted. But this lie not only obscured the hateful behavior of many in the city, it also soft-pedaled the reality that racism could be driven by attitudes other than mere hatred. Jim Crow had been designed to force African Americans to stage public deference to supposed white superiority. When that insufficiently cowed black resistance, segregation was shored up with repressive racial laws so as to normalize white supremacy publicly in daily life as an added insult to the economic subjugation and violent repression of African Americans. Indeed, at the time, segregation was considered a quite progressive measure that hoped to tame violent racial passions into an orderly disaggregating of racial privilege, particularly in cities where racial interaction was frequent.

But African Americans in Nashville did not stand for mere flattery. By World War II, even as segregation's cultural hold powerfully controlled the white mind, there were some signs of erosion elsewhere. Nashville's downtown and underworld were realms where racial interaction occurred in uncertain ways, often weakly or shamefully defended by whites or not at all. Connections between black and white Nashville existed in business and politics—never on an equal plane but, in those connecting places, the racial etiquette of the past held sway. As John W. Cell pointed out, "Jim Crow was a city slicker"—the etiquette was built to preserve distinctions in these realms of racial intersections. Segregated life in Nashville built diverse black populations that fought this etiquette as well as more tangible battles against segregation simultaneously in individual and collective ways. Even as African Americans shrewdly learned to play the game of racial etiquette according to different rules by trading off opportunities for individual survival, the game was still rigged to reaffirm the broader system of segregation and allow whites to luxuriate in their false sense of racial superiority.[10]

This contradiction is captured as chapter 1 surveys the social and political dynamics of Nashville from the late 1930s into the mid-1950s, when racial etiquette had a fluid yet formidable hold on Nashville. The chapter endeavors to capture the lived reality for both whites and blacks in one segregated society. It emphasizes both the racial etiquette that governed the behavior of both races, as well as the spatial layout of the city's urban segregation patterns, in order to give a full picture of life under Jim Crow. Chapter 1 also introduces some personalities key to Nashville's history to show how these figures represented networks of interracial progressives and white conservatives contesting each other over racial issues. All these elements form crucial context for understanding the racial fissures that subsequently develop.

As various versions of grassroots activism in Nashville blossomed into a full-scale movement, black Nashvillians fought segregated mentalities directly in the struggle over public education and public accommodations, along with scores of other battles for better employment opportunities, enhanced voting power, and access to social, political, and economic equality. Chapter 2 is an account of public school desegregation in Nashville during the mid- and late 1950s, the process of which yielded "The Nashville Plan," a model for other southern communities. The chapter focuses particularly on how self-proclaimed white moderates struggled with, and ultimately largely succeeded in, dictating the terms and pace of school desegregation.

After white moderates controlled school desegregation, the local movement had its most triumphant achievement during the 1960 lunch-counter sit-ins explored in chapter 3. Here, diverse tactics and personalities harmonized in pursuit of a common goal by playing directly on the hypocrisies and distortions of Nashville's racial etiquette and making Nashville a different model, now one that showcased the possibilities of disciplined nonviolent direct action. But equally importantly, the sit-ins forged a collectivity in black Nashville that would not be duplicated thereafter. Perhaps more importantly, beyond the stirring moral call of nonviolence and the militancy in seeing nonviolence as a way of life, the campaign united and directed the political and economic power of black Nashville—significant enough to be compelling—toward a single target.

This exceptional moment, and the following battles that continued throughout the 1960s, resulted in unrelenting and constant violent outbursts meant to thwart movement ambitions on a level that few accounts in Nashville then and now dared to acknowledge openly. Chapter 4 brings the themes of chapters 2 and 3 together in surveying ongoing civil rights struggles up to the mid-1960s as activists struggled to extend the lessons and possibilities of the lunch-counter sit-ins into other arenas. Subtle changes in white resistance, continued attempts to sustain the movement, and detailed patterns of how desegregation actually occurred show the mixed results of racial change in these years. The outbursts on some level were acknowledgment that blacks were no longer following the script and that the racial etiquette of the past was fading. Slowly chipping away, the movement scored some victories in the downtown spaces where whites were vulnerable. Other realms such as employment or social clubs were far harder, as whites had little compelling reason to share social space or hierarchy with blacks. But with these developments came a reframing of rhetoric and values from whites besieged by black activism. Whether couched in the usual terms of "freedom of association" and "color blindness," whites tried to use legal and social norms to mask the consistent violence on Nashville streets, to change the conversation to a more elevated tone, and to retain some control over a situation unsettled by African American activism.

Chapter 5 is based on a racial disturbance nominally triggered by Black Power advocate Stokely Carmichael's visit to the city in April 1967, but also depicts how broader issues of class and generational differences pulled factions apart as the city continued desegregating unevenly and uneasily. As the 1960s continued, Black Power—which never had particularly vibrant and organized roots in Nashville despite its appeals—became an excuse for an era of racial politics where whites had new rationales for controlling and dominating black space while stigmatizing black standards. Along with these shifts in racial attitudes and rhetoric came applications of laws and public policies that not only defended against black activism but attacked it directly by targeting the places that had bred the activism. In the Black Power years, a new cohort of black student activists staged symbolic confrontations similar to those in 1960 but according to the new ethos of the era. This was, however, marginalized by the law and order compulsions of the white power structure and students dismissive of differing outlooks from Nashville's black elite. Yet, even as the black elite dampened Black Power spirit in the city, they found themselves vulnerable to wholesale changes that targeted the black economic power directly. How this occurred is treated in chapter 6 as battles over the building of Interstate 40, the local Model Cities program, and the issue of busing all factored into a reshaping of the city that preserved legacies of a racial past.

By knitting these episodes into a fuller analysis, *The Nashville Way* straddles and tries to merge several different scholarly conversations among historians of the urban South and civil rights movement. Such an approach is meant to meld the various historiographies into something more than the sum of isolated yet important themes and use the Nashville Ways to embody how both racial attitudes and racial policies molded the history of this era. This book readily falls within the genre of civil rights community studies, which favor in-depth portraits of individual cities to yield a fine-grained look at how both black activism and white resistance functioned and responded to each other. Like all types of historical scholarship, community studies have inherent strengths and drawbacks. They help provide a useful way to evaluate results—namely, the extent to which the movement spurred change. Focusing on one city also provides the chance to render the sheer range of issues and dynamics against which the movement struggled and to underscore the interplay between individual agency and broader forces. Above all else, this book was profoundly influenced and inspired by William Chafe's classic *Civilities and Civil Rights*, which described the progressive mystique that governed white moderate attitudes in Greensboro, North Carolina—an attitude synonymous with Nashville's moderation. My work extends Chafe's formulations by exploring the class dimensions inherent in moderate civilities, by underscoring the constancy of violence that undergirded those civilities, and by linking those attitudes to wider-scale use of legal means to buttress segregation.[11]

But, to fully render how the Nashville Ways operated, it was necessary to draw from other literatures. In particular, studies about the intricate etiquette that comprised elements of the Jim Crow–era South's racial culture gave insights that applied to the civil rights era when that etiquette was directly under siege. Numerous scholars have underscored how, from its inception, Jim Crow segregation was part of a defensive maneuvering on the part of whites who tried multiple cruel ways to control race relations (and thus political and economic power) as they faced African Americans who refused to surrender to such machinations. The parameters that these scholars trace in sketching how racial etiquette was inculcated, taught, and defended with unrelenting and targeted violence by whites against diverse forms of resistance from African Americans are important to depicting how white and black Nashvillians interpreted their own world.[12] But this book also connects to the post–Jim Crow South and the recent body of historical literature that joins suburban growth and urban changes with race to highlight how the Sunbelt politics of suburbanizing whites drove much of the political, economic, and social history of post–World War II America.[13] Those developments are also Nashville's. White supremacy was updated, moderated, and restrengthened across the South and indeed America, regardless of the "flavor" or "mood" of each place, precisely because of the persistence of movement activism. Place did matter, even as the universal pattern also held true.

Uniting these literatures is necessary to combine black and white realities into one narrative that can better highlight the fullest scope of segregation in U.S. life. My emphasis on southern racial etiquette is meant to depict how a racial culture was made, but, in doing so, I do not mean to downplay the reality that the segregated customs embedded in racial etiquette (however "soft," as Halberstam ascribed to Nashville) were only the most superficial and visible components to a far more abusive system. Indeed, Jim Crow was fundamentally brutal, violent, and exploitative in shadowing every aspect of southern life. This book is meant to highlight this enduring reality as the real legacy lurking underneath Nashville's self-promotional tendencies about matters of race.

Frequently people who lived through this era remark on how life was "totally segregated," as they try to capture the staggering weight of an entire society where racial divisions were stark, unrelenting, and powerfully informed individual destinies. But, even as that view of Nashville or any other place being "totally segregated" highlights the enormity and scale of Jim Crow, the phrase also tends to downplay or minimize how segregated life functioned on an intricate day-to-day level. Racial etiquette dictated that the social realities of race, class, and gender dynamics in southern racial culture were ever-present in everyday life and underscored how people thought about, internalized, and made choices about race. And, as racial etiquette helped dictate social norms, an entire society was predicated on racial values that were falsehoods made terrifyingly real and, especially when reinforced with laws, molded into the fabric of everyday life.

Writing a narrative that encompasses the stories of blacks fighting this reality even as whites reconstructed these fictions is important, but only if we understand that these stories should encompass everything from daily encounters on a Nashville street to how the building of those streets happened in racially specific ways. This approach is necessary to appreciate how the South's racial culture mattered to blacks and whites, how both were inured to and thus shaped by segregation in varied ways, and how that framed their beliefs and decisions about responding to immense social change. And yet, individual decisions come from available options, many of which are dictated by laws, political norms, and public policies that construct our world in seemingly invisible ways yet with profound consequences, even when created by individuals shaped by racial etiquette. Both factors are critical dimensions to understand how legacies of the racial past live in the present. In a sense, then, this book connects the cultural paradoxes of the white moderate South with the racial reorganization of urban space due to the insistent pressures from African American activism. The culture of segregation, borne from generations weaned on Jim Crow and acted out in daily racial etiquette that reinforced such attitudes, was replicated on a citywide scale as whites reacted defensively to black pressures, first over social distance in public accommodation (and other civil rights issues) and later over the physical remapping of the city itself.

When I began teaching history in graduate school, I found myself troubled by student essays exploring the civil rights movement with great sophistication but concluding that those days of discrimination were now banished to the past. In many ways, this book is meant to address that inference. By using Nashville and the respective Nashville Ways as microcosms of racial attitudes and racial arenas,

I hope to use both dramatic and prosaic events to capture the tensions between blacks and whites during this time and place, and explore how decades of local and national issues fraught with racial meaning filtered through black and white lenses differently to condition events and attitudes. The details in these pages are meant to preserve the richness of Nashville's particulars while still speaking to the broader themes that animate the city's racial history and carry the most resonance for historians and citizens. There are undoubtedly stories about race in Nashville that will still need to be told. Rather than being exhaustively comprehensive, my approach hopes to portray faithfully the perspectives of those people who lived this history while binding these individual stories into something more connected and meaningful. It is a difficult balance and one that I hope I have honored. What follows is tied to one specific locale, drawn from local events and personalities, but is also meant as much more. It is the story of a society wrestling with and yet will-fully ignoring its racial reality. Most fundamentally, it is the story of how a racial status quo, after decades of upheaval, was both changed and yet preserved.

ONE

A Manner of Segregation
Lived Race Relations and Racial Etiquette

Someone standing by Nashville's state capitol in the pre–World War II era could easily visualize at least some dimensions of the city's segmentation. The building towered over downtown Nashville and the tall hills overlooking the rest of the city and the Cumberland River. Although the vista's effect might be lessened somewhat by the city's notoriously smoke-choked air, the rare clear day permitted a visitor looking due north to watch the Cumberland snaking up and away, bending to the west in an upside-down U shape that curved around North Nashville. This neighborhood was considered the very heart of African American life in the city. To the east, the river lazily meandered north to form another U shape that encompassed East Nashville, where working-class members of both races lived. It was rather harder to see the conspicuously white parts of the city, which lay farther to the south and west, although they naturally caught the eye by sitting on faraway hills. As with downtown, a sort of geographic segregation meant that most wealthier neighborhoods were centered on higher elevations, leaving residents on less valuable property to contend with the smoggy air. A similar pattern dictated that poor blacks usually lived along the river-bottom areas prone to flooding and along the many railroad tracks that crisscrossed Nashville. There were many ways in which the city was vividly divided in a meaningful manner.[1]

Within downtown, however, where the races might meet in going about their daily lives, segregating was trickier. This was embodied by the uneven and indeed confusing combinations of WHITE and COLORED signs (or the lack thereof). Racially divided space downtown had haphazard patterning. At the train station, even as tellers sold tickets to blacks and whites from the same window, each race had a separate waiting room. Blacks and whites shared telephone booths and bought reading material from the same newsstands, but African Americans had different barbers to trim hair and a separate bench train-side as they waited. At the bus station, however, a cheaper travel option for those of more modest means, segregation was more strictly delineated, with the black waiting room tucked in a far corner of the building. Even by late 1955, after the order from the Interstate Commerce Commission to desegregate travel accommodations, the bus system had a reputation for being "most resistant." Segregated toilets remained and the single lunch counter served blacks, but only at one end. By contrast, in the rail station there were no WHITE and COLORED signs, but local African Americans still used the same restrooms and lunch counters as before. However, blacks traveling through Nashville as interstate passengers occasionally chose to use the general waiting area rather than retire to separate quarters, in accordance with the commission's legal mandate.[2]

Still other forms of transport lacked WHITE and COLORED signs, and here unspoken codes of conduct prevailed. Taxicabs generally took black customers, but doing so was dependent on the cabbie's personal preference—this wholly confused black visitors from other southern cities, where taxis catered to specific races. On streetcars, where segregation was "not as formal in action as it is in word," a silent agreement had blacks fill seats from the rear and moving forward, with whites doing the same from the front and moving backward. Black Nashvillians had fought against this with boycotts and protests in the early 1900s when the practice was first instituted; later generations struggled with the custom. One Fisk student in the early 1940s described the "hot blood" that "flooded her face" when her date scolded her for sitting next to a white person on a bus. His reproach was revealing, as he warned her of potentially powerful repercussions from her breach of etiquette: shaming black men, even though they risked jail or worse if they tried to protect her, but also associating those men with "unmanliness" if they did not defend her. Still, the city, as elsewhere across the nation, witnessed a noticeable increase in streetcar and bus altercations during the 1940s.[3]

The fact that silent understanding could govern racial interaction suggests that *how* Nashvillians moved through segregated space was as revealing as the marking of such spaces. Sometimes racial signs seemed to contradict racial realities. At other times, the very lack of signage was laden with historical meaning, as when the removed signs were vestiges of black political pressure or gestured to white convenience. And yet, this etiquette held sway over the places where the races intersected; those places were relative aberrations in a broader landscape where white and black neighborhoods remained distinct, with boundaries reinforced by both racial custom and public policy. This chapter explores both these dimensions of segregation simultaneously. The intricate details inherent in daily racial interaction show how whites and African Americans could use etiquette for their own benefit; the racial differences of urban sectors indicate how both law and custom converged to impact black and white lives on a broader scale. Each dimension embedded the social dynamics of the city, both silently and tangibly, in the everyday lives of Nashvillians.

The curious dynamic of racial etiquette in the early and mid-twentieth century was particularly conspicuous downtown, which was wholly white-owned except for First Colored Baptist Church (later First Baptist Church, Capitol Hill), the place of worship for much of Nashville's African American elite and a central site for civil rights activism. Yet downtown also represented the civic and economic center of Nashville, and that reality rested uneasily with Jim Crow legacies. This meant that commercial transactions, for example, had curious racial contradictions. White-owned banks in Nashville gladly kept black accounts—but would not provide loans. In the exclusive shops that sold the latest fashions to Nashville's elite, there was never a COLORED sign above the dressing rooms mocking African Americans. Instead, a designated clerk, usually "polite and effusive," would steer black clientele to "special seats in rear" and "special trying rooms." The same Fisk student humiliated on the bus described one store where a white clerk "shifted about, miserably ill at ease" and "hung his head as if he were a school boy" in telling her that she would have to try shoes on in the back. Declining to do so, she found another store just a few blocks away where the clerk calmly invited her to sit wherever she chose as he went to find her size. In plainer five-and-ten-cent stores, however, where separate water fountains were more common, service for black customers often depended wholly on "the disposition of the sales clerk," which in turn usually stemmed from the class status of the black patron.[4]

Segregation had a similar patchwork feel in health and educational venues. Most hospitals in Nashville did not accept black patients. One exception, Hubbard Hospital, affiliated with black Meharry Medical College, was entirely African American. Nashville General Hospital was nearly fifty-fifty interracial, although beds for black patients were contained in an older building connected only by corridor to the newer wing for whites. Here orderlies and maids were black, but never the medical staff. Exclusive Vanderbilt University hospital had thirty-five beds for African American patients; black doctors, while not allowed to practice there, were "received courteously" when visiting. Similarly, public libraries were not open to blacks, but methods of transferring materials to black institutions were not unheard of, whereas "special instances" were made when a black person needed to access the state library, state supreme court library, and Vanderbilt University or Peabody College libraries.[5]

The racial line hardened when it came to food. In the South, where cuisine had a pronounced cultural importance, segregation in eating places was seemingly absolute. No restaurants downtown served blacks. Nor did hotels sell meals or rent rooms to African Americans, although by the mid-1950s there was a curious exception: hotels permitted—"in fact welcome[d]"—the use of banquet facilities for interracial groups, even when the same hotels refused rooms to black patrons. "It seems a fine line of distinction," wrote one local, "but it's held to firmly here in Nashville." Elsewhere, in the Krystal's lunch counters and similar food joints, black customers could order take-out meals but were not permitted to eat inside. Food and money could trade hands, but the fellowship of a shared meal remained forbidden. One white reporter mused that "there is something sacramental about eating together. It is a social act and some of these people have simply been unwilling to make the hurdle that would be involved." Neighborhood stores in black areas "are adjusted to Negroes and give them service they expect," but in white neighborhoods the service might be "courteous but speedy" so as to more quickly usher black patrons out the door. The white southern psyche refused to accept blacks and whites eating together. Partaking in food together was an intimacy presuming equal status.[6]

The cultural realm was equally puzzling. By the mid-1950s, Nashvillians up late at night could tune a radio dial to 1510 a.m., where WLAC disk jockey "Hoss" Allen was spinning Ray Charles, John Lee Hooker, and other black music on his nightly show. Allen was the latest in a succession of now-legendary DJs at WLAC, especially Gene Nobles and "John R" Richbourg. Nobles, in heeding the request of local black college students to play some R&B, had seen his show grow wildly popular, and Richbourg and Allen also played black music on their programs to great acclaim. The latter DJ had a deep southern-flecked voice and sprinkled his speech with black street slang ("Look, it's git-down time! The Hossman is here, so it's time to hop, it's time to jump!") which led many listeners to assume the white boy from Gallatin, Tennessee, was African American. Allen later admitted that he was poorly versed in the double entendres of the vernacular despite hanging out in black music clubs; "git-down time" was actually the street expression for prostitutes beginning their evening shift. His patter was less authentic than it sounded. Nonetheless, WLAC's 50,000-watt signal beamed to twenty-eight states across the nation, so the three DJs, each white but fanatical about black music, were beloved figures. While Dewey Phillips in Memphis, soon to discover and record Elvis Presley for the first time, remains a powerful representative of 1950s musical fusions, the WLAC DJs radiated an equally powerful influence throughout the eastern United States to an eager and diverse audience. Even Alan Freed, often nominally credited as the first popularizer of rock 'n' roll, was a fan. "Freed used to call us from Cleveland every night and ask us what to play," Hoss Allen later remembered.[7]

The DJs indicated a music scene that contained even more of Jim Crow's contradictions. DeFord Bailey, the black harmonica player for the Grand Ole Opry, often had a rough time traveling with his cohort, usually staying and eating in black neighborhoods for safety, although Uncle Dave Macon occasionally pretended that Bailey was his valet so that Bailey could remain with the group. Similarly, when Tommy Dorsey's band played at the War Memorial auditorium downtown, black trumpeter Charlie Shavers performed but was separated from the band on-stage. Other venues like the Subway Lounge (later the Captain's Table) in Printer's Alley had segregated booths for interracial or all-black bands like the Marigolds. Yet musicians of both races played together unseen in the recording studios that would soon make Nashville famous. And the thriving jazz scene in Nashville was relatively tolerant; white musicians would do the high-paying gigs at ballrooms and dance halls before escaping to black clubs like the Palms and Hettie Ray's on 9 Mile Hill to jam with black jazz players. The exception was the musicians' labor union, however, segregated until the late 1940s, which forced African Americans to join the Birmingham local instead. Regardless, a black newspaper reporting on the huge interracial audience at an R&B show commented that "really, more of it is already going on in Nashville than is reported in the newspapers."[8]

The contradiction is that, while this variability made Nashville's segregation marginally more tolerable than the stultifying racial atmosphere of the Deep South, the fluidity itself was taxing. With every walk through a public space, every bus ride, every shopping excursion, the very real possibility of a racial confrontation loomed, subject to the mood, personality, and whims of any individual, black or white. Jim Crow demanded behavior from both races allowing each to navigate—sometimes smoothly, sometimes less so—through pervasive realities of racial difference as needed. Coping with the racial subtext was best managed through the skillful use of etiquette. The famed manners of southerners had practical application in helping Nashvillians steer through the city's segregated terrain while staying faithful to more enduring social differences.[9]

In 1963, novelist Flannery O'Connor illuminated this aspect of southern life:

It requires considerable grace for two races to live together. . . . It can't be done without a code of manners based on mutual charity. . . . It's particularly necessary to have in order to protect the rights of both races. When you have a common code of manners based on charity, then when the charity fails—as it is going to do continuously—you've got those manners there to preserve each race from small intrusions upon the other. The uneducated Southern Negro is not the clown he's made out to be. He's a man of very elaborate manners and great formality which he uses superbly for his own protection and to insure his own privacy. . . . The South has survived in the past because its manners, however lopsided or inadequate they may have been, provided enough social discipline to hold us together and give us an identity.[10]

It is a curious mentality that adopts a racial charity doomed to fail "continuously." Yet, O'Connor's formulation explains why white Nashvillians observed fondly that "Nashville is more cordial in race relations" compared to other cities, and suggests that the notion was at the very core of their identity. The idea was not merely a cliché; it was a cliché that meant something, that hid a deeper truth about how white Nashvillians viewed themselves and how they wanted to be viewed. The self-image was important, not only in terms of race, but in fusing racial and class dimensions together. In a society where white superiority was a foregone conclusion, how you expressed this superiority marked your class aspirations. As one observer commented, "the middle and upper class [white] southerner may insist on the following of caste behavior, but disapproves of the rudeness and discourtesy with which lower class white persons often treat Negroes."[11]

That Nashvillians drew such distinctions showed the importance of class dynamics in Nashville, which rivaled the racial schism in significance and loomed large among both blacks and whites. Indeed, the social relationships forged by Jim Crow had inherent class dimensions embedded in and complicating the racial etiquette. Frequently this was manifested by elite whites clucking disapprovingly at the racial venom from poor whites obsessed with the notion that "they lose face if they kow-tow to a Negro." African Americans recognized that this mentality enabled upper-class whites to downplay their own version of racial arrogance, although blacks often agreed with the assessment of lower-class white insecurities. But African Americans also often sneered at the class differences among their own race, as if to mitigate against the racism consigning them to supposed inferiority.[12]

No matter how arrogant white attitudes were, African Americans were attentive to ways that they could play off the contradictions in daily etiquette for their own benefit. This was particularly true when class and race issues collided. To understand how this worked in everyday life, consider those unskilled lower-class blacks with little opportunity in Nashville's service economy. Ganged together for the most menial of labor, what little contact they had with lower-class whites was impersonal but not necessarily fraught with friction. One black laborer affirmed this by saying, "we treat them that's working with us same as they was colored." But with employers, a different reality existed. This was often shown through naming, where African Americans became "a personality extension" of their employer; common phrasings such as "'he's Ike Johnson's boy,'" or "'he's Jim who works at the Cotton Hotel,'" branded blacks by virtue of their utility as laborers or subordinates rather than as individuals or peers. Yet skilled lower-class African Americans who occupied service occupations (valets, hotel doormen, store managers, and the like) had a stronger connection to white employers and thus "a reciprocity" extending far beyond the usual racial relationship. Often these skilled black workers had great autonomy to carry out their employer's wishes, once they earned the trust and respect of their boss. "In the South," one observer wrote, "such a relationship is recognized and accepted."[13]

This functional working relationship, an intimacy of sorts, was at the heart of southern etiquette and was infused into the racial dynamic even when it seemed to bely racial reality. By conceding their status despite whatever power they actually held, a mammy nursing white babies or a servant handling a white family's food might have a closeness with whites precisely because these employees, by the nature of their work, were class inferiors. Even African Americans acknowledged that genuine feeling between the races might often exist in these situations, under certain conditions and despite the color line: "intimacy is permissible only when both parties know what can and cannot be done, so that the important social distances are maintained." Of course, the very emphasis on ground rules showed that this feeling was never a total intimacy, nor did it preclude other elements of distance between the two parties. And, more frustratingly, southern whites usually distorted this false intimacy into an excuse or apology that either diminished segregation's effects on individuals, or tried to reinforce Jim Crow more generally, or ignored segregation for white self-interest. The variability of those possibilities meant that lower-class African Americans dealt with whites carefully, often preferring to avoid altogether situations where they might be at the mercy of whites. As one black worker put it, the important thing was knowing "which way to rub the fur on the white people."[14]

For upper-class African Americans, the dynamics of Jim Crow cast different shadows. Black elites, by living in their own neighborhoods, attending their own churches, and educating their children in black schools, mostly chose the extent of their interaction with whites. One exception was when they went to purchase goods or services, and this is where the contradictions between class and race held tension and possibility simultaneously. Frequently, black elites, as befitting their status, would opt for stores catering to the better classes and expect color-blind treatment—or, more precisely, a treatment that acknowledged their higher-class status rather than their race. Although white stores were pleased to take money from African Americans, this made for a dilemma: alienating black customers would cut into store profits, but ignoring race contradicted an entire upbringing. In response, white store clerks often behaved with an excessive politeness, often flattering and haughty simultaneously, which helped mask their racial opinions.[15]

African American elites challenged this artifice directly by tweaking the racial etiquette. They would spar verbally with clerks in similarly polite but firm tones, or react in ways that precluded the "naming" that lower-class black employees endured. In one example, a black minister was referred to as "uncle" by a white (which was, along with "aunt" or "auntie," a common term for one's elders in the South, but took a derisive connotation when addressing a black person). The minister shot back with "I didn't know until now that your father and I were brothers. I am pleased to meet my nephew for the first time." He then went on to lecture the offender for "insulting people." Similarly, one black woman introduced herself deliberately as "Mrs. H. D. West" when a white saleswoman knocked at her door. The saleswoman, unable to call Mrs. West by her first name in accordance with racial custom, "turned as red in the face as a beet" and "did not say anything for a long time." In both cases, the scolding occurred because of the transgressor's lower-class status. But there was also the example of a black principal in Davidson County who did a double take after being called "boy" by the local superintendent and snapped, "how big do boys grow where you come from?" He was later forced into retirement for his insubordination.[16]

At other times, different tactical choices were safer, as one black citizen realized when confronting members of the notoriously brutal Nashville police department: "I knew I was in the right but I knew that the officer wanted an excuse to hit me or shoot me, so I kept quiet." Or black elites might choose to ignore or tolerate supposed white racial superiority for some specific advantage, usually a financial one. This was true in the case of a black professor dealing with "very nice" white mechanics fixing his car. The professor noted later, "it might have cost a good sum of money, so instead "I just let them go on and call me 'boy' as long as I was able to profit like that." Frequently, economics dictated etiquette as blacks made a conscious choice between superior class status or degraded racial status, as one observer noted, "Whites believe in Negroes 'paying more' if they are able. Thus the clerk looks at one Negro and calls him 'Mr.' The other Negro is called 'John.' The former pays for his courtesy. The latter gets advantage of 'special things.' Often, Negroes, knowing this, allow themselves to be taken for the less privileged class of Negro, hoping to get an advantage thereby." Of course, whites also exploited this behavior. Said one black professional, white salespersons "are always polite, of course, when they are selling and when a white man has something to sell, he will go an extra mile to sell it." Racial politeness, however superficially rendered, was a way for either race to contradict class and racial realities for momentary and often financial gain. What all this constant negotiation meant simply was that, as a matter of necessity, as one local commentator wrote, "the capacity for social adaptation" is necessarily "possessed to a very high degree by the Negro on all levels." One black Nashvillian echoed this decades later, saying, "you'd gone all your life adapting." Living in a Jim Crow society was an exhausting task, constantly fraught with peril. African Americans had to continually choose which battles to fight and which to leave aside.[17]

Even the simple act of getting teeth cleaned showed the stylized dynamics of Nashville's racial interaction. One might assume that dentists in a segregated city would only serve people of their own race, but the reality was far more complicated.[18] With black Meharry Medical College (which itself had white faculty members) in town, Nashville had an abundance of locally trained black dentists, many of whom treated white patients. One estimated his clientele as approximately 80 percent white and another, with a practice located conveniently in the central business district downtown, treated whites exclusively. Like their elite peers, these black dentists had choices in selecting their clients. Some refused to serve whites outright; others did so while insisting on polite behavior. Others eagerly welcomed white patients for, in a society valuing white over black, this confirmed their professional prowess. One black dentist even recalled receiving a Meharry dean's praise for having several white clients. To sweeten the deal, however, black dentists undercut white fees, charging white patients more than black patients would pay, but less than a white dentist would command.

This meant that the whites who went to black dentists were usually lower-class railroad workers or immigrant laborers who consoled themselves in various ways for breaking the racial barrier. They phoned ahead to ask if the dentist treated whites (thus reassuring themselves that they were not the only violators) or rationalized that black dentists must be qualified because the state board of examiners would instinctively be tougher when testing an African American. Others saw advantages in avoiding "dressing up to go uptown," according to the custom of the day, or in being extra polite in hoping that the black dentist might offer nontraditional office hours or cheaper rates. Indeed, staying open later helped black dentists dodge the issue of segregated lobbies where white patients, although perfectly willing to be treated by a black dentist, often resented waiting alongside blacks for treatment. (These whites were "the ignorant ones, the crackers," sniffed one dentist.) One black dentist went so far as to segregate his office's waiting rooms, which brought stringent criticism from fellow African Americans. It was "difficult living like this," he admitted, a strain brought on by trying to balance economic benefits with social costs. Although white referrals paid well and were appropriate professionally, other blacks branded the dentists as "Toms" or "accommodating Negroes."[19]

White dentists had a different racial standard. Rarely did white dentists see black patients, with exceptions only for the servant of a friend and done for free (to preserve a sense of noblesse oblige) and after office hours (to avoid waiting rooms). Nor would white dentists ordinarily refer a white patient to a black counterpart, for this "would be admitting his inferiority." But even this taboo was broken if the white dentist preferred to avoid a patient, for whatever reason—"everyone they didn't want," as one black dentist attested. Such insults masquerading as professional courtesy were replicated in formal arenas, for white and black dentists never coexisted as peers. Little contact existed between the two groups; there was friendliness between individuals but "never in a group context." Meetings and professional gatherings remained separate. In this way, Jim Crow still held firm.[20]

So a tangled racial etiquette governed social relationships for both races in Nashville. Where segregated lines blurred, class differences often flared, and vice versa, and yet the etiquette was employed by individuals of both races for personal gain. But these personal gains always came at the cost of reinforcing broader white superiority in the social hierarchy. Two anecdotes suggest this arrangement. One concerns a black teenager, working at a white-owned house doing odd jobs and watching over white children, who expressed his puzzlement at the children's epithet for him: "if they don't like somebody they call them 'po' white trash,' if they get mad at me they call me 'po' white trash.' They don't know no better." Compare this with the white Nashville mother overheard scolding her son after hearing him use the word *nigger*: "Don't ever say that again. That's for poor white trash to say and you're not poor white. Remember nigger is common." The first example shows that a Nashville child's psyche might be steeped in class differences even before racial awareness loomed. The second, by lending class considerations to racial terminology, reinforced the idea that style meant everything in expressing racial differences, because the presumption of white superiority remained unquestioned.[21]

Thus Nashville's etiquette was an elaborate sort of racial charade where intricate and stylized behavior from both races lent itself to a daily racial role-playing, complete with carefully chosen words and behavior that seemed to affirm or contradict the segregated status quo according to each person's needs in any given encounter. Black-white interaction thus remained somewhat adaptable in individual circumstances, while still compressed by wider, more tightly prescribed social parameters. Yet behind this daily interaction remained the ugliest contradiction: the silent but ever-present reality that racial etiquette always threatened to break down. A handful of lynchings in the Nashville area during the late nineteenth and early twentieth centuries, followed by whites justifying recurring police brutality for decades thereafter, betrayed the pretense of racial etiquette. Violence, whether real or threatened, always lurked behind the facade of manners. The ultimate expression of white privilege was the ability to withdraw from any semblance of manners to maintain superiority, ensuring that racial deliberations always ended with the same verdict.[22]

The racial etiquette that governed Nashville's race relations was central to everyday lives, encoding social realities in daily interaction and acculturating both races—however fitfully—to life under Jim Crow. Yet, as important as racial etiquette was, it was not the whole story. Even as this interfacing was loaded with social meaning in places where the races met, those realms were often somewhat self-contained. In neighborhoods more decisively segregated by race, a different reality persisted and showed emphatically how legacies of Jim Cow dictated differences in political and economic resources. Descending down the hill from the state capitol to the areas comprising North Nashville, for example, led to a wholly different environment. These areas were almost totally African American, although blacks resided in some small pockets elsewhere in the city. Indeed, one schoolteacher from North Nashville remembered that "everything was all-black" and "when we rode the city bus everyone on the bus looked alike." Indeed, that was in part because bus lines were configured in part to assist black domestics in their commute to white houses. This contrasted with the pattern of train tracks that cut off downtown from North Nashville to isolate both, as only a couple streets connected the two areas. Similarly one medical student recalled, "At Meharry, I was among Negroes I could admire and respect, and the school and Hubbard, its teaching hospital, were so much a world in themselves that I was still more cut off from contact with whites than at home or in New Orleans." Bustling Jefferson Street was the axis off of which the majority of black Nashville's middle class lived. Certainly a lack of capital hampered the growth of black enterprise overall, but some black businesses profited steadily if not handsomely in the Jim Crow era. The neighborhood was enhanced by the presence of Fisk University and Meharry (the latter had relocated to the area from South Nashville in 1931); both bolstered the comfortable, quiet residential nature of this area anchored by these black institutions and the professors and staff who often chose to live nearby.[23]

Away from Jefferson Street, however, there were more squalid areas, including one known as Hell's Half Acre in the latter years of the nineteenth century. Much as black elite neighborhoods centered on Jefferson Street, Charlotte Avenue ran parallel to the south, marking both the northern edge of the downtown's central business district and the gateway for Nashville's seedy underworld before moving west to cross the railroad tracks where poorer blacks, most of them new migrants to the city, lived in tin shacks and run-down housing. Here, thriving if sordid houses of vice were frequent, where patrons could satiate various appetites or find hiding after doing various misdeeds. Charlotte Avenue itself was populated with poolrooms, fleabag hotels, and "uptown clubs," hotspots for gambling and whiskey. Some of these black-owned institutions were important headquarters for black entrepreneurs including Jim Raines, who owned the Porters and Waiters Clubs to the east, and Uncle Teddy Acklen, who had opened the Del Morocco club on Jefferson and hired chefs from ritzy Belle Meade to work at the Blue Room restaurant upstairs. Acklen in particular had a reputation for benevolence, especially for medical students at Meharry. Perhaps most prominent of all was the Grace Hotel, at the corner of Charlotte and 12th Avenues, run by black racketeer Bill James. His fortune came from running the numbers in Nashville's gambling scene, which brought in an estimated thousand dollars of profit per day.[24]

Also in these neighborhoods were "buffet flats," sleazy bars where drinks and women were readily available and patrons from "the upper world" (including the occasional college boys and girls curious for a different slice of life) could mix with shady characters. More serious criminals lurked in "crumb joints" and "ranches," whose reputations were based on their ability to bribe local police officials so as to protect their clientele. Here too were the "circuses," buildings that housed lewd sex shows, and, for those "in the know," clubs that catered to Nashville's underground gay scene. The brothels and worst red-light district in the city was centered on Crawford Street two blocks north of Charlotte, fenced in by railroad tracks and the city dump, where the lines of jurisdiction between city police and county sheriffs were hazy. Although houses of prostitution on Crawford were segregated, it was commonly known that interracial dalliances could be arranged if patrons wished (a white prostitute would enter a black whorehouse through a back door, whereas white johns could enter directly through either).[25]

So racial interaction did not only occur in the white-owned downtown. Some institutions were known as "black and white clubs," where interracial company for all sorts of activities could be found. At Charlotte and Fourth, behind a hash house fronted by Greek immigrants who served as contact men, there was the resident "booking station" where bets were taken. One of many such neighborhood stations in Nashville, it plugged into an efficient and effective network of Jewish-run gambling syndicates across the nation. This station was equipped with telegraph lines to all the racetracks and employed runners with regular routes in black neighborhoods who collected or paid out winnings as necessary. Vice rarely segregated, although one observer acknowledged that the underworld had its code of behavior and ethics.[26]

Whether by silent code or variable racial etiquette, in black-owned or white-owned spaces, racial interaction was shaped by urban landscapes. Yet these landscapes were constantly alive with evolving changes very much in flux across Nashville throughout the twentieth century. To take just one example, another vice district called Black Bottom, just south of Broad around Fourth Avenue, had turned from an Irish area to predominantly African American after the Civil War. But in 1905 the neighborhood became a target, triggered by an announcement that the local Roman Catholic church in nearby South Nashville was planning to open an industrial school for blacks. This prompted many groups to pounce. Prohibitionists eager to dry up the rivers of alcohol that flowed through local bars and City Beautiful advocates anxious to clean up the area more generally joined with white property owners fretting about depressed land values. They found common cause with business owners who noticed that Black Bottom's development was choked off from expansion. The result was a crackdown by police on crime and booze that cleared the area and motivated many in the area to sell and move out. Soon the area, along with nearby Rutledge Hill, become repopulated with merchants as the construction of the Broadway Bridge opened up commercial and residential traffic and helped Second, Third, and Fourth Avenues become renewed as business sites.[27]

This makeover of certain neighborhoods was emblematic of broader patterns throughout Nashville. The denizens of the underworld drawn to certain quarters downtown paralleled other populations shifting around Nashville throughout the twentieth century. The trend known as "white flight" to the ever-expanding suburban fringe was not new in the 1940s; rather, it was an accelerated version of a previous tendency that remained in force for the rest of the century. National, state, and local politics had coalesced in complicated ways during the New Deal era that, while granting millions of dollars for public housing, did nothing to arrest the segregation of Nashville's housing by race and class. In response, whites were drawn away from the city center, lured by tax and mortgage incentives and channeled by streetcar routes and roads for automobiles that pointed to the south and west of downtown. The founding of Vanderbilt Medical School and the relocation of George Peabody College for Teachers helped usher white relocation to these same areas as people settled in homes close to work.[28]

Similarly, African Americans were on the move, occasionally by choice, although options for housing were locked into certain sectors, poorer quality housing stock, and higher costs thanks to discriminatory realty practices. Much like Vanderbilt, Meharry Medical College's shift to North Nashville in 1931 next to Fisk University made North Nashville an attractive relocation site. But with slums nearby, elite blacks also relocated, if their incomes permitted as post–World War II prosperity boomed, settling in neighborhoods such as the Bordeaux area north of the Cumberland. Elsewhere, as whites moved to the south and west along West End Avenue, a mirroring effect occurred to the south and east as black domestics tried to stay in relative proximity to their employer's homes. Especially with urban renewal programs targeting North Nashville in subsequent decades, African Americans would also increasingly pack the somewhat more diverse "salt-and-pepper" areas of East Nashville, particularly the Crappy Shoot slum, or South Nashville's Edgehill or Trimble Bottom neighborhoods. Yet, as the percentage of black faces in many neighborhoods grew, many whites decided, if *their* incomes permitted, to move farther into the surrounding county, clogging city streets on their daily commute each workday from suburban homes. Various shopping and retail centers followed, setting up shop in a ring outside the center city and leaving the urban core, with an increasingly concentrated black population, sliding into economic uncertainty.[29]

So, by World War II, downtown was surrounded by neighborhoods of widely varying quality, as city and state officials worked in gleaming buildings only a short walk from the red-light district, which blended in between distinctly upper-class black areas. On the other side of North Nashville below the river, West Nashville was fast becoming the industrial zone for the city. Across the Cumberland opposite downtown, racially mixed Old East Nashville housed lower working-class Irish and black counterparts in closer proximity but still with distinct neighborhoods. A similar trend followed in South Nashville, while only to the southwest of the city, along the major road arteries extending out from the river and leading to the Vanderbilt campus, Belle Meade, and other wealthy areas, remained expensive, exclusive, and white. It was part of Nashville's character that, despite the curious variability of racial etiquette when the two races did meet, a wider gulf between black and white neighborhoods remained in force in Nashville. The differences between economic and political resources in those areas indeed made for two different worlds.[30]

Despite this paradox, the generally genteel feel of Nashville was tangible in both black and white communities. Unlike Birmingham, for example, where mighty steel companies drove the prosperity of the city as a whole, Nashville had comparatively little heavy industry. Some manufacturing was present, printing, milling, and shoe industries being particularly important, along with some glass and chemical companies. Groceries and dry goods had also helped the local economy after the Civil War; a central location on rail lines had located Nashville as a major distribution center. Diverse insurance and banking companies later followed, thriving in the city and comprising the major players among Nashville's business elite by World War II. Those, plus numerous colleges and universities for both blacks and whites, underpinned Nashville's service economy. An established oligarchy ran the city, usually from the comfort of sprawling mansions in the ultraexclusive suburb of Belle Meade. But many elements of the business elite were highly resistant to changes that were beyond control—some went so far as to lobby bitterly against the new Ford automobile glass plant that promised new jobs but would inflate wages across the city. At the same time, lower-class whites and blacks, migrating from the rural countryside in record numbers before World War II, continued to be drawn into the city throughout the late 1940s. One estimate held that one-third of white Nashvillians made less than two thousand dollars per year in 1950, an amount that hovered close to the poverty line. The Chamber of Commerce, ever mindful of luring new business to town, advertised the city's cheap, available, and placid labor force to potential employers. This image of docility was misleading: strikes, walkouts, and labor-related bombings were not unheard of in Nashville and the police were frequently given a loose leash to suppress such activities. Thus class tensions bubbled underneath Nashville's distinctly white-collar environment.[31]

Nashville's genteel qualities and class tensions were not relegated to the white sides of town. Black Nashville helped the city's claim of being "the Athens of the South" with several higher education institutions in North Nashville. Foremost was private and elite Fisk University, one of the best black colleges in the country and the first African American school accepted into the prestigious American Association of Universities. Similar in stature, prominent Meharry Medical College was also important to the black community in both concrete and psychological ways through its economic and social benefit to the city. The school had a national reputation and, through the first half of the twentieth century, over half of all black doctors in the United States were Meharrians. In 1957 the medical college would admit a handful of whites (for few applicants of either race could meet the entrance requirements), but over the next decades wrestled between its identity as a school fostering black advancement and a chronic lack of funding. By contrast, Tennessee State Agricultural and Industrial school (later Tennessee State University) thrived as the state legislature poured money into black graduate and professional programs in an attempt to "equalize" school funding. The effort was meant to belatedly align Tennessee's universities with the "separate but equal" provision of the *Plessy v. Ferguson* (1896) decision that sanctioned Jim Crow. As a result, TSU supplied a prodigious number of black teachers to Nashville and the wider South. American Baptist Theological Seminary did the same for black ministers, providing an avenue into the wider religious life of the city and beyond, as did the African Methodist Episcopal Sunday School Union and other prominent black religious institutions. Black Nashville also had a highly exclusive social scene, including elite men's clubs like the Agora Assembly and a range of fraternities and sororities.[32]

The number of African American professionals further highlighted the city's conspicuous class divisions. Nashville blacks were generally either prosperous or poor, with few in between (although the comparative difference between white and black upper classes meant that the black elite was often referred to as "middle class"). At Fisk, one student recalled how the institution stressed a combination of racial pride and high-brow culture (encompassing "manners," "clothing," and "fine tastes") along with more general academic excellence. This of course papered over distinct social realities as academic and economic status mixed with awareness of skin color and regional origin. Some saw differences between northern and southern student behavior in daily interaction, and there was a minor fuss on campus in 1946 when a dark-skinned Miss Fisk was selected for the first time. Similarly, one student at Tennessee State commented on the lack of dark-skinned majorettes at the school ("it was understood," she said simply), and likewise commented that "we always had a run-in with the girls at Fisk."[33]

Rifts strained many relationships in the black community. The "town-and-gown" relationships between locals and black colleges and students (many of whom were from outside of Nashville) could be fraught. Dissension between the black elite and underclass was also pronounced, as it was for white Nashville. In one conversation, a white woman broaching the subject of poor blacks was shocked by a black woman's answer: "you are talking about our peasant class, aren't you?" Indeed, class distinctions governed everyday decisions for African Americans even down to the choice of theater one attended (the lower classes frequented the Bijou while the elites preferred the Ritz). These distinctions were highlighted by the lack of economic opportunity in the city, for Nashville's few manufacturing industries shut African Americans out of their factories entirely, the only exceptions being the phosphate and fertilizer plants in town, which required the dirtiest of work. The Vultee aircraft plant, for example, practiced segregation even during World War II. In two places downtown, at 1st and Broad as well as 10th and Church, blacks could congregate in "ganging places" for everyday drudge labor, where employers would round them up in a truck for a day's or week's worth of meager pay.[34]

Along with the colleges and universities, Nashville's refined reputation was helped by the city's reputation for religiosity, which was backed by demographics. By the late 1950s, the city boasted 557 churches, or one for every 322 citizens. The majority of the churches were Baptist, with nearly as many Churches of Christ, and somewhat fewer Methodist, Presbyterian, and Episcopal churches. But religion had even more influence as several publishing and media operations for multiple religious conventions, large and small, based themselves in Nashville, including the administrative headquarters for the Methodist Board of Education, Southern Baptist Foundation, and Presbyterian Board of World Missions. This religious influence, in turn, enhanced Nashville's reputation for education, as most of the city's white colleges and universities were church affiliated. Although Vanderbilt had freed itself, albeit painfully, from its Methodist origins, other denominational colleges, including David Lipscomb (Church of Christ), Belmont (Southern Baptist), Scarritt (Methodist), and Aquinas College (Catholic), along with a host of smaller sectarian schools, dotted Nashville's landscape.[35]

In a city religiously and culturally overwhelmed by Protestantism, there were different social realities for other faiths. A smattering of Roman Catholic congregations called Nashville home and had a real presence. Many Baptists fretted about the noticeable uptick in African Americans choosing to send their children to Catholic schools renowned for stricter disciplinary and educational standards. But there were examples of anti-Catholic bias too, as when the Nashville Ministers Association elected one of its black members as president in 1959; one member acknowledged that "all hell would break loose if we elected a rabbi or priest to membership." Similar issues were apparent for Nashville's Jewish community. Dixie, comparatively speaking, welcomed Jews more than other parts of the United States at this time. But southern Jews, unlike their brethren in the North, understood that their place in society was predicated upon a tacit acceptance of segregation, and Jewish history of persecution often made them rather less inclined to support racial uplift. As one scholar wrote, "Evidence suggests that Nashville's Jews were keenly aware of their precarious place in society. If Jews were outspoken in their protests, they would be linked in the public mind with blacks."[36]

Typical of Nashville, and indeed all of the United States at this time, anti-Semitism remained prevalent if relatively muted. Woodmont Country Club was founded for Jewish members, because they were excluded from all others, and civic clubs either put a "percentage quota" on Jewish membership or shunned them entirely. Neighborhoods disdained Jews almost as much as they did African Americans, although occasionally a sole Jewish family would be allowed to move in with a "gentleman's agreement" that no one else would follow. Decades later, Jews recalled little overt discrimination but understood that they were only one factor in a complex racial equation. One Jewish citizen underscored the point plainly when he told an interviewer that "occasionally I would run into [anti-Semitism], but it was such a rare thing. I reckon they were just too busy hating the 'niggers'!" This situation existed despite some solidarity between the Jewish and African American communities. Quietly, the Nashville chapter of the National Council of Jewish Women ran a day-care center for black children whose parents were employed by defense industries during World War II. Because of such relationships, it was not unknown for some black Nashvillians to speak Yiddish. But such attempts at community solidarity were not publicized, even in the name of religion. Indeed, while adding to the religious quality to the city, the preponderance of churches and church organizations actually led to some discord. Strife often separated individual congregations from religious institutions carrying out denominational policies, and this was especially prevalent for Jim Crow issues. Some heard in the scriptures support for better racial relations; others preferred to separate spirituality from daily life (and thus preserved some legacy of segregation). The religiosity of the city did not always result in spiritual harmony.[37]

All these trends—the uncertain variability of racial interaction, the relentless shifting of both whites and blacks around the city, the persisting class differences, and the unevenness in material resources and opportunities for African Americans—continued as an insistent undertow throughout the twentieth century. Yet, by 1945, this racial business as usual was conflicting uncertainly with important new updates in the local political context, and this would have significant ramifications for both race relations and urban space. Nashville was a relentlessly political town with partisanship ingrained in daily city life. Before World War II, the local business elites who fanned civic pride and ran the city remained a separate constituency from Nashville's politicians. Bankers, insurance agents, realtors, and businessmen moved in exclusive circles and called the shots behind the scenes, although they preferred to focus on economic issues while leaving other municipal matters to the politicos. Powerful insurance companies (National Life & Accident and Life & Casualty) were critical to Nashville's economy, along with scores of smaller outfits. Local banks were regional powerhouses, including American National, Third National, and Commerce Union. Most powerful of all was the shadowy Watauga Club, composed of the city's most senior banking and insurance executives, who often decided the city's fortunes with a handshake over lunch. Some observers contrasted the city's forward-thinking politicians with Nashville's rather stagnant social, commercial, and cultural attitudes, but that distinction was a forced one as local politicians of all inclinations jostled for influence. Their tactics included, in time-honored Nashville fashion, widespread corruption, nepotism, ballot-box stuffing, voter fraud, police raids on political rivals, shady political patronage, political arm-twisting, and straight-out cash bribery.[38]

Such shenanigans in Nashville politics were conditioned by the local remnants of political machines that dominated American municipal politics in the early to mid-twentieth century. Nashville mayor Hilary Howse had presided over this sort of political coalition until his death in 1938 prompted a "chaotic jumble of small cliques and shifting personal alliances." Scandals and factional squabbling now ruled as groups jockeyed for power and, while many soon saw the need for reform, intense disagreement on the nature of that reform was ongoing.[39]

This factionalism gave Nashville's African Americans opportunities to join the political fray. Of course, local politics were familiar terrain for African Americans: they had participated for years, although admittedly at the cost of trading their votes for cash or booze, as was commonplace in machine politics of the day. At the turn of the century, an African American had won election to city council but at the next election found his district "gerrymandered away" even as a "crucial ballot box disappeared." As a result, the black entrepreneurs of Nashville's underworld like Bill James and Teddy Acklen had become particularly savvy during the Howse administration in realizing that votes were the only thing more valuable than cash in Nashville. Armed with a massive influx of money from the numbers racket and a well-oiled bureaucracy of underlings, and brushing off some disapproval from more respectable black elites, the various gambling syndicates in Nashville's underworld were run by enterprising spirits well-connected with city and county governments, both officially and unofficially. This made for a smooth working relationship with the police: in exchange for a cut of profits, raids would be timed strategically so that only a minimal amount of the week's profits were confiscated. Any fines were quickly paid in court, the better to get back in business and to continue "pouring votes" to the Howse political machine. Over time, racketeers became ward-heelers and then bosses, and accounts of white political figures closing down rival white groups in order to keep black machines in their pockets were common. Despite these links to white politicians, however, some segregated subservience remained in force. "Politics is one of the strongest tie-ups between the white and black underworld of Nashville," one observer noted, but "when the Negro underworld kingpins try to organize a political machine of their own, their rackets are promptly smashed. The colored racketeer is sought and coddled as a political ally but is feared and resented as a rival." That was Bill James's fate in 1941 when the Hotel Grace was raided by state police; newspaper headlines followed with lurid headlines about interracial sex at the venue. Whispers around town suggested that a prominent newspaper publisher, and perhaps even high police officials, had been involved in the numbers racket but were unwilling to continue playing along.[40]

Other African Americans wearied of being manipulated by the political machine. One tactic favored by Howse sent municipal workers and quantities of pipes to black neighborhoods on election eve, creating anticipation that new sewers would be laid—with a quick overnight withdrawal of the workers and materials after the election. Such actions pushed many black voters toward reformist politicians. In the pivotal 1938 election to replace Howse, Thomas L. Cummings, the antimachine candidate elected with considerable black support, responded with both rhetorical and substantive rewards for his voters, although all within the rubric of segregation.[41]

But Cummings, less able at managing a supportive political coalition, struggled throughout his tenure. By 1945, important psychological shifts and daily realities were creating a new political mentality among Nashvillians and eroding Cummings's progressive credentials. His appeal had been predicated on vows to clean up the Howse machine's corruption. However, problems remained: extensive municipal problems of pollution, overcrowded housing, deteriorating streets, juvenile delinquents, slums like open sores, and skyrocketing tuberculosis rates now became equally worrisome to the city's elite. The explosion in suburban growth was fueling political factionalism between city and county even as urban services in Nashville were falling apart. This was embarrassingly made clear when Nashville was the first city subjected to the May Act (which in 1941 granted wider federal enforcement power to combat vice activities near military bases) because of a virtual epidemic of venereal disease throughout the city. For a city that loved to extol its charms, such a development was a decided stain on Nashville's good name.[42]

By 1946, the fallout from these crises led to a complicated reshuffling of political coalitions characterized by intensely bitter and divisive fights over local offices. When the dust settled, the conflict between rival political organizations, one based in the city of Nashville and the other in Davidson County, remained. But new city charters dictated a refreshed political marriage between the political and business elite in white Nashville. While these elites had preferred separate fiefdoms in Nashville for decades, the mayor in city hall now had significantly enhanced powers to shape the city's direction as never before, less beholden to suburban Davidson County and with the mandate to expand the public sector for the public good. The courtly and progressive reputation that Nashville had always espoused for itself now was infused with a new rhetoric that praised "economic progress with minimal social change." Manifestations of this new attitude, particularly on issues of race, would prove exceedingly ambiguous in coming years, but more generally there was an increasing mentality that, as scholar Don H. Doyle put it, Nashville's political and economic elite should "advance the general welfare of the community" rather than have "a tightfisted reaction against new bonds and taxes."[43]

Above all else, this new partnership was particularly keen to find federal money to ameliorate local problems and went so far as to retain a Washington, D.C., lobbyist in anticipation of forthcoming funding. Thanks to this foresight, Nashville qualified in 1949 for one of the nation's earliest urban renewal programs targeting the downtown's central business district. First priority went to the wretched areas of the underworld, including Hell's Half Acre and Black Bottom, surrounding the state capitol. This money provided the means to bulldoze the slums where betting and boozing, privies and prostitutes had abounded, now replaced with wide parkways for increased automobile traffic flanked by trees, greenways, private buildings, and parking lots. Previous residents were pushed to other parts of the city, mostly North Nashville and Edgehill, and usually into public-housing projects; the total removed included 427 families and nearly 300 single residents. Major private investment from the retail sector accompanied these efforts to perk up the downtown, led by Fred Harvey, a protégé of Chicago's Marshall Fields. Harvey's department store used clever marketing lures, including circus equipment, garish purple walls, and monkeys in cages to draw customers. The downtown experienced some new life with the shopping, restaurants, and more affordable lunch counters but remained in constant competition against the flashy new malls springing up around suburban Nashville.[44]

Although not unappreciative of urban renewal's capacity to eliminate the worst red-light district in Nashville, black Nashvillians remained wary of incursions into their neighborhoods. Particularly rankling was the Chamber of Commerce's 1946 proposal to issue bonds providing millions of dollars to demolish "the most valuable Negro business section in the city" in order to build a city auditorium. Widespread approval for the plan came from whites, including Mayor Tom Cummings. Black leaders argued that the auditorium would be a fiscal drain on the city and that resources would be better allocated elsewhere. They also objected strongly to not being consulted on a project that would crush the economic center of black Nashville. The *Nashville Globe*, the black newspaper in town, took particular umbrage at the vagueness of promises that black businesses would be resettled. Whites responded to charges of discrimination with the point that, as one scholar paraphrased, "it was an objective fact that the black business district contained undesirable buildings." Despite the black outcry, the bond proposal was defeated only after federal requirements for funding were deemed too expensive to accept. But city fathers took note that the independent businessmen's committee had failed in this attempt and decided that future decisions over development would be controlled directly by city hall.[45]

The sparring over the bond issue showed that the black community played a significant role—if not always a decisive one—in the political and social life of Nashville. The white etiquette that on a personal level flattered blacks while denying them equal status held true especially when it came to maintaining control over racial space. The African American push to broaden and extend their political influence remained constant, especially helped by the 1944 *Smith v. Allwright* U.S. Supreme Court decision eliminating the white primary and by the abolishing of the Tennessee poll tax in 1953. The result was an array of black leaders and political clubs. The local NAACP chapter, for example, had a membership of five thousand by 1947 and benefited from the steady support of the *Globe*. The organization dedicated itself to voter registration efforts with an eye toward cutting the tentacles of Edward Crump, the Memphis political boss who ran political affairs throughout the state. Yet, even in the mid-1940s, the NAACP's efforts were viewed as "wholly negative" by a national NAACP figure, and even years later, the group was decried for lacking "go-getter" leaders. Rallying efforts fell flat. One recruiting trip to Fisk and TSU demonstrated that the association ran "a poor second" to fraternities and sororities on campus. Nor was the issue only the apathy of youngsters. President W. S. Davis of TSU argued that NAACP activism set the black cause back, a belief typical of black elite nervousness about making waves. As the president of a state-supported school, Davis was "clearly afraid [for] his job," observed the NAACP official.[46]

Other black groups tried to better the NAACP. One such organization, the City-County Civic League, formed in 1938 by renowned ward-heeler and city hall custodian W. B. "Pie" Hardison, held some promise. But Hardison was "quickly coopted," as one historian wrote, by white politicians who appointed Hardison deputy coroner in 1941, effectively sidelining him. Another, the Davidson County Negro Civic League, formed in July 1944, and just six months later the Lincoln-Douglass League (formerly the Roosevelt Club) merged with the City Federation of Colored Women's Clubs in an attempt to boost its influence. A somewhat more prominent group, the Solid Block, was founded on May 21, 1946, at the Saratoga Tea Room, and Hardison's League, boasted six thousand members by 1950.[47]

Yet some black political organizing remained less formal and less tied to respectability. Ward-heeler Henry "Good Jelly" Jones learned his trade working as Pie Hardison's chauffeur. Throughout the 1950s and into the 1960s, Jones ran his network from a barbecue joint located on an alleyway off of Jefferson Street. "Good Jelly works hard and comes through and the politicians know that," said one city hall figure. Indeed, they knew it well enough that Good Jelly's various arrests ("operating a disorderly house, possessing untaxed whiskey, vagrancy, petty larceny, impersonating an officer, carrying concealed weapons, and more") never yielded more than a fine, and "mostly his cases have been dismissed by the city judge." This allowed Good Jelly to keep extensive files on all the poor blacks he generously fed, bedded, and had treated at local hospitals, who, in turn, were happy to vote for whomever Good Jelly favored. "Come election day," for an estimated three hundred to one thousand dollars per election, "Good Jelly takes out his big Cadillac and herds his people to the polls." With "his golfer's cap, big flashing smile, and long police record," he was a controversial figure in Nashville to both blacks and whites, with different personas for each. As journalist David Halberstam wrote in a profile, "he is the Negro whom many Negroes like least to think about. . . . In his own blunt word, he is a 'nigger'; what is worse, that is all he wants to be. Respectable Negro society shuns him, yet to some of the Negro poor he is perhaps the only truly big man in their lives." White Nashville was similarly divided on Good Jelly. Noted Halberstam, they "call him a backdoor Negro. . . . they won't have their picture taken with him, and they won't pose with him, even at Negro functions. But they know how to get hold of him." And, as one local black told a white counterpart, "that's the way you people really want him."[48]

The proliferation of black organizations and organizers makes it tempting to overstate black political influence in Nashville. The reality, however, was that the sheer number of groups stymied black attempts to exert power effectively. Instead, the differences promoted a bitter factionalism remarked on by many contemporaries. The Solid Block, for example, whose name was a misnomer, boasted only 18 percent of available black voters as members, and its leadership in 1947 endorsed candidates unpopular with the rank and file. The group's newspaper trumpeted the Block's achievements in getting black police officers hired and increased funds for black schools, but the louder call was for black unity and the avoiding of "selfish and self-conceited" individuals. "Negro citizens must learn to go to the polls and vote without being paid to do so," one *Block Bulletin* said sternly.[49]

A black political presence was a given in Nashville but never cohered into the ability to deliver a bloc vote. Invariably, each black group misstated its own importance, spoke to differing black constituencies divided by class, education, and neighborhood, formed around election time to curry favor with specific politicians, and then atrophied. The African American vote had proved decisive in the 1943 mayoral election but that was the exception. More commonplace was the city council race of 1947 where the black vote split over multiple black candidates in each district with the winner ultimately swamped in the runoff by a white rival. White politicians could "create the appearance of consultation" with black groups, but leave it at that. Moreover, black groups struggled against widespread political apathy in their communities and similar complaints were levied against poorer whites. (Given how most voting activity was fixed, however, that apathy might be better understood as a strategic aversion to political wheeler-dealers about town). Still, in terms of marshaling more clout for blacks, it was a troubling reality. As one black politician said in 1958, "talk about voting and you will put a bunch of Negroes to sleep." In that year, Davidson County had less than ten thousand registered black voters, out of seventy thousand eligible. The right to vote did not translate into an ability to drive economic development within the black community. Voting was a "short-term benefit" that could "deliver the Negro vote to various political machines without requiring any long-range objectives from the machines" as one black observer noted sagely. The social diversity of black Nashville made for a wider variety of personalities and issues in competition with each other, along with a lack of "unifying obstacles" that could compensate for factionalism.[50]

There was seemingly a chance for new possibilities in 1951, when Ben West, a portly attorney with a beaming face and ever-present bow tie, used black votes to defeat Thomas Cummings narrowly. The incumbent mayor had made modest overtures toward improving black conditions and earned the support of the *Globe*. But West, vice mayor under Cummings, had laid the groundwork for his own political base by courting both power brokers and black voters. In 1949, West took the unusual step of formally addressing an audience at Fisk's annual Race Relations Institute and after his election maintained a black cabinet that met every Saturday morning for breakfast. African Americans were put on the transit board and the housing authority. More importantly, working in tandem with the Solid Block, and with the support of the *Nashville Banner*, West spearheaded a 1949 law that changed the districting for municipal elections. As whites continued to disperse outward from the city, leaving a disproportionate number of blacks behind, certain council districts were becoming majority black. This trend made African Americans eager to elect one of their own and to vote for white politicians supportive of that goal—Ben West being the most willing of all. After his 1951 victory, West fashioned a powerful grip on the city, mostly through patronage. This was both a source of opportunity and frustration for black leaders. The issue of black employment in city hall, for example, was governed by a civil service board populated by representatives from the Chamber of Commerce, the local labor council, and post number 5 of the American Legion (each a powerful political constituency). Yet, even as West condemned this arrangement, he secretly controlled it; as one person said, "virtually every appointment made in the past years was in accordance with the Mayor's wishes and direction." Indeed, the mayor knew how to keep his underlings in line; he was reported as saying on the eve of his 1955 election that "if any bananas fall off the bunch, I will personally skin them." Another observer remarked years later that "roughly two-thirds of the present members of the city council are said to be reluctant to speak or vote in a manner that might embarrass Mayor West." Sometimes West was mindful of rewarding his black supporters, however, as when he appointed one black attorney, Coyness L. Ennix, former head of the Solid Block, to the school board and facilitated the election of two black attorneys, Z. Alexander Looby and Robert E. Lillard, to city council seats in 1951.[51]

Freshly minted councilman Zephaniah Alexander Looby loomed large in Nashville's history. Born in Antigua in 1899, he led a vagabond life on a whaling ship before abandoning his billet in Massachusetts and working a variety of odd jobs. After an undergraduate degree from Howard and a law degree from Columbia, he obtained a doctorate in law from New York University. This accomplishment conveniently permitted white southern judges to call him "Doctor" rather than "Mister," which, when used for blacks, was repugnant to many southern whites of this era. In the mid-1920s, Looby departed from Memphis and the smothering political atmosphere created by Boss Crump. Settling in Nashville, he taught courses at Fisk while establishing a night law school for blacks. A staunch Republican and an Episcopalian who loved poker and quoting Shakespeare to juries, Looby was an eloquent and dignified figure. Among his talents was puncturing white pretensions, and the *Globe* chortled frequently about his 1942 lawsuit to equalize teacher salaries in Nashville. The lawsuit stemmed from the reality that black teachers with a master's degree earned lower salaries than white teachers with only a bachelor's degree. In cross-examining W. A. Bass, Nashville's school superintendent, the administrator claimed under oath that "Negro teachers need less money to maintain their standard of living than do white teachers." Looby responded by asking Bass if "he was in the habit of visiting the homes of his Negro teachers and finding out their standard of living"? The presiding judge likewise chimed in to see if Bass knew "where in Nashville could a Negro teacher get a bottle of milk cheaper than a white teacher?" and ruled for Looby's client. Perhaps Looby's finest moment came in 1946. In Columbia, a small town south of Nashville, he defended black veterans who fought back when threatened by whites, setting off a riot that consumed the town. Looby fearlessly attacked the prosecution's case without flinching at death threats and murder attempts and won some acquittals from an all-white jury—a rare feat for a black lawyer at the time.[52]

As a leading figure in both the local and national NAACP, Looby instigated and won a series of lawsuits in 1940s and 1950s Nashville. In addition to the successful teacher salary case, he won the right for black doctors to practice in white hospitals and overturned segregated parks. Looby persisted despite being threatened by letters, phone calls, and a gasoline-doused cross that failed to ignite. Once elected to city council, Looby put forth a constant stream of resolutions throughout the 1950s to desegregate various public spaces in Nashville, including the Parthenon and the airport restaurants. Mayor Ben West, with one eye toward Looby's constituents and another toward Interstate Commerce Commission rulings that forbade segregation in these areas, quickly signed such legislation. West also supported laws forbidding cross burnings and upped the hiring of blacks in city government—although such hires had curtailed powers and were seldom promoted—and ended Jim Crow on city buses.[53]

Looby's fellow black councilman, Robert E. Lillard, West's protégé and a former firefighter who worked nights to obtain his law degree, preferred tactics learned from his football-playing days. As fellow black leader Reverend Kelly Miller Smith remarked, Lillard would hit low while a teammate hit high, and this applied to politics as well. According to Smith, although using "different tactics than Looby," Lillard could "complement" his ally, "softening the relationship between white persons and Negroes by keeping clear lines of communication open."[54]

This sometimes made for a tricky balance, as in 1950 when Lillard's request for a black golf course came simultaneously with Looby's countersuggestion that existing golf courses be integrated instead. Lillard's tactic was decried by the local NAACP as a "disgusting display of Uncle Tomism," especially when Lillard professed that "Negroes do not want to go where they are not wanted." It was perhaps more relevant that Lillard was working on West's behalf in trying to influence Looby's bills that would regulate the administration's city planning, including assuring nondiscrimination in the Capitol Hill redevelopment project. These maneuverings were rather overshadowed when the federal judge presiding over the segregated golf course case launched into an explanation that "white birds, black birds, blue birds, and red birds do not roost on the same limb," which thus explained why "our government does not attempt to make law or enforce law which is contrary to the general will." Such thinking would later be overturned, but the underlying point remained that African American political leadership was not in step. The possibilities and tensions between supporting black advancement and perpetuating machine politics remained constant and difficult to resolve. That both Looby and Lillard as councilmen could license restaurants where they would not be served was an additional absurdity.[55]

As Looby, Lillard, and fellow leaders struggled for a firmer legal and political base, African Americans were growing ever more restless against insults to their dignity during the 1940s and 1950s. In one case, downtown window washers went on strike; in another, a near riot was averted after police arrested a black GI. Another situation occurred when black employees at a café, disgusted with a stream of verbal and physical harassment from a boss fond of calling them "nigger," walked out of the kitchen during the Sunday afternoon high-traffic hour. A black newspaper editorial gleefully reported that the boss "could do nothing but hang his mouth open and plead for them to return (in a nice way this time). The answer was and yet is NO." More ominous was the double standard shown by the district attorney in two rape cases that drew ire from the local NAACP chapter, which complained of "vigorous and unscrupulous efforts" toward prosecuting an alleged black perpetrator, but the "hopeless" handling of a case on behalf of a black victim. Similar disregard for black life was shown in the July 1958 murder of a black youth by police in the city workhouse. "They took his life as if he was a dog," wrote one witness.[56]

Increasingly in this era, conflicts over race relations were given energy by loose rival networks of progressives and conservatives that faced off over such issues as part of more general political calculations. Nashville's two white newspapers provided the most visible manifestation of these networks. Under powerful and mercurial publisher James G. Stahlman, the older of the two papers, the *Nash-*

ville Banner, adhered to a reactionary philosophy of states' rights and individualism. Stahlman, who loved birds so much that he ordered his reporters to chop icy ponds so that ducks would not be trapped as the water froze, had a raging temper and stubborn personality. He detested the federal government so much that daylight savings times (an egregious error, in Stahlman's view) was completely ignored in the *Banner* newsroom and on the giant clock tower that housed the paper, causing much confusion across the city. His influence as publisher, combined with his connections in the business community and his membership on the Vanderbilt Board of Trust, made him a powerful player in Nashville—some called him the most powerful man in the city.[57]

Many observers saw in Stahlman behavior borne from his family's history. The Stahlmans carried three burdens: first, they were immigrants; second, they were German immigrants, which was a particular problem during World War I; and third, they were German *carpetbagger* immigrants. Stahlman's "hyper-patriotism and self-conscious Southernisms" were, some of his friends whispered, "a somewhat sad attempt to become part of an elite group which had never completely accepted his family." Aware of such whispers, Stahlman instead defended his "love of this country and for all its fundamental institutions—sometimes characterized by my critics as superpatriotism or worse." In terms of Nashville's race relations, this meant that, whenever possible, Stahlman used his newspaper to assail the U.S. Supreme Court, federal encroachment on individual and state liberties, and the Communist threat. In his own paternalistic way, Stahlman made efforts to contribute to and thus manage black uplift. As he never tired of boasting, he hired the first black reporter for a white newspaper in the South, Robert Churchwell, chosen because of a tenuous connection with the Solid Block. However, his colleagues at the *Banner* were dismissive about Churchwell, who later wrote movingly about the daily stresses he endured in trying to become a proper journalist. He described being forced to work from home and being excluded from staff events and Christmas parties, all while working for a paper that ran articles quoting a Vanderbilt professor who claimed that Negroes were direct descendants of apes and gorillas. It was a lonely existence as Stahlman's viewpoints matched the perspective of certain traditionally minded politicians, academics, and businessmen in the suburbs and small communities that ringed the city and, along with Nashville's old-money elite, comprised the local country club set.[58]

In contrast to Stahlman's *Banner*, the *Nashville Tennessean* spoke for progressive voices in the city, and the two had a healthy but visceral rivalry. (*Tennessean* partisans referred to "From the Shoulder," Stahlman's column in the *Banner*, as "From the Armpit.") By the New Deal era, the *Tennessean* had become a champion of the Democratic Party and in midcentury threw itself into battles against the Tennessee poll tax, which charged an annual fee to both black and poor white voters. The newspaper's crusading spirit won the hearts of similar-minded Nashvillians and reformist politicians open to remaking Nashville. The *Tennessean* also appealed to those local groups, usually religious or academic, that alternated between periods of spirited activism and benign neglect while working for racial reform. Internally, however, the *Tennessean* charted a more ambivalent course on racial issues with a moderate publisher, a conservative editor, and liberal reporters. The image of the *Tennessean* as a racially progressive paper was often due more to the *Banner*'s counterexample. Only by the mid-1960s would the *Tennessean* become more consistent in advocating substantive racial change. It is perhaps most telling that civil rights leaders in Nashville would later criticize both newspapers for not rendering adequately the movement's essence. One alternative voice, the black-owned *Nashville Globe*, relished its role as the newspaper for the African American community by supporting or scolding the *Tennessean* and *Banner* as it saw fit. As one *Globe* editorial put it, "None of the daily papers here is any better than the other, although some may not be as unfair all of the time as they are most of the time." A few other black newspapers, often organized on behalf of various political organizations, occasionally chimed in but maintained uneven influence over events.[59]

The locals reading these newspapers tied into broader political networks linked with groups across the South. One such group, the Southern Conference for Human Welfare (SCHW), helped spur prolonged efforts to oppose the poll tax. Headquartered in Nashville for some years, along with its affiliated youth group, the Council of Young Southerners, the SCHW's 1942 meeting in Nashville even received straightforward coverage from the *Banner* and *Tennessean*. But the SCHW also found itself subjected to red-baiting and conservative backlashes, especially when Stahlman blamed the group's leader, James Dombrowski, for helping orchestrate responses to the Columbia race riot.[60]

Another South-wide group, the Southern Regional Council (SRC), was a predominately but not exclusively white organization descended from the Council of Interracial Cooperation and the Association of Southern Women for the Prevention of Lynching. The SRC ultimately achieved a wider following than the SCHW, partially through a cautious tempering of its message and also through a scrupulous presentation of factual information to sway consciences (and pocketbooks) to ameliorate Jim Crow. On a local level, chapters affiliated with the SRC tried quiet individual lobbying to achieve the same results. The driving force establishing Nashville's chapter of the SRC was Ella P. Mims, daughter of Edwin Mims, chair of the English department at Vanderbilt. The group, founded on July 27, 1946, as the Tennessee Conference on Human Relations (TCHR) was, Ella Mims conceded, "preponderantly an academic and church group" and "we need representatives of business, state and city government, lawyers, doctors, [and] labor." The group decided to stress their aloofness from the SCHW, who "have succeeded in antagonizing more or less everybody that is in a position to do anything." Particular note was taken of Stahlman's ability to hound those that he disagreed with; it was stated frankly that "the *Banner* is a problem. . . . It's a pernicious influence here and there is a very reactionary element in Nashville that swears by it." The TCHR initiative stalled when Ella Mims resigned her position in order to care for her sick sister. For many subsequent years, Nashville struggled to produce a viable interracial organization. On March 25, 1956, the TCHR met in Nashville to try to shake itself out of its stupor, but the lack of activity continued. Essentially, the Tennessee chapter remained stagnant because of a failure to organize and finance itself effectively as it repeatedly requested the national branch for financial bail-outs.[61]

Other interracial groups, such as the Fellowship of Reconciliation and the Congress of Racial Equality, had at best a feeble presence in Nashville, although they would make themselves known in coming years. Smaller groups created some pockets of interracial cooperation, if not always integration, usually under the auspices of a church or educational meeting where reprisals were less feared, and usually prompted by women. The first desegregated clubs in Nashville were the local chapters of the American Association of University Women and the United Church Women during the early and mid-1950s, followed a few years later by the League of Women Voters. Anecdotal examples exist of blacks and whites sharing dinner at the Jewish Community Center or worshiping at a local Unitarian church. It was known that Vanderbilt would host interracial professional and academic groups but did not encourage their use of dining or residence halls; guests would retire to Peabody or Scarritt to eat lunch. At Fisk, of course, interracial events took place regularly. The Methodist publishing house employed blacks, which "rocked the town for a while," but the organization, "a somewhat self-contained fellowship," remained isolated from Nashville society as a whole.[62]

Yet, while the early role of women and religious figures pushing for desegregation was significant, it should not be overstated. In the late 1950s, as black leaders did reconnaissance on segregation downtown, they found some hints that "women were the chief segregationists," with the discovery that "one large department store had desegregated its men's room many years ago, while the women's room was still segregated." As one store official confided, "Women are by far the greatest complainers." As one scholar has written, the "enforcement and perpetuation of racial etiquette was one of white women's chief forms of collusion in the Jim Crow system." Likewise, religious groups—of the local minister's association, for example—remained interracial in appearances only, rather than through a frank exchange of ideas. White churches, said one black minister, were "politely civil to Negroes but opposed to social equality" and "patronizing to the extreme, and downright exclusive."[63]

Although more unusual, there was one realm for interracial contact that lay ninety miles east of Nashville but retained ties to the city. The Highlander Folk School, run by radical educator and social activist Myles Horton, had been founded as a training school for labor organizers. Horton's educational philosophy stressed the abilities of oppressed people to foment social justice through their own efforts, and he foresaw the attack on Jim Crow as the next great challenge. As early as 1944, Highlander's union workshops had integrated meals and sleeping quarters. Horton also began hosting a series of interracial workshops dedicated to training civil rights leaders; famously, Martin Luther King Jr. and Rosa Parks were participants. Such publicity catapulted Highlander into the national spotlight and enraged local and state authorities. Lingering resentment against the school culminated in 1959 as Tennessee police raided Highlander to concoct trumped-up charges against Horton.[64]

Through the 1940s and 1950s, however, the little institution persevered, steadfastly maintaining its work and mission. Both black and white Nashvillians associated with Highlander worked within the city for racial progress. Cecil Brandstetter, for example, the attorney who would defend Highlander in 1959, was a labor lawyer based in Nashville and carried some local political influence behind the scenes. His young protégé, George Barrett, began his activism as a gopher carrying people to and from Highlander workshops and parlayed his legal career in Nashville into support for labor and racial causes. Likewise, a number of academics from Fisk and other black schools in Nashville were eager contributors to Highlander programs. Perhaps most prominent, Herman Long, a distinguished sociologist and later president of Talladega College in Alabama, served as one point of connection between Highlander and his mentor at Fisk, Charles S. Johnson.[65]

Johnson equaled Z. Alexander Looby in his work for racial change. A prominent sociologist, influential in the Harlem Renaissance before becoming research director of the National Urban League, Johnson was a nationally recognized author in the field of race relations lured to Fisk in 1928. The quiet intelligence and shy dignity with which Johnson carried himself appealed to both his subordinates and the powerful whites from whom he had to wheedle funds for his projects. He would ascend to the presidency of Fisk—the first African American to do so—in 1947, over the objections of some Fisk alumni, particularly W. E. B. Du Bois, who protested Johnson's close ties to whites and a misplaced faith in interracial understanding as opposed to the pursuit of power. Johnson's foremost efforts centered on the Department of Race Relations at Fisk. Founded in January 1943, the department was a think tank devoted specifically to attacking segregation. Johnson assembled a high quality staff, including Herman Long, that collected data on race relations issues and conducted freelance work for cities and organizations around the country. Perhaps the chief example of the department's importance was the Race Relations Institute, which began in July 1944 and met annually for the next twenty-five years. The institute, a conference of international stature, hosted scholars and activists meeting to hear lectures and compare notes. In keeping with Johnson's preferences, the conference kept an elevated tone in the sense that participants dealt with racism with an academic viewpoint from an array of psychological, anthropological, historical, and sociological angles. Yet the meetings emphasized implicitly that the institute should be practically minded; it was conceived as "a laboratory of social action" prompting social scientists to apply their research to real-world issues.[66]

Thus Nashville had individuals advocating for racial justice, albeit with varying degrees of activism, who could take advantage of institutional support linked to black and white progressives throughout the South open to ameliorating racial inequalities. Although other progressive Nashvillians moved cautiously, they did what they could through direct interpersonal interaction that held some promise for more humane race relations in the future. But similar contacts of more conservatively inclined whites also called Nashville home. As Charles S. Johnson tried to connect progressive blacks and whites together with a broader scholarly and activist community, a white professor attempted to do much the same among conservative figures.

While nowhere near as influential as Johnson, Donald Davidson, a poet and professor of English at Vanderbilt, wielded his pen for a very different cause. A member of Vanderbilt's famous 1920s literary group known as the Fugitives, Davidson also was a driving force behind the Southern Agrarians, a group spun off from the Fugitives and collective authors of the polemic *I'll Take My Stand* (1930). This book lambasted northern industrialization's encroachment on southern identity and remains an influential chapter in twentieth-century intellectual history. Eventually, Davidson's Agrarian brethren relinquished their commitment to defending Dixie. But Davidson's personal and intellectual sympathies to the South hardened as the 1940s and 1950s wore on, and he became increasingly devoted to, as one supporter put it, resisting "the whole tendency of things in this country since 1865."[67]

Davidson's regionalist viewpoint had racial implications, and the poet remained particularly touchy on issues of race. His core belief was that African Americans had been severed from their culture and historical identity when slavery took them from their homeland. In lacking such identity, Davidson reasoned that blacks could compensate only by adopting elements of the dominant white culture and therefore would always be intrinsically inferior to whites. While many moderate whites, such as fellow writers Robert Penn Warren and Allen Tate, also held this view, it took on enhanced power for Davidson because African Americans symbolized his wider fear that white southern culture could succumb to outside influences and be lost. Still, other essays reveal a nasty contempt for black people as "kinky-headed" and a deep-rooted distaste for miscegenation.[68]

In 1945, Davidson wrote perhaps his most revealing essay on race, the impassioned defense of segregation, "Preface to Decision." This piece stresses the elements of "Law and Custom," which he argues take precedence over sociological rhetoric about equality. To Davidson, white awareness of racial differences stems from real and irrevocable historical inequalities that foreswear any academic understanding of racial parity. The "historical memory" of the South that understood "history as a causal force" trumped what Davidson sees as the romanticism and abstraction of sociologists who aim foolishly to set law and custom in conflict. Davidson understands that segregation laws "may often cause humiliation or inconvenience individuals. But they originate in positive concern for the whole race, not in ill will toward the Negro race; and they carry strongly implied secondary concern for the Negro race." Indeed, Davidson argues, segregation "represent[s] concessions rather than studied attempts at oppression. In a practical and concrete form, they establish the conditions of tolerance—the conditions without which tolerance might become difficult or impossible." When laws are interpreted in direct contradiction of custom, writes Davidson, the result, as exhibited by the Fourteenth Amendment and the New Deal, yields "totalitarian government," where the will of the people becomes subverted to a centralized authority under the guise of abstract, unrealistic principles. Thus, to Davidson, a society anxious to defend itself from outside infection needs consonance between the racial customs of a people and laws that fortify those customs.[69]

Although Davidson's social writings may seem particularly antiquated, he articulated one version of a broader white mentality and many with similar viewpoints rallied with him. Particularly vocal in his support was *Banner* publisher Jimmy Stahlman, who circulated Davidson's essay in his newspaper. Other opportunities for Stahlman's flag waving came in 1948 when the Dixiecrat Party inspired the imaginations of many southern segregationists. A cadre of like-minded individuals in Nashville, including Davidson, brandished the States Rights party banner. Stahlman also supported the arch-conservative John Birch Society editorially. The *Banner* occasionally boiled over with vitriol against places like the Highlander Folk School and Fisk's Race Relations Institute, although even the *Tennessean* had criticized the latter for some of the rhetoric stemming from the Institution's lectures, especially after one speech described the potential for various minorities around the world to "slap down" whites. But only Stahlman pressured Fisk's president to close the institute, less in response to the speeches than to the interracial dorms that housed participants. Although Johnson won that battle, fighting off such pressure was a constant strain on activist energies, and this would only heighten in coming years.[70]

As Nashville entered the 1950s, the various political and social shifts in the city coexisted uneasily with more pronounced cultural attitudes that regarded change as suspect. Certainly the evolution of white racial attitudes still lagged; as journalist David Halberstam recalled years later, Nashville remained "culturally conservative and more than a little smug, and it liked to think of itself in social terms as representing a genteel part of the older South." It made for a provincialism masquerading as worldliness and this virtue, while prized by Nashvillians, also bred scorn. One visitor, from the *Saturday Evening Post*, observed that "Nashville's greatest weakness and its greatest charm" was the tendency "to view any change with caution and suspicion." The author saw Nashville as acquiescing reluctantly to an "unwilling, halting, resisting sort of progress," one that established Nashville as "a model of civic progress," but remained simultaneously suspicious that "progress replaces something that was better." A meeting of the Chamber of Commerce devoted "considerable discussion" to this article, calling the "unwarranted criticism" not only "unfortunate" but "ridiculous and outrageous and for the most part untrue." The defensiveness showed the importance of white Nashville's collective self-image—and perhaps also suggested the article's accuracy.[71]

Thus Nashville by the 1950s was rife with paradoxes. The city comprised black and white institutions that staked common claim to creating Nashville's character, even as racial and class differences remained prevalent throughout the city. Similarly, the city had a veneer of political and rhetorical progressivism covering a more hardened layer of cultural conservatism. Race made all these qualities stand in starkest relief as the city encompassed two segregated but occasionally overlapping worlds that met in quotidian if slanted ways. When racial interaction did occur, it created interstitial moments that sometimes promised to erode the segregated barrier, but more often served as a salve to the self-image of those believing in the fiction of cordial race relations. As Charles S. Johnson put it, there was communication between races but "no agenda for that communication." Rhetoric rarely seemed in tune with action. The daily intricacies of racial etiquette glossed over more enduring realities about race in Nashville. There was enough variability in the segregated line for whites to praise their own progressiveness, and similarly, many African Americans acknowledged that other towns had much worse race relations. But that flexibility did not preclude the many other ways in which segregation had tenacious hold over both races—in their mind-sets, in their daily existence, and in the range of choices they had in living their lives. The occasional ability that blacks had to navigate social space and preserve one's interests in everyday life was a far cry from having a voice about how more enduring political and economic realities in urban space altered lives in drastically different ways. In coming years, as opportunities for black freedom beckoned and as racial issues shook the city and nation, this cluster of paradoxes would be tested.[72]

TWO

The Triumph of Tokenism
Public School Desegregation

As morning dawned on September 9, 1957, nineteen African American six-year-olds tightly gripped the hands of their elders as they made their way to new and unfamiliar schools. Rocks, spit, and insults cascaded through the air as policemen, protesters, and parents flanked their paths. One white woman in near-hysterics screamed "pull that black kinky hair out" as the schoolchildren passed her. Picket signs at various schools read "GOD IS THE AUTHOR OF SEGREGATION," "KEEP OUR WHITE SCHOOLS WHITE," "THE MAYOR IS A RAT," and "WHAT GOD HAS PUT ASUNDER LET NOT MAN PUT TOGETHER." As one black preacher escorted some youngsters into Glenn School, white teenage boys, backed by a booing crowd, were photographed standing behind the minister, pretending to measure him for a coffin. Hand in hand with her grandchild, a black woman, unnerved by "a gauntlet of hissing whites" and pent up with internal anguish, drew what was reported as a paring knife (it was actually a nail file) from under her shirt and cried, "if any of you jump me, I'm going to use this." That evening, a *Time* reporter witnessed "hot-eyed rabble-rouser John Kasper," who "mentioned the name of one of Nashville's Negro civic leaders and dramatically held up a rope, then hazily talked about dynamite." A parent remembered years afterward that "I have never had people look at me like that in my life. . . . I mean, with hate, like they wanted to kill me."[1]

In the three years after the *Brown v. Board of Education of Topeka* decision, Nashville's atmosphere had become toxic. But it had not always been so. Immediately after the court's ruling and subsequent mandate to desegregate public schools "with all possible speed," both the school board and local political leaders had announced that the decision would be obeyed. But, even with that avowal, the powers-that-be in Nashville dithered, and that indecision fed the determination and commitment of a diverse lot of segregationists who rushed to fill the vacuum. This, in turn, prompted a somewhat weaker counterpush from progressives inclined to let the court's decision stand. Meanwhile, black Nashvillians found themselves trying to direct the situation to their advantage in a racial climate turned increasingly menacing. Hopes and fears of all heightened as the potential embodied by the court ruling drew closer. Amid these crosscurrents of tensions that drew from federal, state, and grassroots pressure, white moderate Nashvillians found themselves nearly paralyzed by the contradictions between the legal compulsion to desegregate and their preference for Jim Crow custom. Finding ways to negotiate this contradiction would prove a tremendous challenge—and ultimately the moderates' finest hour.

Initially, reaction to the *Brown* decision from influential whites was stoic if unenthusiastic. The *Tennessean* declared editorially only that the South should shoulder its new responsibilities with calm grace, a tone matched by the rival *Banner*, which sounded a similar note cautioning against "demagogic appeals" and warning that implementing *Brown* would be a lengthy process that needed to be "satisfactory both to the states and to the Federal Government." Similarly, Tennessee Governor Frank G. Clement's official response acknowledged the supreme authority of the U.S. Supreme Court and counseled patience. The young and ambitious politician's statement remained faithful to his political style, as he had good reasons to tread carefully. Clement favored an old-fashioned, preacherly style of political oratory that played well to his constituents, softening a reputation that exemplified the moderate leadership that generally ruled Tennessee politics. Because he thirsted for higher office, and especially coveted the 1956 Democratic vice presidential opening, he happily cultivated this moderate label. Constantly mindful of how a national audience might warm to him, he still tried not to alienate local voters. Reacting to the *Brown* decision made for a tricky balancing act— and also an opportunity—that Clement would attempt to negotiate over the next three years. For now, he was content to squash a preliminary announcement from his attorney general and state solicitor general that Tennessee would submit a gradual desegregation plan for the court's consideration. It was more prudent for Clement to see how the *Brown* ruling would be implemented before committing to a stance. Throughout the state, political and journalistic conversation about the ruling dwindled to await further developments.[2]

Others moved more decisively. Only hours after the news broke, local NAACP attorney Z. Alexander Looby signaled his intentions by formally requesting that the city and county school boards dismantle their segregated school systems. A similar petition soon came from Robert W. Rempfer, a white mathematics professor at Fisk, who asked that the Nashville school board allow his children to attend a black elementary school two blocks from his home. The request, along with a similar one from Rempfer's colleague Lee Lorch, was quickly tabled by the school board. This was the first of many eight-to-one votes that Coyness L. Ennix, the lone African American on the board, would suffer over the next few years, and the board continued to ignore renewed requests from the Rempfers and Lorches. The resultant attention triggered a setback for Lorch after local segregationists began to sniff into his past. Previously fired from the City University of New York and Pennsylvania State University for his activism, Lorch had been cited for contempt by the House Un-American Activities Committee for refusing to divulge details about past political affiliations. Despite sterling credentials, his contract at Fisk was allowed to expire as he became another victim to the McCarthy era's excesses. After moving to Little Rock, his wife, Grace, would find herself between Elizabeth Eckford and an angry mob of whites as the schoolgirl tried to enter Central High School in 1957.[3]

The school board's inaction contrasted sharply with Nashville's Catholic schools. Even as Roman Catholic Bishop William Adrian promptly ordered that the *Brown* decision be obeyed, his edict left the details up to his subordinates throughout the diocese. Unlike the Catholic hierarchy in Memphis, which ignored Adrian's call, the Nashville deanery announced that two high schools would desegregate in fall 1954: all-male Father Ryan with eighteen black boys and all-female Cathedral with twelve black girls. Another twenty children of both genders desegregated Cathedral grade schools, although other smaller parish grade schools would do so much more slowly. Two other girls' schools operated by the Dominican Sisters also announced that they would admit African Americans, but in subsequent years tended to screen applicants to make sure they came from families "of the professions." Many subsequently considered this first school year a success, but that was only part of the story. Said Father Francis T. Shea, "we determined that everyone would be treated just alike" and "that was our only policy." The attitude led to nominal successes—a black girl at Cathedral was elected to a class office, for example—but underlying anger remained, even beyond the rocks that crashed through Father Ryan's windows every so often. While numbers varied, many white parents withdrew their students in protest, although some later returned. To calm upset parents, the diocese backed off from its policy that threatened to excommunicate Catholics who did not enroll their children in parochial schools.[4]

Within the school, merely admitting African Americans into classrooms did not necessarily alter racial attitudes, and black students later remembered a difficult adjustment. Matthew Walker, for example, recalled one teacher who accused him of cheating after he deftly solved a geometry exercise and, despite some interracial friendships, remembered a persistent "low-level hostility" to his presence. White parents' anger also led to the blatant exclusion of blacks from extracurricular activities and particularly sports. The Father Ryan football team, a local powerhouse in Tennessee athletics, found itself threatened with expulsion from its league with the prospect of black players. Later, the school would oppose such duress, but the immediate response was to cut black students from the team. Although the principal later wrote that this was due strictly to athletic ability, students wondered how this decision could be made after only one practice. Similarly, at Cathedral High School, administrators canceled the prom and replaced it with a desegregated banquet at the Hermitage Hotel downtown to defuse the prospect of interracial intimacy.[5]

Regardless, Catholic officials tried to downplay the desegregation. One priest a year later dismissed the notion that their experience was representative, saying cautiously that "we think it has worked well for us. But I don't want to urge any other school to desegregate, or to discourage them from doing so" because "they've got problems that I have no suspicion of, perhaps, and consequently, the conditions we've worked with may be entirely different." For example, Catholic schools were not coeducational, which temporarily defused some of the racialized sexual anxieties that animated resistance to desegregation. Catholics remained skittish about being racial pioneers in a heavily Protestant town—they "had learned from the time they got here to keep a low profile," as one priest put it decades later, and this meant adopting the racial outlook of the community. Moreover, Catholic school administrators from the beginning told African American pupils frankly that desegregating was due to finances in a bid to consolidate schools and costs.[6]

The uneasy first steps taken by Catholic schools showed how pragmatic decisions to desegregate coexisted with continued latent tensions about new interracial interaction. Both blacks and whites remained wary. Even as African Americans rejoiced at the *Brown* decision, it was hard not to stay watchful. The TSU student newspaper, leery of white race agitators and "the rumor-mongers who tell us that 'we ain't ready,'" warned its readers to "beware of certain things," including the "many of us who have fattened off of segregation" and "hate to see it go in any of its ugly aspects," as well as fellow students "who refuse to realize that overnight we have been thrown into a more competitive world." The cautioning was appropriate, as a small but noteworthy example soon showed. In May 1954, a group of southern educators and journalists, including key Nashvillians such as Charles S. Johnson, Vanderbilt chancellor Harvie Branscomb, and representatives from the *Banner* and *Tennessean*, met in Nashville. They agreed on the need to chronicle the immense transition that southern schools now faced. The result was the Southern Education Reporting Service (SERS). Headquartered in Nashville, SERS maintained a comprehensive archive of information on school desegregation filed by local correspondents around the region and published the *Southern School News*, a newsletter that won wide praise for its objectivity.[7]

But internally SERS struggled with the same changes it documented. A black sociologist of high caliber associated with Fisk, Bonita H. Valien, was released from SERS after leading a human relations workshop in which she stated her opinions about specific school districts' responses to the *Brown* ruling. With the resultant publicity, the SERS board decided that her statement conflicted with the scrupulously neutral stance that SERS wished to cultivate, and Valien's contract was quietly not renewed. The lone African American working for SERS, she had been continually shortchanged of salary, resources, and responsibilities, as her office remained "under repair" for long stretches of time. The *Tennessean* and *Banner* editors on the SERS board had advised that local opinion would frown on a black correspondent working on interracial terms. Charles S. Johnson, fighting for his protégé and a basic principle, pointed out that the Methodist publishing house in Nashville had an interracial work environment and that the black press across the nation would not look favorably on an all-white SERS. But his protests were to no avail. Despite the valuable service provided by SERS, they ultimately symbolized the persistence of racial tradition lurking under the changing racial environment and Nashville's moderate image.[8]

By early 1955, segregationists were marshaling their forces across the state and South. The first salvo in Tennessee was fired when state senator Charles A. Stainback proposed legislation enabling school boards to assign students to schools in ways that prevented desegregation. Stainback based his bill on the police powers of the state, the doctrine granting governments wide scope to legislate against potential social disorder. Stainback, tired of the political tiptoeing following the *Brown* decision, asserted that "this bill is intended to preserve segregation" and "we don't make any secrets about that. This whole thing has been sh! sh! wait! wait! Why wait? The time has come to speak out and act." The legislative hearings prompted exactly that as scores of citizens came to testify for and against the bill. Nashville NAACP leader C. M. Hayes called the bill "in every sense against the word of God" and scolded the dozens of whites who left the hearing room as she began her statement: "they won't stay here to hear both sides." Faced with a challenge to his leadership on the race question, Governor Clement became the first southern governor to stand against segregationist legislators by vetoing the bill (although more quietly he allowed a state bill that gave school boards control over teachers being "suitably placed" in faculties, an ominous development for desegregating teaching faculties). Clement's stance against the state representatives found support from both the *Tennessean* and the *Banner*, the latter newspaper arguing that the Stainback bill was clearly based on "specious reasoning" and waiting to respond to a "federal decree neither then nor now spelled out" was far more sensible. Silence continued to be Tennessee's official response. This did not go unnoticed by Tennessee's sister states, many of whom were busily passing legislation to forestall or minimize the effects of any school desegregation. The attorney general of Georgia went so far as to lament that "Tennessee's position on the segregation problem has embarrassed Georgia to the point that Tennessee is no longer a friend."[9]

The statement signaled the white South's contempt for the U.S. Supreme Court, particularly after May 1955 when the *Brown II* decision decreed that desegregation should occur "with all deliberate speed." That, plus the surge in black lawsuits across the South, sent many stunned whites across the South into a groundswell of angered action. Foremost in the segregationist mobilization known as "massive resistance" were the Citizens' Councils, described as "country-club Klans" for their genteel membership. Based in Mississippi, the councils soon had a string of local chapters throughout the South. While carefully distancing themselves publicly from violent acts by groups such as the newly revived Ku Klux Klan, the councils contributed to the intimidating climate by using economic pressure and political influence. Council members were often bankers, insurance brokers, and merchants who punished whites and blacks unwilling to toe the segregated line and lobbied state and local politicians to do the same.[10]

While these tactics were not unheard of outside the Deep South, they were deployed in a more ad hoc fashion where the council's presence was less visible and unified. In Nashville, the closest equivalent to a council was a segregationist organization known as the Tennessee Federation for Constitutional Government (TFCG), incorporated on June 30, 1955. Its chairman was Donald Davidson, the Vanderbilt English professor who in 1945 had written stirringly about the white segregationist mentality. A handful of Nashville conservatives, especially those active in the 1948 Dixiecrat movement, joined him, including the eccentric attorney, realtor, and abstract artist Jack Kershaw, attorney Thomas P. Gore (cousin to then-Senator Albert Gore Sr.), and businessmen, lawyers, and Vanderbilt faculty members.[11]

The TFCG's curiousness derived from its philosophy and tactics. While members maintained some overlapping relationships with various local segregationist groups, the TFCG remained jealously provincial about Tennessee matters and was often coy about affiliating with other organizations. Although this would later change, the TFCG originally "claimed 'no relation' to the Citizens' Councils" and even incorporated separately from its ostensible namesake, the Southwide Federation of Constitutional Government, because its "exact relationship" to the national group had "not been fully determined." This guardedness was partly because Davidson saw the TFCG as more than just a prosegregation group. He wanted instead to use the massive resistance cause to launch a broader defense of southern culture and conservative principles. "The great argument over 'inferiority' or 'superiority' is not, after all, exactly to the point," he wrote. "The South's determined preference is to maintain white society as white. That preference cannot be removed by the decree of any court." Instead, he wrote, "all the legal problems reduce in the end to one stark question: What kind of government is the United States getting to be?" By giving district courts power to enforce the *Brown* decree by literally formulating policy for school boards, Davidson argued that "a camouflage of idealism and quasi-legal dicta" would permit "a Leviathan-type of federal government" that would prove "increasingly dictatorial in tendency." The TFCG noted that any court ruling making Tennessee segregation unconstitutional in alignment with *Brown* would "invalidate the entire section of the State Constitution upon which our public schools are founded," leaving Tennessee's public schools "without a constitutional and legal basis for existence." The enormous power of the federal government to compel racial association and thus threaten the very basis of southern society proved to Davidson that all his earlier fears as an Agrarian were justified.[12]

Despite the racial paternalism at the core of Davidson's mentality, the legal and constitutional concerns that adorned these sentiments were equally important. The style with which Davidson led the TFCG reflected the substance of his principles. His central motivation besides integration itself struggled between his disgust for the federal government's remote power and his fear of violence in a lawless society. The weight of such issues made him insist that the TFCG be, as the foremost historian of the Citizens' Councils put it, a "respectable" version of the massive resistance movement. This stress remained a constant refrain in every interview or article he gave on behalf of the TFCG. He advocated, as his biographer pointed out, something sounding "suspiciously like civil disobedience." Yet, by confining itself entirely to governmental channels and grassroots persuasion, the TFCG's rigidity proved to be the very source of their eventual failure.[13]

The segregationist mobilization moved desegregation forces into some weak action as both began trying to swing popular sentiment to their side. Even as the TFCG was forming, local leaders of the United Church Women and the Council of Jewish Women called a workshop sponsored by twelve religious and academic groups in May 1955. Five hundred citizens attended the "Supreme Court Decision and Its Meaning for Our Community" panel discussion at the Jewish Community Center. Just under two hundred attended a follow-up meeting broken down into twelve interracial discussion groups. Yet mixed signals were filtering in from black neighborhoods and betraying other ambivalences. In Davidson County (which was Nashville's county, but with a separate school system), the black Parent-Teacher Association declared to the school board that, instead of desegregation, it wanted equal school facilities. The letter indicated that many African Americans were less concerned with laying claim to white schools than getting their fair share of school financing and supplies. Aware of this, the city school board had, in an abrupt about-face, started pumping money into black schools after the *Brown* decision, attempting belatedly to restore the "equal" in "separate but equal" and delay desegregation, a tactic common across the South. While the *Globe* welcomed this move as necessary for the school system as a whole, other issues lingered. From a black child's perspective, desegregation was a daunting prospect. Black schools, despite reflecting severe inequalities in being chronically ill-equipped and underfunded, still served as supportive environments behind the enemy lines of Jim Crow. Here, dedicated teachers could instill African American children with the pride and ability to survive the southern racial order. Black teachers themselves felt lukewarm about desegregation. While staunchly supporting the local NAACP's legal actions, they had private fears about transitioning to a desegregated workplace; they worried about keeping their jobs (justifiably, as it turned out) and dreaded facing potentially hostile white children and principals. Many of these teachers already had a sense of the school board's lack of respect for their expertise; one common tactic was to appoint black teachers to advisory panels on educational topics but then make decisions without the panel's input. Black Nashvillians remained hopeful about *Brown*'s promise, but deeply uneasy about how events would play out.[14]

As African American pupils continued trying to enroll in white schools, and continued to be turned away, Z. Alexander Looby further prodded the school board by filing *Robert W. Kelley et al. v. Board of Education of Nashville* in September 1955. His strategy targeted the Nashville city schools, which was 35.6 percent African American, with the hope that county schools (with drastically smaller numbers of blacks) would follow. The lawsuit featured twenty-one black children as plaintiffs and later included the Lorch and Rempfer cases, as well. In characteristic fashion, the school board reaffirmed its willingness to comply with *Brown* but chose only to appoint a four-man committee to study the situation more closely and await direction from the courts.[15]

The board's response was typical. Beset from both sides by black legal pressure and segregationist ire, most educators and politicians in the city and throughout the South were stalling. Nashville's leaders wrung their hands about whether or how to comply with the law without increasing racial friction. Their sensitivity had only grown in mid-June 1955 after the state board of education approved desegregating Tennessee's public universities. The plan required that graduate schools accept African Americans starting that September, and continue the year thereafter with undergraduate seniors, followed by junior, sophomore, and finally freshman classes in each successive academic year. The rationale was to minimize potential disorder—and desegregation itself—by phasing in desegregation over time. But even this plan produced howls from both sides. From the progressive standpoint, such actions ignored the moral aspect of the *Brown* decision: if segregation was wrong, steps to correct this wrong in a wholesale manner should be taken immediately. Said Looby, "it is evasive" and "neither prompt nor reasonable."[16] Segregationists saw it completely differently: that any submission to an improper and immoral court dictum was equally wrong, no matter how gingerly compliance occurred.

The school board's nervousness was exacerbated by State Commissioner of Education Quill E. Cope's announcement that the burden of desegregating would be borne solely by local school districts; the state board would retain an advisory capacity only. Taking that cue, the Nashville school board maintained its glacial pace. The instruction committee, charged with formulating the blueprint for desegregating, reported on July 14, 1955, that it had sent a questionnaire to forty southern cities to glean advice on dealing with the *Brown* ruling. The committee also moved up by six months a planned census of schools that would give a full picture of the school system's current make-up and began a series of meetings with school principals, PTA chapters, parents, and other citizens. The committee pleaded for "time to work out details, so that we may proceed with caution and guarantee the continued progress of a peaceful, harmonious cooperation for better relationships and the advancement of the best interests of all our children." Coyness L. Ennix, the sole black board member, tried to impel further action by proposing that the board deal more directly with Looby and the NAACP so that "the Board may explore the whole integration question." The motion, waiting for seconding, met with silence. A month later, the committee further hindered progress by deciding that "too many unresolved problems" precluded desegregation from occurring in the 1955–56 school year, which prompted Looby to up the ante with his *Kelley* lawsuit.[17]

The school board's worries contrasted with the quiet reality that desegregation was slowly taking place, or about to take place, in many of Nashville's private colleges and universities. Across town, white students had always been a small but consistent presence in the Fisk student body, mostly through exchange programs with other nonsouthern schools in the United States, but four white women had earned their degrees from the school since the university's founding. And the Fisk Experimental School had been integrated for nine years, by 1956 being one-third white. By the 1955–56 academic year, Fisk had fifteen whites students enrolled, including four undergraduates. In coming years, Meharry Medical College would accept a white medical student and a white dental student. In 1952, Scarritt College for Christian Workers had quietly enrolled black students. This was a more pronounced wedge in segregation, because Scarritt students were permitted to take courses at Vanderbilt and Peabody College for Teachers. A year later, one African American enrolled in Vanderbilt Divinity School for a graduate degree.[18]

Yet, even as the color line in schools seemed to be loosening, it was actually stiffening in other ways. Peabody's story as a small but influential presence in southern education networks is instructive, as President Henry Hill's stubborn timidity made for an uneven course. Hill's dilemma showed how conflicting realities jarred with racial preferences. The Southern Education Foundation and Kellogg Foundation that underwrote much of the school's programs were increasingly unwilling to finance schools that persisted in segregating. But Hill worried that Peabody might lose enrollment (and thus money) if the school desegregated, even as he felt some pressure from some of his faculty and some of his executive committee to do so. To placate them, desegregation for graduate students was approved in fall 1953. Soon thereafter, Hill permitted fourteen African American principals to take a special administrative training session on campus in summer 1954. But even this nominal move was bittersweet, as no whites were included in the program held during a summer intersession. Moreover, the black participants were refused campus housing (and thus forced to overpay for rent in local neighborhoods) and were barred from the cafeteria, gym, and swimming pool. Despite some consternation at even this half step, Hill found solace in the idea that few black students would choose Peabody with Fisk and TSU in town, or that they would qualify if they did so. "I think we can control this situation," Hill confided in 1958, and continued believing for years that social integration need not accompany educational desegregation.[19]

At Vanderbilt, the most influential school in the city that fostered much of the city's elite, the story was much the same but with even more powerful alumni registering dismay. The school's chancellor, Harvie Branscomb, a noted New Testament scholar, had some progressive credentials. But, like Henry Hill, he wobbled between trying to attract grant money to fuel Vanderbilt's growth while assuaging those conservative members on his board of trust who refused to desegregate. When the law school followed the divinity school in accepting a black student, it incensed some law school alumni, many of whom were active in the TFCG and quick to complain. Their letters to Vanderbilt administrators dismissed the "new intellectual or broadminded trend" that was fueling desegregation, saying instead that admission into Vanderbilt was "a privilege, not a right." They also called for a separate association to accredit southern schools and tried to assure the administration that many would donate money to keep Vanderbilt all white and in sufficient amounts to compensate for the "socialistic, leftist money from the North." One wrote that "I want colored people to have every educational advantage and all the fine things of life they can get by working for it just as we all have to do" but added that "My opinion of a little bit of desegregation is like a little bit of a cancer, or a little bit of syphilis, or a little bit of pregnancy." Yet, even as the most inflexible segregationists held these views, Vanderbilt officials understood that segregation could be maintained even after black students were enrolled and at a quieter volume. One administrator cautioned that desegregation would be "limited to courses not available in Nashville in other institutions" and further confided that "It is generally understood by all of us" that only a few blacks would be eligible to attend Vanderbilt, and those few would be even "further limited" to the best applicants and those who "possess enough judgment and common sense to be trusted in this situation." He also acknowledged that "what most alumni fear is the presence of young negro men and women in undergraduate student life and activities," a development he did not foresee happening.[20]

As this quiet attitude slowed the African American presence in private universities, the state's public universities took a different path to the same result. During the 1956–57 academic year, Tennessee State had two white students from nearby Madison College taking classes on campus through a course-sharing program. More revealing was the University of Tennessee's branch campus in Nashville, which had a total of sixteen part-time and full-time black students by mid-1950s. Here the university carefully adhered to the strictest sense of legal rulings by admitting only those students who could not find similar degree programs at Tennessee State or Meharry. The effect, then, was to curtail African American numbers at each school even as they technically desegregated.[21]

As the Nashville school board continued to vacillate, they leaned heavily on one influential attorney. A member of the Davidson County School Board and the Southern Regional Education Board, Cecil Sims was mulling carefully over the Supreme Court's reasoning. He paused especially on a crucial component of the decision, and the source of much segregationist displeasure, that drew from psychological and sociological data to show that segregation embedded a deep-rooted inferiority complex in black children. Sims deduced from the court's phrasing that "the inferiority complex resulted not from actual attendance in a segregated school" but instead "from the legal requirement under which Negro children were *forced* to attend separate schools." In other words, the stigma lay not in the bricks and mortars of segregated schools themselves but in the mentality of difference that segregation fastened on blacks and whites, regardless of the quality of each race's school system. If this were so, Sims concluded, no plan with any sort of racial assignment would ever be considered legal, and he mocked other attempts to circumvent the Supreme Court ruling by preserving segregation without using the word directly. As he put it, "you can't pretend to go out of it and stay in it."[22]

Instead, Sims found himself enamored by the midwestern example of Evansville, Indiana, which had come as "near to solving this problem and preserving the public school system as any place I have ever seen." Evansville had used a grad-ual grade-per-year desegregation plan in conjunction with some creative zoning to allow parents to choose schools according to their personal desire. Years later, the result was minimal racial friction with a still predominantly segregated school system. This was the answer, Sims thought, as the city sent a delegation to Evans-ville to learn more. The *Brown* decision, he proposed, in an idea adopted widely by the Nashville school board and similar-minded southerners, "does not require integration." Instead, it "merely condemns compulsory separation solely because of color." There was no need to advocate for desegregation, and the fact that black school resources had been a fraction of those for white schools over decades of ne-glect was similarly beside the point. The simple act of giving every child a choice of schools fulfilled the current legal mandate, Sims argued. Whether the children would choose to endure a newly desegregated environment was an entirely dif-ferent matter and not, strictly speaking, one of concern for school boards. The legal structures allowing for desegregation could also be designed to permit racial preferences to persevere.[23]

Sims' revelations would soon prove seductive for a school board grasping for answers. And revealingly, his thinking echoed aspects of Donald Davidson's seg-regationist mentality in ways that suggested common intellectual ground as well as differences. Both stressed how racial law and racial custom were interlock-ing components that reinforced white supremacy. As Davidson fought to restore laws that reflected the will of the segregationist South, Sims more dispassionately understood that token desegregation could still converge with a mellower manag-ing of racial change. Sims allowed that "it is true that Negroes have fought for this democracy just as have the white people." And he likewise mused that "It may or may not be true that the Negro is inferior by nature—I don't know." Nothing in his experience could allow him to affirm the idea. What he did know was that the Supreme Court's authority was absolute and defiance was pointless. But he also trusted that racial custom would outlast racial law. Thus he adopted a legal model painstakingly proper in its moderate etiquette; he knelt to judicial authority while still firmly hand-in-hand with southern custom.[24]

As 1955 ended, Nashvillians of both races watched as the desegregation pro-cess hung in suspended animation and the school board appealed for patience to avoid "ruining schools and friendships." On one side, the board had Nashville NAACP leader Reverend J. F. Grimmett calling for a "manly stand" to support the *Brown* decision. On the other, segregationists found vocal expression in a Janu-ary 23 caravan and demonstration at the Tennessee State Capitol. Waving signs that read "SEGREGATION OR WAR" and "GOD, THE ORIGINAL SEGREGATIONIST," 250 white supremacists (mostly from Memphis and Chattanooga, but augmented by reinforcements from Georgia and Mississippi) noisily protested for an audience with Governor Clement to demand new laws supporting segregation. Davidson and the TFCG eschewed the demonstration, as noisy rallies offended their sensibilities, and these instincts were no doubt confirmed when the protesters nearly attacked two journalists, one of whom was African American, before a state policeman intervened.[25]

It was a "mob scene," albeit one smoothly managed by Clement. Knowing that the segregationists were gathering, he invited them into his office where they "could shake my hand if they want to" and where they were surprised to find a priest, minister, and rabbi waiting alongside a number of reporters. After allowing the segregationists to vent, Clement responded with a long speech scolding the protesters for helping the NAACP's cause with their actions. He added that "I do not believe in pressure tactics and a governor who submits to pressure rather than following reason would not be worthy of the office." Going off the record, he especially upbraided them for circulating a photograph that pictured an interracial couple lying on a bed, which Clement felt brought "indignity on the women of Tennessee, all races, by suggesting that anything would make them pose for such pictures." Having made his point, and chastising the segregationists for their behavior, Clement ended the meeting with a prayer and sent the protesters away thoroughly "whipped," as a journalist wrote. "Spelled out in Clement language, this pitch was about like having the visitors wash their mouths out with soapy water." It was a classic Clement maneuver, maintaining the appearance of fidelity to a higher morality while staying politically uncommitted with maximum room to operate. But it was a temporary victory.[26]

Progressives in Nashville also tried to hold the moderate ground as community workshops allowing citizens to voice their opinions on the *Brown* decision continued. A summary of one declared that, while "opinions vary as to the degree and strength of goodwill in our community," successful examples in Nashville of desegregated organizations, interest groups, and the city school administration meant that compliance should not be delayed. Yet ideas for how to facilitate this, mostly concerning interracial church group meetings and concerted efforts to enlist public support, were thrown out; there was a fear that citizens meeting for "an airing of different opinions" might "get out of hand and inflame prejudice." Apprehension reigned, even as participants agreed to request that both city and county school boards begin desegregating in fall 1956. These meetings also prompted the formation of the Nashville Community Relations Conference (NCRC) in April 1956. The purpose of the NCRC was "to retain the friendly relations our community has achieved in many fields, and to help resolve, in a lawful manner, unresolved problems, prejudice, discrimination, and group tension, upon a friendly, firm, and lasting basis." The group preferred a sideline role, content to work behind the scenes and by petitioning and supporting the school board as needed.[27]

The spectrum of racial perspectives in Nashville was evident in an open forum at a March 8, 1956, school board meeting. Reverend C. T. Baker, representing the Nashville Association of Churches, gave some encouragement to the board, but his words remained tepid. He called for "some action to integrate" but pleaded vaguely for "working together as people under God." With more measured force, the NCRC's Whitworth Stokes argued that the board would be "subject to criticism" if it "let moderation become immobility." He "felt the solid people in the community would stand behind the board" if the plan would "move forward slowly in compliance with the law." Joan C. Harap from the League of Women Voters pledged support from her group and asked the board to consider "the best opportunity for all of Nashville's children." Professor John Compton of Vanderbilt counseled instead that the board's attitude needed to focus on "what is just and what is right" rather than what is "happy and enjoyable," and, given that "integration will take aeons," a "gradual, sensible, and intelligent basis seems possible and required."[28]

From the segregationist side, Davidson, in keeping with the TFCG's emphasis, warned of a lack of legal authority for board actions because state funds were specified for segregated schools only. Citing a Gallup poll that 75 percent of Tennesseans preferred segregation, he urged the board to wait for the 1957 meeting of the Tennessee General Assembly, which he expected to "legislate according to the will of the people." His fear was that Nashville would become "an uneasy island of integration surrounded by a tumultuous ocean of protest and discontent." Two other segregationists speaking as individuals also voiced their views. A. L. Utley said bluntly that if school desegregation occurred, "whites and blacks would intermarry and that they would be better off if they never had been born." Mrs. Claude Finney said simply that desegregation was "retrogression" rather than "progress" and that three groups were pushing such ideas: "misinformed northerners," politicians "who want the people's votes," and religious folks "who are a ticklish group to handle and who, perhaps do not look to how integration would affect the next generation." The meeting ended with TFCG attorney Sims Crownover praising the gathering as the best possible defense against "a situation like that in Tuscaloosa," where violence had broken out as Autherine Lucy desegregated the University of Alabama.[29]

The pattern of insistent efforts from segregationists and feeble response from progressives continued throughout 1956. Educators, who undoubtedly had both among their ranks, remained caught in the middle and frozen by the spotlight on them. Consequently, desegregation remained mired in deliberations and procrastination. Nashville's chief school administrator W. A. Bass accused his fellow city and county superintendents in Tennessee of "dodging the issue," saying that "We're like ducks sitting on a pond. No one is giving us any advice and counsel in this matter." The school board even managed to use Looby's *Kelley* lawsuit as a pretext for delay, reasoning that a court ruling might provide them with a framework for action. But, when Looby continued trying to move forward in concrete ways, the school board begged for yet more time. At one point, it suggested a plan for desegregating first-graders only. Looby agreed to this, with the stipulation that a specific date be set for subsequent desegregation of all grades. The board members decided to evade instead, even in reiterating that they would comply with the court order. They stressed the need to wait for the forthcoming school census and public hearings. They warned of moving too quickly in the face of enormous pressures from all sides. They rationalized that a plan with unanimous support for wider credibility was needed. They argued disingenuously that, because Nashville had provided separate but equal facilities in the past, the school system should not be held to a punitive standard now that judicial standards had changed.[30]

A switch in court jurisdictions remanded the case to Judge William E. Miller and postponed a potential decision by seven months. With that postponement, however, the room for maneuver was shrinking as spring turned to summer. The state, one journalist observed, "teetered on the tightrope of moderation." Governor Clement, feeling the pressure, asked Tennesseans to "put faith in their governor." His attempts to maintain the middle path were attacked by the TFCG, who needled him endlessly. TFCG Vice Chairman Jack Kershaw dubbed him "'No Comment Clement' and 'I'm-Not-For-Anything-Or-Against-Anything-Frankie.'" Another TFCG member lambasted Clement for his contradictions, pointing out that Clement had vetoed the Stainback Bill on the grounds that integration was a state problem but now refused to overturn "local authority." TFCG attorney Sims Crownover's call to abolish the public schools rather than submit to desegregation indicated the heated rhetoric.[31]

Even in this climate, the die-hard segregationist cause was flagging. The shrillness of segregationist cries had an inverse relationship to their effectiveness. A June 1956 TFCG rally featured former Dixiecrat Strom Thurmond, who took the stage before a wildly enthusiastic crowd as "Dixie" played in the background. *Banner* publisher Jimmy Stahlman introduced Thurmond, remarking that "I am not so much concerned with whether a man is black or white as I am with the continued and gradual chiseling away of the rights of the state as they apply to the freedom of you and me." Yet, as the TFCG tried to fight segregation through lawsuits, they were shot down by judge after judge, which meant that Tennessee courts became the first to overturn the state's constitutional provisions for segregation. Dismissed first by the judicial branch, followed by voters in 1956 who elected only two

TFCG candidates to the Tennessee General Assembly, the group began planning a lobbying campaign for the next legislative session beginning in January 1957. But that came only after the worst fears of most Tennesseans were realized as a new and sinister energy was infused into the segregationist movement.[32]

In fall 1956, national attention riveted on Clinton, a small town in East Tennessee outside of Knoxville. Nearby Oak Ridge, a federally owned city that was created by the War Department to support the Manhattan Project, had quickly complied with the *Brown* decision and desegregated its schools the previous year—the only Tennessee city that had done so—with relatively little fuss. Now a court order, instigated by a Looby lawsuit, compelled Clinton to follow Oak Ridge's example and reluctantly the town made preparations to do so. As they did, a dark chain of events began to unravel as a stranger with "faintly hypnotic eyes," a "hurt-spaniel look" and a "boyish charm" appeared in town. Starting from a payphone in a local drugstore, followed by quiet consultations with certain town luminaries, and finally with rallies in the town square, he began a campaign of racial discord to turn Clinton's citizens against desegregation.[33]

The stranger, John Kasper, remains an enigma to history. New Jersey–born and Columbia-educated, he had once led a bohemian lifestyle operating bookstores in Greenwich Village and later in Washington, D.C. As his political philosophy turned drastically to the right, he began editing a cheap paperback book series devoted to radical right-wing propaganda. Simultaneously, Kasper developed an unhealthy fixation with Ezra Pound, the brilliant and mad poet indicted for his anti-Semitic and pro-Fascist radio broadcasts in Italy during World War II. Writing obsessive letters to his idol, who was banished to a psychiatric hospital, Kasper gushed that "You are god and the greatest of all men. You are MASTER, SAGE, WISDOM, POWER" and "I praise you. I worship you. I love you." From his bookstore, Kasper also became tied into extremist networks whose tentacles extended throughout the country. His contacts included prominent conservative radicals Rear Admiral John Crommelin and the infamous race baiter Asa "Ace" Carter (a Klansman, maverick Citizens' Council leader, and later a key aide to Governor George Wallace in Alabama). Drawn to Clinton after reading a newspaper story about the town's impending desegregation, Kasper began his work. In alliance with selected supporters, and by preaching a gospel of hatred toward Jews, blacks, and elites, Kasper exhorted his growing band of followers in Clinton to assert their voices. As a reporter noted, he appealed to the "crackers and red-necks and wool-hats" by speaking "like a demoniac poet" to their "deepest dreads and most primitive instincts."[34]

What Kasper did not tell his followers was that he was a fraud. In his bookstore days, he regularly hosted parties with African American friends as they discussed art, literature, and jazz. He lobbied his friends to join the NAACP and held collections for Emmett Till's mother. He even dated a black woman, Florette Henry. Many of his former black friends were stunned at his new notoriety: "He used us. . . . He used us all," said one. One journalist, after Kasper's background was exposed by the press, saw his rantings as a cynical conniving, "a carefully calculated technique to get attention," and concluded, "It is obvious he has no more belief in such statements than any sensible person would."[35]

It was too late for Clinton. Seething from Kasper's speeches, a town that had been reluctantly complacent about desegregation now began crackling with racial hatred. On August 29, 1956, the third day of classes, the situation exploded into riots after Kasper's followers attacked black schoolchildren walking to their new high school. An overwhelmed police force was inadequate against the mob and, as rallies continued to protest Kasper's jailing, Ace Carter nudged angry citizens even further. A black couple driving through town were encircled by angry crowds who, rocking and overturning the car, swarmed upon the driver with fists and rocks. Mayhem persisted for days. Governor Clement eventually sent the highway patrol and national guardsmen in to quell the uprising. But threats of bombing and violence hovered around the town as boycotts and similar turmoil within the school, stoked by Kasper's young recruits, persisted for years afterward.[36]

Repercussions from Clinton swirled over Nashville. The TFCG, whose vice chairman Jack Kershaw had implored Clinton's citizens in vain to maintain order before the riot began, was now guilty by association in the wake of Clinton's chaos. The TFCG, in turn, became bitterly distrustful of Kasper and even more disgusted with Governor Clement for allowing desegregation to go forward. Clement, however, had once again showed a calculated blend of calibrated decisiveness. He sent in forces only after requested to by Clinton's aldermen and stressed that the troops' mission was solely the upholding of law and order. This avoided the scene of soldiers escorting black children to schools as later occurred with federal troops in Little Rock. He continued to hold a sort of moral high ground as the segregationists squabbled. Meanwhile, Kasper, once released from Clinton's jail, cast his eyes toward Nashville, where Looby's lawsuit were finally breaking through the board's postponements and could be delayed no longer.[37]

Shortly after Tennessee was rocked by Clinton's eruption, the Nashville school board's instruction committee tendered a final report on October 29, 1956, advocating what would soon be known as the Nashville Plan for desegregation. After years of equivocation, the Nashville Plan proposed limiting desegregation to the first grade only, which equated to approximately 3,200 pupils. But the heart of the plan was in details of zoning and transfer provisions, and these further blunted the possibilities of desegregating. Under the Nashville Plan, each child was assigned to a school near his or her home. These assignments derived from newly drawn zones dividing the city in such a way that every previously all-white school now had at most a handful of black children. There was some debate about how the zones originated: while the board insisted that school capacity and not race formed the basis, cynics found this doubtful. Regardless, the prevalence of segregated neighborhoods meant that each school varied widely in its racial makeup, and that would change over time as white Nashvillians continued to leave the city limits for suburbs. Moreover, the board explained that any first-grader could transfer to another school according to two simple criteria: if he or she had been assigned to a school previously reserved for the opposite race, or if he or she would be in the racial minority in his or her new school.[38]

Nashville's administrators rationalized that, by confining desegregation to the first grade, children not yet socialized into segregated settings might adapt better, whereas older grades would have posed an obstacle for black children supposedly unused to academic rigor. But opting for desegregating the first grade only also conveniently postponed questions of interracial and "potentially explosive sexual attractions." The board also stressed that this first-grade plan would remain a test case, subject to examination after the first year.[39]

In its simplicity, the plan was deviously elegant. Although Looby branded it "entirely inadequate" and decried the use of first-graders as "guinea pigs for experimentation," the plan served the board's interests well. In keeping with the court order, racial assignments for each school no longer existed on paper. But in practice, several layers of protocols restrained desegregation. Due to the zoning, only a few black children would be eligible to attend formerly white schools in the first place. And the transfer rules were an additional escape valve for both races—either for African Americans who preferred more familiar environments or for whites to avoid attending the formerly all-black schools that Jim Crow had rendered inferior for decades. It was a deft construction of legal obedience that still clung to racial custom, as it meant that racial branding was no longer written into law but could still dictate individual choices. And the plan took as unvoiced inspiration the belief that both whites and blacks, given a choice, would prefer the company of their own race. The school board had devised a plan that was consistent with its moderate values. Now it waited, hoping that these values would be upheld by others.[40]

As 1956 drew to a close, the TFCG, having been thwarted by the courts, tried to enlist the state legislature's help instead. In a pamphlet titled *The Crisis in Tennessee*, the segregationists proposed bills for consideration when the Tennessee General Assembly reconvened in January 1957. Davidson declared grandly that "there is a course of last resort, higher than the Court of our State or any Federal

Court, even the Supreme Court of the United States—and that is the Court of the People." In calling for legislators to counter the Supreme Court, which "cannot be permitted to be the judge of its own illegal acts," the TFCG's bills would allow the governor to close schools and the legislature to deny funds to desegregated schools. Davidson stressed the last of these provisions, calling it the "most powerful" statement that the assembly could make because it was "unchallengeable by any other authority or agency of government." He warned that "a surrender at this point" would begin "the reduction of Tennessee to the condition of a feeble and compliant satellite and parasite of an all-powerful and socialistic Federal government."[41]

With these proposals, the TFCG advocated the doctrine of interposition, the fanciful but fashionable legal theory advanced by segregationists in recent years. Interposition essentially tried to revive legal arguments from the nineteenth-century nullification crisis in arguing that any state had the right to assert its sovereignty by ignoring federal laws deemed illegal and hostile to the interests of the state's people. It was a bankrupt theory and was debunked effectively by a pamphlet from the white moderates in the NCRC that noted that the TFCG's proposals would not only illegally bypass the *Brown* decision but would centralize power in the governor's office and potentially destroy the public school system. Still, the proposals excited the die-hard segregationist legislators and that meant that Governor Clement had to take matters in his own hands to circumvent the revolt.[42]

Clement moved with customary shrewdness. He proposed five separate bills, the cornerstone of which was a "school preference" plan that allowed parents to voluntarily send their children to a segregated school. This was bolstered with a "pupil assignment act" that permitted school boards the power to assign children to schools as they saw fit. Both seemed supportive of segregation; yet, the language was such that how the bills would be implemented remained highly ambiguous, and whether they could withstand legal scrutiny remained doubtful. Each of the five passed, helped by Clement's veto of harsher bills. Nettled by the governor's political skill, the legislature ratified an anti-integration resolution called the Tennessee Manifesto (which had no legal significance whatsoever) and promptly adjourned. Clement's actions recalled his adroit handling of the Clinton episode: these laws gave him some political cover by suggesting that he was defending segregation, yet they were empty ones that could not stand. As the *Tennessean* forecast, the school preference act "was either unconstitutional or meaningless." The *Globe* concurred, advising black Nashvillians not to waste energy opposing the bills, since they merely "accommodate a species of politicians who must take a stand for segregation." The newspaper likened the situation to a two-hundred-pound man who ignores being flogged by a diminutive wife because "she seems to get a lot of satisfaction out of it and it doesn't hurt me one bit." With his legislative sleight-of-hand, Clement looked decisive, but he could now stand aside and allow others to catch the flak as they defined how—or if—these laws would actually work.[43]

The governor's political posturing paralleled other legal developments. On January 21, 1957, weeks before Clement's successful end-run around the legislature, Judge Miller accepted the Nashville Plan's terms for desegregating the first grade during the following school year. But he rejected the idea that the board could reconsider options after a year, requiring instead that a plan for all grades be submitted by December 31. With the first year of desegregation mandated, the NCRC began trying to convince prominent civic leaders to sign a petition professing support for "law and order" that did not reference desegregation directly. Nonetheless, many businessmen and educators "found reasons for not signing," and the white PTA remained particularly petulant in refusing to sponsor meetings to discuss the issue. The conversation remained defensive, at best expressing only weak and token gestures from white moderates. But, with a specific deadline and visions of Clinton seared in their minds, segregationists became even more agitated. Backed by increasingly strident editorial support from the *Banner*, the TFCG formed an offshoot group, the Parents School Preference Committee (PSPC). Noting that the Nashville Plan contradicted the state preference laws that Clement had pushed through the legislature, the PSPC labored feverishly into the summer trying to convince the school board to opt for the latter. The segregationists of course favored the legislature's laws because they dangled the hope that schools could voluntarily remain segregated, in contrast to the Nashville Plan, which granted that desegregation would occur but tried to suppress that desegregation to token levels. The board, alarmed by a PSPC petition with six thousand signatures supporting the preference plan, momentarily began questioning its own strategy. But, by the end of July and after consulting with attorneys, the school board decided that the Nashville Plan was more likely to gain legal approval.[44]

As the summer continued, the segregationists mixed fury and despair as their ranks divided. John Kasper, drifting into Nashville on June 29, began working as he had in Clinton. He assembled a small cohort of faithful including two itinerant preachers, Fred Stroud and John McCurrio. Stroud had been ousted from Nashville's Second Presbyterian Church in 1936, forming in response a splinter congregation called the Bible Presbyterian Church. McCurrio was according to police files an "unemployed transient" and "self-styled evangelist." Given the revelations about Kasper's interracial past and the stain of violence that lingered from Clinton—to say nothing about the non-Nashville origins of the trio—relationships among segregationists in town remained contentious. During Kasper's trial for his racial agitation in Clinton, the TFCG had arranged for his legal defense but, after his fraudulence was uncovered, they refused to represent him. At one point, even the Ku Klux Klan ousted Kasper from a meeting. The TFCG, convinced that most Nashvillians would never follow the rabble-rousing outsider, tried to preserve an elevated tone articulating their racial sentiment. Clyde Alley, a physician and chair of the county chapter, asserted that "there is a vast difference between race prejudice and race pride. I may have much more pride in Nashville than in Knoxville, but that certainly does not mean that I am prejudiced against the good people of Knoxville." Moreover, "we certainly don't endorse the Kasper-type individual in any shape, form or fashion."[45]

Such pronouncements showed that the class differences between segregationists had now fractured the group. As Kasper began building his following in Nashville, he resorted to the same formula grimly successful in Clinton, appealing to lower-class whites with hatred toward blacks, Jews, and elites. One bystander in Clinton had remarked that Kasper's entourage showed that "this isn't a race conflict as much as it is a class conflict!" This was confirmed by a Nashvillian who saw the Kasperites as the "low-income folk, the type generally called 'red-necks,'" the "young men and women of the long-sideburn, duck-tailed haircut set, bully-boys and girls who operate in packs." Still another commentator pointed out that "Kasper couldn't get enough lower-class anti-Negro money, so he had to move up a notch and go after some middle-class anti-Semitic money, too." Kasper himself preferred more grandiloquent terms, saying "the poor people in Nashville had no organization to represent them. There seems to be a lot of snobbery about classes here and these people who are the real salt of the earth are the ones who really suffer in integration." In particular, Kasper launched attacks on Mayor Ben West for his appointment of blacks to political positions and called Jack Kershaw, vice chairman of the TFCG, a "bleeding heart" for letting these appointments go unchallenged. Elite white Nashvillians watched Kasper with horror. "His chief success," remarked one progressive, "has been in dividing the white South within itself"; he serves as "a foil" to those other southern moderates whose "own defiance and revolt may appear like sweet reasonableness" by contrast.[46]

The TFCG also fell victim to the divisions. Disgusted with Kasper "hogging the spotlight" and whipping up lower-class racial hatred, Kershaw lambasted Kasper's "disservice to the cause of responsible segregation and the South." But the TFCG also had problems with the best mouthpiece for their organization. Although James Stahlman of the *Banner* had taken up the PSPC's cause in the past year, he remained wary of certain members of the TFCG and "never subscribed to some of the extreme positions of Mr. Davidson." As such, the publisher's editorials zigzagged inconsistently between decrying the *Brown* ruling and supporting the

TFCG. It is likely that Stahlman's business connections reminded him that closing the public schools would ruin the city, keeping the publisher from endorsing the TFCG's willingness to do just that. Meanwhile, the *Tennessean* and *Globe* furnished editorial support for those trying to dodge segregationist pressure. The *Tennessean*, which merely adopted Cecil Sims's argument that the *Brown* decision denied only compulsory segregation, concentrated on ridiculing the TFCG's efforts. The *Globe*, for its part, cautioned blacks to understand when white students transferred to avoid black teachers or when black children preferred African American schools whenever they were equal in academic quality to white schools. "Level-headed parents and teachers of colored children elsewhere have not demanded 'letter-perfect' decisions in carrying out the demands of desegregation," said the *Globe*. "It is best that the same policy be adopted here in Nashville." The *Globe* also applauded the moderate NCRC's work and approvingly declared Superintendent William H. Oliver "a changed man" after segregationist threats pushed him into supporting the forthcoming desegregation.[47]

The segregationists tried to compensate for their lack of unity with a surplus of fervor, and the school board struggled to not cave under the pressure. Wrangling between the PSPC and the school board persisted throughout the summer of 1957. The realization that many PSPC members lived outside of Nashville led to questions about the group's constituency. Both the board and the PSPC called for the other to request that Judge Miller approve the legislature's preference plan instead of the Nashville Plan. While open to segregationist proposals, the school board remained exasperated at holes in segregationist logic, doubting both the legality and wisdom of alienating the judge by advocating a plan of dubious constitutionality. The PSPC in response argued that the law was constitutional until the courts decided otherwise but only the school board had the purview to incorporate the school preference plan in its dealings with the court. Superintendent Oliver instead lobbied the board to stay the course, reminding it of the momentum behind the Nashville Plan.[48]

Although the first day of school was not until September, the August 27 date for school registration loomed as the situation slid further into fear and tension. "Nashville is the big show this year," Kasper crowed at one point. "It's the 1957 battleground—I can smell it; I can sense it; I know it." According to the new zones, no school had more than twenty-five black children within its area. Most had five to fifteen. Three schools had only one. These small numbers made black students convenient targets for torment, and as publicity and rumors about new entrants began to escalate, dozens of harassing phone calls to black families and school officials began to take a toll. One mother, for example, had a caller, self-described as a "Klu-Kluxer," threaten to "beat your little girl to death and string her up by her toes. Then we'll burn your house." Another asked simply, "Why do you want to push your little burr head with white folks?" A third threatened to throw acid on a child and burn a cross on the family's lawn.[49]

On registration day, the affected schools had small groups of white housewives and "a few delinquent teenagers" milling about the entrances, passing out racist pamphlets and handbills advertising Kasper's next speech. Kasper's flyers were virulent, deriding the "Vanderbilt-Fisk socialists," the Jews on the school board, and the board's "lack of manhood" in not taking "a jail sentence if that's what it takes." They were also apocalyptic: "woe to those who conquer with armies and whose only right is their power. They will lie in unmarked graves and the wild grass will grow over their dead bodies." At Fehr School in predominantly black North Nashville, Kasper appeared, quizzing school officials for information and going ignored. At Glenn School, which had more African Americans in its zone than others, a situation almost flared before tempers could be restrained. One segregationist started shouting "let's throw them all out." A policeman stared him down and told him to stay quiet, then "wilted" and protested that he didn't "really mean to throw them out." With Superintendent Bass in attendance, six women (surrounded by even more reporters) wearing KEEP OUR WHITE SCHOOLS WHITE buttons tried to ask for names and addresses to "organize a student boycott." One was quoted as saying that "The Lord didn't intend for us to integrate or there wouldn't have been two colors." A journalist discovered that one of the noisiest protesters had lived in the area but had moved farther out into Davidson County. Another recorded an exchange between Bass and a young white woman who asked, "what's happened to our state's rights?" Said Bass, "madam . . . that was settled at the Battle of Appamattox [sic] in 1865." Almost startled, the woman, in a "suddenly subdued voice," said "That was a long time ago." Ominously, the crowd gazed silently as two black girls walked into the school to register.[50]

Across the city, even as school officials claimed that registration went off "without a hitch," only slightly more than half of expected registrants showed up. Thirteen black children registered for white schools, while the other hundred and twenty-five eligible children chose to stay in black schools. As the first day of classes drew nearer, six more children joined the courageous few, meaning that school desegregation in Nashville would be accomplished by fewer than twenty black first-graders spread throughout the city. Each affected school was in a working-class neighborhood. Over the next days, segregationists were out in force as Kasper and Fred Stroud continued stalking Nashville streets, meeting nightly on school grounds where black children had registered. The rallies and continual bomb scares were tangible signs of white intimidation. (Local police had considered dispersing the meetings but decided not to create a situation allowing Kasper to fill a martyr role as he had in Clinton). A journalist recorded that the ranks at Kasper's rallies were swelling and "the temper has become more fiery." Reports of a student boycott and rumors of threats from African Americans reverberated through the city. Mayor Ben West, arriving at a scheduled meeting with the PSPC, was stunned to find over a hundred Klansmen and Citizens' Council members waiting, but recovered his composure enough to reassert support for desegregation rather than "chaos and anarchy."[51]

The turmoil that accompanied registration made many shiver at the thought of what the first day of school would bring. Reverend Kelly Miller Smith, the most influential black minister in Nashville, later described the agony he and his wife faced in deciding whether to send their daughter to a desegregated school. "Do we have a right to do this to her?" they pondered. The answer was yes, because "in the long run this was the thing that should be done and she needed to get exposed to the kind of world that we're living in." Moreover, later generations "would be recipients of the good that she would be doing." But Smith acknowledged the dilemma, worrying "about the danger to the child, the physical danger, the possible psychological danger to her. And what right does a parent have to do this?" But there was also the "possible psychological danger of withdrawing her" and "keeping her out of situations of controversy." Another black parent remembered how, after she withdrew her child from a previously white school, the constant phone calls from segregationists were replaced by black elites trying to get her to reconsider. "I don't remember you offering to come by here and help stand guard," she retorted (although many local black toughs had offered to do just that). The principle of school desegregation remained far more abstract than a child's safety.[52]

Parents gripped by similar anxieties had one small but influential group on their side. The Congress of Racial Equality (CORE), formed in 1942 in Chicago, was devoted to applying Gandhian ideas about nonviolent direct action to U.S. race relations. Efforts by the local CORE chapter to assist school desegregation would remain virtually the group's sole contribution throughout the 1950s and 1960s as they were continually dogged with low membership and aborted plans. But, in this crisis, CORE's steadfast one-on-one interaction with parents and children was nothing short of crucial. As parents voiced worries about job recriminations, the incessant threatening phone calls, and the pressure from neighbors, CORE members tried to assuage fears, clarify misinformation, and be supportive through "drastic fluctuations in morale." The activists emphasized that, in Nashville, segregationists were only a minority against broader civic support for the school board and that CORE would continue to help over the long term those students and parents attempting desegregation. They also stressed that the first-grade experiment would be the basis for future integration and they tried to embody that hope: one member said "I think the fact that we were an interracial team, from the same organization, did more to influence them than anything else." But mostly they tried to foster personal strength amid the uncertainties. They noted that "Of course it would be fine if the most important people in town were active workers for desegregation. But there is little chance that they will be, so the victory depends on you." Nor were other groups, perhaps especially the NCRC, truly helpful: "organizations interested in school desegregation and human relations do not reach the great body of people who will be affected by the desegregation process." They stressed the power of individuals to change history, even against seemingly insurmountable odds, exhorting that "If we expect to build the kind of society we want, we must put forth effort ourselves" and to "not underestimate your power and the power of your own group."[53]

CORE also documented many instances of presumptuousness from white officials as the first day of school loomed. Some threatened legal injunctions against black parents who contemplated enrolling their children in previously all-white schools. White principals, upon receiving black parents, began filling out transfer forms without asking the parents why they were visiting. In one particularly grotesque incident, when meeting in a black neighborhood, Superintendent Bass, peering outside at a violent rainstorm, commented on the appropriateness of the weather "because very soon it's going to be raining little nigger babies in our schools." The fact that he blushed with embarrassment after realizing what he had blurted out was of no comfort to African Americans in attendance. CORE also noted more covert ways in which desegregation was being constrained. Not only through zoning and transfers, but the very fact that desegregation was confined to first grade was a chief obstacle. Many black parents found themselves unable to support desegregation because first-graders often required an elder sibling to accompany them to school or watch them in the evening. The first-grade only plan instead meant that parents had to plan for logistics of multiple schools by hiring a babysitter, an unfortunate prospect for dual-income households, or by leaving some children unsupervised. This had been anticipated by the school board. In April, one member asserted that, because "beginner pupils usually go along with their older brothers and sisters for protection" and "negro children and parents have pride in their own schools, wholesale shifts of children from negro to white schools are unlikely." A local NAACP official thought this factor alone accounted for almost half of those black parents who chose not to desegregate.[54]

CORE's efforts to shore up morale were brave but minimized by the broader backdrop of fear, both silent and voiced. Among whites, sentiment against desegregation persisted and at its best was quietly disapproving. In late August, the Nashville Association of Churches sent a mailing to 350 clergymen, urging them to read a prepared statement, mild in tone, calling for a peaceful response. The *Tennessean* followed up with an informal survey of the clerics; half of them had said nothing. By contrast, both the Kiwanis Club and the Men's Club of Monroe Street Methodist Church passed formal motions opposing desegregation. So too did the *Globe* concede that most blacks would prefer separate schools if they were truly equal. Segregationists were especially beside themselves, and the September 4 standoff in front of Central High School in Little Rock, Arkansas, haunted Nashvillians fearful of what might occur in their own city. Said Bass: "we are in the backwash of a thing that's going on too close to us," and "the Little Rock situation is giving the impression of possible victory to those people who would defeat the Supreme Court decision." Most revealing of all was when Chester Mason, chair of the PSPC, spoke at a school board committee meeting. Asked if he would acquiesce to desegregation if the Nashville Plan went forward, Mason's answer was that he hoped that the "lid would blow off" if that occurred. The comment showed how violent strains simmered beneath supportive clichés for law and order among segregationists and moderates alike.[55]

When the school board asked for Judge Miller's opinion about using the voluntary preference plan instead of the Nashville Plan, the PSPC's hopes expired. Indeed, as widely anticipated, on September 6, three days before classes opened, Judge Miller ruled that the legislature's school preference plan, in granting authority to maintain segregated schools, was "patently and manifestly unconstitutional on its face." His decision tied together two strands: the TFCG's efforts to resist desegregation through legal channels had failed, and Governor Clement's laws, in being ruled unconstitutional as designed, had absolved him of responsibility for what the first day of school might bring. The governor could now ignore the TFCG's pleas for him to demonstrate "Christian love and respect for the Negro race" by appealing Miller's ruling and using his police powers to block desegregation. Now nothing prevented the Nashville Plan from going into effect. Before the ruling, Superintendent Bass had revealed his unease about what would happen, acknowledging that "the resentment is deep, much deeper than many of us had supposed" and that "many I believe have absorbed the Kasper line." But he also professed his belief in Nashvillians: "I have lived with them for nearly half a century. I know they are good citizens."[56]

September 9 was the day of reckoning at eight schools across the city, and the fright was as suffocating as the morning's humidity. Picket lines and fistfights roiled the crowds gathered in front of the schools. Journalists on the scene described the "poster-carrying, vacant-faced women with uncombed hair" parading around as cars marked with KKKK (Knights of the Ku Klux Klan) and police cruisers trolled city streets at uneven intervals. There was "no feeling of protest, only fear," one reported. Another wrote of a man telling him confidently, "This here's the South, buddy, I mean the South. Somebody's going to get hurt before niggers goes to our schools." Black parents tried to soothe anxious and bewildered children; Rosemary Lewis even told her son Calvin that "the mob was there to wish him well his first day in school." Around Jones and Buena Vista Schools, the restless crowds stayed relatively under control even as a grandmotherly white woman exhorted parents to withdraw their children; about a dozen complied. Far worse was Caldwell Elementary next to Sam Levy Courts, a low-income housing project, from which "a horde of ranting women" numbering at least a hundred poured out. "Some member of my family has gone to this school for the last 22 years," wept one, "and now they're sending niggers in." At Hattie Cotton and Clemons schools, paperwork technicalities kept two black children from enrolling. As they ducked out the back entrance, the mob gave them short chase, one protester sobbing at their presence and clutching a piece of glass. Indeed, many of the protesters rushed between the schools looking for targets to vent their feelings. Said one black parent years later, "I was in awe of the hatred."[57]

An "untrue but hardy" rumor surging through the crowd at Caldwell, that a black woman had slapped a white child, led many to start muttering threats and others to withdraw their children, as the mob rushed into the school. As parent Mahlon Griffith led his children Jacqueline and Stevie into Glenn, a detective shoved aside a white man who blocked their path. "Look at this," the segregationist cried triumphantly, "they push the white people around but take up for the niggers." Years later, Griffith remembered the throngs with a shudder: "John Kasper brought out the worst in a lot of white people, and it was ugly and frightening." His wife would soon be fired from her job because of their stand, and only intervention from supervisors saved his at the post office. Yet no arrests at either school occurred; police tried only to contain the wrath. A journalist noted the strange unspoken tension between the keepers of the peace and the disrupters: "Cops did their duty, and did it firmly, but there was no real antagonism displayed." Instead, "a strange sort of rapport was established and it seemed to be understood that they were all southerners together." A reporter noted that there "was no sense of victory on either side"—only fearful resignation as both sides "had done what they had to do." Still, there was an "exodus" of children from Glenn as Kasper and Stroud made appearances. According to a journalist, the latter's "benedictions dripped more blood than love" as Stroud declared grimly that the crowd should "read the word of the Lord and be ready to die for the Lord."[58]

With the color line officially breached, Monday night was "sheer madness" as three hundred attended a rally downtown where John Kasper ranted a gospel of invective as white children dashed through the crowd passing out racist literature.

His words were pungent with insult even as he carefully worded his threats indirectly. A *Tennessean* reporter had heard one supporter rush up excitedly to Kasper to say, "John, I don't want to have any trouble here but my kids aren't going to school with Negroes, and if I have some dynamite, I know how to use it." Not only did Kasper repeat the remark to the crowd, he further held up a noose and referred to "talk" he had heard about hanging Z. Alexander Looby. "If one of these niggers pulls a razor or a gun on us, we'll give it to 'em," he cried. Soon, a black figure was hung in effigy on nearby Church Street. Inflamed, some among the hundreds of protesters lingering around the racially mixed neighborhood of Fehr Elementary began pitching bottles at black motorists and burning cars. (Fehr's black custodian had been assaulted that afternoon after taking down the U.S. flag.) Officers at the scene waited hours before calling in reinforcements and arresting three people.[59]

And then, incredibly, it got worse. Shortly after midnight, a dynamite blast thundered throughout East Nashville. "A hellish explosion—just like God had whispered in my ear," as one citizen put it; "it sounded like the whole world ended," said another. Hattie Cotton Elementary School, where Patricia Watson, not yet six years old, had attended that day (without previously registering since she had moved into the school zone just two weeks prior), stood with one wing in smoking ruins. "Moderate" Nashville now had the dubious distinction of being the first city with a school desegregation-related bombing since the *Brown* decision. Both the school's principal and Patricia's mother confirmed that everything had gone smoothly in class that day. (Only later did the principal confess to receiving a phoned threat the night before as she had taken Patricia home after the child missed the taxi that her mother had sent for her. "Well, now you won't be carrying the little nigger home anymore!" declared the anonymous female caller.) The explosion meant that, as the second day of school started, the racial climate had changed. The community attitude, "blasted into a changed mood," had shifted, belatedly "shocked into a new appreciation of law and order" with leaders "backed by a city of conscience aroused as rarely before." One bystander commented that the "explosion was a godsend to Nashville. It drew the battle lines. The choice was between integration and anarchy. The anarchists dwindled in number and status." James Stahlman, from the *Banner*'s front page, bellowed that Kasper should be "run out of town . . . NO SCUM, NO RENEGADES, NO RAGTAG."[60]

As protests continued and a carload of armed blacks was imprisoned, police activity was noticeably firmer as arrest numbers climbed. Barricades manned by "hard-faced weary" officers ringed each school. Segregationists complained of police brutality. The PSPC implored Clement to send troops into Nashville, saying "the presence of Negro children and their presence alone is the cause of violence in Nashville." The widespread crackdown against any potential unrest was helped by restraining orders from Judge Miller. "This is a matter of sheer lawlessness . . . we're up against thugs," one school official was quoted as saying. And another: "That damn Kasper found more support here than we expected and he capitalized on it."[61]

Rotating police forces kept "a cascading constant flow of approaching sirens" sounding in the warm September air. Caldwell School was again the worst, although no black students were enrolled after transfers had been denied, but the police made "tough, quick arrests" of the ringleaders to stifle the crowd's restlessness. Glenn was quiet, as were the few demonstrators at Jones. When a black pupil left the school with two women, a white child called to bystanders, "smell anything? The niggers are coming." As they walked past, a white woman said, "I bet their hearts are beating like a hammer." No other comments were made—just a steady, unbelieving stare as the new student walked away. At Hattie Cotton, where the bombing had occurred, "people are shocked. Kids have been coming along and go home crying." The most dangerous situation was at Fehr, when Reverend Edwin Jackson escorted Linda McKinley away with her grandfather as classes let out. The white bystanders trailed them for a few blocks and, away from the police presence, let loose with rocks at the trio, prompting the minister to brandish a pistol before the police caught up with the group and arrested the preacher. Jackson later apologized publicly for his actions and reaffirmed his commitment to nonviolence but told a story of attacks on his church and continual harassment of his parishioners that had led him to the breaking point. It was consistent with muttered threats from African Americans ready to retaliate violently against such threats.[62]

Klansman Charles Reed, sent to the Nashville police by the FBI, confessed that he had seen John Kasper with three sticks of dynamite. Unlike for Fred Stroud, who had declared during a court hearing that he would make no more statements except from his pulpit, the local cops subsequently made life rough for Kasper. Arrested for vagrancy and assorted charges, he posted two thousand dollars bond. While trying to leave police headquarters, he was arrested again for illegal parking, paying another five hundred dollars. Less than twenty-four hours later, county constables awoke him by arresting him for inciting riots. Out of cash, he was committed to the workhouse as he learned about Judge Miller's injunction against him. After being shuffled from city, county, and federal courts, with a crony helping him make an additional $2,500 bond, he left Nashville on September 18 with two detectives trailing him as he crossed the county line. As a Nashville journalist put it, "for the first time in history, a white man was given nigger justice."[63]

A year later, Kasper surfaced briefly at a meeting at Clark Methodist Church, watching silently as officials instructed the public on proper procedures for that year's school registration. The meeting was halted after a bomb scare, although no explosive was found. Two weeks before, the segregationist had convened a KKK meeting that drew thirty-four people, but after the church meeting, his influence waned as he rotated jail terms and trials for his various misdeeds. In one federal prison in Florida, he received a "sound thrashing" from a black inmate. Between imprisonments, he made occasional appearances among his stalwart faithful in Nashville. The *Globe* maintained a close eye on Kasper's whereabouts and highlighted disapprovingly that one of Kasper's "lieutenants," a grocer, had a "brisk trade" in a black neighborhood. Back in Nashville to serve out a sentence in 1960, he was assigned to garbage detail in a black neighborhood, much to the glee of locals. "Let's barbecue him," catcalled one onlooker. "He's the one that tried to keep our children out of his schools," said another, "now look at him picking up trash." Regardless, although several prime suspects were also arrested, no one went to trial for the Hattie Cotton bombing.[64]

The crisis passed as school enrollment returned to 90 percent of normal within a week. But most remained jumpy even after the first days of school. Over the year, the number of black children in previously all-white schools shrank to nine. Many applauded Hattie Cotton's quick reopening a week after the explosion. But nobody mentioned that this occurred without its African American student, for Patricia Watson had moved to her grandmother's house to attend an all-black school. On September 26, W. H. Oliver, slated to replace W. A. Bass as superintendent on January 1, professed that desegregation had failed: "in my opinion," he said, "we were doing a better job in our city schools (before desegregation) than we could have done with both races together." Another school official echoed the pessimism, saying that blacks "are not doing well, scholastically and emotionally." In North Nashville, one resident, a former missionary from South Carolina, opened her house to teach twenty white students from five different desegregated schools for ten dollars a month each. On October 3, the Glenn School PTA lost three officers because of racial tensions. Meanwhile, a black parent's backyard toolshed was set ablaze after the first week of school. Throughout October, a series of cross burnings flashed throughout the city.[65]

Encouraged by these rumblings of discontent, the PSPC redoubled its efforts, convincing the school board to try another voluntary desegregation plan. The PSPC based their idea on the pupil assignment law, the second of Clement's ambiguous bills that had passed the legislature months ago. The PSPC's plan would establish one system for whites, another for African Americans, and a third where parents of both races who favored desegregation could send their children. The group argued that such a plan was democratic because it embodied "free choice," conformed to religious practices by "lov[ing] thy neighbor as thyself," and was compelled by no "arbitrary force" from outside the South. It was also clearly absurd to the point of desperation: bureaucratically unwieldy, fiscally prohibitive, and illegal to boot, it was "almost identical" to the Tennessee preference law already declared unconstitutional by Judge Miller. The PSPC still yearned for legal preservation of school segregation when there could be none and for the federal courts to take the full brunt of responsibility for desegregating Nashville's schools. On December 4, the board, still stunned by September's turmoil, accepted the proposal and tendered it to Miller, who promptly rejected it as well as the other Clement laws. Chastened, the school board offered instead to continue the current plan at the rate of one grade per year in a gradual "stairstep" manner. The *Globe*, its sentiments betraying a growing sense of cynicism, likened the idea to a pet owner who amputates his puppy's tail by snipping off little bits at a time to make it "less painful for Little Fido."[66]

As dissension bubbled under a city uneasily desegregated, another blast sounded through the city. On March 16, 1958, dynamite shook the Jewish Community Center shortly after it closed for the day. Minutes later, phones rang at the offices of the *Nashville Tennessean*, the United Press International, the Temple Ohabai Sholom, and the home of Rabbi William B. Silverman. The anonymous caller calmly identified himself as a member of the "Confederate underground" and threatened "any other nigger-loving place or nigger-loving person in Nashville. And we're going to shoot down Judge Miller in cold blood."[67]

It was yet another shock to a city still trying to believe that it had desegregated smoothly, but one that also exposed deeper fault lines in Nashville society. Foremost was the unspoken pact among Nashville's Jews to dampen their distaste for segregation in exchange for acceptance from the broader community. This split, according to one scholar, took place across an urban-rural divide: Jews newer to Nashville, or living in smaller towns outside the city, usually merchant businessmen, resisted black uplift in contrast to city Jews, who tended to be more disapproving of segregation. The division became somewhat more pronounced with Rabbi Silverman's arrival after he made some quiet but visible attempts at interracial fellowship. Although some in his congregation dissented, he consistently obtained votes of confidence from the temple board for his activities. After the Hattie Cotton school bombing, Silverman had stepped up his work through back channels, urging more forceful leadership against Kasper and his followers. In response, a harassment campaign began, including a stream of anonymous anti-Semitic literature decrying "jewpapers, the jewboard of education and the kike control of this city" stuck on car windshields throughout the city. The so-called "nigger-loving rabbi" later told an interviewer that "unfortunately there wasn't a minister in town that came to my defense. Later one man did," and Silverman commented, that man "was soon removed from his post."[68]

Despite Silverman's leadership, he still gave some conflicting messages. Whether these were based on his personal feelings, tactical choices, or what he sensed from his congregation is impossible to say. But in sermons following the community center bombing, he mixed endorsements for civil rights with some equivocation. Having at one point said directly "I FAVOR INTEGRATION," he later counseled that "[Jews] need not initiate or take an overly conspicuous role in advocating integration." He was more critical of the "two extremes" he saw in his flock, those lamenting that "the Jews of America are doomed!" because of anti-Semitism, and the "escapist jittery Jews" who blamed Silverman and the center for "[bringing] all the trouble upon themselves." Actually, Silverman confessed "with a profound sense of shame" that, excepting one sermon and one PTA address, he had "not made a single public utterance" advocating desegregation and had failed to be "active in behalf of social justice as my faith demands." As such, Silverman said he stood with what he believed was the "vast majority of this congregation" for "decency, law, morality, and social justice" and insisted that Jews "not prostrate ourselves and crumble into whimpering, fear-ridden devotees of doom." Nonetheless, the Jewish predicament was only a specific version of contradictions afflicting most of white moderate Nashville.[69]

In some ways, the community center bombing seemed more symbolic than anything. Damage was modest and quickly repaired, and no one was killed or injured from the blast. The community outcry in response to the bombing was fervently expressed, even though, as with the Hattie Cotton school bombing, no arrests were made. The community as one voiced shock and indignation, and city and state leaders alike offered rewards for the bomber's apprehension, echoing the Jewish community's point that this was an attack on all of Nashville, not only Nashville's Jewry. There was irony in the fact that this particular community center was only nominally Jewish. Its governing board was in fact interdenominational, and some debate had occurred about whether to call the center Jewish in the first place. Nor were any African Americans members of the community center, although some had attended interracial civic and social functions there. The possibility of black membership "was unlikely before the dynamiting; it is impossible now." But with Silverman's harassment, Kasper's anti-Semitic rantings, and a rash of attacks on synagogues across Dixie, the bombing further frayed the nerves of southern Jews and Nashvillians.[70]

As the decade closed, Judge Miller approved the Nashville Plan's grade-per-year rate, meaning the school system would fully desegregate in 1968. Displeased with this protracted timetable, Z. Alexander Looby appealed to the Sixth U.S. Circuit Court of Appeals, requesting that all grades be desegregated immediately. On June 17, 1959, the appellate court upheld the Nashville Plan. The ruling's logic would have made Cecil Sims proud. The decision asserted simply that "if the child is free to attend an integrated school, and his parents voluntarily choose a school where only one race attends, he is not being deprived of his constitutional rights." Although "one might disagree with the gradual process," it was not "so unreasonable" that Miller's decision was erroneous. Looby immediately asked the U.S. Supreme Court for a ruling. In a divided vote, the court refused to take the case, although three justices voiced reservations about the transfer provisions. The reality is that the zoning, however calculating in its attempts to stifle desegregation, was also trying to capture a continually moving target. The appeals court noted that shifts in neighborhood demographics, as whites continued shifting from city to suburbs, meant that each school now had African Americans in its zone. That the original plan had left ten or so schools all white, and that zoning suppressed the number of African Americans in white schools overall, remained a secondary issue. But the actuality that any process of school selection rooted in zoning could hardly be "voluntary" for African Americans, since discriminatory housing policies kept them residing in certain sections of the city, remained altogether unacknowledged.[71]

Legal sanction made the Nashville Plan attractive to many school systems that adopted it as a blueprint for desegregating. The plan also helped Nashville's national image as a supposed model for progressive school desegregation, particularly as the shadow of Little Rock loomed in the popular mind. In city schools, the plan continued to work slowly as its proponents had hoped and its opponents had feared. For the second year, only 28 of the 150 black students eligible for white schools chose that option. This contrasted with the 70 white children assigned to formerly black schools, all of whom transferred. A resigned *Globe* editorial identified the tokenism as indicating the deeper problem of "colored citizens being generally situated in their communities in Nashville with white citizens in theirs." Segregationists, too, were disappointed as Tennessee state leaders toyed with anti-desegregation legislation before dropping the measures.[72]

Thus did this chapter of Nashville's school desegregation story end dubiously, with disquiet on all sides. Superintendent Oliver, for example, called desegregation "exceedingly tedious, very painful, and terribly difficult." He referenced the fact that black and white teachers made the same salaries as evidence of Nashville's good race relations, conveniently leaving unmentioned the contentious lawsuit that won this victory despite the school board's testimony in opposition. And his assertion was doubly galling because of the issue of black teachers. The *Globe* registered disappointment over the lack of desegregated faculties, which was even more pronounced given that both the school administration and some professional teachers' groups were racially mixed. School officials, when faced years before with the prospect of having white children under black teachers, had declared that whites would refuse any such arrangement. Those sentiments persisted.[73]

Moreover, black-white interaction in schools, won at a hard cost, remained uncomfortable. Observers of black children in desegregated schools saw evidence of loneliness among the first-graders, who mostly played by themselves. Conducting research on local black families, Vanderbilt sociologist Eugene Weinstein found patterns suggesting that "better-educated, more stable, lighter skinned parents" were more likely to desegregate. Conversely, those families opting for segregated schools were more likely to be lower class, from a rural background, and more politically alienated or apathetic. He also found that, while choosing the most favorable school for the child's education was the foremost explanation for each family's choice, the need to separate siblings into different schools was a major factor hampering desegregation, as predicted.[74]

The *Southern School News* similarly documented that, although most black parents opting to transfer did so out of justifiable fear, at least one did so strictly because the child would be surrounded by lower-income whites. Reverend Kelly Miller Smith later noted that his child had "no negative reactions within the school itself"; instead, the groups peripherally associated with schools, the "PTA, Girl Scouts, etc." were the source of friction. He also judged that, for whites, "while many have accepted the change, there has been no change in attitude 'deep down inside them.'" The principal of the Glenn School concurred, commenting that "there's still some tension in the neighborhood. It's not expressed in words. It's still there—but silent." When the NAACP held workshops trying to increase the percentage of blacks enrolling in white schools, school officials voiced displeasure, seeing this as meddlesome. Even some white liberals noted a "breakdown of communication" between blacks and whites. The lingering feeling was that Nashville parents "have shown less disposition to desegregate than at the outset."[75] Thus hope for more expansive racial change ended on this downcast note by the end of the 1950s.

The central paradox in Nashville's school desegregation story is that, even as the crisis made many of the racial, class, and religious conflicts that saturated Nashville society boil over, the end result could still be construed by white moderates as a victory worthy of Nashville's good name. The fretting dissembling of white moderates, as local and state authorities ducked responsibilities and passed the buck, created self-fulfilling prophecies by opening a space for racial turmoil to convulse the city. But that very turmoil also confirmed the self-beliefs of white moderates. For them, the ability to square personal racial preference with legal approval meant that they could remain smug in their paternalism. Even as they frowned at outsiders who had derailed desegregation, moderates were reassured that their core values remained intact—that *how* desegregation should occur mattered more than the change wrought. One did not need to throw dynamite to frustrate the hopes promised by desegregation. A Vanderbilt professor of religion, Roger L. Shinn, watched with dismayed marvel as local leadership rallied against the interloper John Kasper, providing a window into white Nashville's soul. Wrote Shinn, "the city had loaded its sins on the sacrificial goat and had driven him into the wilderness." And, in doing so, Nashville, "feeling wholesome and purged of guilt, could return to respectability and start refuting the image it had presented to the world." Instead, Shinn concluded, "Nashville now lives by a myth. The myth is obviously false, but it serves the purpose of maintaining moderate harmony. The truth could scarcely have been so effective. Nashville survived its first crisis of integration by an unreal picture of its own virtue."[76]

Black Nashvillians concluded something far different. They had acted the right way and said the right things, even when faced with choosing between the safety of a child or family and the abstract hope of a better education and a greater good. Practically, the array of tactics employed by African Americans were all sound choices: the *Globe*'s defense of moderate politicians, moderate educators, and the city's belated but effective response to Kasper's activities; the Davidson County PTA lobbying for more money instead of desegregating; the support for the NAACP from African American teachers while they worried about their future role in Nashville's educational system; even the reasoned decision to keep children in black schools for reasons of safety or logistics. But it still added up to a mixed victory and, while the failures of white leadership were manifest, deflating these delusions was as difficult as desegregation itself. This meant that black Nashvillians listened with skepticism as national media acclaimed the city as a model for race relations, remembering instead the sounds of dynamite and the voices of threatening phone callers, and the sight of their teachers left ignored when faculty assignments were made. In some ways, for all the changes in the racial landscape, their story was still much the same story—sometimes free to choose their destiny, but still curtailed by both invisible and tangible racial boundaries. It suggested that a different assault on the convergence of racial law and racial custom was needed.

That day would soon come.

The Shame and the Glory
The 1960 Sit-ins

The shattering sound of crashing plates in February 1960 signaled that something unusual was happening in downtown Nashville. "They must have dropped two thousand dollars' worth of dishes that day. It was almost like a cartoon," remembers student leader Diane Nash. "One in particular, she was so nervous, she picked up dishes and she dropped one, and she'd pick up another one, and she'd drop it." It made for surreal feelings, Nash thought: "It was really funny, and we were sitting there trying not to laugh, because we thought that laughing would be insulting and we didn't want to create that kind of atmosphere. At the same time we were scared to death." The clamor came as skittish white waitresses first faced African American students sitting at lunch counters waiting to be served. Nash also recalls tearful cashiers and sweaty store-managers; strange feelings wormed through whites viscerally uncomfortable in encountering African Americans both literally and figuratively seated in forbidden space.[1]

It was a scene replayed across the South as waves of black students energized with a new assertiveness confounded white sensibilities by taking their place at lunch counters and brazenly challenging the usual racial deference. Yet, Nashville's experience was unique. In time, this episode would be at the forefront of the city's civil rights legacy and held up as a national and indeed international model for nonviolent direct action. The campaign was an especially important formative experience to a core nucleus of leaders associated with Nashville who later became key civil rights figures as the movement spread South and beyond. But the lessons of this episode should not be confined to this legacy alone. If nothing else, the situation highlighted the ability of African Americans to marshal multiple tactics to confront the hypocrisies of Nashville's racial etiquette.

The backstory to Nashville's 1960 sit-ins began when Reverend Kelly Miller Smith was part of the founding of Martin Luther King's Southern Christian Leadership Conference (SCLC) in 1957. Tall and enormously "dignified and sophisticated," Smith had emerged from Nashville's school desegregation crisis as a leading spokesman for black Nashville. Backed by his congregation at First Baptist Capitol Hill, the lone piece of black-owned property in Nashville's downtown and the place of worship for much of the city's black elite, he moved among poor blacks and white power brokers with equal ease. *Tennessean* reporter David Halberstam, who later wrote *The Children* about the Nashville sit-ins, remembers Smith as the "gentlest and most subtle" of leaders and, perhaps most important, he "was not very territorial" about his activist turf. Inspired by the SCLC founding, Smith convened a meeting of local black ministers on January 18, 1958, at Capers Memorial CME Church to form the Nashville Christian Leadership Council (NCLC). Ongoing tensions over school desegregation figured prominently in everyone's mind, along with the general muting of protest activity that had prevailed across the South in the post-*Brown* era. Frustration about the Nashville Plan's mixed results, fears about John Kasper's vigilantism, and worries about angry black ministers who had acquired guns in response fed the NCLC's collective resolve for resolute but respectable black protest.[2]

Yet deciding on what exactly made the NCLC special remained more difficult. The group immediately began assisting local voter registration efforts, but also aspired to a new path. Key members had activist experience. Metz Rollins, secretary of the United Presbyterian Church in town, for example, had participated in the Tallahassee bus boycott in 1956, and fiery C. T. Vivian, an editor at the black National Baptist Convention, had similar experience with sit-in protests in Peoria, Illinois, in 1947. Highlander Folk School also played a role in incubating nascent black struggle by sponsoring workshops that linked Nashvillians with other personalities working for racial justice elsewhere. Smith noted that the NCLC wished to use "methods heretofore untried" so as to highlight "the spiritual implications of the struggle" for the "grassroots of the community." However, although the ministers advocated "Christian social action generally," as Smith later wrote, "nothing was said about nonviolence at this time. The fact is that none of us knew enough about it to bring it into the discussion in any meaningful way." Another issue was whether the NCLC should coordinate or compete with other black activist groups in an "over-organized town" where the various civil rights organizations lacked energy.[3] A national official branded the local CORE affiliate, so pivotal in the school desegregation crisis, as "a sick, sick" chapter, with "no action, no imagination, and no projects." The local NAACP chapter was also problematic, although Smith served as president while establishing the NCLC. Smith found that when the NCLC stressed its moral and religious focus, some wondered if the implication was that the NAACP was "immoral and anti-religious." More pragmatically, some worried that the NCLC's efforts, particularly in emphasizing voter registration, would merely duplicate other work. But Smith's conversations with King in 1957 led him to believe that "the NAACP is not equipped to do the whole job"; both ministers agreed that "removing the legal barriers may be *desegregating*, but it is not necessarily *integrating*." So the NCLC persisted. Given that the Tennessee legislature had shown some preliminary willingness to ban the NAACP, as Alabama had done, finding complementary ways to advance the movement seemed sensible.[4]

Throughout early 1958, the NCLC tried to broaden the group's membership by welcoming varied supporters in hopes of enhancing the group's effectiveness. Two early white figures on the NCLC board included Nelson Fuson, a physics professor at Fisk. Fuson and his wife, Marian, were Quaker pacifists active in liberal causes. The Fusons were joined by Reverend Will D. Campbell, a Southern Baptist minister from a poor rural Mississippi family. Serving in World War II and attending Yale Divinity School made Campbell question his segregated upbringing and, uncomfortable with the life of a small-town preacher, anxious to work for racial justice. Just three months after the *Brown* decision, he took a position at the University of Mississippi as director of religious life, but his superiors grew increasingly displeased with his efforts to alter the racial status quo. He decided to leave Ole Miss after anonymous locals expressed their disdain for Campbell's activities by slipping human feces, anointed daintily with powdered sugar, into a punch bowl at a party Campbell hosted. Hired instead to open a southern office for the National Council of Churches, Campbell settled in Nashville in 1956. In short order he had deposited his money in Nashville's lone black bank, hired a black secretary, and joined Kelly Miller Smith's church. He would, over the coming years, serve as a roving troubleshooter for southern communities grappling with desegregation issues, laboring behind the scenes to counsel townspeople during racial upheavals.[5]

But the crucial step in the NCLC's development occurred when the group welcomed two influential out-of-towners as members. Glenn Smiley and James Lawson were both affiliated with the Fellowship of Reconciliation (FOR), an international group dedicated to using nonviolent direct action to promote human rights and social change. FOR's early work primarily supported conscientious objectors during the world wars but, inspired by Mohandas Gandhi's challenge to British colonial rule in India, the group became eager to use nonviolence to topple southern segregation. Although Nashville's local FOR chapter, like the city's other activist groups, had struggled to make headway, national FOR officers had early stature in the wider movement. As Martin Luther King began his rise to prominence during the Montgomery bus boycott, it was Smiley, a white Texan minister and conscientious objector during World War II, who encouraged King (along with black activist Bayard Rustin) to explore nonviolence. Smiley convinced King, for example, to withdraw an application for a gun permit after King's house was bombed. Throughout the 1950s, Smiley and Lawson traveled throughout the South, conducting workshops to inspire a concerted nonviolent struggle against Jim Crow. On March 26–28, 1958, one such meeting took place at Nashville's Bethel AME church, cosponsored by FOR, NCLC, and Anna Holden, a local CORE official, and featuring Reverend Ralph Abernathy, a chief King lieutenant from Montgomery and vice president of the SCLC.[6]

Reverend James M. Lawson was "the special ingredient," as Kelly Miller Smith later put it, that made Nashville's example so unusual. A black Methodist minister from Ohio, Lawson's life path had been transformed as a ten-year-old after he slapped a white child who called out "hey, nigger," as Lawson walked past. The enduring lesson from the incident came later with his mother's reaction, as she asked him quietly, "What good did that do? We all love you, Jimmy, and God loves you . . . with all that love, what harm does that stupid insult do?" (Her response contrasted with that of Lawson's father, also a Methodist minister, who was more inclined to self-defense when appropriate, despite his wife's disapproval.) His mother's voice stayed with Lawson, and as a college freshman he joined FOR after hearing veteran pacifist A. J. Muste speak. He soon manifested his beliefs by serving a jail term after refusing to defer or accept his draft into the Korean War. Later, as a missionary in India, Lawson followed with keen interest Gandhi's career, knowing instinctively that Gandhi's work might resonate in U.S. race relations. The realization crystallized after news of the Montgomery bus boycott reached Lawson half a world away. After returning to the United States, a meeting with Martin Luther King convinced Lawson to come south immediately. Following Glenn Smiley's advice, he settled in Nashville as FOR's field secretary for the South. After enrolling in Vanderbilt Divinity School (only the second African American to do so), he began working with small groups of local ministers on behalf of the NCLC to apply the gospel of nonviolent direct action to local race relations.[7]

The NCLC's first effort reached out to fellow white clergymen. On November 29, 1958, five NCLC ministers refused segregated seating at the Oral Roberts Evangelistic Crusade, which prompted a range of responses. One white audience member "turned his back" rather than shake hands, but later "'courteously' waited" as an NCLC member donated money to the collection plate. Meanwhile, "nervously smiling ushers" tried to coax the black preachers from creating a scene. One, encouraging Smith to move to the blacks-only balcony, said, "Oh Lord bless you: I just know your people would be happy to have one of their pastors sitting with them." He was unmoved by Smith's observation that blacks and whites "are all brothers." Exactly who mandated the segregated seating remained unclear: an Oral Roberts representative told Smith that the arrangement deferred to local custom, while another usher said instead that "it was a requirement of the Oral Roberts team." When Smith asked the ushers if Oral Roberts saw "any connection between salvation and the practice of segregation," the response was a terse "no." The experiment ended with no clear result.[8]

After this attempt, the NCLC zeroed in on three objectives: increasing voter registration, facilitating black employment, particularly in the Nashville Police Department, and desegregating the lunch counters and restrooms in downtown stores. Although the shift to today's era of food courts in suburban malls was occurring at this same time, downtown dining was still a fixture in 1950s America. Each of the major retail anchors in Nashville's central business district, Harvey's and Cain-Sloan department stores, provided restaurants for their customers. The lunch counters in more modest five-and-dime stores offered cheaper dining. Each option allowed a full outing for patrons, especially for townspeople from Nashville's outskirts who made special trips, usually on Saturdays, to shop and eat. In spring 1959, the NCLC chose these dining venues as the next venue for action.[9]

Tactically, the NCLC's decision made sense, for the lunch counters were a conspicuous example of segregation's humiliating absurdities. African Americans shopped freely in these stores but even after purchasing goods were not permitted to rest their feet and fill their stomachs. The contradiction had not entirely deterred black Nashvillians; later estimates found that 15 percent of one store's business derived from African Americans. But the combination of moral hypocrisy and financial vulnerability was a potent wedge for NCLC activity. Moreover, the stores provided a dramatic theater for the morality play that the NCLC planned to stage. The neat row of lunch-counter stools evoked the segregated line; large storefront windows permitted plenty of witnesses in both legal and spiritual senses. Moreover, the prospect of both races eating together threatened one of segregation's most taboo codes. But the lunch counters symbolized much more than that. As Lawson heard countless stories from African American women recounting the shame, outrage, and degradation prompted by shopping excursions downtown, when they rushed pleading children away from white restrooms or endured snobbery from clerks while dress shopping, "he knew he had his target."[10]

The NCLC opened the campaign with an attempt at dialogue between Harvey's and Cain-Sloan. Fisk students had already announced contempt in 1957 for Harvey's black self-service food counter, located in the store's basement, which had lasted only a few months thanks to poor sales. But the women's restroom in Harvey's remained segregated, as did both restrooms and the restaurant in Cain-Sloan. The two stores responded differently to the NCLC. At Harvey's, manager Greenfield Pitts acknowledged "some recognition of the problem and some willingness to seek to explore alternatives to segregation." By contrast, John Sloan of

Cain-Sloan met the NCLC coolly, insisting that "good merchandise at good prices" was the sole concern of black customers. As Smith later put it bluntly, the NCLC had received "a courteous no and a curt no." One merchant called the NCLC's requests "comic," saying that integration would likely occur, "but not in our lifetime." Store officials admitted freely that "their concern was economic, not moral"; they feared losing white business if they desegregated and doubted that black patronage could make up the difference. Financial doubts, personal preference, and social conformity were powerful obstacles to the NCLC's diplomacy. The ministers noted that "both stores expressed the willingness to desegregate after the rest of the city had changed in this direction."[11]

Unimpressed, the NCLC decided to press forth, but the group needed more volunteers. The idea to include students was almost an afterthought. But when Smith and Lawson began enlisting volunteers from local black colleges, by Smith's admission, they were "caught by surprise by the intense interest" in response. Although only a handful of students had attended the first meetings in fall 1958, the schools soon became fertile recruiting grounds. Lawson's initial approach was low-key. His first talk, for example, consisted of a simple assertion that all the world's greatest religions had a single universal value: justice. Workshops studying this theme and similar ones took place at Clark Memorial Methodist and First Baptist every week. Open to all, the meetings slowly began to gather a following as Lawson offered lectures and case studies about the power of nonviolent resistance to alter history. He cast a wide net, sharing examples of William Penn, Henry David Thoreau, antislavery proponents in the antebellum United States, anti-Nazi resisters in Europe, and Jesus Christ. His students read Chinese philosophers Mo Ti and Lao-tzu and theologian Reinhold Niebuhr. Gandhi's example was particularly vivid, especially his concept of satyagraha (literally, "truth insistence" or "steadfastness in truth," but often translated more loosely and effectively as "soul force"), a value of inner calm and resolution that permitted one to embrace nonviolence as a way of life. Lawson's lessons ended with an example much closer to home: the Montgomery bus boycott. The cumulative effect not only showed nonviolence's long legacy but also provided a specific blueprint for action. As John Lewis remembers, the collective education was "mind-blowing."[12]

Lewis, the son of sharecroppers in rural Troy, Alabama, was studying for the ministry at American Baptist. A devout young man, Lewis had practiced sermonizing as a boy by addressing chickens in his yard as he fed them. He even baptized his fowls—until he accidentally drowned one. Although shy and a little halting in his social graces, prone to teasing from peers for his country ways, something about Lewis caught Kelly Miller Smith's eye after he took the minister's class at American Baptist. "That young man," marveled Smith, "is pure of heart." By fall

1959, inspired by the workshops, Lewis convinced his best friend, Bernard Lafayette, to join. Lafayette, a young Floridian, was a generous and smart student
who had declined a full scholarship at Florida A&M in favor of the seminary. Another emerging leader, Diane Nash, a former beauty pageant queen from Chicago,
joined the workshops after being appalled by a date's casual acceptance of segregated restrooms at the Tennessee State Fair. It was part of her more general unease
at feeling "stifled" at Fisk, in comparison to her native Chicago's South Side. "I
came to college to grow and expand," she recalls, "and here I am shut in." She ignored her fellow Fisk students who told her, "why don't you just go to class during
the week and to parties on the weekend?" Even as the desire to fight segregation
conflicted with her skepticism about nonviolence, she continued participating
in the workshops ("they were the only game in town," she said later) and gradually was won over. Several male students sampled the workshops just to get closer
to Nash, but she became intently focused on Lawson's teachings and immune to
such distractions. Another older American Baptist student also joined up: Jim
Bevel, a streetwise, eccentric, and brilliant Mississippian who had split his child-
hood between the Mississippi Delta and Cleveland, Ohio. Bevel's self-professed
desire in life was to be a "chicken-eating, liquor-drinking, woman-chasing Baptist
preacher." He was described by Lewis as "nuttier than a nut," especially after Lewis
tired of Bevel's attempts to teach him the art of seducing females. Also initially
skeptical about the workshops, Bevel started reading about Gandhi and became
increasingly engrossed. Lewis, Nash, Lafayette, and Bevel would soon be at the
very core of student leaders in Nashville.[13]

The students in the workshops made for an unusual fellowship. Except perhaps
for the American Baptist contingent, none were considered among the campus
elite, and other students regarded Lawson's crew with some derision. Residual tensions from life in class-conscious Nashville made the group's relative unity even
more pronounced. Fisk was conspicuously elite, with a pedigreed background of
scholarship, but was also regarded by some as little more than a finishing school
for students to join exclusive Greek organizations and marry well. TSU was somewhat more middling in wealth and stature, while American Baptist remained poor
and struggling. Disparate origins also conditioned the group mentality. Paradoxically, students from other regions of the country, dismayed by the blatancy of
southern-style discrimination, were sufficiently nettled to join the workshops and
fight Jim Crow, whereas their counterparts from the Deep South also saw Nashville's mellower version of segregation as a chance to induce further change. The
combined energy jolted native black lethargy. As one adult later put it approvingly,
the students "got this town rolling."[14]

Lawson's educational process was rigorous, extensive, and highly personal. Early discussions stayed abstract but, as the students internalized his lessons, they could not help but relate the teachings to southern racial issues. Like any good teacher, Lawson listened as much as he spoke. He allowed his students to question, he challenged them, and he tried to guide them to their own independent understanding of Jim Crow and the racial beliefs that segregation enshrined. The students were impressed, as Lewis remembers: "He just had a way about him, an aura of inner peace and wisdom that you could sense immediately upon seeing him." But that sort of presence was necessary to defuse the jaded reservations of the young pupils. Again, the point bears repeating: few if any of these students had an instinctive tendency toward nonviolence. Instead, these beliefs were taught and honed, first by Lawson in these workshops and later through subsequent years of struggle (mental, emotional, and indeed often spiritual). Above all else, the process helped the students intuit what became a core belief: that any personal succumbing to the racial status quo, whether implicit or explicit, in small or large ways, only sustained the segregated system. As one put it decades later, "if you fell back in fear, you contributed to your own slavery." Every flinch at *nigger* reaffirmed the word's poisoned power. Every dollar that went to a segregated store paid interest to Jim Crow. The sum of untold silent and public humiliations shrank souls into complacency and fear.[15]

But the fear bred by segregation also ravaged whites and left them spiritually malnourished, racked with deeper insecurities and psychological anxieties. "If segregationists were truly powerful or confident or well-loved," Lawson argued, why did they resort to violence? "Folks," whether white or black, he might have added, "who believe so much in violence fail to recognize that in violence someone always loses." The day-to-day navigation of racial etiquette, however necessary for survival or psychological comfort, only reinforced the broader racial system. Indeed white supremacy drew its power from a potent stew of fear, meek compliance, and sheer blindness as two races were locked in relentless tension by the silent threat of violence. It was not a racial problem but a human problem, as historian Wesley Hogan observes, "the problem of submission" to an unjust and immoral system. The students now understood white southerners as sick with sin, trapped in Jim Crow's vise so powerfully so as to be unaware of their affliction. Whether through fear, violence, "dishonesty," conformity, willful or unknowing ignorance, Jim Crow stifled whites in ways less powerful than for blacks, but equally real.[16]

This understanding, however, suggested that nonviolent direct action could break the cycle to redeem both black and white souls. Although drawing from a range of historical antecedents, Lawson infused his teachings with the New Testament spirit, the living demonstration that humans served God through their Christian love for one another. Using nonviolence meant that the Nashvillians sought to "take the suffering upon ourselves and never inflict it upon our fellow man." And melding Christian belief with nonviolent direct action, as Lawson taught it, formed a coherent worldview for living one's life, not just resisting racism. Instead of a tactic, the Nashvillians learned that the philosophy of nonviolence should be a fundamental life principle, all-encompassing in mentality and behavior. "The ends you seek must be involved and inherent in the means you use," as one put it decades later, and the phrase that particularly captured the emotional and transformative power of nonviolence was "redemptive suffering." As John Lewis explains, "we must honor our suffering . . . there is something in the very essence of anguish that is liberating, cleansing, redemptive."[17]

There was power when a practitioner fit nonviolence into a personal worldview, squaring belief with action and drawing inner strength from refusing to participate in an unjust social practice. But the chance to use that action to challenge the oppressor, to prompt whites into realizing their own silent psychological suffering under segregation, was another revelation. Nonviolence was not "passive resistance" (the phrase often used interchangeably with "nonviolent direct action"); there was nothing passive about it. It was direct spiritual provocation. Nonviolent confrontations were *opportunities* to derail the racial etiquette and delve into white psyches. By refusing the usual racial roles, by directly contradicting racial stereotypes, by exhibiting a higher morality while transgressing social codes, African Americans could "dramatize the sin" of segregation, by making whites aware of their own complicity in a racist system and by forcing them to choose the extent to which they would defend Jim Crow. And by bringing the ever-present threat of violence into the open, nonviolent behavior hoped to trigger "inward shame" in the segregationist and create an unexpected relationship between victim and attacker, as the latter questioned themselves and their actions and their souls. Nonviolence inverted the racial order, creating a new space where blacks could "take ownership" of "their own public life," unlike the racial etiquette of the past. With nonviolence, "everything done to destroy actually develops you." By physically absorbing spit, punches, and kicks, protesters gave witness to the totality of their Christian forgiveness and exposed the full ugliness of segregation. Politically resisting segregation also made for the ultimate display of spiritual love. The individual inner calm of satyagraha, when applied to collective nonviolent demonstrations, could bring social tensions to the surface in hope of healing.[18]

Armed with this awareness, the students now found Lawson's lessons moving from the abstract to the practical. Instead of cowering, nonviolent direct action promised a way to confront racial stigma directly, taking strength by transgressing racial taboos. The group began acting out "socio-dramas," role-playing exercises in which students adopted the persona of a segregationist tormentor or a nonviolent protester. The students shouted racial epithets at each other, poured liquids over heads, and slapped their peers in attempts to test inner wills and resolve. Lawson taught his students to adopt a protective posture, cradling internal organs from harm while maintaining eye contact with the attacker. Visualize the assailant as an infant, he suggested; see them in their purest form before segregation raised them on hate and fear. By embodying forgiveness, protesters might ignite the spark of humanity in even the most hardened segregationist. As Lewis remembers King preaching, nonviolence meant that you "must love the unlovable" and that meant to literally "love the *hell* out of them."[19]

In honing this intellectual understanding and moral commitment, the students became increasingly eager to act. As the workshops intensified, a mostly unnoticed dress rehearsal of sorts occurred at Harvey's on November 28, 1959, and hinted at what was to come. A few students sat down, were refused service as expected, conferred politely with the management, and left quietly. Another took place on December 5 at Cain-Sloan's, with momentary confusion when one student was served after being mistaken for a foreign-exchange student. After the accidental breach, the manager reiterated the store's policy of segregation and the students withdrew. The practice run, consistent with nonviolent techniques, fully established the store's continued commitment to segregation, and the group agreed to conduct a full-scale strike upon returning from winter break.[20]

January came and went, and only unexpected news from outside Nashville triggered action. On February 1, four black students in Greensboro, North Carolina, staged a sit-in at the local Woolworth's. Neither entirely impulsive nor organized, exactly what precipitated this sit-in remains obscure. But Douglas Moore, a minister from nearby Durham active in FOR, saw an opportunity and began counseling the foursome about the philosophy of nonviolent direct action. Whether or not the students were aware of it, sit-ins were not an unfamiliar tactic for resisting segregation; CORE had used the tactic in Chicago in 1942 and in subsequent, isolated instances in southern and midwestern cities. But, this time, the four Greensboro students excited imaginations and almost immediately sit-ins erupted across the South. As Greensboro's protests continued, Moore phoned his friend Jim Lawson, asking for Nashville's support. Lawson in turn called some of his student contacts: Luther Harris and Peggy Alexander, leaders of Fisk's Youth NAACP group, and Paul LaPrad, a white exchange student at Fisk and one of the very first to attend Lawson's workshops. Immediately a hastily gathered meeting in Fisk's chemistry building began to gauge student interest in commencing sit-ins locally. Apparently, when the subject of nonviolence was broached, "most of them laughed," but by the end of the meeting everyone was "taking it seriously."[21]

Although the students were anxious to begin, the decision required NCLC approval and here some generational dissension appeared. Apprehensive adults in the NCLC pointed to the meager $87.50 in the group's treasury, insufficient for the legal fees and bail money that large-scale action would require. The students would have none of it. "I'm tired of this business of waiting," said Jim Bevel and his compatriots agreed. Bernard Lafayette made repeated analogies between their situation and Christ's, prompting one minister to "facetiously" refer to the student's "crucifixion complex." Practical reasons for delay meant nothing to the youngsters. Mostly unencumbered by jobs and domestic responsibilities, they were somewhat insulated from potential reprisals. As Bevel put it, "something will happen . . . that will provide the solution" to scarce funds and legal representation. The ministers could do little but assent.[22]

Preparations commenced, with meticulous planning. Lawson and his protégés began crash courses in nonviolence for dozens of new faces impatient for action. Lewis recalls that "we were speeding up our schedule, yes, but we were determined to do this right. . . . We did not want to unleash hundreds of eager, emotional college students without properly preparing them in the ways of restraint." Organizers also found subsidiary roles for those unwilling to risk their futures or doubtful of their ability to absorb potential violence without lashing back. Some would write newspaper articles for hometown newspapers. Those with cars were assigned to ferry people; others manned phone networks to circulate information throughout the black community. Still others were designated as runners to pass messages and updates between First Baptist headquarters and the downtown stores.[23]

It began at 12:30 p.m. on Saturday, February 13, 1960. Groups of nonviolent soldiers sat in First Baptist pew rows. There were 124 of them, ten of them white, each dressed in Sunday finery that included "coats and ties for the men, stockings and heels for the women." In leaving the church, they had a last opportunity to leave behind pocket knives, nail files, and anything else that might be construed as a weapon. Each team had a designated leader charged with maintaining group discipline and communicating with store representatives and journalists. Tramping through six inches of snow that had fallen the previous night, the students moved double-file through Nashville's downtown. Kelly Miller Smith remembers them walking with a "casual haste," which he likened to "a Saturday football game when it is near kick-off, or a movie when the feature is about to begin." Entering through the Arcade, downtown's covered mallway leading to Fifth Avenue North, Nashville's main shopping street, the students dispersed to Kress's, McClellan's, and

Woolworth's. In each store, the students purchased sundries to establish that they were paying customers, proceeded to stools, and sat.[24]

And, in that moment, somehow everything changed, and yet nothing did. As John Lewis, group leader for the Woolworth's contingent, remembers, "No one got up. No one said anything." One waitress "stopped dead in her tracks. 'Oh my God,' she said to no one in particular, 'here's the niggers.'" At each store, the designated leader asked to be served and at each store the staff declined. The staffs were, as one leader put it, "courteous, but not particularly nice." Lewis detected "no anger in them, just bewilderment, nervousness, and maybe a little bit of fear." When two students went to the ladies' restroom, they encountered a white woman who cried, "Oh! Nigras, Nigras everywhere!" before rushing away. An elaborate chess match occurred at McClellan's as waiting black students occupied the seats of vacating white patrons. Seeing this, the manager passed instructions for white customers to hail a waitress before leaving so that the store could fill the seat customers with waiting whites instead. The demonstrators used three of their white partners to thwart this evasion and obtain more stools. Police officers summoned to the scene scratched their heads, eventually advising the stores that they could do nothing. The groups stayed in place for about two hours. At Woolworth's, the waitresses closed the counters and shut the lights, leaving the students sitting while the curious milled about watching or occasionally yelling taunts.[25]

Back at First Baptist, it was "like New Year's Eve—whooping, cheering, hugging, laughing, singing." Lewis remembered the "sheer euphoria, like a jubilee," with everyone "elated," asking "What's next? . . . What do we do next?" At the second demonstration on Thursday, February 18, over two hundred students took part. They returned to the three stores and added W. T. Grant's, again arriving around lunchtime to maximize their exposure to daily clientele. Diane Nash, walking through downtown, recalled whites recognizing her from a *Tennessean* photograph and calling out "That's Diane Nash! She's the one to get!" This time, the five-and-dimes not only closed the diners but stacked merchandise on countertops as if to block out the sight before them. McClellan's actually unscrewed the seats at the counters, and a secretary for the company told a reporter that even though the students were there, "we aren't supposed to discuss or even think about it." Two days later, now with an estimated three hundred and fifty participants, the students sat again for four hours and purposefully lingered especially at McClellan's just because workers there were mean. John Lewis worked on a sermon as white hecklers gathered, increasingly emboldened as police watched carefully. Around 1:30 p.m., the students attempted to surprise Walgreen's with a sit-in but the counter there, like the others, quickly closed; the protesters remained "officially ignored" by the stores. Around 3 p.m., an argument broke out between two white boys and Carol Ann Anderson, a white Fisk student, which triggered the store's closing and her group's withdrawal. A few individuals, such as Will D. Campbell and representatives from the interracial local United Church Women group, loitered at the edges of each store, maintaining silence but serving as observers. They were especially aware of the police turning their backs on the demonstrators. Although nonviolent discipline held, white animosity heightened and threatened to spill over.[26]

The fourth sit-in on February 27, soon known as Big Saturday, was the breaking point. With the city abuzz during the previous week, white retaliation was being planned behind the scenes. The merchants, meeting with Mayor Ben West, demanded that the students be arrested. West later protested that he had refused, as his attorneys advised that anyone could legally request service at lunch counters. But West also suggested that it was illegal for anyone, regardless of race, to sit at a lunch counter closed to all patrons. The qualification illustrated West's dilemma, for his political base relied on two key components, one being James Stahlman and his *Banner*. Not only had West run against arch-enemy and *Tennessean* candidate Thomas Cummings in 1951, but he had worked at the *Banner* while in school. Now, Stahlman, with his business constituents behind him, was livid about the sit-ins. But West also owed his election to Nashville's black voters and, with the sit-ins, neither group could be appeased without alienating the other. Moreover, Nashville remained on edge because of problems in Chattanooga, where, on February 24, authorities using fire hoses put down a near-riot that accompanied local sit-ins. "Ben really got caught in this one," one anonymous local politician observed. The mayor had to do something, yet any move risked serious political implications, none of them favorable.[27]

The weeklong hiatus meant that dangerous repercussions for the next sit-in loomed. As Kelly Miller Smith put it later, "word had been rather generously passed around" that demonstrations would resume on February 27. This Saturday made for an attractive if hazardous protest day, as the students knew well; downtown would be congested with the usual weekend shoppers and white teenagers curious about the sit-ins. There was rich potential for reaching a wider audience, along with the very real threat of violence. On February 23, students met with Chief of Police Douglas Hosse and asked for a policeman to be present in each store. According to a later student account, Hosse answered with "a flat 'no' on the grounds that a policeman entering a place of business for no reason damages business." The *Tennessean* claimed instead that Hosse had said only that he lacked the manpower but reassured the students that protection would be available. He also provided copies of city ordinances that would be used as grounds to arrest the students for "inciting others to engage in riotous, violent or disorderly conduct." Turning to student leader Curtis Murphy, Hosse said, "is this all worth a twenty-five cent hamburger?"[28]

A more ominous tidbit circulating through city networks stemmed from the meeting between the merchants and the mayor. Will D. Campbell, drifting around the courthouse, caught wind of the rumor and alerted Lawson and Smith. His information was confirmed by Molly Todd, the wife of a Harvey's official. During the sit-ins, Todd often made discreet phone calls to First Baptist after her husband, prominent in the Nashville Chamber of Commerce, came home with the day's gossip. The news was grim: Stahlman had prevailed upon Mayor West to acquiesce to a chilling arrangement that allowed white hecklers a few minutes alone with the protesters, uninterrupted by police, before arrests took place.[29]

The news made for a test of wills and commitment. The NCLC was unanimous in wanting to hold the students back. The students were split down the middle, as an initial vote after hours of arguing and conscience-checking was eight to five in favor of demonstrating. Characteristically, they continued discussion until they reached something approximating a consensus to continue. John Lewis, for his part, remained "calmed by the sense that the Spirit of History was with us." Hoping to maintain discipline among their swelling ranks despite these new threats, Lewis, possessing keys from his janitorial job at American Baptist, filched some paper from the mimeograph room and made up a list of now-famous instructions:

DO NOT: 1. Strike back nor curse if abused.
           2. Laugh out.
           3. Hold conversations with floor walker.
           4. Leave your seat until your leader has given you permission to do so.
           5. Block entrances to stores outside nor the aisles inside.
DO: 1. Show yourself friendly and courteous at all times.
           2. Sit straight; always face the counter.
           3. Report all serious incidents to your leader.
           4. Refer information seekers to your leader in a polite manner.
           5. Remember the teachings of Jesus Christ, Mahatma Gandhi and Martin Luther King. Love and nonviolence is the way.
           MAY GOD BLESS EACH OF YOU.[30]

On February 27, everyone downtown braced themselves for a scene. Woolworth's, McClellan's, and Walgreen's were "jammed with people." Grant's and Cain-Sloan quickly closed down as the students approached, and Kress's was roped off. White packs of teenagers, "obviously previously organized," in Kelly

Miller Smith's appraisal, prowled the sides of the five-and-dimes. Will D. Campbell had seen the "ill-kept" bunch earlier getting free haircuts at the Barber College. A few had written "Chattanooga" across their jackets, in salute to the racial disorder in that city from three days before. Unlike previous sit-ins, the demonstrators entered in smaller groups attempting to downplay their obstruction of lunch-counter traffic. They instead staggered their seating, leaving vacant stools as open invitation for whites to sit next to them. Policemen strolled down the aisle occasionally to preserve a three-foot demarcation between the protesters and the white gangs. C. Thomas Baker, a minister affiliated with the Nashville Association of Churches and apparently mortified by the impending danger, also went up and down the aisle. Speaking earnestly and with unintended irony, he exhorted the students "to apply Christian principles!" in trying to get them to desist.[31]

After the police vanished mysteriously, as if on cue, the first target for the mob's rage was white Paul LaPrad, "the nigger lover" seated next to Maxine Walker, a black Fisk student. His attacker, in LaPrad's dispassionate account, "grabbed me from behind and pulled me off the stool. I tried to hang on to the stool but I couldn't. He hit me on the head several times with his fist. I did not try and fight back." As others waded in, a nearby camera filmed the encounter for broadcast on the national news that evening. After finishing, the attackers left the store. Minutes later, the police reappeared, ordering the demonstrators to leave. The protesters obeyed—and promptly resumed their sit-in at a different store. At McClellan's, a man blowing cigar smoke at an unresponsive student began to flail his fists with "jabs more suggestive of frustration and bewilderment than the actual intent of hurting." At other lunch counters, punching and shoving became increasingly forceful, with angry aggressors pouring coffee and smearing condiments onto seated students. White onlookers watched "approvingly" while "non-participating Negroes in the crowd were silent." Shortly after one o'clock, doors to the waiting fleet of police vans were thrown open and the students ushered inside, accompanied by the applause of whites.[32]

These cheers quickly turned to disbelief as a second contingent of students quickly took over the newly unoccupied seats. Even as police escorted the first round of singing students to jail, runners had sprinted back to First Baptist or dialed the church on payphones, calling for reinforcements. Rounds of arrests took place at Woolworth's, Walgreen's, and McClellan's. Each time, a fresh batch of demonstrators made their way to newly empty stools. Smith recalls that "I got a big kick out of listening to some of the Caucasians in the crowd talking. And they just could not, could not conceive of this, of people going to jail singing." Whites were flummoxed by the zest of students who accepted arrest and continued to flock to the lunch counters without wavering. Yet this made jeering whites grew bolder against the new demonstrators. "Get back to Africa!" and "You chicken?" were constant refrains. When knocked off stools, the students returned calmly to their seats; as ketchup was poured onto their hair, they stared ahead impassively. Despite their bluster, the white gangs preferred soft targets. At one point, a white hoodlum focused on a black bystander, not connected with the sit-ins, who watched from the side of the store, and "menacingly waved a cigarette in his face." The black kid—who clearly would have been unimpressed with Lewis's mimeographed instructions had he seen them—snapped back quickly with "White folks, let me tell you three things. In the first place, I am *not* one of those integrationists. Therefore, I am *not* nonviolent. And therefore, if you touch me with that cigarette, I'll cut your goddamn throat." When a neutral party ran to a policeman outside, entreating him to stop the brewing melee, the officer responded that he "was busy 'directing traffic.'" A student overheard another officer telling a white heckler, "Go ahead, no one is going to bother you if you hit them."[33]

Will D. Campbell, perched on the second floor of Woolworth's for a better view of both the upstairs and downstairs lunch counters, watched with amazement as an elderly white woman, in the store to buy an egg poacher, moved among the throng. Like Campbell, she tried to quiet the crowd by chastising the white thugs after they landed a blow or spat out an insult, saying, "how would you feel if that was your sister?" Campbell recalls that "she more than anyone controlled that mob." Questioned afterward, she professed unawareness of the impending demonstration but, as a member of FOR, had relied on her training to forestall the crowd's growing rage.[34]

And so it continued, in each store, throughout the afternoon.

Between four and five o'clock, news that the police had left again filtered through the excited gathering. At Woolworth's, the stand-off between protesters and the sneering bystanders grew even uglier and sickening. David Halberstam, scribbling notes furiously, watched as "for more than an hour the hate kept building up," and that "slow build-up of hate was somehow more worse than the actual violence." Every so often, whites crossed the line to give a shove or a kick, or to stub a cigarette on black flesh. Each time they moved in, shouts of "here it goes, here it goes" filled the room, as if the expectant crowd was baiting the demonstrators as hatred and fear rose to the fore. Jaunty cries ("here comes Old Green Hat!" and "Looks like it'll go this time") sprang up to hail an apparently familiar young white man who swaggered in "looking like the modern-day pictures of Robin Hood with a big feather sticking in the band." Strutting up and down the aisle as he asked "What's going on here?" and perhaps even playing to the crowd, the ruffian began to hit the students, first in the backs, then deliberately striking at throats and eyes as bystanders watched gleefully and in horror. Drawn to one student who was visibly fraying under the strain, Green Hat pounced, jerking him off the stool and sprawling him on the floor before swiping a knife that slit the student's coat as the demonstrator rolled away in desperation. As the rabble converged, screams and gasps heightened amidst a crowd that had turned into a "wild animal mob." Just then, a white college-age preppy kid in a suit and tie lunged and, seizing Old Green Hat by the neck, punched him below the eye, yelling, "You son of a bitch, if you don't get out of here, I will stomp the piss out of you." Old Green Hat, offering some resistance, took more punches, as the white intervener said, "Goddammit, get out of here or I will kill you." Whereupon Old Green Hat looked out the window—where there were no policemen in sight—and cried, "here come the cops!" as he and his band fled the store.[35]

As Old Green Hat improvised his exit, the arrests ceased and the collective downtown tried to recover some composure as the singing from Nashville's city prison grew louder. Because the jail was segregated, the three white students were separated from the seventy-eight African Americans crammed into cells. Even as the officers busied themselves making racial jokes, that was of no consequence to students, who remembered instead expressions of astonishment from police as the demonstrators moved calmly into the wagons. The act felt like being "caught up in something noble and holy," John Lewis remembered, and indeed over time many of the students became insistent that they be arrested, which some called "witnessing." If the psychological rush of sitting at taboo places was powerful, the students were now exultant at the chance to overturn the symbolic stigma of prison and make it instead into the ultimate metaphor of southerners imprisoned by the Jim Crow system. This maneuver was a heady one for the students: they had been raised to stay away from prison, to avoid an arrest record that might keep them from a good job and to be frightened of the rough police justice that could occur in Nashville jails. But now students embraced their jailing as emblematic of their commitment and sang spirituals to signal their passion and that they had freed themselves from fear.[36]

Not only did the students invert the stigma of prison by walking willingly into cells, they further testified to their beliefs by refusing bail—turning prison "from a pit of sorrow to a haven of liberty," as one national CORE official wrote approvingly. The very idea stunned many. Even Thurgood Marshall advised the students against this tactic when he spoke in Nashville weeks later: "once you've been arrested, you've made your point. If someone offers to get you out, man, get out." John Lewis remembered hearing this speech and feeling that Marshall "just did not understand" what the students professed through their actions. The sly inversion of prison's power represented a more wholesale overturning of racial etiquette more generally. But refusing bail was also a smart tactical move that avoided straining community resources by allowing any cash raised to be used for the Movement instead of supporting segregation by going into Nashville's city coffers. White Nashville certainly understood the symbolic import of prison as the powers-that-be reduced the fines from one hundred to five dollars. Later that night, after the workhouse remained filled with students chanting "jail without bail!," the students were freed outright.[37]

Despite early dismay, the black community's reaction was, by all accounts, profound. "At first, the parents and many of the adults were very withdrawn," Kelly Miller Smith's secretary recalls. "They thought the kids were being silly—until the kids started going to jail." After hearing about the sit-ins over the radio, one black undertaker rushed up to Kelly Miller Smith, reaching for his wallet. Smith, eyeing the motion, quipped, "well, you've got the right idea." An estimated fifty thousand dollars poured into NCLC coffers the first day, with a steady stream of donations from around the country for weeks thereafter. Less than forty-eight hours after Big Saturday, on February 29, the Internal Revenue Service swarmed over local banks, searching for evidence of financial wrongdoing that might explain this cash bonanza. At Fisk, worried students cheered after President Stephen J. Wright professed his support for the students and their conduct, although he would later sternly remind his charges about the drop-off in class attendance with the lunchcounter demonstrations. At Flem Otey's grocery store, a longtime fixture in the black community, employees made up sandwiches for the jailed students. Many agree that the arrests marked the moment when the sit-ins finally unified local African Americans into a mass movement.[38]

This was undoubtedly true—and yet there was also more to the story. Even as the spirit took hold of an entire community, there was still a range of diverse perspectives to be reconciled over the coming weeks. To take one example: even if they supported the demonstrations in the abstract, the presidents of black colleges necessarily had to handle the situation with a light touch. They had to walk the finest of lines in disassociating formally from the movement and potentially illegal activities while not ignoring the transformations on their campuses and while coaching students on how to walk a similar line. Nor did they want the movement (and especially potential arrests) to interfere with grades and class performance. Too firm with their pupils and they might be seen as unsupportive; perceived as too lax and they could alienate their predominantly white funders. This was especially tricky when it came to policies that could be variously interpreted regarding dismissals for misconduct. For the most part, students understood this dilemma and did not hold it against Presidents Wright of Fisk and Davis of TSU. There was general agreement that the presidents handled the delicate situations as well as could be expected, often moving through back channels to insulate problems as necessary. One student did recall some informal restrictions at Fisk, as house meetings were called when demonstrations were planned and led to privileges withheld if the meetings were missed. There were also reputedly directives that demonstrators should seek counseling and orders that students should go into town only in pairs, although these measures were attributed to an especially protective dean who handed down these strictures in President Wright's absence. While there was conflicting information about whether TSU and Fisk were losing money as a result of the demonstrations, President Wright confessed to one interviewer that he had been subjected to hourly phone calls of harassment for a brief interval and required some police protection. All these factors showed the tricky double game that the presidents had to play, soothing politicians, fundraisers, faculty, and students all at once by supporting or distancing themselves as necessary.[39]

Similarly, the activist students would find themselves working hard to maintain solidarity among their peers. It was impressive that students were now independently meeting, setting agendas, and carrying out tasks, and frequently this was being accomplished by those not traditionally considered leaders on campus. The student council representatives from the schools were often excited by the protests without necessarily being committed to direct action. Often, scholarship recipients were understandably timid about leading demonstrations. Similarly, the Meharry Medical College students gradually became drawn in after the outrage of Big Saturday: they were especially good at raising money or lending cars when necessary, despite some worries that they "could not afford to participate," and they tended to fall back on the idea of calling attorneys to help the demonstrators. And while TSU was best represented in sheer numbers among the demonstrators, there was some friction as more Fisk students gravitated toward leadership with more resultant publicity, especially since most meetings were held on the Fisk campus. It was less a case of a split between more cautious and aggressive types; rather, those two groups were trying to appeal to a wider majority that weighed each decision and moved carefully.[40]

The younger demonstrators, now calling themselves the Nashville Student Movement (NSM), also decided to maintain their own group distinct, not only from the NCLC, but from the wider community. Essentially, the NCLC was the organization that "provided liaison" with other civil rights groups and raised money for both themselves and the student demonstrators. But the students kept separate by sharing a representative with the NCLC. A Central Coordinating Committee met regularly to reconcile differences and speak in unison. This organizational structure had tangible benefits. For example, 6 a.m. meetings, when combined with a network of informants, allowed for quick responses to disseminate statements to the press and wider community. The NSM also favored an unusual egalitarianism drawn from Gandhian techniques that rotated leadership roles among the group to keep everyone equally invested and to reduce personality conflicts. Decisions were made by consensus, often after drawn-out conversations to reconcile internal divisions and soothe egos. Debates on how to act consistent with Gandhian principles were common. The prolonged attempts at formulating consensus were "a trying thing at times" with some "pointed discussions," students admitted at the time, but it made for a tighter-knit group when decisions were ultimately made. It also meant that leadership emerged organically from those most active in the consensus building and resultant action.[41]

This structure, however, was hard-won and a necessary move after some turmoil and division had revealed themselves, particularly between the students, NCLC, and the broader community. Whatever synergy was accomplished across the generations was inconsistent and required careful and continual nurturing. There were special committees for discrete tasks, including a citizens' committee that handled the NCLC's finances because of lingering suspicions about preachers and money affairs. The new structure was Diane Nash's idea after she realized that the students were formally in the custody of university deans after being arrested. The structure had to be flexible in order to accommodate the fact that the movement was not always in harmony. Inevitably, egos differed and clashed. The students were eager to act, eager to move, and annoyed with what they saw as the NCLC's "continually temporizing" in response to various real or imagined problems. Some NCLC ministers saw this as the usual "late teenage attitude towards adult domination," but nonetheless "a subtle feeling of challenging adults" was constantly present. Fortified by their newfound energy, the students rather jealously guarded their terrain. They chafed at the NCLC's attempt to restrict expenditures, rolled their eyes at the paperwork needed to justify costs, and were frequently too excited to communicate and consult with their elders. Having continued this work, and after putting their bodies literally on the line, they resisted attempts to take away this new joy of resistance. The students were very clear that their endeavor was something new, and their excitement would not be content with incremental legal change or narrow interest-group placating. Instead, they insisted that the movement was theirs and only secondarily belonged to the community. All these issues would continue bubbling under the surface as the sit-in campaign continued.[42]

Even as the shock of Big Saturday dissipated, anxiety continued to reverberate throughout the city. The collusion of police power with white toughs demonstrated a flagrant abuse of power, which was topped by the resultant court proceedings that opened the following Monday, February 29. The trials, by any standard, were travesties of justice. Even as City Judge Andrew Doyle quickly dismissed loitering charges against the students, charges of inciting to riot still remained. Doyle then recused himself, using the rationale that Judge John I. Harris had signed the police warrants approving the arrests and thus should preside over the trials. Harris, no friend of the defendants, conducted the proceedings with pronounced disregard for the judicial process. Not only had he prejudged the situation by apparently expressing the night before how he would rule on the cases, but, with the revelation that the arrest warrants were unavailable, he permitted amended ones to be entered into the record. Days later, he would require cash bonds for all defendants under twenty-one years of age, an unusually punitive step. Angered that defense lawyers had instructed their clients to plead the Fifth Amendment, he fined those counselors for contempt of court. At one point, as Z. Alexander Looby tried to conduct a cross-examination, Harris interrupted to assure the prosecutor that Looby's points would go unheard. He later turned his back as Looby argued his case. Fed up with the judge's behavior, Looby threw up his hands in disgust, provoking Harris to threaten more contempt of court charges. The defendants' lawyers immediately began steps to dismiss Harris for his blatant bias after the eighty-one students were found guilty.[43]

As judge and lawyers sparred, over two thousand black protesters milled outside the courthouse in solidarity with the students. The *Globe* remarked on the black community's unity and the fact that the courthouse stood on the former location of a nineteenth-century slave market. Meanwhile, "tension charged the atmosphere" of the city as whites "haunted" the Fifth Avenue and Arcade areas, lurking in corners and making their presence known whenever blacks appeared, although no sit-ins occurred.[44]

On the same day as the trials started, Mayor Ben West, who had been conspicuously absent from the city on Big Saturday, consented to meet with black citizens at First Baptist. The NCLC offered to close the meeting to the press to avoid the appearance of intimidation. But West allowed reporters to stay and publicize his defense of himself. Reminding the audience of his opposition to John Kasper, "in which they were no longer interested," a reporter noted, West drew an analogy between his efforts to stop the demagogue and to quell the sit-ins. Although he did not think it "fair" to refuse service to paying customers, he could not permit anyone to "flout the law," regardless of "race, color or religion." West went on to say that "I do not think my Maker is going to judge you or me by the color of our skin when we get up there. We are all alike. The only thing that makes us different is how we act." But the focus of the meeting soon shifted to Lawson, who "spoke with bitterness," wrote a *New York Times* reporter, in accusing "the 'power structure' of Nashville" of "try[ing] to end the sit-downs without considering the morality of the issue." Local newspapers covering the meeting seized on a quotation from Lawson, who said that "the law has been a gimmick to manipulate the Negro and keep him in his place in the South." The *Banner* in particular fumed, perceiving Lawson as disavowing the rule of law; the paper quoted the minister rather cavalierly as saying that he would "advise students 'to violate the law.'" The next day, Lawson issued a clarification trying to recast the issue: "I do not say that I have disrespect for the law as such"; indeed the idea that he "advocated lawlessness or the incitement of riot" was "contrary to my own understanding of God's call to me in the Christian ministry." Instead, Lawson's statement reiterated that he was addressing the false etiquette in Nashville's race relations, arguing that the sit-ins were meant to alert consciences that African Americans were "deprived of normal services by custom." Nor did he mean to "invite a riot," claiming that "for my part [I] will never do so." But further miscommunication occurred after two students tried to minimize the NCLC's role in the sit-ins even as Lawson described the long-term planning of his organization in some detail to interested reporters. The two were later "ousted" from the group for not being "in swing," but nonetheless the rare example of dissonance sent confusing messages to those whites incapable of understanding the sit-ins as an example of black frustration.[45]

As Lawson presented his statement on Tuesday, March 1, abbreviated sit-ins took place downtown. The police, having made their point on Big Saturday, now patrolled downtown tightly. The following day, the students switched targets to the Greyhound and Trailways bus terminal lunch counters. They refused to leave even when informed of a bomb threat, which gave the police sufficient pretense to arrest sixty-four of them for disorderly conduct and violating fire marshal laws. This led to a hurried meeting between Chief Hosse, Judge Doyle, and City Attorney Robert Jennings Jr., with Davidson County District Attorney Harry Nichol weighing in by phone. They conferred in part because confusion persisted as to whether any statute actually required segregation at lunch counters or whether segregation was at the discretion of the store owner. But the real goal was "to see if there was any law under which Rev. Lawson could be arrested." As David Halberstam noted, they tried to use what worked against Kasper: "arrest a few, get a leader." After the meeting, the city prosecutor handed down the somewhat stiffer charge of conspiracy to violate state trade and commerce laws. This applied, not only to the students arrested at the bus terminal, but retroactively to the February 27 defendants and Lawson. Nichol immediately voiced skepticism about the validity of the charges. "This whole thing seems a lot different than the Kasper business to me," said Nichol; "it looks like everyone did violence but the Negroes" and "they got pushed around pretty bad by some whites from what I've seen and heard." Clearly there was some dissent among authorities: reports persisted that

Jennings lobbied for "a tougher stand" against the demonstrators, whereas Nichol "did not co-operate." Still, it was "not known who gave the word to re-arrest the students Friday."[46]

Even as this supposed mystery persisted with the flurry of activity, James Stahlman continued pursuing his own version of southern justice. The sit-ins were galling enough, but the fact that James Lawson was a Vanderbilt student maddened Stahlman, a member of the university's board of trust. The editor loved the university deeply and felt that any African American privileged to be a Vanderbilt student should not be implicated in civic disorder. The *Banner*'s coverage of the sit-ins showed Stahlman's single-minded obsession with Jim Lawson. His most frequent rhetorical attack equated Lawson with John Kasper's legacy of havoc in Nashville. By "out-Kaspering Kasper as the ramrod of strife directed from the outside," wrote Stahlman, the "flannel-mouthed agitator" Lawson led the "paid agents of strife-breeding organizations." The *Banner* also played up certain elements of Lawson's background, running a United Press International wire story stressing his missionary work abroad, while the *Tennessean* chimed in with the detail that Lawson had conversed with students active in the Chattanooga sit-ins. Both the *Banner* and *Tennessean* emphasized Lawson's behavior during the March 1 meeting with Ben West, where he apparently used hand motions to signal speakers to tone down their rhetoric or get back on topic, as if he was some sort of brainwashing communist maestro conducting his minions' responses. That sit-ins were sweeping across the South, combined with the use of Lewis's mimeographed instructions circulated among the protesters, seemed proof to Stahlman that Nashville's sit-ins were "an organized effort projected from outside sources." Such descriptions and depictions, to everyday white Nashvillians, must have seemed all too reminiscent of tactics associated with Communists. The NCLC in response tried to downplay the interconnections between Nashville's protests and other cities, leery of having its regional networks tainted by Red-baiting.[47]

Other white Nashvillians echoed Stahlman's thinking. One attorney who helped prosecute the demonstrators, Walter C. Leaver Jr., remarked that the defendants were "thoroughly indoctrinated on how to conduct their lunch counter demonstrations" and "told what to do and what to say." While questioning Paul LaPrad extensively during the trials, Leaver became "convinced there's a lot more behind [the sit-ins] than has hit the surface." The insurgency, to Leaver, recalled recent threats from the Soviet Union that "our grandchildren will live under American socialism." If the "unlawful conspiracy" of the sit-ins "can threaten and intimidate and literally smother" Nashville businesses, "then Khrushchev is indeed a prophet." Leaver was particularly dismayed by the "tailor-made adjectives" of "nonviolence" and "passive resistance," used "to assume the cloak of martyrdom," which he saw employed by the demonstrators "within camera range, or while accompanied by their eager reporters." The attorney contrasted this language with his personal experience of phone calls offering to kill Leaver "for less than $500.00." Leaver concluded that, despite sounding like a "deranged alarmist," he could not believe these were "spontaneous student demonstrations."[48]

Of course, hard-core segregationists were even more aghast at the turmoil than bewildered moderates. L. V. DuBose, TFCG member, wrote to local political figures insisting that Tennessee state law required lunch-counter segregation—although, throughout Nashville, there seemed to be no clear consensus on this point. DuBose dismissed the idea that the sit-ins were about "a few Negro schoolchildren wanting to buy a coke or hamburger because they are cold, or hot, or hungry, or weary." Instead, DuBose called that idea a "cliché" and "a gimmick covered by semantics [and] reconnotation of words, hung on the bleeding hearts of professional do-gooders and political expedients who would have us lie supinely while we are bound hand and foot." The violent imagery in DuBose's wording resonated with his segregationist allies. "It is probably no coincidence," the TFCG argued, that the sit-ins occurred simultaneous to "the rape of Constitutional government about to be perpetuated in Congress" where civil rights bills were being debated. Another segregationist adopted a similar metaphor when he warned that "the colored person who forces his way into a social situation where he is not wanted displays a peculiar lack of understanding of the civility common to decent people." Not only did the verb "force" evoke sexual violation, but the speaker underscored an implied threat that civility had limits and should be broached only by African Americans only at some peril. The strident rhetoric showed how the usual etiquette was becoming unwound with the shift in African American behavior. The fear bred in whites by Jim Crow twisted observations into hysteria as whites desperately searched for laws and moral condemnation that would buttress racial custom.[49]

Less hysterical but still dismissive reasoning came from other whites from afar. One white in a neighboring county argued that the students should content themselves with a separate lunch counter—"if not, it will show that their desire is to socialize" and "the more they attain the more they want." He concluded that, because the demonstrators often came from places other than Nashville (indeed, he might have noted, sometimes from outside the South), "consistency demands, I think, that they be given the Kasper treatment" and run out of town. Other segregationists agreed that those sitting in were trying to "bludgeon their way into acceptance by whites." Above all, these examples demonstrate that the NCLC's stress on morality fell on many unhearing ears. Segregationists remained unmoved by nonviolent direct action. The TFCG argued that "by their very maddening 'passivity,'" the protesters "have provoked intemperate words and violent acts, just as they were calculated to do." With this, segregationists of course had a point in the abstract about the calculation and the results, but the emphasis remained fixated on the social cost of violent outbursts, while the moral and human issue went completely unacknowledged, perhaps even incomprehensible. The intensity of the segregationist sputtering showed how completely the racial etiquette had been defied and morality redefined. But the response remained much the same; by excusing the turmoil on Nashville streets and deeming the protesters as responsible, they continued to understand African Americans on white terms only and suggested that the pervasiveness (and permissibility) of white violence should always guard against faltering in racial law or custom.[50]

Friday, March 3, brought more pressure and posturing. Given that Lawson had an outstanding arrest warrant, Stahlman prodded Vanderbilt to expel the activist from the divinity school. The publisher's crusade was aided by John Sloan, the recalcitrant owner of Cain-Sloan department store and also a member of the Vanderbilt Board of Trust. Lawson's dismissal triggered a backlash from Vanderbilt faculty that quickly became its own minidrama of personalities and internal conflicts, and the storm of criticism from across the country hurt the school's reputation for years. On March 4, four police sergeants arrived at First Baptist to arrest Lawson roughly, walking through the sanctuary with hats on heads and cigars in mouths—a pronounced disrespect for the church that only further infuriated African Americans. As the officers escorted Lawson outside to a waiting police car, a press photographer caught the five in tableau near a marquee announcing Sunday's sermon, titled "Father, forgive them." The arrest occurred simultaneously with the report that Tennessee governor Buford Ellington had met with TSU's president to express his disapproval of student sit-in activity. Intimidation now came from all sides.[51]

Amidst these developments on March 3, the students, who had opted to serve prison time rather than pay fines, were released by Ben West. The mayor also named a biracial committee to mediate between merchants and students, apparently swayed by entreaties from the Nashville Association of Churches as well as the TCHR and NCRC. Such efforts had failed earlier in the week after white ministers could not reach the mayor. News soon followed that prosecutions would be suspended temporarily in hope that the biracial committee could resolve the impasse. Prominent Nashvillians made up the mayor's committee, which included two blacks: Stephen J. Wright, president of Fisk, and W. S. Davis, president of Tennessee State. However, these appointments produced some grumbling from the African American community that a black clergyman would be more representative of black opinions. Prominent white citizens were also on the committee, including businessmen Lipscomb Davis and F. Donald Hart, labor lawyer and

Nashville Community Relations Conference president George Barrett, and B. B. Gullett, head of the Nashville Bar Association. Madison Sarratt, the widely respected vice chancellor emeritus of Vanderbilt, chaired the committee, which convened on March 8.[52]

Diane Nash and Audrey McDonald from Fisk, Cupid Poe and Kenneth Frazier from Tennessee State, and Jim Bevel and Bernard Lafayette from American Baptist testified before the committee. Diane Nash particularly impressed Sarratt as she stressed the issue of "dignity" and the "living evidence" that should mandate total integration: "the breaking down of segregation has taken place on city buses, college and university campuses in the city, and at the airport very easily and immediately without complications." The committee was especially interested to hear of the February 23 meeting with Chief Hosse and that the students had attempted earlier negotiations with the merchants at Kress's, McClellan's, and Woolworth's to no avail. But the committee noted some clashes in testimony about whether the students demonstrated with "the *intention* of being arrested . . . [or] the *possibility* of being arrested." Regardless, members recognized that the sit-ins "are not a 'panty raid' type of college student expression; on the contrary, they appear to spring from deep-seated convictions and are not likely to be easily brushed aside." Afterward, the students praised the committee but reiterated that, in Nash's words, "no form of token desegregation [would be] acceptable." The students emphasized their dedication to the "long-range objective" of "full equality."[53]

The following day, merchants addressed the committee and remained close lipped after the meeting, professing only that they were "good neighbors." John Sloan and Greenfield Pitts continued to argue that desegregating "would hurt business." Representatives from the dime stores stressed their fidelity to "local customs established by local people" and complained about having to bear the onus of changing social norms. On March 12, a third meeting occurred. News that the students had rejected a plan for partial desegregation created some consternation about what should happen next. The situation remained in suspended animation.[54]

Even as the committee continued deliberating, the students kept up their protests. It was a bit of a surprise when, with little fanfare, on March 15, two Fisk students were served coffee at the Post House restaurant in the Greyhound bus terminal. Previously, the restaurant had done everything possible to avoid this: in one case, calling out an African American cook to wait on the students and, in another, neither refusing nor closing the store but simply and suddenly sending all of its waitresses home "sick." But quietly the owners acknowledged that a federal Interstate Commerce Commission ruling in 1955 required railways and airports to provide equal service to all. The restaurant workers instead endured harassing phone calls as they labored to prevent news photographers from capturing the moment on film. Student leader Rodney Powell said that the entire black community had been aware of their legal right to eat at the Post House and this new venture was simply trying to test that possibility. The next day, a white waitress served Matthew Walker, Peggy Alexander, Diane Nash, and Stanley Hemphill, but the situation soon ignited. When a journalist tried to photograph the scene, a waitress armed with a seven-inch knife became agitated, "running and screaming" at the reporter. Soon a band of "well-dressed" whites, attracted to the mayhem, accosted the foursome, telling them that "they had sent for a monkey cage to put the monkeys in." The white group then attacked both black men. While the newspaper account claimed that Hemphill had used dishes as weapons, the students told a far different story of being jumped without provocation. Walker, offering no resistance, suffered "a bad cut on the lip" that left the floor streaked with blood. Three black kitchen workers walked out of the restaurant "without saying a word" after this scene. One waitress's lone reported comment was that the black customers never paid for their hamburger and grape drink.[55]

The students' attempt to sustain activist energy was in part a reaction to lingering dissension in the movement, some of whom were uneasy about this new version of protest. Tactical differences made for some conflict, as some ministers such as Vivian and Lawson wanted to keep morale focused and the spirit of protest inflamed. Others cautioned that the point had been made and worried that increasing protests would trigger more violence and potentially drive away supporters. So too were NAACP attorneys privately skeptical about nonviolence—Avon Williams, Z. Alexander Looby's law partner, secretly disparaged Lawson as "Cloud 90"—and were nonplussed about students opting to stay in jail. (Indeed, some suggested that Looby and Williams prodded Thurgood Marshall's rebuke of this tactic.) Usually this attitude translated into a restrained relationship with the students, relegating the attorney's advice to legal matters only. Professionally—and probably temperamentally too—they were not inclined to support strategic law breaking. Regardless, as meetings and demonstrations became spontaneous and fervent, it was not always possible to coordinate with others, nor was that always the inclination among the students. It was a restless energy from the students that was only fitfully channeled in certain ways.[56]

In much the same way, it would be wrong to say that there were distinct divisions within the wider black community—but nonetheless subtle overtones from different outlooks, egos, and personalities inevitably could be heard. Indeed, with the overlap of NAACP and NCLC leadership and membership, there was never a clear line between the two. But, as mass meetings of the NCLC swelled with attendees, there was some annoyance among NAACP members that the NCLC was now considered synonymous with the black community. It was a strange mix consistent with Nashville activism: there was little palpable conflict, and occasional complementary organizing, but there were subtle shades of emphases even as groups worked toward an ostensibly common goal. Kelly Miller Smith agreed that the lack of friction meant that there was a "working—though not organized" relationship, especially since the NAACP was somewhat more "restricted in activities." Another black leader confided privately that black Nashvillians were fragmented in nuanced ways. It had nothing to do with rivalries—it was "just that it was not unified." As some contemporaneous observers note, a later call from Vivian Henderson that everyone should work together and be less concerned about who was getting credit perhaps signaled some dimension of the problem and some egos involved.[57]

The wait for the committee report dragged on through March. The NCLC, not wanting to alienate the merchants, the biracial committee, and the city at large, restrained students ready to resume protests. Instead, the NCLC tried a different appeal, this time to the city's religious conscience. On March 20, as churchgoers walked to morning services at eleven churches of various denominations across the city, they were met by African American bystanders with fliers asking for prayers supporting Nashville's desegregation. Seven churches invited the petitioners to worship with them, although the pastor of the Downtown Presbyterian church sniffed that, while interracial fellowship was fine, the "propaganda promoting certain sociological ideas" was more repellent. Representatives of two other churches were more pointedly mean to the black visitors. Only the Roman Catholic and Unitarian pastors commented that the event remained unremarkable because biracial worship was not uncommon in their churches. Ten days later, a prayer service held outside Ben West's office window, if heard, yielded no response.[58]

On March 25, shortly after two o'clock in the afternoon, sit-ins resumed at downtown lunch counters with over one hundred participants. "The hope of many has grown dull," announced a statement passed out by the demonstrators. "We have no choice but to again witness in a dramatic, yet loving, fashion." The students were "called of God to continue this 'resistance in love.'" The statement affirmed that the protesters "wish the counters open to more trade—including our own" and wanted no harm to anyone, asking instead only to "stop pretending to have good race relations." As the sit-ins occurred, Kelly Miller Smith testified before the biracial committee, which asked him "what the Negro community would be satisfied with." Smith later observed wryly, "I thought it was quite late for that question." Madison Sarratt, when hearing about the renewed sit-ins, said that "It looks like we are back where we started" and that he was "just as confused and befuddled as when we started." It was genuine bewilderment, as Sarratt opened up privately to fellow committee member George Barrett, asking, "You are a young man and you don't have all the prejudices that I have acquired over the years. Explain this? How can we satisfy these youngsters and not scare the John Sloans and Greenfield Pitts to death?" The now-routine bomb scare followed, as did at least one assault, although police were noticeably more protective of the demonstrators on this occasion and arrested only four blacks at Moon-McGrath's drugstore.[59]

An enigmatic phrase in the statement indicated the NCLC's frustration with certain developments: "there are few signs that the Mayor's bi-racial committee can expect the genuineness of certain merchants." The discord derived from the sense that the merchants were hindering the biracial committee's activities. The stores were content to stall negotiations because they wanted to keep business flowing throughout Nashville Extra Value Days, a regular event that yielded an estimated extra two million dollars in sales annually. The NCLC explained its actions by saying that "we never agreed to stop the sit-ins. We merely went the second mile by giving the committee ample time to release a statement concerning the moral and democratic rights of all Nashville's citizens." The group suggested that a fairer truce to the sit-ins would close the lunch counters entirely while the committee deliberated.[60]

These issues were overshadowed by the presence of a crew filming the movement. The team, sent by CBS to film a news documentary called *Anatomy of a Demonstration* to be broadcast in late April, had bypassed Nashville's CBS affiliate WLAC in return for exclusive access to NCLC meetings. This displeased the local press, blocked from these meetings because the NCLC feared that local merchants, if aware of impending sit-ins, would fill the lunch-counter seats with their own people. Chief Hosse was also clearly irked by the outsiders' presence, saying that they had come in "like thieves in the night." Hosse was no doubt displeased because the continued open surveillance of NCLC meetings and church services from officers "scowling like some kind of grade B movie henchmen" had failed to expose this development. Tennessee Governor Buford Ellington, who had been publicly silent about the racial unrest, now asserted that the sit-ins were "instigated and planned by, and staged for, the convenience of the Columbia Broadcasting System" and accused CBS of "the most irresponsible piece of journalistic trickery I ever heard of."[61]

The outcries, scapegoating, and finger-pointing were all spasmodic reactions to a slow but relentless suffocating of business in downtown Nashville. On April 5, stories in both the *Banner* and *Tennessean* reported another protest tactic in play, an economic boycott that thus far had eluded public notice. A news blackout on the boycott, agreed to by both the *Banner* and the *Tennessean*, resulted less from sinister racial motivations than the newspapers' dependence on grocery-store advertisements for profits.[62] The articles reported on a mass meeting where Dr. Vivian Henderson asked all those declining to purchase goods or services downtown to rise. Nearly the entire audience, estimated at over five hundred, stood. Henderson, an economist at Fisk, had collected data showing that a significant chunk of profits for downtown stores came from black dollars. The seven million dollars spent by black Nashville downtown constituted 5 percent of Cain-Sloan's business and as much as 15 percent of Harvey's. Similarly, the lunch counters at the five-and-dimes comprised 40 to 50 percent of each store's total profits. Initially, Henderson suggested that the boycott was only partially successful. But over time, discipline tightened. When multiplied with the repercussions of the sit-ins, economic pain rippled throughout downtown. Profits from the bus routes used by black shoppers to go downtown dried up. Sympathetic whites in the religious and academic communities also withheld business. The violence accompanying the sit-ins, along with an unusually cold winter, dissuaded many other whites from their usual shopping excursions downtown. Moreover, these factors all converged just before Easter, a traditionally strong season for clothing sales, combining to bleed the downtown dry.[63]

The boycott's origins remain unknown. Some suggest that the idea came from four black housewives during their regular bridge game, each persuading ten of their friends to participate. Others more clearly attributed the boycott technique to a NAACP call during a mass meeting as a useful way for adults to participate in the cause. Officials from NCLC denied continually that they had started the boycott, which actually posed some problems for the group. One leader said later, "We had considered an economic boycott as a methodology and probably would have used it if it had not started elsewhere. But we were planning on this as our ultimate weapon. We still wanted to dramatize the moral issue through the sit-ins." Kelly Miller Smith professed that "quite a few negroes did not grasp this point and used the boycott as a means of striking back at the white community for real or imagined trouble in the past." The NCLC adapted by defining the boycott in moral terms, calling it instead an "economic withdrawal," where blacks held their dollars back from propping up Jim Crow. As C. T. Vivian put it in a speech: "I've been asked, 'Isn't a boycott rather destructive?' I say this is not a boycott to club men down. This is an economic withdrawal against evil." Perhaps more tellingly, news of the boycott was paired with a recent election in which Ben West's candidate for sheriff was soundly beaten due to black votes—a development that signaled the beginning of the end for West's reign. The range of tactics used by black Nashville were gaining some collective traction.[64]

Supporters aggressively enforced the boycotts, sometimes in ways not entirely consistent with nonviolent strategies. TSU student Leo Lillard remembers that "we had to send some educating committees to downtown to convince them that that was not the thing to do. We didn't hurt them, but we did kind of snatch their bags and tear things away from their arms and let them fall on the ground and say, 'Stay out of town.' And course the word got around pretty quick you don't go downtown anymore." A visiting CORE official recounted a cabbie showing him a strip of torn silk, explaining that three black women, confronting a fourth holding a newly bought dress, "snatched the box from under her arm and tore the dress to shreds." Whether "true or not," the CORE official mused, "a rumor is spreading. 'If you buy downtown, those Jefferson St. thugs . . . will beat you.'" It appeared that, just as the boycotts reinforced the message of the sit-ins, so too did a certain aggressiveness by others complement the nonviolent demonstrators.[65]

Amid this first public acknowledgment of the boycott, Ben West's biracial committee released its long-awaited report on April 5. The document, in its earnest equivocations, echoed the attempted compromising during the city's school desegregation. The committee proposed a ninety-day trial period during which the lunch counters would have three sections, two for people of each race wishing to remain segregated and one that was integrated. The committee further called for the establishment of a permanent biracial committee that, after the trial period concluded, would examine the lunch-counter issue and other racial issues throughout Davidson County and decide on a future course of action. The committee also recommended that the arrest records of the demonstrators be dropped on the condition that no further sit-ins take place.[66]

No immediate comment came from the merchants or the NCLC as each studied the report. One Fisk student said that the feeling on campus was one of "disappointment." The only committee member to voice an opinion, George Barrett, endorsed the proposal but lamented that a chance for "a bigger step" had been avoided. Later, Barrett, meeting with the NCLC, revealed that internal politicking inside the committee meetings had been intense and deeply divisive. While the merchants acknowledged that they "could not return to the 'status quo,'" they "withdrew any compromise of changing after the CBS incident." Barrett expressed his personal opinion that desegregation was still possible. At the meeting with Barrett, Lawson reported that the students insisted on total integration. Committed to this goal, and eager to exploit the apparent schism in the merchant ranks, the NCLC issued a statement requesting a meeting directly with the merchants to resume negotiations. The offer was accepted by four merchants who met on April 9 with both students and NCLC ministers.[67]

The parlay had little effect. After it concluded, the NCLC announced that sit-ins would continue. Although in favor of making the biracial committee permanent, the NCLC found the other proposed solutions derisory. They reasoned that "the suggestion of a restricted area involves the same stigma of which we are earnestly trying to rid the community. The plan presented by the Mayor's Committee ignores the moral issues involved in the struggle for human rights." The NCLC pointed out that the trial period, by its nature, would encourage "irresponsible elements" to ensure the plan's failure and also presumed that "the principle of desegregation is on trial and we submit that it is not." Still, the NCLC had to convince even well-meaning white liberal groups of the proposal's inadequacies. The merchants countered that their own situation was "unenviable" and that "it was most impractical for a small group of stores to assume the role of leading such a social change." Some merchants claimed to journalists that the proposal resembled a previous one that had almost been accepted by the NCLC the first time. Yet Smith said instead that support for a lasting solution was not apparent in the April 9 meeting. One account said that the NCLC had rejected a merchant offer to "let the colored people eat at the lunch counters [if] they agreed to stay out of the dining rooms," which presumably meant the finer restaurants in the downtown. If so, such an offer ran counter to the NCLC's broader mission to desegregate the entire downtown.[68]

Faithful to the NCLC's promise, on April 11 at noon, small integrated groups of protesters, numbering four to six each, returned to downtown. The seven stores affected closed their lunch counters immediately but quickly reopened them after the demonstrators left. At Walgreen's, the students returned several times, prompting the counters' closures. The "cat and mouse game" continued with these new tactics, as "there appeared to be no desire on the part of the stores to have the Negroes arrested and no desire on the part of the Negroes to get arrested." One elderly white woman moved between McClellan's and Woolworth's, hissing to demonstrators that "they'd know what to do to you in Mississippi." Turning to a police officer, she continued: "Don't you wish there were three Mississippi plantation managers here to take care of this thing?" He replied, "Lady . . . take a walk. You're too old for me to arrest you." Picket lines appearing throughout downtown supported the sit-ins. Despite a heavy police presence, a few altercations resulted as white pickets, "imitating their every move, mocking the Negroes," carried their own signs of "Run Out Jiggs" and "We Don't Like Jungle Bunnies." The competing lines led to isolated pushing and shoving, as Virgil Glenn, an unemployed truck driver and failed thief, attacked Wilson Yates, a white Vanderbilt Divinity School student, after a verbal exchange. Both were arrested, but the fine against Glenn was dropped after Yates told the judge he forgave his assailant.[69]

The gesture was lost as violence engulfed the city over the next few days. An estimated one thousand people, many of them young white teens with the day off from school, packed downtown the next day to watch the pickets and sit-ins. A black high school student on a second-floor balcony at the Arcade became the target of taunts, spit, and paper missiles shot with rubber bands. He responded by dropping a cigarette butt on his tormentors. When a spitball hit the student between the eyes, he answered with a bottle. Enraged, thirty whites, screaming "kill the coon," burst upstairs, thrashing around with assorted weapons. Some accounts said that the horde dangled the student over the balcony, escaping when warned by the crowd that the police were en route. The student, having tried to defend himself with a bottle and a screwdriver, "collapsed" in the arms of police and was carried off to be charged as a white woman yelled, "you're arresting the wrong person." Bedlam persisted throughout downtown. McClellan's received a bomb threat. Police arrested two other whites who snatched picket signs from black protesters and tore them up, one of the miscreants caught after a "flying tackle" from an officer. As day turned to evening, carloads of seething people, some black, some white, and variously armed with guns, knives, pipes, rubber hoses, and bricks, roved through town, menacing members of the opposite race. A *Tennessean* editorial pleaded weakly for another committee with community support to stop the violence that "could well destroy the middle ground meeting place for solving any of our difficulties." One reporter noted that Mayor West was vacationing in Florida.[70]

Anxieties persisted throughout the week despite a lull in sit-in activity. The NCLC suspended demonstrations, partially to avoid potentially even more violence surging throughout the city, but also because much of the Nashville leadership was in Raleigh, North Carolina, at a meeting that would yield a new civil rights group called the Student Nonviolent Coordinating Committee (SNCC). But the fear soon spiked higher, as a vile sound, lately all too familiar to Nashvillians, echoed through the early morning of April 19. At 5:30 a.m., a tremendous explosion from a package with as many as twenty sticks of dynamite obliterated Z. Alexander Looby's home. The detonation damaged neighboring structures and shattered over a hundred windows at nearby Meharry Medical College. A two-foot hole in the ground, littered with brick and concrete detritus from the house siding and foundation, testified to the devastating power of the blast. Yet, incredibly, Looby and his wife, asleep in the back bedroom, escaped alive only because the package missed going through a picture window "by about four feet." Nashville's fire chief said that, "if it had gone through that window, the explosion would have killed everyone in the block." As a police inspector confirmed, "these were killers. You don't throw that much dynamite to scare somebody." The usual round of condemnations followed, with scathing editorials and rewards offered. False bomb threats the following day at Belmont College, the women's dormitory at Tennessee State, and Hubbard Hospital at Meharry kept alarm and animosity at fever pitch. Despite vague reports of an old-model car in the area before the bombing and the discovery of dynamite caps in a vacant one-room house in East Nashville, no leads developed. No one was ever arrested for the bombing. Looby later told an interviewer that he thought that the police could have found the perpetrator, but they were "looking the other way."[71]

If nothing else, there was no question that all the earlier undercurrents within the movement ceased to exist after the Looby home bombing, seared away by the explosive assassination attempt. Participants were emphatic that the bombing resolidified everyone on behalf of the movement, even as it further stirred the souls of those roused by the emotional impact of the sit-ins. The black community responded with a march that started at one o'clock with fifteen hundred people at Tennessee State University. More people joined as the procession wound through the city in absolute silence. At Pearl High School, students streamed past the principal ordering them to return to class. By the time the marchers arrived at the city courthouse, the fifteen hundred had at least doubled in size. Mayor Ben West, informed by telegram, met his black constituents, who smoldered with anger as they readied for a pointed dialogue. As they waited, Guy Carawan, a young white supporter from Highlander Folk School, unslung his guitar and began picking out a tune. The song Carawan chose was an old black church melody used by union workers for years: "We Shall Overcome." Voice by voice, the marchers joined in as the song "seemed to sweep across the courthouse square," echoing and magnifying the throng's determination and unity after their whisper-quiet walk. As David Halberstam writes, "it was an important moment: the students now had their anthem."[72]

The exchange that followed ranked with that of Big Saturday in its dramatic and symbolic power. As the rear marchers continued filling the area, Reverend C. T. Vivian read a statement protesting the mayor's passivity in evading the lunch-counter crisis and accused him of "ignoring the moral issues involved in segregation," "not using the moral weight of his office," and "encouraging violence" through a "lack of decision." West, bristling visibly, began to argue his position, saying, "I deny your statement and resent to the bottom of my soul the implication you just made." After referencing his credentials in facing down school segregationists and "maintaining order," West told the crowd that "we are all Christians together. Let us pray together," prompting Earl Mays, a Fisk student, to yell, "how about eating together?" West ignored the jibe, but Vivian began pressing West further: "is segregation moral?" "No," West responded, "it is wrong and immoral to discriminate," and, as Diane Nash also began to quiz West, the mayor called for all citizens to "have no bigotry, no bias, no hatred." When Nash asked him if that included lunch counters, West countered with "little lady, I stopped segregation seven years ago at the airport when I first took office and there has been no trouble there since." "Then, mayor," asked Nash, zeroing in him, "do you recommend that the lunch counters be desegregated?" And Ben West said "yes," and then back-tracked slightly: "that's up to the store managers of course, what they do. I can't tell a man how to run his business." The admission, so brief and unexpected, seemed almost to be lost. Vivian continued pressing the mayor, asking him if segregation was Christian. West retorted by defending his past record on race relations, saying, "Look what I've done. Ask my friend Alexander Looby, ask Avon Williams." A student shot back with the shout, "Can we ask Judge Harris too?" But then Cupid Poe, TSU student, doubling back to the earlier comment, inquired if West "had just recommended the end of the eating facility segregation." Responded West, "right, right, that is absolutely right!" and the crowd burst into sustained applause. "It was a question that I had to answer as a man and not as a politician," West later stated.[73]

This exchange did as much as anything to convince some of nonviolent direct action's power. The insistent grilling from Nash and Vivian was faithful to Lawson's training, which taught the value of communicating in the form of questions. Interrogations in this form provided a way to touch a conscience, as the respondent, faced with a choice, weighed an answer. The yes-or-no question mirrored the students' moral certainty in segregation's evil. Nash's resolve meant that the mayor could no longer dodge the stark moral issue before him. West's answer proved to the students that the irrepressible truth of segregation's evils could not be shirked, even by whites. As one participant puts it decades later, Vivian "indicted" West while Nash gave the "chance for a pardon," although the verdict on West remained open over coming years.[74]

That evening, Martin Luther King Jr. spoke at Fisk University to a packed crowd numbering over four thousand. (Indeed, one theory posited that Looby's house was targeted with the assumption that King would stay with the attorney.) The venue was moved from the War Memorial Auditorium downtown on short notice because of the "controversial nature" of the talk. Almost predictably, a bomb threat interrupted the program for almost an hour as "hisses and boos" rang out against the delay. Trying to keep things light, C. T. Vivian wisecracked that it was "probably one policeman making a call to another policeman." The audience, including the press covering the event, rose with a spontaneous "thunderous ovation" when Looby appeared on the podium. "It was an ovation coming from the hearts and souls of a grateful bunch of Nashvillians," said the *Globe*, and Looby wept in front of the audience, overcome with emotion. King, in his speech, called the Nashville sit-ins "the best-organized and most disciplined in our Southland today," professing that "I come not to bring inspiration but to gain inspiration from the great movement that has taken place in this community." He praised the students who "lifted the jails from badges of dishonor to badges of honor," and applauded their reaction against African Americans who "sold their birthright of freedom for a mess of economic pottage." Exhorting his listeners to commit to nonviolence, he said that "we will meet your physical force with soul force" and "wear you down with our capacity to love." King concluded in the words of an old spiritual that cued the organist: "let's keep moving; let's walk together children, don't you get weary."[75]

Underneath April's turbulence, diplomacy had continued between the store-owners and the NCLC and, faced with escalating violence and declining profits, merchant intransigence was slipping. For more productive meetings, the store representatives insisted on a few things. The first condition was that no whites be included in the talks, because "they started preaching to us about the moral-ity of the question" and "we didn't need anybody to orate to us about that." The merchants, surprised to hear that black university presidents "were not represen-tative of the Negro community," requested leaders with wider support from black Nashville. Kelly Miller Smith, Coyness Ennix, and two students thus spoke for the NCLC. Greenfield Pitts, the manager at Harvey's, acknowledged that "We were pretty well agreed among the merchants that we would have to cooperate with the inevitable" and Smith later said that "when they expressed this view, we immedi-ately suggested that if they recognized it as inevitable, wouldn't it be better for all to start planning for it now." It was a typically firm if humane admonition from Smith, who later said that he felt the negotiations were equally important as the boycott (even as many of his supporters disagreed) as he "got to really understand them" over prolonged and sustained encounters and tried to humanize the Move-ment's issues to them.[76]

The merchants cited a few reasons for their change of heart. The Looby bomb-ing was foremost. "This act did more to change the climate of community opin-ion than any other single factor," noted journalist Wallace Westfeldt, who wrote a postmortem of the entire episode. King's speech also contributed by visibly rally-ing the black community, ending the fiction that the sit-ins were "a student affair, and quite possibly one led and organized from outsiders" (although it remained a sad commentary on white attitudes that they needed an outsider to shore up their appreciation of local black issues). Attendance at King's speech and participation in the boycott gave the merchants "an inkling of how deep" sentiment support-ing the sit-ins ran. Merchants also drew some comfort from a public forum in late March on Nashville's race relations, sponsored by the NCRC and widely attended by the community; said one merchant, "It does make you feel good to know there are at least 500 folks here who are willing to talk about it in public." A lack of co-ordinated segregationist resistance also was "a hopeful sign." One merchant confessed that those morally sympathetic to the movement would not have deseg-regated without the sit-ins. "We didn't need the pressure," he said, and instead "wanted the Negroes to pressure the community." But that was an altogether different source of frustration and confusion. The storeowners complained about the uncooperative Chamber of Commerce, which "didn't do a damned thing to help this situation even though they knew we were having the economic hell beat out of the downtown area." There is some evidence that Cain-Sloan's business actually went up by 12 percent in April, which would have been due to increased white patronage. But more generally, the merchants felt that the white community generally in favor of segregated norms gave them "no help" and "just stood back." The contradiction was that, even as merchants claimed that local custom kept them from segregating, they had little or no visible support from those locals. As such, a final agreement came on May 7, when economics finally won out over morality. As one merchant acknowledged, "we had to change whether we wanted to or not."[77]

It was a curious contrast with the student perspective. Even after the Looby bombing put everyone on the same page, disagreements lingered about what should constitute the final goal of this campaign. Observers noted disagreements within the activists between those who saw the campaign as a victory, good for morale and a base to build of off, versus those preferring to hold out for more substantive change. Moreover there was continued student wariness of NCLC decisions even when the students lacked a policy of their own. In the end, there was talk that an informal disagreement to leave alone the Iris Room and Carousel, two private dining restaurants downtown, was "a compromise" meant to "let the students have something before they went home" for summer break. There was a constant balancing act between maintaining enthusiasm and achieving tangible goals.[78]

When the transition came, it was done with characteristic attention to manners and appearances. On May 10, at 3:15, carefully selected African Americans purchased a bite to eat at six stores, waited on by white servers and sitting next to white patrons. The scene was quiet in part because it had been stage-managed to avoid disturbances. The agreement specified that African Americans could be served at the off-peak hours of ten and two on Wednesday and Thursday, and at any time on Friday, in exchange for staying out of downtown Saturday to avoid unruly patrons. A store official remarked on the lack of response from white customers, which was sheer publicity given that the merchants had prearranged for sympathetic whites to be eating as blacks were served. Detachments of United Church Women and similar women's groups acted as observers, watching carefully while drinking coffee or spooning ice cream. The women took their job seriously, as shown by one who confronted a wayward Baptist minister: "What are you doing in here? This room is for the Unitarians!" Undercover police also mingled in the stores, and the one minor episode that occurred took place without monitors present. Local media helped by not publicizing the plan, although the *Tennessean* ran brief pieces acknowledging the events after they occurred. The merchants requested a total blackout, but the news leaked out from outside media. In other stores downtown, black shoppers resumed buying goods. By May 18, the elaborate preliminaries ended and desegregated eating proceeded as if nothing had ever been any different. The lone hold-out was W. T. Grant's, which refused to change its policies, and boycotting of that store persisted. Grant's capitulated a month later after the New York City CORE chapter began its own campaign against the company's Harlem stores. There were also some scattered instances—and successes—where African Americans tried to be served at restaurants and drive-ins outside of downtown. Other reports suggested that there would be pressure on the state attorney general to shore up state statutes preventing desegregated dining but, since such laws were "obviously invalid," it was also predicted that the attorney general would prefer the entire affair to "slip as far into obscurity as possible." On June 13, the last of the conspiracy charges were dropped.[79]

It was a quiet ending to a tumultuous episode, and the reasons behind this were rich. The sit-ins, as both a political and economic issue, could not be solved by the usual means of the past as the African American community maintained steadfast with boycotts, protests, and political power. Not only was the white belief that the African American boycott could not be sustained proven false, but no organized counter-boycott from segregationists occurred afterward. Moreover, the conflict masked a more fundamental interdependence: the physical compactness of downtown, the outward movement of whites to the suburbs, the concentrated black population in the city center, and the relative lack of black competition meant that downtown merchants relied on black shoppers. Moreover, the Belle Meade bankers who ran the city had sunk a considerable amount of short-term loans into the downtown after World War II, and their indecision about intervening and worries about long-term economic repercussions crippled the Chamber of Commerce's deliberations. All these factors convinced the white elite to relent.[80]

It is curious that conflict over a few lunch counters could bring a city to its knees. But of course, nothing about the sit-ins was about the stools alone. The undeniable reality is that, despite this triumph, segregation remained deeply knitted into the fabric of Nashville society. Yet a narrow view focusing on a limited tactical victory misses a more salient point: that the movement was personally and absolutely transformative for the activists themselves. There was something special, almost indefinable, about the sit-ins in Nashville, and particularly in the levels of training, discipline, and organization shown there. This ethos to the Nashville Movement remained elusive but very real. Many saw it as especially religious, which was part of it. But the spirit bred in Nashville was more broadly a streak of unshakeable moral belief, forged in a crucible where personalities and commitment to racial struggle were melded together in powerfully new ways. Diane Nash underlines the point in noting that many protesters elsewhere had an intellectual rather than emotional understanding of nonviolent direct action, but in Nashville, the workshops had fused a powerful connection in which the group "loves each other—a real bond." And, Angela Butler emphasized, there was a noticeable difference in thinking from the students who participated in the workshops from those who had not. To be sure, there was some variation, as many preferred to view nonviolence as a "technique" rather than a "way of life," but the core group who wanted to explore the philosophy further were shaped here as never before. It was an unlikely story of how people from different backgrounds, diverse social contexts, and a range of beliefs could meld a new existence. "It was sharing in the Movement which apparently drew them together," as one of their teachers wrote, and it was a sharing that equally inspired the individual and the collective with a belief that every person "has a talent to be facilitated," an inner strength to lend to a higher cause. The living embodiment of the "Beloved Community" gave a sense of wholeness to participants who could meld their religious, political, and ethical values into one. It is no exaggeration to say that the Nashville sit-in movement proved to be a model for activism as much as the Montgomery Bus Boycott. In 1961, these same students would rescue and extend the Freedom Rides, capturing the attention of the entire world, before moving to Mississippi, Alabama, and a number of civil rights flashpoints throughout the decade.[81]

Yet, while the sit-ins remain a special chapter for the participants and their role in history, it has a slightly different relationship to Nashville's racial history. Despite the unique quality of Lawson's workshops, the relative unity of the black community in 1960 was not centered on a widespread commitment to nonviolence, even as this commitment would soon be seen as the hallmark of Nashville's activists. One account captured a black teen lounging in a pool hall who said, "I don't understand why they just let themselves get beat up. . . . Like man, that just don't go with me. I don't think I'll ever go back to Fifth Avenue." Charles S. Johnson's son, Robert, himself a promising sociologist, traveled to Nashville to investigate the movement and commented on the loyalty inspired by the sit-ins, even from those not inclined to agree philosophically with nonviolence: "in Nashville, the sit-in students spoke almost lovingly about the so-called 'rougher element'" who appeared 'around the fringes of the movement.'" Wrote Johnson, "they did not even pretend to be non-violent, but they delegated themselves to be protectors of the students sitting at the lunch counters, and they rigidly supported the boycotting of the stores—and saw to it that all other Negroes did likewise." Black communities unified around the movement, even as they chose various ways of expressing that sentiment.[82]

More broadly, among black Nashvillians, there was a sense that fresh tactics and new generational mentalities were eroding the racial etiquette that had shaped Nashville's Jim Crow patterns. Student activist Leo Lillard, Robert's son, leapt at the chance to sit in because "it was my chance to get back at Nashville. It was my chance not to have any adult lie to me about what the problem was. It was my chance to make the problem different, to correct it." Lillard elaborates separately that "I myself had grown too complacent with it. I was living with the southern way of life," and that "I see now my generation has been too apathetic about conditions as they existed." While "my grandmother and my mother were proud of getting special favors from the white man," Lillard stresses instead that "The young Negro doesn't want any favors, he's become keenly resentful of any special consideration." Lawson in particular (although technically not of this student generation) would become outspoken in declaring that the sit-ins were "against Uncle Tom Negroes, against the NAACP's over-reliance on the courts; and against the futile middle class technique of sending letters to the centers of power. We have the Negro middle class with us now . . . but almost none of them understand how it happened."[83]

It was a story of shame and glory, to use one of Kelly Miller Smith's favorite phrases, in displaying the tension between law and custom that underwrote white supremacy in the South. A local journalist saw this clearly in writing that, in Nashville, "the racial segregation situation is paradoxically confusing." The sit-ins exposed a contradiction: that breaches in the racial order "are the result of specific legal action and quiet changes in custom," whereas rigid segregation "stands fundamentally on custom alone, although it is bathed in a thin light of strictly interpreted legal propriety." Jim Lawson, decades after he directed the sit-ins, said it more plainly: that no laws requiring segregation existed in Nashville, only custom—the police enforced laws not even on the books. Only the inversion of racial etiquette brought this paradox fully into the light. It was one thing that the lunch counters were a space where Jim Crow's hypocrisies were especially self-evident, but these hypocrisies converged at the juncture of law and custom. It was significant that all aspects of Jim Crow were targeted by the black community's relative unity: the bankrupt laws by attorneys, the moral issues highlighted by the preachers, the power of the black dollar as shown by the boycott, the symbolic power of the sit-ins and resistance more generally as embodied by the students, and the on-going commitment sustained by all.[84]

Thus the shame and the glory. The shame of a white citizenry still at best only meekly troubled by injustices in their midst. The glory of the movement, with a step forward and an inflamed passion for transforming those injustices. And beyond both the shame and the glory: more work, and more struggle.

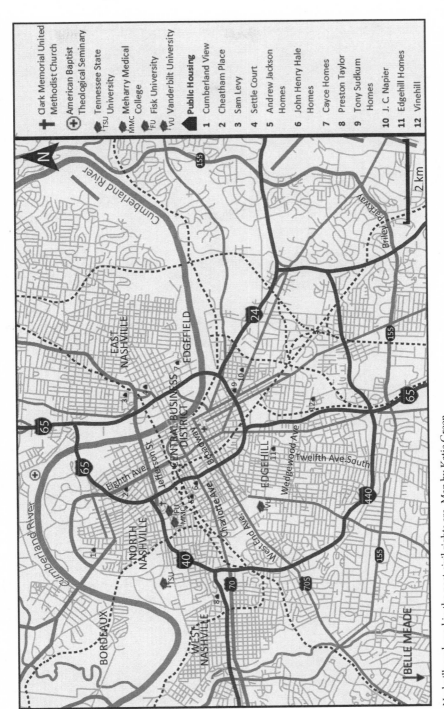

Nashville reshaped in the post civil rights era. Map by Katie Green.

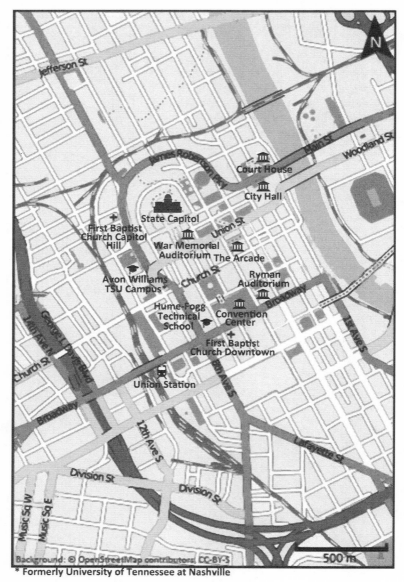

* Formerly University of Tennessee at Nashville

Nashville's central business district. Map by Katie Green.

Capitol Hill slum before urban renewal. Nashville Public Library, Nashville Room.

Outside Glenn School on the eve of public school desegregation. Nashville Public Library, Nashville Room.

September 9, 1957. Mrs. Grace McKinley escorted her daughter Linda Gail McKinley (second girl) and a friend to Fehr Elementary School through an irate crowd of segregationists and protesters of public school desegregation. Nashville Public Library, Nashville Room.

February 13, 1960. Nashville students held the first organized local sit-in. One hundred and twenty-four protesters, mostly African American college students, converged on Woolworth's and Kress's downtown to sit in at the lunch counters. Nashville Public Library, Nashville Room.

Agitators attack a sit-in demonstrator, February 27, 1960. Photo by Vic Cooley, *Nashville Banner*. Nashville Public Library, Nashville Room.

March 3, 1960. Student demonstrators were arrested and escorted into a paddy wagon after a nonviolent protest at the Greyhound Bus Terminal. Students continued demonstrations in an effort to desegregate all public accommodations. Nashville Public Library, Nashville Room.

The home of prominent Nashville attorney and councilman Z. Alexander Looby, who defended many of the sit-in demonstrators in court, was bombed at around 5:30 a.m. on April 19, 1960. Photo by Bob Ray, *Nashville Banner*. Nashville Public Library, Nashville Room.

The May 8, 1963, demonstration where Vencen Horsley and Joseph Tanksley exchanged words . . .

. . . before "crashing through a large mirror outside a vacant building," as news accounts at the time reported. Both photos, before and after, Nashville Public Library, Nashville Room.

April 28, 1964. Before demonstrators and police officers clashed, in what was known
as a "lying-in" students sealed off downtown Nashville by sitting and lying in the street
at the corner of Church Street and 7th Avenue North, in protest of the city's segregated policies.
Nashville Public Library, Nashville Room.

FOUR

The Kingdom or Individual Desires?
Movement and Resistance during the 1960s

On a Sunday in 1961, "John Barnett" decided to worship at a downtown Presbyterian church in "Knoshville, Kennessina." A black New Englander who had left his church back home to study at seminary, he was happy for the chance "to be a listener instead of a pastor." Upon entering, Barnett was confronted by a "stocky grizzled-haired man" who demanded that he leave. Shaken, Barnett withdrew, but immediately the minister followed after him, asking for forgiveness and inviting him back inside, where "the stocky usher was waiting belligerently." Agitated, the usher said, "you're not bringing him into this church, are you, Reverend? That's what's wrong with the church today! A nigger! You goin' to stand for that?" After the preacher held firm, the usher stormed out in disgust while Barnett was escorted to an empty pew. As the first hymn began, an elderly woman with a metal cane made her way down the aisle to sit next to Barnett—which greatly relieved him because his first instinct, in hearing the cane clacking closer to him, was to duck from an impending assault. After the service ended, he was "cordially greeted" by some congregants while others, "stony-faced," avoided him. Leaving the church, "with the warmth of many handshakes still felt in his fingers," Barnett found a note slipped in his pocket by the elderly lady:

> Please let me say to you why I came to sit beside you. I do not think integration is best for any of us. . . . But as a Christian I want you to know that I feel this to be God's house and I would never want to exclude anyone. We are before God, all of us, "sinners saved by grace."
>
> But I would like to say to you one thing. If you came because of your right to come, it is one thing. But we all as Christians need to put first "the Kingdom of God and his righteousness." I am afraid your coming has done something to greatly upset our church. You know the division and unhappiness it causes. Which is more important, "the Kingdom," or our individual desires?

I have loved sitting here and worshipping with you as some day I hope we will worship him in Heaven. But please think what it means. I hope you will use your fine voice for His glory. May God bless you.[1]

It was a telling exchange. From the usher's belligerency to the quietly earnest doubt of the elderly lady, there were countless ways that African Americans were not embraced in Nashville's everyday life. Both these individuals discounted John Barnett in favor of a congregation's racial sanctity, preferring a lack of divisiveness rather than the harder work of expanding the possibility of what a community could be.

This chapter explores how this theme played out more broadly in diverse realms across Nashville. The 1960 sit-ins had prompted the dream of an "Open City"— open in heart, mind, and potential for all of its citizens. The movement's insistent pressures toward this goal told a rich story of tireless effort and not a little heartache and conflict. Channeling multiple versions of activisms into a collective endeavor was a herculean task. This work, however, derived from how white Nashvillians, defensively responding to the movement's activities, found themselves scrambling for new answers and updated justifications as race continued to electrify nearly every aspect of Nashville during the early to mid-1960s. Employment issues, political realignments, public accommodations, everyday social groups; all were besieged with possibilities of change. Examining each of these realms and the historically contingent battles that took place in each shows how whites defended their beliefs in this era of shifting race relations in mixed ways. As politicians, businessmen, and everyday citizens tried uncertainly to deal with movement pressures, the combination of responses included violent lashing-out and a grasping for legal and moral language that tried to tie racial issues to other standards of behavior. In the Kingdom of Nashville, it was difficult for any number of individual desires to give way to a greater glory.

Sustaining momentum from the lunch-counter campaign was difficult, and the summer of 1960 brought a lull in racial activism. Student interest in expanding voter registration and employment opportunities witnessed a brief uptick, the former supported by black attorneys keen to build on this work in politically astute ways. But the summer break meant that many of the students imprisoned during the previous February had left the city, sapping the movement's dynamism. Kelly Miller Smith also observed that a relative lack of drama restrained activism in students and adults alike.[2]

By fall 1960, with students back in town, the movement redoubled its efforts on several fronts despite worrisome trends. The NCLC, expanding its campaign to the "stand-alone restaurants" populating Nashville's downtown, reported that the store representatives who had helped during the lunch-counter situation were now refusing to talk. Consequently, the NCLC and NSM, in "good conscience" and with "Christian concern," began new sit-ins. There was little or no coordination among white responses; one monitor said that "merchants hesitated to bring charges against the demonstrators, and police refused to arrest the students without warrants." Instead, some stores found cruelly creative answers. At one Krystal's, as other servers "stood around and laughed," one waitress "went wild," drenching students with water and cleaning powder before switching on the store's air-conditioner for good measure. Following up later, John Lewis and James Bevel found themselves locked inside the store as a fumigator churned out "dense clouds of insect spray." As Lewis and Bevel gasped for breath, the manager opened the door only after firefighters prepared to break the windows.[3] Similar altercations were widespread over the next week as sit-ins occurred at local restaurants and pharmacies. At Mickey's on Fourth and Church, demonstrators were "pushed out" by whites after police declined to make arrests. The Tic Toc's owner brandished a rifle to chase students away. "Door guards" were hired by establishments to block students from entering, aided by "jeering and shoving" crowds who materialized to participate in brief scuffles. In one case, protesters were locked inside a restaurant until after midnight. At the Trailways restaurant on December 7, a white taxi driver attacked Bernard Lafayette; police arrested both despite Lafayette insisting that he had not responded with violence. Minutes later, a white Fisk student hit from behind regained consciousness to kicks from bystanders. On the following day, while supervising the trials of demonstrators, Judge John I. Harris repeated his obstructionist tactics by calling for new charges after the fact and badgering defense attorneys about student intentions.[4]

The one-year anniversary of the sit-ins brought a more prolonged campaign to desegregate the movie theaters along Church Street. Demonstrations started only after negotiations stalled, and again the students took pains to circulate fliers explaining their actions. "We solicit your sober consideration and cooperation," the students asked, "in erasing one more stigma of racial discrimination and in witnessing the growth of human dignity." They noted among themselves that Cecil B. DeMille's *The Ten Commandments* was the featured film. Theater owners responded instead that it was "community policy" for cinemas to be segregated.

Dubbed the "stand-ins," the NCLC used continuously circulating lines to clog lobbies and ticket windows after blacks were refused admission. The protests continued in waves over the next few weeks, with varying estimates of fifty to one hundred and fifty participants. Some theaters deliberately closed down in counterprotest, while others stayed open for business and tried to ignore the demonstrators. Behind the scenes, white coconspirators lobbied the SRC for information about the national movie chains that owned many of these theaters, hoping that additional pressure could be brought from different angles.[5]

As the stand-ins continued, tensions grew. Although newspaper coverage remained sparse, one participant called the situation "a blazing battle." Kelly Miller Smith wrote to NCLC supporters to report what the media would not: "violence has been the normal occurrence. In fact on several occasions even the police have joined in the violence against the students." John Lewis later recalled the "roving gangs of young white hoodlums out for some evening 'sport'" who attacked reporters and demonstrators, pinning black marchers against walls, kicking, beating, and breaking eyeglasses. On one occasion, some whites jumped Nelson Fuson, apparently on the grounds that "this is the colored people's fight and eventually they are going to win anyway so they don't need no help from the white people." Police, absent during the altercations, reappeared in time to make twenty-eight arrests at two theaters for "blocking fire exits." This was despite one reporter's observation that the demonstrators stayed "well away from the box office and did not block anything." The arrests were later voided on a technicality.[6]

Amid the acrimony, the NCLC continued appealing to Nashville consciences, pointing out that "the Athens of the South" and "a city of churches" still had "unthinking and immoral men" who felt only "contempt" as blacks were "heckled, molested, and then arrested." One flier asked simply, "when will Nashville decide to be a really good city?" Ultimately, the demonstrations held to the lunch-counter precedent: the economic and somewhat lesser moral pressure of the stand-ins, combined with calm but firm negotiations, forced the movie theaters to succumb. According to a Fisk student, "the intangible satisfaction outranked the tangible ability to sit anywhere in the theatre." By spring 1961, the Nashville Ballet, Circle Theater and Theatre Nashville had desegregated. Soon after, some (but not all) of the city's drive-in theaters followed suit without demonstrations.[7]

Elsewhere, however, an uncertain mix of progress and friction remained. The movie theater victory overlapped with continued intransigence from restaurant owners. On February 15, 1961, overeager protesters, particularly determined to make their point at the movie theaters, had been rebuffed after trying to duck under the ticket line ropes. They shifted instead to the Trailways bus terminal and were served at the "normally segregated" lunch counter. Students then shifted to the Greyhound counter, where they were served, albeit only by black workers. When a fight broke out, the white protagonists were "escorted out of the building" without being arrested. Even as late as March, restaurant managers downtown were still emboldened enough to eject seven students. Every breach in racial custom was circumstantial and required continual testing.[8]

There was one place where the colored line remained inviolable. On July 18, 1961, six blacks led by Leo Lillard bypassed the "colored-only" swimming pool at Hadley Park and tried instead to enter Centennial Park's pool. After being turned away, the six left quietly but promised to pursue future negotiations, with demonstrations as a "last resort." The response was quite unlike Nashville's usual equivocation: the next day, the board of park commissioners closed all municipal pools with a terse announcement citing "financial reasons" that mystified other municipal officials. The city finance director said that this supposed budget predicament was news to him. The city parks superintendent demurred with "all I know was in the announcement." While Mayor Ben West claimed he had not been previously informed of the decision, he refused to comment when asked about the financial issues. It was poor form from a normally adroit politician, as Nashville politicos understood that the move had occurred at West's behest. The pools remained closed for years. The *Tennessean*, no friend of the mayor, lampooned the decision by waxing Shakespearean: "to swim or not to swim, that is not the question. . . . To dive; to swim, perchance with demonstrations: Ay, there's the rub . . . such makes us talk of money woes and youthful deprivation we have, than say the honest cause; Thus conscience does make cowards of us all."[9]

More antagonism in summer 1961 met efforts to merge direct action with employment issues. This campaign targeted H. G. Hill grocery stores, which had been subjected to similar protests in the 1920s. In another typical example of segregation's hypocrisies, the company, located in predominately African American neighborhoods and with a disproportionate number of black customers, refused to hire black workers. The students, trying to rally the community, scolded their elders for their inaction, saying sternly that "to pat the kids on the back" was insufficient. Instead, "you should be out there with them."[10] Picketing at H. G. Hill grocery stores by August was shadowed by packs of sneering white gangs. Some nonviolent restraint was still apparent early on; when a mob member accosted a white demonstrator with "so you want to be black. Well, take this," and sprayed him in the face with paint, the demonstrator merely thanked him. By August 5, the climate had grown more charged and, at the Hill's store at 16th and Grand Avenues, taunting from white gangs degenerated into violence as bystanders "went wild with assaults." The police joined in, arresting both demonstrators and attackers but "manhandling" protesters, sending several to the hospital. Watchful reporters accused the police of tampering with crime scene evidence. The NCLC responded to the violence with an impromptu sit-in at a police station, prompting yet another wave of jailings. The trials were postponed to allow police to correct mistakes on the warrants, for they had "not actually determined the reasons for the arrest."

Musing aloud to a mass meeting, Kelly Miller Smith said only that "it's strange the mayor would always be out of town when there's trouble."[11]

The racial climate remained raw throughout the week as both picketing and harassment continued. The venom took a toll on the demonstrators; many had not undergone the extensive workshops on nonviolent direct action that preceded the lunch-counter campaign. John Lewis had some quiet consternation about new recruits eager to participate in demonstrations but quick to curse whites or to dispense with Sunday-best clothing. One person who particularly vexed NCLC leaders was a brash and quick-tongued Howard University student named Stokely Carmichael, who was eventually asked to move on from Nashville. As Lewis writes, "I could see that discipline eroding, crumbling a little at the edges where the outsiders were stepping in."[12] At the trials, some charges were dismissed after the police testified lamely that "it takes two to make a fight, so we just arrested all of them." One *Tennessean* snapshot introduced in court showed Nashville police in various stages of beating demonstrators with feet and billy clubs. Only after some prodding were the parties named under cross-examination, but it remains unclear if any repercussions befell these officers.[13]

Lewis's observation about nonviolent discipline was confirmed by an eyewitness account from visiting civil rights leader Jim Forman, fresh from a visit to Monroe, North Carolina, with NAACP leader Robert Williams. Forman compared the attitudes of Nashville demonstrators with Williams, a celebrated advocate of armed self-defense "committed to taking some white lives should [he and his followers] have to die." Forman wrote that "such was the mood in Nashville Wednesday evening as I joined the picket line. People who have been involved in the non-violent movement for two years were saying: 'Jim, I am tired of being beaten. The police will not give us any protection. If this thing continues some reprisals will come.'" Forman also described a six-year-old white girl who chanted, "SPOOKS. SPOOKS. GO HOME SPOOKS," as grinning thugs waved knives at demonstrators, later slashing Forman's sign and showering him with soda spray. He also referred to a swelling group of "at least four hundred blacks" of all ages that watched and occasionally interposed themselves between the white gangs and black demonstrators. The Hill's store, for their part, gave away eggs to anyone promising to throw them at the protesters. "How ironic is it to see Negroes buying eggs," said one student flier, "at a store which will freely give them to any who would use them to humiliate Negro persons."[14]

The inconclusive effort against the H. G. Hill stores spoke to broader efforts to increase black employment in Nashville. This was a persistent issue despite the movement having scored small coups. Political pressure occasionally helped gain municipal job opportunities for blacks, but private-sector employment remained problematic. During the lunch-counter campaign, for example, two black police officers were promoted to detective (although their new position "would not give them supervision over white officers") and were immediately assigned to the "sit-in case." In mid-June 1960, the local bus company had hired a black driver and, in late summer, Kroger grocery employed a black clerk after threatened with pickets similar to those against the H. G. Hill stores. The latter store eventually also made some hires, but displeasure persisted and activists confessed that the task had "never been brought to the desired conclusion."[15]

Increasing the quality and quantity of black jobs was a daunting task. In April 1960, a two-day conference had discussed the appalling prospects for black employment in the city, as Vivian Henderson, the Fisk economics professor who had nurtured support for the 1960 boycott, examined the issue in detail. His report revealed the problem's scope, as over 80 percent of Nashville blacks worked in "menial, unskilled positions," which in turn comprised over 80 percent of *all* the unskilled jobs in the entire city. Those blacks obtaining more skilled jobs — the "professional, proprietor, clerical and similar skilled occupations" — were in "segregated employment areas devoted almost exclusively to serving Negroes." To underline the problem, Henderson noted that, since 1957, a bare 4 percent of twelve thousand newly created jobs in Nashville had gone to blacks, virtually all unskilled positions. Moreover, blacks were barred from the "training positions of new industry" even when such programs specifically targeted local people.[16]

An attempted answer, by fall 1961, came from the Nashville Community Conference on Employment Opportunity (NCCEO). The NCCEO was especially driven to desegregate Hume-Fogg, the vocational school in Nashville. But the group also emphasized a desire to capitalize on the lunch-counter successes by focusing on companies lining the retail corridor along Church Street as well as other employers vulnerable to federal government intervention. An April 1961 meeting with Vice President Lyndon B. Johnson supported this last goal, as LBJ had been tasked with leading the Kennedy Administration's push for companies to sign voluntary "Plans of Progress" to boost black hiring. The same initiative soon led to Kennedy signing Executive Order 10925, which first used the term *affirmative action* in mandating black employment opportunities in all companies possessing federal contracts. Nashvillians spoke to the vice president about the city's lack of black jobs, even in federal agencies and contractors. Copies of formal complaints from workers describing widespread discrimination were given to Johnson, with egregious examples at the local Internal Revenue Service, the U.S. Postal Service, the Nashville Housing Authority, and the veteran's hospital. Even the U.S. Employment Service had two Nashville branches—one downtown and the other in a black neighborhood. The lack of black employment was galling given the number of blacks educated at area colleges.[17]

Nashville's AVCO industrial plant was a particular example of what the movement faced. A manufacturer of airplane parts and home appliances, AVCO employed 42 blacks (out of 2,600 workers), all as low-wage menial laborers. While signs for WHITE and COLORED facilities in the plant had been taken down, apparently for Vice President Johnson's visit, the facilities remained segregated. This meant that, although cafeteria lines were racially mixed, "local Negro maintenance personnel still eat in a separate small room," presumably "by preference." Blacks also changed clothes and used the toilet in a boiler room rather than venture into the white locker room. But such behavior mixed with more systemic problems. For example, AVCO classified its jobs in a way that siphoned blacks off into separate worker categories. This, combined with the traditional practice reserving "seniority rights," meant that upward mobility for blacks within the company, as an AVCO official acknowledged, was "awkward if not impossible." The "vicious circle" meant that black workers did not qualify for continued training in their own department and yet could not be hired for newly created jobs in other departments because of insufficient training. It meant that, despite an official policy of nondiscrimination, the "practice will remain discriminating."[18] Even in a desegregating context, social space and opportunity was always arranged in hierarchical deference to white superiority.

Improvements did occur, if unevenly. After sixteen AVCO workers filed complaints with a federal committee, four workers were upgraded to better jobs—notably, however, none of the four were among the sixteen protesters and indeed were lower in seniority. More significantly, these promotions were all within the appliance division, which was known to have a higher rate of lay-offs and lacked a training program for career advancement that was reserved for a separate division. And these changes came in the context of harsher treatment toward all black workers in the plant. Only after consenting to a Plan of Progress incorporating more African Americans at all job levels, whetted by a recent ten million dollar contract with the federal government, did AVCO have sufficient incentive to comply. The company apparently did so: a later check found that, on a grassroots level, desegregation was largely accepted by the workers and a separate eating room had been eliminated so as to foster social interaction. Although a white boycott on the night shift showed some displeasure, it apparently "worked out all right" for others. An ongoing working relationship continued; gradually movement activists expressed some approval of AVCO's first steps, although conflicts and federal lawsuits continued throughout the decade.[19]

Still, follow-up reports from across Nashville tempered cautious optimism with abject dismay. After a "vigorous community-wide economic and political program" threatened boycotts across the city, some companies granted jobs to blacks. Local soda and milk companies employed black salesmen; retail establishments hired blacks as clerks and in similar white-collar posts. Local and state governments began fulfilling promises to do the same, as when Clifford Allen hired a black tax assessor for his office and the Tennessee State Prison in Nashville recruited black prison guards. Other diplomatic exchanges suggested that there were job opportunities in state government and elsewhere provided that blacks could be convinced to take the civil service test to qualify. Yet these modest successes were hard-won. Even companies with federal contracts showed little initiative, responding only after being pressured. Perhaps worst of all were public utilities that as monopolies remained largely immune to boycotting from disgruntled customers. Southern Bell and Telephone, for example, "flatly refused" to consider hiring more African Americans. Similar contempt came from local labor unions, which, despite "lip service," practiced discriminatory practices "on a very large scale in Nashville," often in collusion with management. As one example, some claimed flatly that no black person could become a licensed plumber or electrician because of a restricted apprentice-training program.[20] Trying to overturn these long-standing patterns of racial discrimination made for halting, piece-meal progress. Partial breakthroughs only highlighted the work to be done; results occurred only with "economic, political and direct action" used as mutually reinforcing prods for change.[21]

Yet black activists had their own internal factors to contend with, and occasionally concerted efforts did not mean all was harmonious. As local civil rights groups lobbied intensely behind the scenes for new hiring policies, students remained unsure about next steps. By fall 1961, many of Nashville's student leaders had moved to other battlegrounds, rescuing the Freedom Rides and going south to challenge Jim Crow elsewhere. The ones who remained found themselves uneasy about adult ways of doing things and the chafing present during the lunch-counter campaign now resumed. The students saw their occasional protests as part of a comprehensive assault on segregation, which they thought should include a complete boycott downtown. While enthusiastically supporting voter registration efforts, they were aggrieved when the NCLC leaders, trying to sustain unity, demurred against further protests. On an immediate level, the two emphases were not incongruent; indeed, the NAACP highlighted the use of boycotts and demonstrations as a useful complement to negotiations. But adults preferred to use a selective boycott to punish or reward businesses accordingly depending on how they responded to the movement and abandoned the boycott entirely when some jobs were given to blacks. (Only later would the NCLC return to "the total withdrawal" boycott strategy.) As before, students saw it differently and were contemptuous of this choice, branding the adults as content with "back-patting," "tokenism," and a return to the "tea and cookies"-type false pleasantries that marked past incremental change.[22]

The real problem was that the Nashville Movement was no longer a mass movement. In a sense, the lunch-counter example loomed silently as a distilled example of segregation's hypocrisies, symbolically powerful in ways that cut across racial, class, and gender lines, where economic and moral pressures were levied in tandem against a tangible target, so that everyone could find a revitalized spirit of protest. But now tactical differences spoke to wider ruptures in temperaments. The students defined the problem in terms of deficient commitment and fervency. "The sense of sacrifice is missing," John Lewis thought. The lack of a mass movement, to students, meant that *one had to be created*, even if it meant, as Lewis argued strenuously, that the students should continue without coordinating with other groups. The collegians were not included in employment negotiations anyway, as they dismissed black leaders who crowed about winning a few more jobs here and there. The students argued instead that "a bigger push" would yield "a bigger piece of the pie" and were exasperated about the false "sense of accomplishment" that, in the case of H. G. Hill, led to an attitude of "why push it any further, and harder"? The joy of resistance had also faded somewhat—students remarked that most of their peers frowned upon those who dropped out of school to work for the movement. That some compatriots involved in the Freedom Rides had been expelled from school was also intimidating. But Lewis stressed not only the lack of leadership, but the lack of a leader, period—no one to rally thousands to action with short notice. "We just keep fooling ourselves that we have a nonviolent movement," he groused. He acknowledged that the "drama and novelty" had "worn out," but wanted to impel change from the ground up, to have more people to "witness," to "stand up," and "be present."

Others had a different mentality. One minister argued that the most conspicuous lesson from the lunch-counter campaign was that economic factors were foremost. Indeed, "the moral argument is just about conceded to," he said, but this admission from merchants was lost because "we are not getting press coverage." Emphasizing economic motivations fit more comfortably with elite preferences. Indeed, the minister suggested that the NAACP had no issue with nonviolence. It was rather the etiquette associated with the strategy; the style of picketing, of direct action, of putting bodies directly on the line, was not to the NAACP's taste. The middle-class quality of Nashville's black community, and the function of this class within Jim Crow in general, created certain parameters for activism.

If the white-owned downtown was dependent on black business, the core of the African American community still had relatively little interaction with whites; indeed their livelihood was mostly based on other African Americans in segregated neighborhoods. Whether as academics, college administrators, businessmen, or other white-collar professionals, black Nashvillians were frequently part of the community fabric through institutional, professional, and organizational ties that meant that their corresponding racial activism had a different cast.

These conflicts were pronounced even as many went to great lengths to overturn them. Forming the Nashville Civil Rights Coordinating Committee, a forum for leaders of NCLC, NAACP, NCRC, NSM, and NCCEO, seemed a promising step. The common goal was Operation Open City, a full-scale assault on segregation in all sectors of Nashville. Kelly Miller Smith had some initial optimism. "Make no mistake about it," wrote Smith, "the functioning of the Coordination Committee is far from perfect, but we believe that the potentiality is good." But it was misplaced sentiment.[23] An ongoing debate about how to apply boycotting persisted. James Lawson went so far as to say that the 1960 lunch counter sit-ins had created false progress and "the NCLC made an error in settling for integration in a half dozen restaurants, a few jobs and the removal of a few signs." Instead, "what should have been insisted upon was an entirely new direction on the part of the whole city." Minutes from NCLC meetings revealed agonizing that "we don't have a pattern of action that will get results." When asked if the NCLC was "concerned about unity," Smith responded that "the problem we are facing cannot be worked out in a Board meeting."[24]

Such issues made their work harder. Significantly, a Chamber of Commerce official had hinted to Kelly Miller Smith that a public accommodations law would best bypass ongoing resistance to serving black customers. Movement leaders eagerly presented Ben West with a proposal advocating such a bill, drawn from a similar ordinance in St. Louis, but "no known action" resulted. The NCLC also tried to spur the mayor about the pool closings, more hirings in the police department, and other components of the Open City program. But, when combined with the NAACP's ongoing efforts, the multiple fronts made coordination harder. Several examples show frustrated activists with no idea what others were doing. The NCLC, for example, was unfamiliar with the NAACP's efforts to desegregate Hume-Fogg. Even a year later, Kelly Miller Smith, when asked about the status of the Voter Education Program, a SRC program to facilitate black voter registration in the South, had no idea: "needless to say, we were not asked to participate with the sponsoring groups." Many thought that numerous groups lobbying the Chamber of Commerce on different issues gave the impression of a divided black community and provided an excuse for white inaction.[25] Students, for their part, continued direct action on several fronts downtown throughout 1962, all of which were met coldly and made little headway. One new improvisation, the "sleep-in," occurred at downtown hotels as clerks refused to register the students and white patrons flung liquor bottles at the demonstrators.[26]

A particular and protracted site of struggle was the Wilson-Quick Pharmacy downtown, which embodied how white business owners saw their stores as an extension of themselves and their economic and personal livelihood. This perhaps explains why guards posted at Wilson-Quick soon became standard and on January 6, 1962, ejected protesters with enough force that a few white bystanders left, vowing never to return. In late February, four demonstrators were hospitalized after a confrontation involving knives and bricks as "police, though on the scene, did not intervene." The NCLC complained about the white press's silence about the incident and the propensity of both the *Tennessean* and *Banner* to report "arrests and court action only." The NCLC countered with a number of tactics, including enlisting sympathetic white doctors at Vanderbilt to register complaints with the pharmacies. Physicians at Hubbard seemed more reluctant to get involved, offering "off the record" advice on the issue. Movement sympathizers recorded that Wilson-Quick continued insisting that their pharmacies were desegregated, except for the lunch counters, and the store was awaiting action from other drugstores. The company's representatives suggested that the professional association of pharmacists was the best target for changing business practices, although activists noted that Wilson-Quick was known as the "real force" in this group.[27] Feeble protests continued throughout 1962 at restaurants and drugstores but even Martin Luther King's Nashville appearance in 1962 did little to inspire concerted action.

By fall 1962, desegregation battles had fallen into grinding attrition as old ways of behaving persisted. "Voluntary resegregation" in seating still occurred on city buses. A sign "with the word 'COLORED' erased" remained posted by the Union Station railroad waiting room and African Americans still used it in Jim Crow fashion. Although the bus terminals dispensed with signs, Greyhound still had a functionally segregated waiting room and lunch counter. White politicians, sensing the racial stalemate and not inclined to resolve it, were cautious about pledging allegiance to either side. Some failed to show as promised at NCLC meetings, and even some politicians who opposed a public accommodation bill "represent councilmanic districts where the Negro support is crucial"—apparently they had little fear that blacks would punish them electorally for their stance. Another local politician, Clifford Allen, split the difference by pledging personal support for the bill but questioned whether it would stand up in court.[28]

One reason for the impasse was a larger issue with a racial subtext that diverted energies in the early 1960s: a proposed effort to merge the city of Nashville and

Davidson County, as well as smaller incorporated towns in the area, into a single metropolitan entity. This effort became known simply as Metro.[29] The same measure had failed in 1958 despite rare unity from the *Banner* and *Tennessean* plus support from both Mayor Ben West and County Judge Beverly Briley (the county's equivalent of a mayor, although with less power than West). By 1962, however, a second campaign for metropolitan government folded into other political dynamics. After being boxed in by his opponents, Ben West was forced to throw his weight against consolidation. The mayor's popularity was already sinking due to displeasure over his handling of the 1960 sit-ins and bitterly controversial new taxes. Now, with urban renewal programs and other expenditures straining the budget, West had no choice but to annex areas aggressively to create new revenue for the city. Cleverly, his opponents (particularly Briley and the *Tennessean*) fed the resulting resentments to encourage support for Metro. In response, the mayor mobilized the remnants of his political network. The *Banner*, as usual in lockstep with West, was joined by white ward boss Gene "Little Evil" Jacobs and his black counterpart Henry "Good Jelly" Jones, and, in a more unlikely alliance, a number of archconservative John Birch Society types, including John Kasper. The result was a hotly contested political battle.[30]

Briefly stated, the call for Metro was motivated by a growing chasm between city and county (and neighborhoods torn between the two), driven by the white-flight trend that "became a virtual avalanche between 1940 and 1950." By 1960, the suburban population of Nashville outnumbered the city's, with the result that Greater Nashville was one economic entity fractured into two competing political machines. City and county wrangled often. A typical problem was sewers. Because Nashville rested atop a bed of limestone, extending adequate sewage systems to keep up with the relentless outward growth of the city was expensive and elaborate. Similarly, private fire companies in the suburbs worked by subscription, and anecdotes of firemen watching impassively as the houses of nonmembers burned abounded during the Metro debate. Varied financing of school districts and utilities, police departments with confusing jurisdictions, taxes on homeowners that only benefited select neighborhoods, and similar issues made for a mishmash of inefficient services for both city and county. Yet opponents of Metro questioned the constitutionality of the merger and the merits of expanded government; these arguments mingled with a broader distrust of the city and what it represented. Many disliked the idea of consolidation because of a cultural mentality that cultivated "pride in their independence from the 'big city folk." Some tried to paint "consolidation as communistic." (Typically, although many players in the Chamber of Commerce favored consolidation, there were rumors that "many of its influential members did not want to get involved in the politics necessary to bring about the adoption of the plan," in keeping with elite white Nashville's preference for keeping politics at a distance from business.)[31]

When combined with political divisions, race factored into the Metro issue, although to what extent is difficult to say. Generally speaking, African Americans opposed consolidation. Black political organizations stressed that Metro would hurt black voting power thanks to white flight. As whites settled into suburbs, the increasing percentages of blacks remaining in the city made for numerical advantages in certain districts and an easier path for electing black representatives, advantages that Metro would negate. A rumor persisted that Metro consolidation had extra urgency because whites feared a black mayor. When asked in the mid-1990s by a historian about Metro consolidation, one observer agreed that this factor predominated, saying, in an unfortunate choice of words, "I'm going to call a spade a spade." When later asked about the positive effects of Metro, he said that "well, it's kept a black person from getting to be the Mayor. That was what they wanted." Other people challenge that belief, pointing out that annexation of local communities had begun after Metro first failed in 1958. Many felt that, had such a program continued, black voting power would have been weakened anyway.[32]

Yet even as some used this rationale to urge African American support for Metro—an argument only sweetened by the chance to oppose West—the issue still exacerbated political divisions among blacks. Some influential black leaders, particularly Vivian Henderson and Z. Alexander Looby, lobbied for Metro and stressed that black representation would be preserved through Metro districting. The logic was that if "you can help create this" than "you'll have some significant voice," whereas "if you let it happen through annexation, the city will continue to just spread out to the white suburbs and the black vote will be diluted." Others suggested that consolidation, by expanding Nashville's industrial base, would create job opportunities for blacks and whites. Others, particularly City Councilman Robert Lillard and his Davidson County Democratic League, took the opposite position, enlisting Boy Scouts to spread tracts opposing Metro as Ben West compelled city firemen and policemen to do the same. Lillard was a West ally, having exchanged political support to ensure West's benevolence toward Lillard's district. While such horse-trading was the norm in Nashville, many lamented that the Metro issue brought intrablack political divisions into the open. Black councilman Mansfield Douglas later said that Metro made local black politics falsely reduced to a supposed "struggle [of] the Looby faction versus the Lillard faction," with Lillard portrayed as an "Uncle Tom" and "from the old school."[33]

Although 55 percent of black voters rejected Metro, the merger still passed on June 28, 1962. Widely acknowledged today as crucial to Nashville's subsequent prosperity, the decision was lauded then by city leaders as further proof of Nashville's progressivism. Black influence remained during Metro's planning, which went to considerable lengths to placate black voters, and this was especially thanks to Z. Alexander Looby. The attorney, who many believed could have been the first black mayor of Nashville had the city-county divide persisted, originally opposed consolidation. But prominent businessmen convinced him otherwise, pointing out that he indeed could be mayor but of "a dying city." Instead, Looby, with help from Lillard, was a persistent lobbyist. He persuaded his colleagues to zone Metropolitan Council districts to preserve black majorities and entreated his counterparts to help him justify the commission's decisions to black voters. He struck down a proposal that half of the new council be comprised of "at-large" representatives, fearing that this would further reduce the prospects of black politicians. And Looby was unapologetic in doing so: at one point, studying a proposed zoning line, he requested that it be moved over exactly one block. One member responded, "Mr. Looby, do you have a good reason that it needs to be moved over, or is it really just gerrymandering?" To which Looby replied cheerfully, "it's gerrymandering."[34]

Metro seemed to augur a new political era; it also ended Ben West's political career. As historian Don H. Doyle noted, there was no small irony in West's loss—his opposition to Metro combined with his handling of the sit-ins and pools tarnished the legacy of an otherwise forward-thinking career. West's successor as mayor, Beverly Briley, an East Nashville native and Vanderbilt alumnus, was well-prepared for this chapter of Nashville's history. Armed with the *Tennessean*'s support, Briley had been "a principal figure in the destruction of the old county machine that had been in place for over thirty years" and had advocated a number of progressive issues during his political career. His election, coupled with the move to metropolitan government, gave Nashville more reason to trumpet its civic virtue to the nation. The only discordant note that could mar this image would be further contentiousness over race relations.[35]

In the new political and economic context of a metropolitan Nashville, activists recognized possibilities. Nashville's move toward Metro took place against the backdrop of the important U.S. Supreme Court case *Baker v. Carr* (1962) that led to new reapportionment of voting districts. Political power was being remapped in Nashville and elsewhere. Black professor Herman Long underlined the point by noting that decentralization was now the chief theme in Nashville in terms of "population, residential development, commercial and business activity, and even political control." With the shift to suburban development that kept blacks in the city's urban core, "the central fact is one of inescapable interdependence of the Negro population and the business community." As such, the city's recent effort toward becoming a convention city, as seen in the building of a new city auditorium and urgent efforts at urban renewal programs, was significant. Attracting business, church, and professional groups to the city would be difficult with the lack of public accommodations for African Americans. Long noted that the Methodist Board of Education, for example, headquartered in the city, had a small meeting in Nashville (where "no hotel or downtown facilities are used" so that no delegates would be offended or ostracized) but reserved its national meeting for Cincinnati. This convergence of racial and economic interests would command the movement's attention in sustaining momentum, even as whites found themselves facing uncertain realities and scrambling to find new rationales for old ways of thinking.[36]

As politicking over Metro concluded, civil rights demonstrations, accompanied by low-grade violence, again heightened. By winter 1962–63, weekly weekend protests at downtown restaurants, starting on November 24, comprised "a series of skirmishes" followed by small numbers of arrests. Only back-channel diplomacy restrained these events; it was an open secret that the police would be permitted to break up demonstrations as forcefully as necessary, but cooler heads soon counseled wiser action. Even as Nashville restaurateurs dug in their heels, they chose a new rhetoric that belied events. The manager at Cross-Keys restaurant for example refused service to demonstrators in a "calm, pleasant manner," saying that "I feel they are infringing on my right to operate a private business as I see fit." The shops taking refuge under the philosophy of private property meant that police officers could not arrest demonstrators without a warrant for trespassers, unless violence broke out. This exception made blacks fair game and spurred whites toward callousness as only turbulence prompted police intervention. One, who gave his name to a reporter as Johnny Rebel, barred a demonstrator by saying, "we don't serve niggers here and you ain't going to get inside." Fire extinguisher spray became a favored weapon against demonstrators; guards hulked inside Wilson-Quick Pharmacy and Tic Toc, B&W, and Simple Simon restaurants. Those sitting in were locked out, "removed bodily," locked inside stores, or, in the case of one young black woman, hit by a white man yelling "get the hell out of the way here."[37]

Even as movement demonstrations and store intransigence escalated, the low-grade violence seemed to make whites anxious to justify their actions in new terms. A revealing pamphlet from the management of B&W restaurant issued to its white clientele explained calmly that the restaurant's choice to segregate was made "without malice" and without "exercising a capricious prejudice." Unlike the lunch-counter hypocrisy between sales and service, the management professed that "we sell only one service—namely prepared meals to our selected patrons" and stressed this made for "legal equities which we are entitled to maintain and defend." Bidding for white racial solidarity, the restaurant argued that attempting to maintain these rights was also "defending yours." And, in criticizing the demonstrations, the management claimed that no legal or moral rule justified "mass demonstration, mob tactics, or human blockades," as "mass action" threatened to destroy anyone's rights. The document cited student attempts to be seated as "forced entry"—an incongruous overstatement, since these entries would have given more business to the restaurant—but mostly focused on the disturbances and "resultant economic loss" as white patrons stayed away. More to the point, the pamphlet asked about the demonstrators "why haven't they sought relief in the courts?" and declared that "if our position is wrong, it should be so declared by legal proceedings and not by irresponsible efforts to block our doors," although the pamphlet also allowed that the store would "comply with all legal directives."[38]

The B&W document, in its reasoned and polite tone, rhetorically positioned itself as setting aside emotional racial feelings for more dispassionate racial opinions. It did not, of course, acknowledge the persistent, ever-present violence against downtown demonstrators. But it was also an attempt to impose new moral standards on racial customs that were being fought over in Nashville streets. The implication that morality was far less compelling to a storeowner than fidelity to a legal mandate was clear; apparently conformity to a new standard was necessary to change racial behavior. But the equal implication was that whites maintained the prerogative to grant black incursions on white spaces in white terms only.

The year 1963 brought sporadic demonstrating as the frustrated movement tried to regalvanize black activism against such attitudes, and the problem would get worse before it got better.[39] One particular target was the YMCA and YWCA, which the NCLC had been working on for two years. The Y in Nashville maintained separate facilities for blacks, which struck many as especially hypocritical in light of the group's Christian orientation. The YWCA had desegregated its cafeteria in response to the lunch-counter campaign but not its residence halls or recreational facilities. In 1962, eight African Americans attempting to spend the night were referred to a subsidiary suburban facility with independent management. By 1963, open conversations within the YWCA were taking place but with little result, particularly because of worries about desegregated swimming pools. Despite a professed interracial policy expressed in 1965, only financial reasons made the YWCA desegregate in 1967 even as the organization opted to relocate to suburban Nashville.[40]

Moreover, the NCLC continued challenging the same intransigent restaurants downtown. In early March, a demonstration brought only sixty marchers, and newspaper coverage noted that it was "obvious that the leaders were disappointed" by the meager turnout. Ceremonial stops in front of Wilson-Quick, Cross-Keys, B&W, and similar hold-outs were followed the next day by a prayer vigil outside the official inauguration of Metropolitan government. One batch of demonstrators on trial for an October 21, 1962, sit-in at B&W were punished with a harsh sentence of ninety days in jail, provoking outrage from the black community and dismay even from both white newspapers. (The appeal in this case eventually ended up in the U.S. Supreme Court.)[41] Animated, the NCLC tried to seize the initiative, announcing on March 19 an "immediate and full-scale assault." The group proposed a barrage of sit-ins, "kneel-ins" at local churches (to "stir church leaders from their complacency"), "drop-ins" (where sympathetic whites asked to talk with store managers), as well as tedious but crucial diplomacy with city officials. Kelly Miller Smith lobbied "to get some hopeful note which could be reported" but the Chamber of Commerce demurred from helping him because the issue was "sociological, not economic." On March 23, eighty-five marchers downtown participated in "probably the largest segregation protests" since 1960. News reports told of John Lewis being "pelted with eggs," and of a failed attempt to enter Wilson-Quick, where "two women clerks held the door and refused them entrance." Kelly Miller Smith, clearly trying to sustain mass support, called the march "a people's cause and not just a leader's cause." The NCLC's threat of boycotting became realized a week later at a mass rally, when over four hundred voted unanimously to support the measure.[42]

Masked by this public drama of demonstrations, the interplay between activists and power brokers continued, as captured in one conversation between Kelly Miller Smith and L. C. Langford, owner of the restaurant of the same name. The owner expressed some shock that, despite his attempts to convince the local restaurant association to facilitate desegregation, some black protesters had entered his restaurant. Smith responded that "some kids [were] not under control," calling them "too enthusiastic" and assuring the owner that "the word has now gotten around" to avoid Langford's business. The owner continued pleading his situation, saying that, although he was now "rather an outcast" with the Association, he would continue to work on other store owners and company presidents. Smith in turn offered to organize future tightly controlled demonstrations, asking if that would put the owner in a better bargaining position. Langford requested instead that demonstrations at his store be avoided entirely, so that his pleas for desegregation would not be seen as driven by "a selfish motive," as had happened during the 1960 negotiations. Smith, although indicating he had to abide by the collective NCLC decision, promised to present the owner's case.

Langford also noted how divisions among the owners created indecision because of fears that, as individual restaurants capitulated, they would become patronized entirely by blacks as whites went elsewhere. (Indeed, movement activists had long suspected bigger stores and restaurants of staying on the sidelines with the hope that demonstrations would drive smaller businesses bankrupt and create chances for business monopolies.) Smith tried to assuage these fears, reassuring that "Nashville blacks mainly want to establish their right to eat in any restaurant but in practice would mainly support their own places." Smith also acknowledged that the owner's information was correct, that the NCLC was "mainly testing" and "that those who serve the colored will be bothered no longer." When necessary, Smith adroitly shifted the conversation to find common ground with the owner. They both chortled about perennial political candidate Clifford Allen, who had opened his restaurant to blacks because "votes have no color—they are all counted." Both lamented the distorted coverage from reporters: "can't believe everything the papers say." And both agreed that racial issues in the South would be "solved sooner" than in other parts of the United States, because, as Smith put it, "[blacks] know exactly where we stand, which is not always so in the North."

The conversation prompted Langford to fumble at explaining white behavior. "I like good colored people as much as good whites," he claimed. "Have had a colored maid 16 years, built her a house where her children have playmates." He was "a little afraid of what some of our customers might do" in terms of potential violence and maintained to Smith that "some hotheaded people can't be controlled. Just as you can't control all your people." (Given that Langford had gotten drunk after the initial miscommunication occurred and fumed aloud that he would have local wrestlers attack the students, he may have known this tendency firsthand.) But in terms of desegregation, "it is not a case of not wanting to do it for a lot of us. It is that we are afraid of losing our white customers." And yet, "it is definitely coming and right thinking people should accept it."[43]

The revealing exchange showed schisms within the owners' ranks. But it also implied that, even as the immorality of segregation was taken for granted, it never trumped more lingering fears about enduring racial custom and worries about economic logistics. It is hard to fault restaurant owners for worrying that their livelihoods rested on uncertain changes, but resorting to questions of racial custom and economics were a salve of sorts in avoiding a deeper personal choice. Moreover, the transcript showed Kelly Miller Smith's clever navigation of racial etiquette in working with Langford. In Smith's words, black factionalism became an aid rather than an obstacle. Shrewdly, Smith conveyed to the owner that "it was interesting for us to learn that part of this was an economic situation, not race prejudice"—whether or not he believed this, it was an effective ploy to reaffirm what the Langford's owner confided in him. He even asked for advice about how and where to carry out future sit-ins. Nor did Smith challenge the concept of the freedom of association that governed most white actions; in fact, his statements suggested that African Americans felt the same way. While it is impossible to say whether this was a tactical choice or a deep-seated belief for Smith, it nonetheless reinforces the minister's skill in working with his counterpart—a sympathetic firmness that made for an effective interracial working relationship.

But such conversations were rarely taking place with all the struggles left to fight. Beyond public demonstrations and private lobbying, the NCLC advocated another economic withdrawal encompassing the entire downtown, suburban shopping centers, and any neighborhood groceries choosing not to employ blacks. The NCLC justified the boycott because of "token changes" that did nothing against the "prevailing pattern of segregation," continued intransigence from stores (Moon-McGrath and Wilson-Quick were specifically mentioned), harsh sentences against demonstrators, and continued police arrogance. The conclusion for many was that a boycott was the "only really effective instrument" for instigating change. As Smith put it later, "the dominant pattern in Nashville is still segregation. Nashville citizens still think in the terms of segregation," and "we can eat in a few places downtown but you still had better ask somebody before going in."[44]

Overwhelming support at a mass meeting, however, did not represent the community as a whole. Kelly Miller Smith also worked tirelessly to convince different constituencies that the boycott was necessary. A contrarian view came from one Fisk student, overly preoccupied with "buying an Easter outfit," who thought sit-ins and boycotts were anachronisms and that "we can now solve the problem through talks and negotiations." Diplomacy toward Smith's fellow black elites had to be even more delicate, as shown in a letter to grocery store owner Flem Otey. Smith pointed out that 80 percent of Otey's goods were purchased from a businessman owning, among other things, Wilson-Quick Pharmacy, one of the holdouts downtown. While thanking Otey for his contributions to the movement in Nashville and acknowledging that "it is your affair where your goods are purchased," Smith also dangled the "live possibility" that Otey might soon face a boycott of his own store.[45]

While never impolitic, Smith vented more straightforward frustration at Bernard Schweid, the white owner of Mills Bookstore downtown and husband to an active TCHR member. Schweid had written Smith with the view that boycotts were a "'tired technique'" and "unimaginative." Smith, although patient, did not mince his words, pointing out that Schweid voiced concern only after the prospect of losing profits surfaced: "everybody minds his own business until some sort of crisis is at hand." After countless ignored requests for meetings, the NCLC was forced to "rap for attention," as Smith put it—"it is an attempt to get the attention of the leaders of a system." Smith acknowledged that Schweid's Jewish heritage gave him some empathy toward victims of prejudice but nonetheless "it would be difficult to communicate the desperation which we as Negroes sometimes feel" and added that "you could not possibly know the things which humiliate us and the limitations which we have" in responding to segregation.[46]

Behind the promised boycott was pressure on Mayor Briley to establish a permanent human relations committee as part of the new Metro government.[47] On May 8, 1963, events escalated sharply as citizens, energized by the use of fire hoses on African Americans in Birmingham, Alabama, began new waves of fervent demonstrations. The protests reached new levels to express sympathy with Birmingham blacks and to "point out that all is not well in Nashville." One shaken citizen wrote Briley that a lunch meeting for a Chamber of Commerce group was "completely blocked by a solid line of negroes arm in arm forming a semi-circle blocking the entrance." After a "brief physical struggle," the police had to "pull me through the human chain." Incensed at the crowds milling around watching the scene, he termed it "lawlessness in its darkest form." The ranks of demonstrators swelled due to seven hundred grade and high school African American students who "played hookey," fleeing their schools to join the protests as had occurred in Birmingham. Most rallies took place before the same beacons of resistance: Wilson-Quick, Cross-Keys, and B&W, as well as Simple Simon and Krystal's. Some Pearl High School students, watching their peers led off to jail, implored the police to arrest them as well. Feeling ran equally high among watching whites, and the crowds became restive. The first missiles, paper bags filled with water, were soon replaced with "bricks, eggs, and soft drink bottles." Downplaying the turmoil, one protester claimed that "this is Nashville, not Birmingham," and "We don't expect police dogs or water hoses."[48]

Perhaps not, but the situation grew grim. Subsequent demonstrations on May 10 became heated as blacks tried to "shove their way" into B&W; "each time a door was opened to a white patron, the Negroes would surge forward in their unsuccessful efforts to enter." Reports of "flashing knives" and bomb threats circulated. Rocks crashed through windows at First Baptist Church and at the home of an NCLC minister. Some blacks had "belts wrapped around their fists" in fighting "white hecklers"; others "attempted to climb into the patrol car in an effort to force police to take them into custody." Police Chief H. O. Kemp acknowledged that "we can handle the demonstrators, but with the gangs of whites milling around, it makes our job extremely difficult." Ed Shea, a Chamber of Commerce official and head of the mayor's interim biracial committee, released a "strongly worded" statement excoriating the demonstrators as "wild-eyed radicals and extreme rabble-rousers." Briley said simply, "I am disappointed but have not lost patience."[49]

The NCLC struggled to maintain a message of nonviolence amid the turmoil, searching for signs that it was reaching white consciences. Metz Rollins argued that "even the men who guard the doors at some of the restaurants have come to know us" and "the demonstrations bring white people into proximity with Negroes, making them realize that you are more than a black face, that you are a personality." On May 10, a rock had hit Rollins in the head, and he admitted to a spurt of anger within him, wanting to "have a real donnybrook" to "show them what it felt like," but his training and composure quickly returned. He argued that those who instigated fistfights were untutored in nonviolence and that the NCLC had been unprepared to train all those eager to join protests: "numbers have a real effect on discipline."[50]

The recourse to damage control was needed, for whites were often more upset by schoolchildren participating in demonstrations rather than by violence or the reasons behind the protests. The *Banner* editorialized its refusal to believe that "it is the responsible Negro leadership that is sending children to harass two or three restaurants, and by conduct completely out of hand, precipitating incidents of which riot is born." The irony, of course, was that former Nashville student James Bevel had pioneered this tactic in Birmingham. "What's to be gained," the paper asked rhetorically, "by interrupting the peaceful commerce of this city in an effort to wreck the business of a few eating places?" After citing hopeful signs of racial progress, the editorial concluded sternly, "sanity must prevail." The column was revealing; by disassociating black leaders from events downtown, the newspaper implicitly downplayed the demands made by the "responsible leadership." And the disapproval of demonstrations that used child protesters left little room to take the substantive reasons motivating the protests seriously. African Americans were sharply critical of this condescension. "Where did all of this concern for the black children of America come from?" John Lewis wrote decades later.[51] White standards of behavior on matters of race seemed more important than black complaints.

As Beverly Briley shuttled between parleys with the NCLC and downtown businessmen, trying to maintain "the uneasy truce" that temporarily halted demonstrations after the May 10 debacle, dread pervaded the city. Above all, there was an insistence that "Nashville 'must not become another Birmingham.'" The students voted to continue demonstrating against the wishes of both the NCLC and the white leadership. On May 13, when the marchers took a different route after completing their demonstrations, they were "attacked by white parties and many retaliated." The situation quickly degenerated into "several fights" and "one pitched battle" as the mayhem "surged perilously close to the riot stage." Police arrested two hundred fifty people during the chaos, both black and white, as some African Americans chanted "take us too." Trash cans flew through the air with "large rocks and boards"; as windows shattered, both blacks and whites threw glass shards at each other. As dusk came, a reporter wrote of fighting that "surged across the street, stalling traffic" as "in the eerie glare of headlights, fist-swinging forms darted across the street." After chasing the remnants of the demonstrators back into black neighborhoods, the assailants contented themselves by heaving assorted objects at the backs of those fleeing, "driving police and newsman behind parked patrol cars," while "rocks, short of their marks, began thudding against police vehicles."[52]

It was another bad night, by any criteria. Because of the violence and their sense that Briley was "doing as much as any mayor in the South can do," the students relented. Faced with a blunt warning from Metz Rollins that "we're sitting on top of a racial powder keg," Lewis reported that the students, "in order to show our faith, to purge ourselves of our sins . . . called off the demonstrations for the night." Kelly Miller Smith, trying to disassociate the NCLC from the melee, released a statement to "condemn the recent attacks by white ruffians" and "likewise condemn the retaliatory acts by a few undisciplined demonstrators and non-demonstrating spectators." The atmosphere was so tense that the NCLC decided that venerable First Baptist could no longer be the staging ground for protests—it had become too conspicuous a target for retaliation.[53]

As racial turmoil swirled within Nashville and across the South, whites wrestled with what it all meant. On May 19, First Presbyterian minister Walter Courtenay stepped to his pulpit to deliver a measured yet agonized sermon on race. Given his frankness, and the fact that parishioners circulated a reprint of the sermon attesting that the white minister spoke their own thoughts, his speech is worth pausing on. Courtenay opened by confessing that he was raised on segregation "by inclination, conditioning, and choice" although hastening to add that he had "never intentionally been discourteous" to blacks nor "abused them" or "taken advantage of them." But with racial disturbances convulsing Nashville and Birmingham, he had begun to question his own thinking, even when his thoughts led him to places "contrary to your nature and your history." His realization was that "hound-like I have followed my prejudices across the years," which meant that he "read pretty much only that which supported my prejudices" and "unconsciously judged the black race by its worst, not by its best, nay, not even by an honest average." This led him to condemn the Christian church's role in aiding and abetting slavery, "the blackest chapter in the Church's long history."

Yet Courtenay also fell back on a classic moderate ploy by equating injustices on both side of the color line. While opposing the use of "hoses," "dogs," and "clubs" against demonstrators, he likewise was appalled by the use of children in demonstrations being used as "pawns of advantage" by adults. (He said nothing about what the use of hoses against those children said about southern racial custom.) While fully crediting the black race for their religious beliefs and racial uplift since

Reconstruction, he was careful to divide blacks by class, suggesting that only "their best" (which he termed "a small group") deserved the full ability to participate in American life.

Traces of racial superstitions preoccupied the preacher. Among slavery's evils was that ensuing generations intermingled white, African, and Native American blood and, "with that mixture," the minister professed, "came the amalgamation of the worst and the best, including the diseases, the superstitions and the fears of their ancient homelands." Indeed, with reference to African Americans, "The mystery of the jungle still remains in them, its rhythm and its haunting tendencies" and Courtenay proposed that the jungle setting of Africa, and "the languid ways of the tropics," made for an uneven adaptation to present-day America. The connection between land, history, and culture remained ever-present in the white mind.

With these caveats, Courtenay spelled out where he now stood. He allowed that he appreciated the African American desire for equal rights in public accommodations. Nor could he preclude voting rights for African Americans, especially in reasoning that "eighty percent" of white voters were not worthy of the franchise and yet still could vote. He acknowledged that blacks had the right to boycott but stressed that to "invade" and "disrupt" a business was a far different matter. On a more visceral level, however, he found himself "resenting being pushed, shoved, and coerced into a position of acquiescence" and "I dislike people trying to cram their opinions down my throat even though their opinions are justified." With regard to the demonstrations, he argued that no one had the right to "disrupt the business and tranquility of a community," for resolving such turmoil was "the business of the American courtroom." More searchingly, he admitted, "I cannot understand their wanting to be where they are not wanted." He noted that he was not a member of the Rotary Club nor recognized as a minister in other denominations. Nonetheless, "I do not feel discriminated against." Further, "I believe that groups have a right to privacy, to admit whom they desire. I believe there is nothing basically wrong with a whole white church, a wholly Negro church, or a wholly Indian church. I do not see that integration as such solves social problems or advances the cause of race relations."

His conclusion, then, was that "what is needed from both sides" was simply "more reasonableness, more common sense, more courtesy and appreciation, more conversations, patience and fairness." Furthermore "the lawless and those related most closely socially and intellectually on the lower side of both races should not be permitted to create situations that dishonor our country and alter our image abroad injuriously." He closed the sermon with a reference to Acts 8:26–29, an account of an Ethiopian eunuch converted to Christianity by St. Philip the Evangelist, as a lesson for interracial conversation and understanding. "My plea this day," he ended, "is for an end to those words and ways that make us play into the hands of communists and a following of those ways that place all of us, black and white, in the hands and under the guidance of Christ."[54]

Thus the white attitude in 1963 Nashville, besieged by doubts and yet able to bend only a certain amount against generations of calcified racial belief. Courtenay's speech was revealing because his growing awareness of the wrongs embedded in southern racial custom was counterbalanced with his dismay at movement demonstrations. Overwhelmed by racial change, he fell back on a belief in the color neutrality of the law and a moral equivalency between racial injustices that tried to equate white and black experiences (while distancing from lower classes). The etiquette of racial demonstrations, while peeling away at white consciences, was also overwhelming the message of brotherhood. It prompted in the white mind a false and limited logic that allowed rights for black individuals but not for the race. And it mimicked the mental contortions of the Jim Crow era where every shift allowing for some dimension of equal treatment only reforged white defenses of racial privilege simultaneously.

Despite the outcry over demonstrations, the sad reality was that violence led to results. A temporary Metropolitan Human Relations Committee (MHRC) was established on May 16, prompted by the disarray. Rumors of a "tentative agreement" that had downtown businesses giving up resistance stirred. One account said that, "they will relax the racial barriers if they can do it in an atmosphere of calm. For economic reasons they have refused to drop the barriers while tension is high." Mayor Briley later recounted the extent of his diplomacy, which started by calling "all the bank presidents and the business community leaders who were high level" and saying "boys, we've got a problem and we might as well look into it right now." In contrast, he characterized his comments to black leaders as indicating that "I wanted to help them but that we were going to have to do it peacefully." When faced with resistance from a few businessmen, Briley asked them, "which way do you want to bankrupt? If you don't let the blacks eat, they're going to fight. If you do, you may lose your business, I don't know." By enlisting bankers, Briley brought more pressure on the restaurants to avoid bankruptcy. When the owners responded that, "they'd just about decided to let the blacks in but they were afraid that they'd be flooded by blacks right off," Briley said he would get black leadership to avoid this situation. It had little to do with racial morality, Briley asserted: "that's what I call damn good sense."[55]

The *Tennessean* supported Briley and the MHRC by citing other cities with similar organizations, claiming that "the committee approach to progress in race relations is one of reason, freedom from violence." The newspaper also took pride in Nashville's example by casting a disapproving eye toward Tuscaloosa, where

"Gov. George Wallace continued to breathe heat and defiance yesterday" in denying a black student entry into the University of Alabama. "There is not so much difference in the cultural backgrounds of Tennessee and of Alabama," remarked the newspaper, "the difference is in leadership." In criticizing Wallace, the *Tennessean* implicitly praised local whites by stressing that their counterparts in Alabama "have not yet tempered their emotions with feelings of justice, honesty and morality."[56]

The MHRC proved to have real clout. No fewer than six local bank presidents joined the panel, which was led by a former head of the Nashville Bar Association. The urgency from President Kennedy's planned visit at month's end prompted the business community to become involved directly. With this economic and political influence behind the MHRC, black leaders kept up the pressure, emphasizing that "the situation is urgent. The Negro community is extremely restless." Results accrued rapidly. On June 11, there was an announcement that a "majority" of downtown hotels and restaurants, pushed by the Nashville Hotel-Motel Association, would "voluntarily" desegregate. Herman Long, a member of the MHRC, spread the news that Memphis and Knoxville hotels were also desegregating. Soon reports surfaced that the most stubborn downtown stores, including B&W, Cross-Keys, and Wilson-Quick, had agreed that "limited numbers of Negro couples, for the time being, be invited in during certain hours each day."[57]

Among these incremental changes, however, everyday whites seemed to be hardening in their beliefs. This was represented particularly in letters to Nashville representative Richard Fulton as the U.S. Congress discussed a possible civil rights bill. The letters followed a standard pattern: a disclaimer discussing the author's general racial attitudes, followed by an opinion on current racial events. One correspondent, for example, "considered [him]self a liberal in regard to civil rights" due to his support for the *Brown* decision and his "sympathy for the educated Negro" (although the caveat implied a lack of sympathy for poorer blacks). But this relative permissiveness clashed with the deeper belief that "the stupid concept that people are equal in social standing in any community is utterly ridiculous, as every thinking man should know." As such, the author felt "that the philosophy that you're going to get something for nothing is what is inspiring the racial unrest in our country today." The problem was twofold, that "blacks don't want equal responsibilities along with equal rights" and that white Americans were "not solely responsible for the economic, social and political plight of the American negro. There are too many facts to the contrary." The proposed solution, destroying the freedom of association, was like "burning down the barn to kill the rats."[58]

Another letter writer professed that "I am most familiar with the Negro . . . I have no objection to their self-improvement and ambitions for better living conditions." But he went on to say that "we whites are not going to have our neighborhoods pulled down to the common nigger level," which again emphasized a preoccupation not just with race, but racialized class distinctions. After reciting a list of typical clichés about black barbarity, he asserted that "no one could convince me that the white man doesn't have the right to live by himself" and lamented "why is the white man so bad?" Still another white Nashvillian who declared himself "strong for civil rights" nonetheless expressed resentment at the idea that the federal government "*will discriminate in favor of those who have been discriminated against.*" The very idea "horrifies me," wrote the citizen, "and in my opinion is completely indefensible." While acknowledging the "keg of dynamite" in the racial situation, he fretted more about "legislation [that] will infringe our truly basic liberties, rights and freedoms."[59]

Regardless of the starting point, the attitudes of these authors converged as African Americans threatened to come into closer proximity. Whether garbed in philosophical, political, social, or economic beliefs, these whites saw little connection between their worlds and black worlds and had a consuming fear that minority rights would overturn majority power. The contradiction is that the fears barely matched racial reality, as a comprehensive report compiled by the TCHR showed. In documenting the extent to which segregation in Nashville remained intact, the report asserted three key conclusions. First, "progress in desegregation is achieved in direct ratio to the pressure exerted by the Negro communities" and required "active white support." Second, the report observed that another critical factor facilitating desegregation was the federal government and conversely desegregation was "increasingly difficult where it is clearly a matter of private or local determination." Third, and above all else, the report stressed that, for all the successes in Nashville, the only sustainable conclusion, manifested "with extreme clarity," was that integration was "still only token."[60]

These conclusions were borne out by Nashville's uneven desegregation patterns. The exhaustive survey showed that only thirteen of over fifty hotels and thirteen of seventeen motels in Nashville welcomed blacks. The Nashville Symphony, Cheekwood Botanical Gardens, and the Grand Ole Opry were open to black patrons while the Montague drive-in movie theater remained closed to blacks. For local teachers, there was "no possibility of staff integration for 1963–64." Among the restaurants, "most of the large downtown" ones had desegregated. Hold-outs persisted in the suburban and upper-class West End and included Morrison's and Cross-Keys, B&W in Green Hills, and the Belle Meade Buffet, even though the first two had downtown locations that had desegregated. Golf courses and public parks had been accessible to blacks for some years (thanks to a Looby lawsuit), but pools remained an issue. Although reopened with some fanfare by Briley, they only allowed "desegregated classes for children under twelve. Otherwise the pools are closed to all." White alarm about racial miscegenation still dominated white practices for places where intimacy might be present. Similar uneven examples occurred in hospitals; although Vanderbilt University and St. Thomas Catholic Hospitals had unevenly desegregated, the birthing and maternity wards remained generally separated by color and also permitted black nurses and technicians, but not black doctors. (In the meantime, both patients and nurses remained segregated at Nashville General and Madison Hospitals.) In matters of spirituality, Unitarian, Brookmeade Congregational, and all the local Roman Catholic churches, as well as the three synagogues, "have all opened their doors" to black worshipers. Yet most other churches maintained racial distinctions by "receiv[ing] Negroes as guests only," including Christ Church Episcopal, First Baptist, Downtown Presbyterian, Westminster Presbyterian, West End Methodist, Belmont Methodist, McKendree Methodist, First Lutheran, and the Evangelical and Reformed church.[61] In sum, African Americans were nominally being desegregated into the city as citizens, taxpayers, and patrons, but not as fellow human beings. The southern mix of intimacy and status still held true: whites could accept black nurses more easily than black teachers, and they would not stand as equals next to blacks before God, no matter how politely African Americans were welcomed into church.

An altogether sunnier portrayal came from the *Tennessean* two months later, which began with "this is a story of progress—in the area of race, in the city of Nashville." The article deservedly credited the MHRC for the motel and hotel desegregation and also cited some employment of African Americans in department stores and insurance companies. It smoothly glossed over the swimming pool situation, quoting the Metro park board as having to deal with only "one small incident and it was settled around the conference table." No mention was made of the caveats for pool attendance; instead the newspaper wrote airily that now "private pools and lakes" were being used "for recreational swimming." The *Tennessean* also quoted business managers as claiming that desegregation was moving successfully and that the only problems derived from the "failure of the general public to accept the change" but this had not translated to a "decline in business volume." As Briley summarized, "this voluntary approach has been the key to our success, and we feel it's the only way to bring about lasting accomplishments."[62]

Thus the exhausting tasks in desegregating the city continued slowly. By pressuring larger hotels and restaurants, especially those central to Nashville's economy, activists hoped that "smaller ones in suburban areas" would follow suit. In this way the movement hoped to expand from the downtown outward and across the broader spectrum of segregated life. Isolated pickets tried to shame specific establishments when necessary. Banks and insurance companies, with their chairmen on the MHRC, moved to hire blacks. Usually professional associations, like the Hotel Motel Association or the Nashville Retail Druggists Association, ushered in desegregation. Such policies were "not compulsory on any particular member of the Association" even when "adhered to by a great number of the stores." By December 1963, the metropolitan government had joined some of these retail associations in agreeing to an official policy of hiring without discrimination.[63]

Perversely, the incremental changes were just enough to both fulfill and disrupt the movement by mid-1963 and well into 1964. One white observer noted that the white business elite was happy to presume that professing openness to hiring blacks equated to equal access to jobs; "they do not see the underlying problem of poverty." Disarray now reigned as "progress to a totally 'Open City' has almost ground to a complete halt."[64] Activism in Nashville now began to show increased splintering along racial and class lines. Organizationally, dissent over continued attempts at boycotting persisted. Some tried to dispel the notion that "the NAACP and the NCLC are working on opposite sides of the fence" but the best they could assert was that the NAACP "did not call the withdrawal as an organization, but it is untrue to say it is opposed." Criticism of the boycott derived from the supposedly mixed message that the tactic sent; some felt that it was inappropriate given the progress spurred by the MHRC and that a citywide boycott only penalized those who desegregated, however grudgingly. The NAACP preferred to focus on issues regarding employment primarily, along with housing and hospital desegregation. The consensus seemed to be that "the piece-meal approach to race relations is no longer legitimate or workable" yet there seemed no agreement on other ways to move. As the new NCLC president Andrew White put it, "please remember that the struggle for civil rights legislation, anti-discrimination legislation, and for jobs must be one struggle, not three different struggles."[65]

As divisions widened, insularities within black factions became increasingly apparent. This was especially evident among college students. One Fisk activist, Michele Allen, saw a change arising from the 1963 sit-ins as black nationalism began gripping younger African Americans. With a small cadre of "six or seven" Fisk students as "the only ones demonstrating," she thought the struggle against black apathy and white violence made many jaded; these students were "respected" but thought of as "crazy." Nonviolent direct action seemed increasingly quaint as Allen recalled that entreaties to "bring meaning between white men and black men" would "really hypnotize" her and her comrades—"and then they would hit us." An Afro-American Student Movement conference in 1963 helped cement the trend as proponents argued that the "movement should be all black." In short, Allen identified a "groping towards blackness" at Fisk as the decade continued. These issues would remain compelling ones for African American students as the decade continued.[66]

Class divisions among blacks remained an issue, evident in public criticisms of black religious figures and leadership in general. The *Capitol City Defender*, a black newspaper, wrote scathing critiques of both "the gutter Negro" and black leaders who "build fine homes away from the masses and then, at the same time, come back to the slums and claim leadership roles." These "so-called Negro leaders give a little money to . . . charities each year, maybe one or two college scholarships, and then sit back on their laurels." Cried the *Defender*, "These folks are so busy making money that they forget their social responsibilities! There are also the respectable folk who have given up the Negro race for comfortable, middle class race-mixing." More broadly, the *Defender* asked emphatically, "We wonder sometimes where we can FIND THAT MISSING FACET IN NEGRO SOCIETY CALLED LEADERSHIP." And indeed, the dearth of leadership across Nashville was a problem. The MHRC, after its initial spurt of activity, now fell silent. The *Defender* noted, "Negroes are wondering what became of the Mayor's biracial committee" and the only response was "a blank stare or a 'no comment' answer." The NCLC's Andrew White admitted that "our mass meetings are not attracting the masses." The movement had suffered a blow when Kelly Miller Smith moved to Cleveland (where, he observed wryly, his children attended segregated schools for the first time), but Smith, unhappy in the Midwest, returned to First Baptist in January 1964. In addition to Smith and the student leaders from 1960, C. T. Vivian had moved to Chattanooga, and Claude Walker and Metz Rollins had also left. Overall, the *Defender* lamented, "It is all quiet on the Nashville front!"[67]

Yet, through it all, civic pride in Nashville persisted even as race relations soured. National media hardly helped this tendency, as in the December 1963 *Jet* magazine article that branded Nashville "the best city in the South for negroes." Other cities might have taken "bigger strides" or "gone further," said the magazine, but Nashville had the "most comprehensive and diverse integration achievements." Some local blacks scoffed at the notion, decrying the "complacency that indicates that Negroes in Nashville think they 'have it made' in the area of human dignity and progress" and pointing instead to the two black churches that remained under round-the-clock police protection. Such sentiment made little headway against Nashville's relentless boosterism. As one white liberal put it, "That's part of our trouble here in Nashville—we believe in being decent and refined and currently non-violent, but not really doing much about inequalities. We are all so *pleased* with ourselves!"[68]

Above all, a discernible lack of white religious sentiment favoring integration concerned many. *Jet*, in its Nashville profile, hit this point harder than any other:

"Most backward in racial progress are white preachers and their narrow-minded white congregations. Though there are interracial ministerial groups on the city and state levels, white ministers as in most communities generally remain aloof and seemingly untouched by the 'national disgrace' Nashville mayor Beverly Briley has asked them to help remedy. From the white churches, there is almost utter silence as a whole." Andrew White echoed this criticism, calling for renewed appeals to the three institutions that ruled Nashville: government, business, and religion. "The tragedy of church life in Nashville," said White, "is that there is little or no communication between white and Negro preachers, and white and Negro Christians." Other black ministers concurred, noting the fact that "two of the largest national denomination boards are located here and have almost no contact with the problems of the community." And, although a few members involved themselves in the local sit-in controversy, there was "no direct action on the part of either Southern Baptist or Methodist boards." Between black and white religious institutions, "officials hardly know each other."[69]

Rumblings of discontent continued on a subterranean level into spring 1964. Amid the grueling work and the dissension, there were warnings: John Lewis, in a February speech, declared that Nashville "is not yet free—not yet an open city" and was "sleeping in the midst of a revolution." Flem Otey agreed, saying "Nashville hasn't accomplished much" except for "a few motels and restaurants that would have opened anyway." Events at Vanderbilt showed mixed results. Announcements that three blacks had been offered admission as undergraduates clashed with news that a dean had pressured a white Vanderbilt student to break off her romantic relationship with a black TSU male. The couple had been seen kissing on campus, prompting "various rumors intimating personal harm to the Negro." Similarly, at Peabody, the glacial pace of change meant that the few African Americans who enrolled remained "all but invisible on campus," as they were able to eat but not room on university premises. While there was some grudging willingness to admit more blacks, there were also suggestions that "higher admission standards and rising tuition" would be limiting factors, along with proposals that each black enrollee submit to a personal interview as the administration stalled on formulating new policies for school dorms and the university pool. As the NCRC head put it, "the quiet in Nashville of the past half year has mislead many of us into believing 'great progress has been made' in intergroup relations here," but instead, "our city's present explosive situation simply shows what was already present. We were slow to see and read the danger signals. We now see hatred again in raw form in our city."[70]

The building anger found expression in late April as a new wave of sit-ins—the worst yet—rocked the city with a new spirit of defiance. The targets were the same restaurants that still refused to serve blacks. On April 27, an estimated one hundred and fifty to two hundred demonstrators, mostly young people, conducted "roving" protests at two Krystal's restaurants, one at Fifth Avenue and another at Church Street, as well as the Tic Toc. The events were marked by "several pushing incidents." Around eleven that morning, the marchers moved to Morrison's, where they "blocked the entrance, some standing on other demonstrators' shoulders" as "others moved into the street, sitting down and halting traffic, ignoring the pleas of police, whose ranks continued to swell." A fire truck entered the scene, but no hoses were aimed at the protesters. Contemptuous, the activists taunted the police, calling "bring on the dogs" although the police department had none to sic. Several arrests on West End Avenue followed, highlighted by the jailing of Lester McKinnie, local SNCC leader. The assistant chief of police claimed that McKinnie struck him in the stomach, which the TSU student found laughable: "why would I attack a policeman with him armed with a club and a half a dozen others standing around?" Isolated fights occurred and a brief "lie-in" on the jail floor continued the civil disobedience, followed by a protest at police headquarters against those "being beaten and slapped by police." Swift condemnations of the protests followed from different quarters. School superintendent William Oliver raised the possibility that charges of truancy and contributing to the delinquency of minors might be appropriate. More troubling, the NAACP issued a statement disassociating itself from the upheaval. Reporters noted that the principal at Washington Junior High, in attempting to stop his charges from participating, was "subjected to abusive action" by civil rights leaders and called "a communist." Other civil rights leaders warned not only of more demonstrations but "that the 'tempo' of the demonstrations would pick up."[71]

Police anger rose with the unruliness. Three hundred demonstrators, mostly comprised of junior high and high-schoolers, eager to "dramatize the need" for a public accommodations bill, took to the streets at 10:30 a.m. on April 28, squatting in Church Street to disrupt traffic. Lester McKinnie, apparently acceding to his attorney's advice, stayed out of the march but took the opportunity to exhort his peers before they left. "Seemingly there are certain people in Nashville who don't know why we are demonstrating," McKinnie said, dramatically indicating his own head wrapped in bandages for emphasis. "We're going to demonstrate again today whether they use billy-sticks or not." After being "apparently stunned by Monday's demonstration," newspapers recorded, the police "began marshaling forces in the face of the more serious situation." It took only ten minutes for fighting to begin and reached a zenith after Police Chief Donald Barton made an arrest at Seventh Avenue North and Church Street. This prompted the protesters to surround the police wagon, "its siren screaming unheeded," and blocking the path by "climbing on its bumpers and hoods, beating on the sides and lying in its paths." The police first responded by forming a phalanx, interlocking arms and moving outward so as to push out of the scrum. But, increasingly infuriated, they began resorting to roundhouse swinging of clubs. Although hoses were screwed into fire hydrants, calmer heads chose not to use them. "No one wants to hurt these children," one officer declared later, "but what can you do when they come bearing down on you in droves?" The "noisy downtown melee" left scores injured, including seven cops, one with cuts and another bitten on the hand. Two ambulances ushered wounded protesters to Hubbard Hospital, with several "bleeding and holding their sides and stomachs." In all, twenty injuries were treated and twelve arrests made. Reports of the disorder reached Mayor Briley and John Lewis, both of whom abandoned trips to deal with the situation.[72]

The disruption continued. Three to four hundred demonstrators flooded Morrison's on West End Avenue at noon on Wednesday, April 29, with fifty arrested. Long "human chains" snaked around the block in front of the entrance and into the streets as "traffic completely stalled." The protesters held wallets open to show their money, calling out "would you let an American citizen in?" Police fashioned a "solid wall of patrol cars" between the demonstrators and watching citizens; they also monitored black schools to arrest those trying to exhort schoolchildren to join them. At one point, a black officer turned on a colleague in anger about "the way white policemen were pitching these 12 year old Negro children into the paddy wagon." Mayor Briley took a stern line, insisting that "law and order will be preserved," and "no brutality will be tolerated on the part of anyone." He also branded the civil rights leadership "ill-advised and irresponsible." The *Tennessean* moderated Briley's view, decrying that "several times street incidents developed into near riot" as well as the "deplorable sight of police wielding billy clubs on youngsters." While agreeing that demonstrations were necessary to take "steps forward," the newspaper also pointed out that these new demonstrations lacked the adherence to nonviolence shown in 1960. The use of children, scolded the *Tennessean*, meant that there was no "clear understanding of their aims" in protesting. The newspaper called to all Nashvillians: "each should examine his own conscience as to how he can best help bring that about. Nothing should be done by anyone that is calculated to hurt rather than help Nashville find its way."[73]

The police crackdown had some effect. A total of ninety-six were arrested, as well as the first conviction from Tuesday's demonstrations for contributing to the delinquency of a minor. On April 30, brief demonstrations were held, marked mostly by a crowd of fifty blacks and fifty whites who "faced each other threateningly on the plaza of the courthouse." Attempts to rouse more blacks failed. The *Banner* reported "obvious disappointment" at a rally held at Fisk that yielded few recruits; the anonymous caller whose bomb threat sent police to end the meeting need not have bothered. Pearl High students watching activists from the windows cheered as the marchers passed the school but remained in their classrooms. White attitudes continued to be dismissive; one Chamber of Commerce official stated flatly that demonstrations "will obstruct progress toward the very goals that the demonstrators are seeking." Briley branded the demonstrations as "designed" to "turn Nashville upside down" and hinted darkly that "a conspiracy" remained behind the disorder. When one leader averred to Briley that the children left school "voluntarily," the mayor dismissed the claim, saying "we have proof to the contrary."[74]

Although reports circulated that the demonstrators were lobbying for a bill to desegregate all public accommodations in the metropolitan area, a *Tennessean* editorial noted gravely that the demonstrators provided "no clear indication of their objectives." Although the newspaper still affirmed that black rights needed redressing, it viewed the disruption of traffic as a "senseless violation of public laws which trample the rights of many and threaten the safety of all." The *Tennessean* hoped that "reason and sincerity will prevail" lest racial harmony be "shattered by the forces of extremism and obstinacy." The *Banner* took a more dismissive attitude by pointing out that the demonstrations were not "peaceful," viewing "their purpose as mysterious as their spontaneous outbreak anew, whatever or whoever triggered it." "Hardly can they incur sympathy, or attract support," the *Banner* editorialized, "on the pretext of disturbance for disturbance's sake."[75]

Violence, isolated but intense, continued unabated. Pickets on May 1 were "kicked or slugged" as their lines snaked around the intractable stores. John Lewis, assaulted in front of the Tic Toc and "bleeding from a split lip," continued directing marchers in ever-moving circles (so as to conform with city ordinances) in front of four different Krystal's, the Tic Toc, and the Arcade Grill. Some of these establishments closed; others kept guards posted. Informed of an injunction against their cohort obtained by Morrison's, one activist scoffed, "We are not going to obey anything like that. They ought to know better. I don't know what's wrong with these people." The protesters soon learned that the charge against them was a state disorderly conduct charge rather than a city ordinance for blocking traffic. The local NAACP continued to disapprove, calling the marches "unorganized and disorderly." Whites remained aghast that black children would be involved in such mayhem. White liberals tried instead to argue that such measures showed the severity of the lingering race problem. As George Barrett told his fellow members on a state human relations panel, "There is an absence of commitment by the total white population" and "rabble-rousers are beginning to gain control."[76]

The quality of the demonstrations now changed markedly, probably in no small part due to Lewis's influence in reinstilling discipline. On May 2, for example, one hundred thirty demonstrators strolled in front of Morrison's with signs in hand, stopping courteously to allow the white-only clientele to enter and exit. Only two arrests occurred as a crowd including Fisk President Stephen J. Wright watched silently. Morrison's found itself subjected to a new innovation on Sunday, May 3, as white college students and faculty descended on the establishment with a "sip-in." The tactic consisted of protesters taking tables during the cafeteria's peak hours and leisurely sipping at a drink, denying use of the table to hungry white patrons. While settling the tab, the protesters handed the cashier a card asking that the "blight of segregation" be ended as a "disgrace to our city." The sip-inners left around 5:30, in time to avoid arrest warrants sworn out against them and to see Martin Luther King address two thousand people at Fisk. The preacher reaffirmed the need for a public accommodations law, saying "It may be true that law can't make a man love me, but it can restrain him from lynching me," and "Now is the time to make Nashville an open city." Inspired, one hundred marchers, after a quick sit-in at the Tic Toc, rallied at the Davidson County courthouse.[77]

Other evidence of white support for the movement came on May 5 when four local religious figures led a march through downtown Nashville. The four (Lawrence Jones, the Fisk chaplain, and three white clergymen, Sam Dodson, Albert Siener, and Randall Falk, who were Methodist, Catholic, and Jewish, respectively) had called for a weekend of interracial services and, despite professing that fellow religious figures had responded enthusiastically to the idea, the results from that Sunday were unimpressive. Similarly troubling were later reports that Sam Dodson was being ushered out of his congregation's door due at least partially to his racial activism.[78] This march came a day after the NAACP's picket campaign against downtown sandwich shops (where Krystal's employees hurried customers out a back door before closing in response) and included one hundred and thirty participants. A prayer vigil and meeting with Mayor Briley followed as the marchers called not only for "peaceful and orderly demonstrations" but also an acknowledgment that "we can no longer satisfy the demands of our democratic society with tokenism." The marchers demanded a public accommodations ordinance and complete desegregation in all school grades and throughout Metro government, especially at Nashville General Hospital. The demonstrators also specifically called for "replacing or renovating existing swimming pools where necessary." Briley informed the marchers that his mission was to "uphold the law" and that "the community conscience is yours. I cannot speak for the community conscience." This did not faze the ministers; in fact, Falk and Dodson said they remained "pleased" with Briley's reaction. It was, the ministers said, "up to us" to stress the moral issue. The encounter, along with news that the Candyland ice cream shop—segregated for fifty years—and the Arcade's Tic Toc restaurant now agreed to serve blacks (although the Tic Toc on Church Street remained resistant) gave the day a positive contrast to the recent disorder.[79]

With discipline restored, some signs of white support, and indications of crumbling resistance from some businesses, May 7 brought joyful, nonviolent protests in front of Morrison's. As "orderly" picketing continued, thirty-six protesters, including six children, offered "no resistance and continued to sing" as they were arrested and hauled away. At Tic Toc, customers ganged up with employees to shove demonstrators out of the store. Similar behavior on both sides persisted throughout the week. Swelling numbers of protesters kept the downtown alive with protests nearly every day. Sip-ins at Morrison's continued as the restaurant's attorney, Walter C. Leaver Jr. (the same attorney who helped prosecute the 1960 lunch-counter trials) kept police busy with arrest warrants for those practicing civil disobedience. One guard posted as a screener scrutinized each customer carefully, turning some away with the admonition that "we reserve the right to refuse service to anyone." One white woman "snatched two signs from the hands of demonstrators and destroyed them" and was promptly arrested. Even attorneys Z. Alexander Looby and Avon Williams caught the fire after arguing heatedly with Judge Andrew Doyle about his lack of neutrality in court. Cited with contempt, both attorneys opted for jail rather than pay the fine. C. T. Vivian, watching from the galleries, jumped up and implored the crowd to join them. "There are a lot of people who feel the same they do," said Vivian, referring to the lawyers. "We want to go to jail too." Doyle obliged, sending Vivian to be locked up with Looby and Williams. Briley's representatives quickly went down to bail the trio out without their knowledge or permission. Marches and arrests continued amidst meetings between the NCLC and Briley, with the mayor issuing public statements calling for "vision" and "leadership." But Briley also tried to marginalize the protesters, showing on his weekly television program pictures of the protesters "with hands upraised" and commenting that this "reminded him of some fascist salute." The whole conflagration, said Briley, was "disorder bordering on riot—the sort of thing that cannot be tolerated in this community."[80]

Consternation was widespread, especially after Arthur Krock, a *New York Times* journalist, criticized Nashville's disorder in his nationally syndicated column. "There was no truce and the peace was a fitful peace," wrote Krock, noting that Nashville "had in fact more violence than many southern cities." Krock wrote of businessmen overly concerned with profits instead of morality and court injunctions needed to keep calm on the streets. The *Tennessean* and *Banner* reacted immediately with their own editorializing, the *Tennessean* particularly fretting about Nashville's national image where "negro leadership was irresponsible, where police brutality was rampant" and "where communication between the races was non-existent." The *Tennessean* continued that "Nashville needs to end useless law violations and end also needless insults to citizens who deserve respect" and that "every day that this city indulges in the false theory that everything is going to be fine, and that the crisis will disappear, it risks an explosion that can come from racial hatred."[81]

The demonstrators maintained some headway despite continued tension between adults and students; issues of disciplined adherence to nonviolent and respectful behavior remained the problem. A NCLC meeting acknowledged that "demonstrations were having some effect and should be continued." But the NCLC also noted that they "could not continue to support the students being out of school" and registered their displeasure with "the conduct of the students" as well as the "abusive use" of First Baptist. A "lack of adult leadership" was also conspicuous, while some local black groups scolded black collegians for their loose attitudes about smoking and swearing. But the strange behavior of a new cohort of student activists had benefits too, a local white supporter reported: "some strange and wonderful creatures have come into town, as SNCC workers, to aid in the campaign. Real weirdies. The only positive function they serve as far as I can see is that the merchants now consider Lester McKinnie (the local leader) an understanding reasonable soul after dealing with the Bearded Wonders." Overall, the campaign had fallen into "a pattern of attrition," Jones recorded. "I have little doubt that most of the sizable restaurants will be desegregated by Chamber of Commerce negotiations within the next two weeks, but that is still not satisfying to the Negro leadership, and the Chamber of Commerce men simply cannot recognize that this business of gratuities is not what the students or adults want."[82]

By mid-June, demonstrations downtown had quieted, as most of the restaurants that still defied integration were now "counter service hamburger places," in addition to one drugstore and one hotel. Cross-Keys and B&W had abandoned their opposition while Morrison's still fought. Belle Meade Buffet was now supposedly open to blacks but still refused to seat groups that had a large proportion of African Americans. Similarly, other places that had desegregated exhibited grudges with quiet insults, permitting students to be seated but then openly ignoring them or, as in the case of Krystal's and Chambers Steak House, overcharging them. Race hatred remained volatile; at Old Hickory beach, "more than a thousand 'wool hat' boys and their women were engaged in chasing Negroes around the beach," throwing rocks and pop bottles. The *Capitol City Defender* chuckled grimly because Metro policemen served as unlikely saviors by driving the black victims to safety (their ride had already left before the attack commenced). New reports surfaced that "several public swimming pools will be reopened and that the program for swimming instructions of children will be continued during the coming summer," while two others would open "to adults" on an "integrated basis." As for black employment opportunities, numbers were small but there was an "opening of new fields," as well as some desegregation of Nashville General Hospital's staff.[83]

Local and national events merged in the 1964 Civil Rights Act, signed into law by President Johnson on July 2, 1964, and the federal law made those restaurants that had battled desegregation for so long relent. Morrison's, Tic Toc, Krystal's, and Chamber's Charcoal House served black patrons as activists responded with magnanimity. "This is a marvelous testimony to the goodwill of the city," said NCLC minister Andrew White. "It shows the climate is ready for progressive strides toward full citizenship for all members of the community." The positive spin from the civil rights leader was not entirely borne out by reality. Three smaller operations, the Whip, Tripp's, and Burger Boy still held fast, the latter directing blacks to a "side window." Similarly, the Montague drive-in movie theater, an independent operation, still refused blacks. "We hope the defiant ones will reconsider their actions," said White, "so the community will not have any black mark."[84]

It was a historic event, a triumph—and yet also cautionary. After all the work of countless people and all the unrest that had racked the city, the Civil Rights Act swept away the more conspicuous vestiges of a segregated order. Underneath the surface, however, other changes ebbed far more slowly. White defiance remained particularly eddied in places where status and intimacy came into close contact. Hospitals continued to be particularly fraught. Tennessee's three Baptist hospitals, for example, accepted blacks for emergency-room treatment but transferred them to black hospitals as soon as possible. In 1961, these three had decided to integrate chapel services within the hospital but otherwise kept the policy intact.[85] At St. Thomas, a Catholic hospital, the pattern was somewhat different. An official hospital account claims that a black nurse employed at St. Thomas had requested to have her baby in the hospital, which was granted despite "a little grumbling here and there." Whether true or not, the isolated exception was overshadowed by a longer history of contentiousness. In late May 1963, African American Catholics had met with St. Thomas administrators urging them to desegregate. They mixed the practical and the moral in the discussion, saying that it "must occur immediately and totally before something more than just demonstrations occurred," and that "The people have waited long enough . . . they won't wait any longer." Contemporary minutes contradicting this official account suggest instead that, in 1965, a black employee requested admittance to the obstetrics unit at St. Thomas hospital, but the supervising doctor refused. This prompted her to go to a different doctor who "has boasted about bringing her in." Hospital minutes showed that other doctors were worried and "do not think that we are ready to take them in, but if they can pay we will have to admit them since we do in the other units." Equally worrisome was the hospital's consternation when black surgeon (and Tennessee state congresswoman) Dorothy Brown applied for staff privileges at the hospital, as funding requirements forbade discrimination.[86]

In 1966, the issue was still rankling black leaders. Avon Williams in particular fumed to Mayor Briley about irregularities in local hospital employment (especially among nurses), segregation in wards and restrooms, "actual meddling" into interracial "social relationships" by white supervisors, and a lack of black doctors. The latter was especially frustrating because of an agreement under which Vanderbilt medical students would intern at Hubbard Hospital, an arrangement bankrolled by Metro funds. The so-called integration of doctors flowed only in one direction.[87]

Smaller social realms showed similar enduring trends, especially in professional circles. In 1964, the Chamber of Commerce first accepted black members, including some who had been in business for over sixty years. A year later, the Nashville Dental Society narrowly denied membership to two blacks, against the approval of the board. Only in 1966 did the Nashville Bar Association resolve to include African Americans, prompted by a call from white Vanderbilt Law students. The bar had not formally blocked black lawyers from membership but, as meetings were always held at white-only country clubs, racial custom had applied the same effect. In Nashville's elite Rotary Club, where racial issues were discussed openly, not until 1969 would members even discuss the possibility of having black Rotarians. The next year, the proposal was accepted unanimously but ran into procedural issues, as Rotary bylaws stipulated quotas and required a unanimous vote for membership. Those opposing Rotary's desegregation expressed both an opinion that black candidates were not properly qualified and an aversion to socializing with African Americans when wives and children were present at functions. The result was that two black candidates were rejected for membership, which prompted a rash of resignations in protest and years of procedural bylaws being passed amid much infighting. Only in 1981 would African Americans be admitted to the Nashville Rotary Club (and it took yet another six years for women's acceptance).[88]

The same quiet resistance occurred in nonelite contexts. Local Girl Scout officials had by October 1962 eliminated the administrative apparatus that kept all-black troops in a separate district, but developments to desegregate the groups persisted informally throughout the decade. Similarly for Boy Scouts, membership campaigns had increased ranks in the early 1960s, but most individual troops remained segregated through December 1964 with black troops excluded from campsites, events, and activities. It was particularly noted that black boys who attended desegregated schools were excluded from membership. Only in mid-1965 would this change: "There was no formal announcement of integrating Negro troops into the white organization but it has been happening." At one function, "They were received courteously, too much so perhaps." Changes became apparent after that date, but summer camps remained racially separate for years.[89]

Perhaps most revealing for "the Protestant Vatican": in 1965, Kelly Miller Smith's sermon at First Baptist shared the contents of a letter that he had recently sent to H. Franklin Paschall, pastor of the "white" First Baptist church in town just five blocks away. The letter proposed that the two churches merge. They were, after all, the same denomination, and Smith exhorted his flock to think of the powerful symbolism of a racially unified church in Nashville. Weeks passed before an icy response from Paschall declined Smith's proposal, claiming that "we believe there are too few good churches in Nashville, not too many." Paschall, just four months later, would ascend to the head of the Southern Baptist Convention. In 1968, he wrote a letter to a parishioner defending segregated Baptist churches with the assertion that "for the most part, Negroes do not want to be integrated into white Baptist churches and lose their identity as Negro denominations." While the pastor was not entirely incorrect, of course, his silence about the different path that the two downtown Baptist churches might have taken was equally significant.[90]

In Nashville, the city of churches, it was just another exclusion despite "the Kingdom of God and His righteousness." As the local movement fought along parallel and only occasionally synergistic efforts, the social gradations among black Nashvillians, and the sheer number of issues at stake, made for a diverse activism that often braked rather than accelerated change. While this mix was a source of both creativity and frustration, the goal of making Nashville "an Open City"—a space free for both races to navigate through and aspire from as they wished—made only partial headway. The movement traded on student energy and generational mentalities in formalized ways much as blacks traded on class distinctions in the Jim Crow era, stressing similarities and differences as needed to move forward against white behavior and to call other African Americans to action. But this proceeded fitfully as activist tempos varied. Frequently victories were followed by lags in activism, as Smith lamented, "a period of aggression and then a period of apathy, it seems."[91] The number of battles fought—in demonstrating in Nashville streets, the wearisome backroom cajoling of politicians and businessmen, and daily interaction with whites—was arduous to sustain.

As the uneven changes in Nashville's color line showed, whites were confused and dismayed about black aggressiveness in breaking down the social distance that both races had owned for themselves during the Jim Crow era. The nature of the insistent and increasingly aggressive use of nonviolent civil disobedience ended up being redeployed by whites against the movement. As struggles in the streets reached fever pitch, whites—eager to disassociate from the frenzied visceral reactions that racial conflict often provoked—reached instead for the comfort of other values, particularly legal ones, to support their thinking. In some cases, this was seen in the quiet lobbying for laws governing public accommodations—an implicit admission that they were on immoral ground but also rhetorically a way to shift the conversation away from accusations of racism and prevent competitors from using the situation to their advantage. The white economic elite of Nashville, when it needed to in 1963, showed as in 1960 that the ability to coax people in line would always retreat to its usual hands-off attitude after the crisis had passed. Politically, the indifference was more consistent from whites; indeed black political influence came mostly in a conserving sense as Z. Alexander Looby negotiated to preserve black voting districts and maintain some black political voice. Within the context of downtown's decentralizing, political and economic space was being reshifted; African Americans would not have the pressure points that had worked in 1960.

And of course racial custom still reigned in other realms. It governed the most recalcitrant restaurant owners, certainly many companies in terms of employment opportunities, and most of all social realms. On a grassroots level, whites used the breakdown of racial etiquette to make negative assumptions about African Americans as a race rather than individuals. Even as individuals made headway in an uncertainly desegregated society, the broader system remained flexible enough to withstand more fundamental shifts. As racial custom began breaking down, whites called for the neutral arbitration of color-blind laws; as laws began to break down aspects of the segregated order, whites suggested that custom and individual preferences should still be heard. The fluidity of the racial situation found whites scrambling for new rhetorical and substantive ways to adjust to a changing order even as few found themselves able to free themselves from racial legacies. The response increasingly in Nashville, with some exception, was that whites found ways to retain distance—socially, spatially, and even in terms of shared values and the ability to converse—from the movement even as some segregated space crumbled. This tactic of distancing did not necessarily directly exclude African Americans, but it found ways not to be inclusive, and that maneuver was in its own way excluding. Thus the spirit of Jim Crow hovered over a newly evolving fusion of law and custom.

FIVE

Black Power/White Power
Militancy in Late 1960s Nashville

During an early evening in April 1967, as Jefferson Street seethed with unrest, milling groups of African American students watched and occasionally joined in as some of their peers hurled contempt at helmeted riot squads. As police lights cast ominous flickering colors over the scene, a middle-aged African American leader pleaded for calm over a borrowed bullhorn, even as a female student tried to wrest the microphone away from him. Off to one side, a police captain contented himself with an ice cream cone as he watched the adults and students arguing vehemently with each other. In one exchange, an elated black student gloated that "we are going to take over North Nashville!" The bravado prompted an older black citizen to retort, "what the hell will you do with it?"[1] Even as a new rhetoric was in the air, capturing imaginations across Nashville and indeed the nation, Black Power remained both evocative and elusive, resonating differently among diverse individuals and encompassing many gradations of belief about how to translate an ideal into reality.[2]

The above scene, and this chapter more generally, nominally centers on Black Power leader Stokely Carmichael's visit to the city in April 1967. This emphasis on an outsider suggests that, although a small cadre of Nashville students advocated this new militancy, the charismatic leadership of key Black Power figures trickled down only slowly to influence the grassroots. Most immediately, the Carmichael episode represented a broader-scale version of police repression that had constituted the daily reality for black Nashvillians for decades. But the conflicts generated by Carmichael's visit and the police response resonated in different ways for local activists, local politicos, white liberals, black students at predominantly white universities and those on black campuses, and black Nashvillians in general—each in their own way trying to move forward in a society only marginally desegregated. As the widening gaps between militant voices of both races washed away common ground for more moderate voices and past versions of interracial cooperation, social and political fragmentation in Nashville was becoming even more pronounced.

So if on an immediate level the story of Black Power's impact on Nashville is rather muted, the wider context is far more revealing. Black Power was another articulation of blacks attempting to break from the racial past, this time by rejecting the experience of integration itself. In openly advocating social and political distance from whites, and turning it into an affirmation of black identity and independence, African Americans asserted themselves as independent from whites and the slanted racial etiquette that the movement had struggled to update. Despite different rhetoric, Black Power values, which in Nashville were nurtured especially in local black universities, meant to rally against the segregated system just as in 1960. This time, however, black elites were not won over by the spirit of the youngsters, as generational outlooks between African Americans were now in open and direct conflict. And Black Power rebelliousness was judged by whites on white terms only and dealt with, in the name of community integrity and safety, in the same way. Not even patently obvious realities about segregation were permissible for blacks to verbalize openly. So, by the late 1960s, schisms that had always existed on some level loomed larger in pulling Nashvillians apart, and not just white from black (although that change was itself profound). Activists of both races now found themselves struggling through another phase of the movement, somehow different from the previous era and yet depressingly familiar.

Even as the civil rights clashes from the first part of the decade waned, a more insidious and frightening reality persisted. The Metropolitan Police Department, notoriously brutal, continued to rule Nashville streets. As early as 1964, writing to Mayor Briley, Kelly Miller Smith had voiced his fear about "lurkers" in a car outside his house but added that "I did not call the police because I, frankly, did not have the confidence that calling them would solve anything." His reluctance, Smith reminded the mayor, came from recent cases of police harassment against African Americans, including one in which officers "took three boys many miles from home and left them stranded" and another where a boy "was brutally beaten with brass knuckles and sent to the hospital. This was done for laughs, some of our people were told." None of these culprits had been disciplined, and Smith wrote simply, "Mr. Mayor, it is very unpleasant to feel that one has virtually no protection in times of danger."[3]

But Smith's understated rebuke only hinted at the issue's extent. On February 2, 1965, a male Kenyan exchange student at Fisk accompanied a white female friend to the train station. When the woman was blocked from boarding (for the "sin," one white Nashvillian wrote sarcastically, of being "seen in the presence of Negroes"), the African student protested and was assaulted by police officers and arrested. A similar situation occurred eight months later when police arrested Ralph Odour, another Kenyan exchange student at Fisk. When Odour asked for an explanation, four police officers beat him severely enough to hospitalize him for five days, and ultimately charged him with loitering, resisting arrest, and cursing. Local African Americans responded with a November 2 rally that was "one of the largest marches ever known in Nashville." The Kenyan government, disturbed by this trend, filed an official protest with the State Department.[4]

Several more grotesque incidents occurred, only some of which made the newspapers. One included the rape of a fourteen-year-old African American girl by a policeman; another came from an interrogation where a cigarette lighter was allegedly used on a victim's testicles. Officers at one jail had a euphemism for suspects "taking a ride in the elevator," where the detained would be beaten, away from witnesses, in a contained space where blood could be easily hosed clean, and the elevator had grown heavy over the years with the thick weight of continually reapplied fresh coats of paint. More commonplace were planted evidence, raids without search warrants, documented suspicions of officers participating in shakedowns and theft rings, casual adherence to legal procedure, and quieter instances of low-grade cruelty.[5] The constancy to the sickening brutality continued well into the 1970s, accompanied by nonchalance from city officials. After three black teenagers were shot during May and June 1971, Mayor Briley defended the police by saying, "Well, what do you want them to do, ask for a birth certificate?" He had previously lectured African American leaders for complaining about brutality, suggesting that this hurt police recruiting. Guilty officers were only occasionally disciplined or prosecuted. One white observer described the overall composition of the force as one-third professional, one-third "thugs," and the other third as a loose mix between the two. Fisk students agreed; one editorial referred to the typical Nashville police officer as "disguised K.K.K., who sometimes calls himself a white policeman" fond of "cracking his billy stick across our head to pacify his sadism." The accumulated resentment festered among black Nashvillians powerless against the badge and gun. Perhaps nothing else unified African Americans so powerfully, for nothing else made one feel so helpless on a basic level.[6]

No one was safe from police monitoring. Beginning in July 1965, as local and state authorities watched closely, several small Tennessee towns witnessed a series of Ku Klux Klan rallies to drum up recruits and revitalize chapters. Mayor Briley warned that "these merchants of hate are not welcome," for Nashville was a "peaceful, law-abiding community which works out its own problems among its own people." A Chamber of Commerce representative likened the KKK to "a colony of vipers," saying that "the Klan and its masquerading ilk can bring no bonafide good to a community such as ours that not only believes in democracy but practices it." Undaunted, twelve robed Klansman met on October 17, 1965, at a gas station on Nolensville Road. About fifty of the five hundred bystanders applauded the speaker, with the rest "watching silently." The Klan leader apologized to the crowd, saying "if you expected someone to stand here and spew hate, I'm sorry you're disappointed." He then launched a barrage of insults toward Briley and President Lyndon B. Johnson and asserted that "Negroes should be back in the fields picking cotton." Yet the Klan leader also professed "more respect for Negroes than for 'that white trash that goes along with them.'" An estimated fifty to one hundred whites became members after the rally concluded.[7]

Similarly, the fading Citizens' Councils, the Mississippi-based organization formed in 1954 to protest the *Brown v. Board* decision, also tried to revive locally. Monthly council meetings, averaging about twenty-five attendees, featured an uncouth attempt at the "freedom of association" argument that white restaurant-owners had advanced in previous years. One council advocate said simply that "if a man is of another race 'you can't be a brother to him and there isn't any sense in talking about it.'" Another put it more bluntly, "we don't hate the Nigrah; we just want them to stay where they are." A reporter who attended a council meeting received a deluge of materials espousing various right-wing causes and beliefs, including a number of anti-Semitic tracts—a member helpfully explained that "the Council itself is not anti-Semitic, though some of its members are." The group formally disassociated itself with the Ku Klux Klan but one leader mused aloud that "I think it's silly of people to say they don't believe in violence, period." Former representatives from the now-defunct Tennessee Federation for Constitutional Government, the same segregationist organization that had insistently tried to make its own way in the 1950s, were active in the council. But the latter group traced the same ineffectual pattern as the TFCG in failing to gain a wider following. As one member sighed, "Nashville is the worst city in the world."[8] Although a vocal minority of hard-core segregationists remained in the city, they nonetheless viewed Nashville's climate as consistently inhospitable.

Yet behind that frustration lurked another story. The "neutralization" of the Klan, if not the council, was due mostly to police captain John Sorace, a fast-rising, Dostoyevsky-reading Brooklynite who headed the intelligence division and was described variously as "darkly handsome," "unsmiling," "cold-eyed," and as a "brainy humorless carpetbagger." His assistant, Lieutenant Bobby Hill, a naval frogman during World War II, had the distinction of being Tennessee's first black police lieutenant. In these years of racial tension, Sorace's vigilance toward black militants and white reactionaries helped his career's ascent and he had significant pull with Mayor Briley. Indeed, at one point, some of the mayor's political allies met to warn Briley about Sorace's influence and to voice concerns about illegal police spying tactics. The chance for intervention was lost, however, when Briley— who by then was struggling openly with alcoholism—revealed that he had taken to carrying a pistol. A dark paranoia seemed to grip the mayor and with him the entire city. The police had instituted a protocol that could nearly triple the on-duty force with an hour's notice and city officials were "so sure of trouble," one reporter noted, that, when an order for riot helmets was delayed, they demanded and received a temporary shipment of Michigan state police helmets instead. Local activists noticed increased levels of harassment by late 1966—at least one phone was obviously tapped and some city insiders knew about the panel truck specially fitted with lenses, microphones, and similar clandestine surveillance equipment. One Nashvillian summed up the mood after being invited to a meeting of leftist groups in 1968; he wrote nervously that "I have a hesitation to attend for fear of being a marked man by the local police and the spying eyes of the local power structure." The worried citizen referred specifically to Sorace, calling him "a man of violence and the strong-arm man of the Mayor" and a "bully of the town whom all seem to fear, even the individual police officer." The troubled author noted that Sorace "appears anxious to provoke a riot and then a massacre."[9]

The writer's anxiety derived from an April 1967 incident that started innocently enough with IMPACT, a student-run lecture series at Vanderbilt that hosted prominent speakers on contemporary issues. This year's slate featured, among others, Beat poet Allen Ginsberg, journalist Rowland Evans, Martin Luther King Jr., Strom Thurmond (the South Carolina senator, Dixiecrat leader, and segregationist icon), and Stokely Carmichael. But Carmichael's acceptance had been formalized only six weeks before the event. Thus it was not until March 17, when publicity for the event began, that the Vanderbilt Board of Trust discovered the university would be providing a platform for a speaker who many deemed controversial. *Banner* publisher Jimmy Stahlman, still a powerful Vanderbilt trustee, was especially perturbed. Editorially, Stahlman thundered against the decision, citing Carmichael's "inflammatory appeals to violence" with "language so contemptuous as to be beyond the borderline of outright sedition." Stahlman, who took particular issue with Carmichael's frequent use of the term "honky," argued that the SNCC leader "has capitalized on the color line to engineer and exploit turmoil." Others joined the fray. The Tennessee Senate passed a resolution condemning Carmichael and his "racist poison." and, after his visit, called for deporting him to his native Trinidad. One Nashville politician pointed out that this was impossible, since Carmichael had become a U.S. citizen after his parents were naturalized— but added that otherwise he would favor the motion. The local American Legion Post 5 likewise protested, with one member saying, "We have stood against the enemy around the world and we're damned sure going to stand against it in our home town!" and "We are ready to fight any person who attempts to destroy our ideals; if we are ready, we shall neither be dead or Red!" Black Nashvillians waited to see if an African American would be barred from addressing a Vanderbilt audience, but Chancellor Alexander Heard upheld IMPACT's right to invite whomever the students wanted and he was supported with student and faculty petitions. The chancellor had convinced Harold S. Vanderbilt that withdrawing the invitation would only sully the university's reputation. Yet many remained apprehensive.[10]

Upon coming to Nashville, Carmichael stopped first at TSU and Fisk to give SNCC recruitment speeches. In both cases, university administrators formally distanced themselves from the student leader. April 8 was Vanderbilt's turn, and Carmichael's speech, commensurate with his gifted ability to talk to various audiences equally effectively, allowed listeners to hear what each wanted to hear. A learned and devastating critique of both white society and the civil rights movement, the talk was mostly a rendition of his essay written for the *Massachusetts Review*. Arguing that "blacks are defined by two forces—our blackness and our powerlessness," Carmichael proposed that only by fusing these two elements together could African Americans create some measure of racial change. He derided past forms of civil rights activism and scoffed at the unconscious paternalism of those whites supposedly sympathetic to racial progressivism yet entrapped in a white supremacist mentality. The white liberal's conception of integration, Carmichael argued, ignored that blacks had independent cultural worth; the goal instead "was to integrate the acceptable black people into the surrounding middle class white community."[11]

But Carmichael further charged that the earlier phase of the civil rights movement fed into these white pretensions by adopting the role of the "suppliant, the dependent." While the idea caricatured the movement, the accusation no doubt resonated in Nashville, where nonviolent direct action had been used so effectively before lapsing into stalemate. Said Carmichael, the early movement's aspirations were "to make the white community accessible to qualified black people" so that gradually "a few more blacks, armed with their passports, a couple of university degrees, would escape into white middle-class America and adopt the attitudes and patterns of that group and one day the Harlems and Watts stand empty— a tribute to the success of integration." This was, concluded Carmichael, in language pointed and scathing in referencing the Holocaust, "the final solution to the race problem in this country." He specifically criticized black Nashvillians and the practice of racial tokenism and patronage in local politics. With segregated Nashville neighborhoods, Carmichael noted correctly that black participation in electoral politics was necessarily constrained because "the white political machine stacks and gerrymanders the political subdivisions in the black neighborhoods, so that true voter strength is never reflected in political strength." Thus sidelined politically, black Nashvillians lacked real electoral clout and were relegated to marginalized areas in a "constant state of insurrection." Their choice was either to remain in "concentration camps," with the "only power" in their grasp being "the power to destroy," or to become "organized and powerful communities able to make constructive contributions to the total society." As Carmichael undoubtedly knew, black political influence continued to be both divided and absorbed by Nashville's rival political machines, which meant that their influence had only a meager impact on the decisions most immediately critical to black lives. As one person put it, blacks "could help a politician win," but with "no way to benefit from having done so."[12]

Carmichael's style of delivery was as important as his sharp critique. His winking insouciance, evident even in the transcript of his talk, marked a new rhetorical technique from earlier eras. He cut down viewpoints that he deemed pretentious or hypocritical, even as his rapid-fire sound bites had their own flair. With exaggerated coolness at his speech's opening, he thanked the preceding speaker, Allen Ginsberg, "who also turned me on." (Ginsberg had tried to add to the weekend's mojo by putting "a two-handed, finger-wiggling Indian hex sign" on Strom Thurmond during the senator's speech.) When interrupted midsentence by a Confederate flag unfurled from an audience balcony, Carmichael quipped, "that's all right, as long as you don't burn my churches." He taunted the *Banner*, calling it an example of "the modern day theater of the absurd," and informed the newspaper that his talk would be "on an in-tel-lect-tual level." He also turned racial stereotypes on their head, applying them to whites, when he declared that Vice President Hubert H. Humphrey's initials stood for "handkerchief head Humphrey" and snorted that "he is a yes man without answering any questions." Carmichael's sense of the dramatic was best displayed when he asked a student to say the word "constitution" for him, explaining that he could "only say a part of this word" but "when I become five-fifths I will be able to say the whole word." The blunt delivery of a new rhetoric, while calculated to play with his audience's expectations, fulfilled them simultaneously. By calling out authority figures, he tweaked white standards to skewer white hypocrisies, even as his flaunting of conventional etiquette only reinforced white delusions about proper behavior. No longer would civil rights protesters cast themselves as paragons of respectability in their neat dress and nonviolent behavior, as in the 1960s sit-ins. Here instead Carmichael played the role of swaggering wisecracker who spoke important words. The problem was that few whites would tolerate hearing them.

It was, by all accounts, one of the tamer speeches in Carmichael's repertoire.[13] But the atmosphere had been altered by the collective paranoia and later that evening events began to spiral out of control. Back in North Nashville around 7:30, just hours after Carmichael's speech, the black owner of the University Inn tavern at 1728 Jefferson Street saw a Fisk student who had given him some trouble a year ago. (The owner had accused the student of shooting at him and breaking a window at his establishment, but the subsequent lawsuit had been thrown out for lack of evidence). Unwilling to abide the youth, the proprietor had police expel the student from the premises. Later statements by city officials stressed that the student was "ejected, not arrested," although at least one student account said that the student was "thrown out and beaten by a mob of white 'cracker' cops." The police remained at the scene to assist with another problem, a soldier asleep at a table. After being awakened and presumably asked to leave, the soldier "became belligerent," prompting the officers to call in military policemen to arrest him. So far, it was a typically rowdy night as in any town with colleges or military bases nearby. But, in the meantime, the Fisk student had returned to the tavern accompanied by picketers who quickly began demonstrating outside the tavern, calling the owner an Uncle Tom for using the police. One reporter heard a "shrill-voiced Fisk co-ed," Andrea Felder, over the din "like a Greek chorus" shouting about the "cowardice of black men" who failed to stand up to police. Many or most of the demonstrators were SNCC members, which the police would have known because of their shadowing of the group, helped by a network of informants.[14]

Riot police had been on standby for two days; their nearly instant appearance at the scene had an antagonistic effect. The police claimed later that "three attempts to create an incident in other business houses earlier in the evening" proved that the picketing had been planned well in advance. Students countered instead that, with the publicity attending Carmichael's speech, the police were already on edge and "ready to pounce." The area soon became crowded with bystanders eager to see the fuss. Much of the commotion was "almost like a street party," as one student wrote, but closer to 17th Avenue and Jefferson, there was "much tension" as SNCC leaders confronted police. As groups gathered on surrounding blocks over the next hour and a half, police trigger fingers became itchier. One policeman was overheard saying that "all I needed was a machine gun to mow down these niggers."[15] The verbal abuse directed at the students was constant and ugly and, after a movie finished and released students on dates directly into the middle of the scene, often directed toward black women.

At 9 p.m., Sorace ordered additional riot squads to assemble in the area. The situation remained fluid as most of the crowd milled around loosely, but arguments were escalating. Student leaders, complaining to Sorace about the police presence, demanded that the captain "produce" the soldier from the University Inn, "because we believe you beat him." Prominent black leaders like Edwin

Mitchell, a Meharry radiologist, and Reverend James Woodruff, chaplain of Fisk's St. Anselm's Episcopal Chapel, tried to calm the crowd while convincing Sorace to withdraw the helmeted police. Some witnesses recorded that the captain agreed although, while ordering the police lights ringing the area shut off, he also made sure his men remained on the scene's outskirts. Blacks in the crowd goaded the policemen, especially trying to get the few African American officers to join the restless crowd and calling them "black honkies."[16]

But the tension would not—perhaps could not—dissipate. By this time, police in the immediate area numbered four hundred and, under Sorace's orders, blockaded the neighborhood. This fueled the crowd's resentment, as they began rocking a police car.[17] Although the exact sequence of events remains unclear, two incidents triggered chaos. Although traffic had been routed away from the area, a passing city bus, blocked by students in protest, continued to be waved through by police without regard for those in its path, supposedly because narrow streets made a detour impossible. As the police threatened student leader Leroy Wilson with arrest, he smashed the bus windshield with a brick. One police officer in civilian garb responded with a pistol shot in the air, which dissipated the energy slightly; one observer saw the crowd as almost "jovial" about the release of tension. But friction soon returned as the crowd shifted to 18th and Jefferson, screaming and spitting at the solitary officer guarding the intersection. After Sorace redeployed his forces to maintain the line, the officers were answered with stones sailing through the air. Soon a nearby telephone booth stood with its glass shattered and pitted from the onslaught. When a rock hit Edwin Mitchell in the head, it was clear that negotiations were finished. It was then that Sorace "let loose" as the scene slid into chaos. The police swarmed into the area with nightsticks, shotgun volleys, and tear gas, although the chemicals drifted back into police ranks. It was a "head whipping session," as a white student later put it.[18]

Faced with the onslaught, the crowd initially retreated to the rock wall bordering the Fisk campus but then surged forward "with a new boldness," as a *Newsweek* journalist recounted. Reports of blacks "tugging a terrified white man out of his car" and "injuring a newspaperman" made national media. Similarly, one observer saw white youths somehow break through a police barricade to shoot a black student in the neck. Police officers and FBI men later testified that SNCC members moved back and forth urging others to take part, which was confirmed by a TSU student: "some of the leaders urged the indifferent members of the group, there out of curiosity, to move to the front of the line and help their black brother fight 'Briley's Gestapo.'"[19] Some SNCC members, however, argued that they were trying to get students to calm down and go home. Although critical of the police presence, saying there was "no need for the estimated thirty riot-equipped policemen who were in the area," Mitchell later "admitted" he saw police commit "no improper acts." Other accounts differed. The *Newsweek* journalist agreed that, despite SNCC's connection with the tavern incident, the "melee never got out of hand until Sorace deployed his force." In this instance, "out of hand" included reports of police who "entered a restaurant in their attempt to capture a rock-thrower and began clubbing all of the restaurant's occupants." After pellet guns were allegedly fired—reports cited shots coming from behind the walls bounding Fisk and from the TSU women's dormitory—police broke through windows to conduct full-scale raids on both campuses. The police later disavowed any sort of dormitory raid or even the use of tear gas, although the number of sources claiming otherwise strains the department's credibility. The crowd's anger continued, "apparently without any particular target to their protest except the white policemen's presence." One participant, asked by a journalist what had set off the commotion, responded that "the white people are running our university." As the news started circulating, Jimmy Stahlman phoned Vanderbilt Chancellor Alexander Heard, who wondered aloud if "some incident could have triggered this?" Contemptuous, Stahlman responded with "your guest, Stokely Carmichael. Now reap the whirlwind," and hung up.[20]

Disarray continued over the next two days, although disproportionate media attention cast it wrongly as worse than the first night. Some suggested that the later disruptions were less a political protest against police and university administrators by this point and instead a collective response in defense of the university against intruders, including both the SNCC and police. Still, the toll of injuries and arrests mounted as periodic unrest, now centered more around TSU, crept up Jefferson Street. Six police cars responding to a reported shooting were assaulted with rocks. One account claimed that twenty-nine fires were set, and a particular act of arson on a lumber pile at a TSU construction site was apparently coordinated with "an organized effort to flood the Fire Department with false calls" and alleged gunshots at fire trucks. Sporadic havoc continued, with bullets from snipers and random acts of window breaking. Three whites were shot "but not seriously hurt" by a black youth, and one local black business was bombed by "bottles of burning kerosene," perhaps connected to growing dissension between students and the black elite. The *Tennessean* contrasted the eerie quality of the scene's decline into a tense truce as "couples out to stroll" walked through neighborhood streets while "only a few blocks away" there were "helmeted officers with sawed-off shotguns."[21]

Both Fisk and TSU "issued warnings that 'outside' influences and further violence will not be condoned" and took steps to "seal off the campuses to outsiders at night." Stahlman recorded in his personal papers a warning from TSU president W. S. Davis that the educator "had great difficulty in preventing a large segment of the student body at [TSU] from going over to the Vanderbilt campus to assault the student body there." Student groups at both schools formed posses to maintain order, which in one case resulted in SNCC members being driven from the dorms by Fisk football players. Criticized for his silence by Edwin Mitchell, Mayor Briley finally issued a call for law and order on Monday. Campus roadblocks and a negotiated withdrawal of police gradually alleviated tensions, although further negotiations were needed to free jailed students as continued diplomacy from the city's black ministers tried to quell anger in North Nashville.[22]

Police punctuated the situation by raiding a house at 1720 Jefferson Street identified as a SNCC hangout. Some nearby apartments had been previously stormed on the pretext of drug searches, with twenty-five arrested despite the fact that "no narcotics were found." At the house, the police claimed to discover Molotov cocktails with local SNCC member Andrea Felder's fingerprints on them. The problem was that the reporter tagging along with the police left momentarily to call into his editor and upon returning was presented with the bomb-making materials. Asking why these were not found in the initial search, he was told that the students must have dropped them out the window to avoid detection. He later confessed privately his hunch that the items were planted. Simultaneously, SNCC activists George Washington Ware and Earnest Stephens, returning to Nashville in a station wagon filled with SNCC literature, were pulled over and detained (Stokely had been dropped off on the edge of town before the arrest; an associate helped him dress up in African robes to assume the guise of a tribal elder in fleeing via the Nashville airport.) Details about their arrest continued to leak out over the next few days and inflame white anxiety about black conspiratorial plots. The station wagon, for example, had been rented by Reverend Woodruff and a pistol in the car was traced to a former SCLC official now working with the Deacons for Defense, a group advocating armed self-defense to protect African Americans. Sorace, however, falsely compared the Deacons as the "counterpart to the KKK white organization." Unsubstantiated reports later surfaced that the local SNCC chapter had begun "Operation Nashville" to "make the city a target for disorder"; their activities supposedly included organizing gangs and teaching black children martial arts as well as surveying white-owned businesses in North Nashville as potential targets. Also inflammatory was the news that TSU president W. S. Davis had facilitated a three-hundred-dollar honorarium for Carmichael, although a state investigation assured Governor Ellington and others that the money came from alumni donations rather than state funds.[23]

Similarly, as news of Carmichael's speeches at TSU and Fisk leaked, white Nashvillians learned that Carmichael had referenced the outcry over his Vanderbilt talk by saying to black students, "I told you so, the honkies are trying to tell you who you can listen to and who you can't." Other news accounts quoted him as saying that "this is a chance to get whitey" and "you have to go for the honkies who are keeping you in the ghettos." More quietly, some black students noted that actually Carmichael had been talking about their "frivolous activities" and their lack of political activity. That was, as one student present at the scene later told a journalist, "like slapping us in the face," and the police repression had only confirmed Carmichael's warnings. Yet whites chose to believe instead that Carmichael's racial rhetoric alone had incited and inflamed the situation.[24]

The Black Power leader ultimately responded by suing Mayor Briley and the police department; publicity over the lawsuit gave Carmichael another platform, particularly after his colleague H. Rap Brown, on the verge of becoming the head of SNCC, reiterated that Nashville would continue to be a site for SNCC organizing. But the headlines went to Carmichael as he accused Nashville police "of staging the April race riots in an attempt to assassinate him," specifically referring to police surveillance, the use of gunfire to "flush SNCC members out in the street," and the planting of Molotov cocktails at 1720 Jefferson Street. It was not mere hyperbole—neutral parties in Nashville later concluded that the Ware-Stephens search was probably illegal and that SNCC members were particularly being targeted for arrest. Carmichael took pains to articulate that "the police in Nashville started the riot; we started a rebellion." But instead the press fell over themselves questioning the always-quotable Carmichael, at one point asking him if for "assurance" that "blacks will not use their power maliciously" against whites, to which he responded simply, "you don't have any." When questioned about the use of self-defense, Carmichael said, "if [a white man] doesn't want his arm broken, then he should keep it in his pocket." But he also used his press conference to talk about the 1965 Watts riot, explaining it as a "rebellion" by people with "no other alternatives open to them." He mused aloud about a potential "coalition with poor whites" so as to "get economic strength in a country which is the richest in the world" and noted the hypocrisies of whites who feared Black Power violence even as "they drop bombs full of peace and love on Vietnam." But these ideas were overshadowed by the media's obsession with the more incendiary rhetoric of Black Power. Although SNCC's lawsuit against Briley and the MPD eventually failed, it served as a useful stage for Black Power's public relations and similarly as media fuel for white obsessions about black retribution.[25]

The Carmichael incident reverberated through the city for months, even beyond the immediate aftermath of approximately eighty arrests and thirty injuries. Even from afar, those involved in Nashville's 1960 sit-ins tried in vain to impart lessons from Carmichael's visit. James Bevel used Carmichael's own trick of subverting racial stereotypes, dismissing Carmichael as "attempting to become a white man" by advocating violence. But Bevel also criticized black apathy in Nashville, saying, "When I was in Nashville a few years ago, black people couldn't use the same restrooms as the whites. But no one would admit it. The blacks would pretend they didn't have to urinate and the whites saying they knew nothing about the problem." James Lawson, by contrast, described a wider pattern of whites and blacks deadlocked in conflict. He argued that those Black Power adherents who preached "open violence and guerilla warfare" only "alienate[d] further those who are clamoring for 'law and order' as a means of repression." The issue for Lawson was that Black Power adherents were wedded to "intangible goals," in contrast to the 1960 sit-ins, noting that the "purpose of a protest is not achieved with a sit-in alone." If society failed to return to nonviolent direct action in a climate saturated with violence, Lawson warned that the only alternative would be "making law and order the chief issue of the time"—a development that would only curtail black advancement. Kelly Miller Smith instead, years later, had a more restrained perspective, that nonviolence had been "a technique to get something done" rather than an all-encompassing philosophy for many. "I don't think the people here are more violent, I think they are a lot less nonviolent," said Smith; "There is less of a disposition to sit passively by." He added that "I still believe in nonviolence, but mostly for what it does to the individual. I believe less in its effectiveness, and I know more of its limitations."[26]

For many African American students in Nashville, there was anger and anguish at the violation of their campuses according to "the design of Stokely Carmichael." One wrote that "the riots had no purpose" and further "the university was raped and we had a great hand [in] it." A Fisk student complained instead that the University Inn incident "was a Negro problem. It should have been handled by Negroes. There was no need to call in white police to solve the problem." Others balanced specific anger at Black Power advocates who had helped roil the waters with equal bitterness about the wider social context surrounding the riots. The Nashville NAACP stated that "the tension, despair, and resentment which has been accumulating for quite a period of time in the Negro community was bound to cause some form of civil disorder." NAACP attorney Avon Williams, Z. Alexander Looby's junior partner and fellow civil rights activist, likewise said that Carmichael's "bully boys were here and they knew what he wanted," but he also castigated "the blindness of white people who have refused for months to see trouble coming." Indeed, older African Americans had as much reason to feel debased as younger students did. In the months following Carmichael's visit, black adults who lived in the area found the insurance policies on their cars, homes, and businesses canceled abruptly. Inman Otey, who had the misfortune of driving near the scene with a broken taillight, was pulled over, ordered out of his car by police, and beaten, an assault that continued at the police station after Otey insisted on knowing the charges against him. Although he was found guilty, the charges were dropped; no action was taken against the officers. Similarly, a TSU student who bore a resemblance to Stokely Carmichael was detained at gunpoint and held for four hours without being charged or allowed an attorney. Upon his release, he was told to cut his Afro so as to look less Black Power-ish. The TSU *Meter* called police brutality the "common enemy" between the "black college campus and the ghetto," noting that Fisk's location "on a high embankment" had "at one time protected them from the realities and evils of Jefferson Street.'" Fisk students concurred: the situation had "shot Negroes into reality," said one and another noted that "for the first time Fisk was identified with the black community of Nashville."[27]

Yet it was an uneasy identification. What was more significant was the near-complete rupture between the black elite and the handful of Black Power advocates. It was significant that a hastily convened meeting was the first-ever conference with representatives from the NCLC, NAACP, and the two rival black political organizations in town (the Davidson County Independent Council and Davidson County Democratic League). Less a meeting and more an argument, it was by all accounts an "abusive" exchange of views that revealed a generational power struggle. Robert Lillard derided the "group of pink and red crackpots infiltrating college students" as the assembly turned quickly into diatribe after diatribe about the incident's excesses. Edwin Mitchell, pointing out that a black student had thrown the rock that hit him, asked "how does the burning of $30,000 worth of lumber on a black campus fit into the education of Negroes?" Other speakers referred to anti-Semitic "smear sheets" that circulated among the black community and attacked black leaders, specifically Mansfield Douglas, Edwin Mitchell, and Inman Otey. Still another story referenced a black physician rushing to assist those wounded in the riot who was held up and harassed by Black Power adherents thinking he was white. A few more militant blacks left the meeting as it became clear that no serious discussion of the Black Power ethos would take place.[28]

Other examples showed similar intraracial discord. A journalist related a cocktail party exchange where Carmichael refused to rule out assistance from Communists in support of the Black Power agenda and this reluctance was a major problem for the "middle-class, college educated three button Negroes." The remark signaled the black elite's genuine distaste for leftist thinking and that they saw those radical tendencies in Carmichael. Similarly, white Fisk professor Theodore Currier, skeptical about Black Power's objectives, noticed that the militants had particular contempt for middle-class African Americans. He cited examples of black businessmen being threatened and a Fisk dean who had a rock thrown through his window.

It was known at the time that Inman Otey had an "evasive" and "generally un-cooperative" meeting with FBI agents during which, under visible "emotional strain," he voiced his worry about SNCC's new direction and the "black conspiracy" to take over Nashville. He was particularly concerned about the "increase in strangers" he saw at the meeting, along with a number of peers that he was surprised to see participating. For their part, student activists in general were contemptuous toward the Fisk and TSU administrations in "favoring bigotry because they refused to condone violence." One insisted that the riot was engineered by Nashville's leaders expressly to frighten the local black middle class. This was not necessarily paranoia considering the use of counterintelligence programs that deliberately tried to sow dissension within groups, a development that activists were dimly becoming suspicious about at the time. The same TSU student who faulted his fellow students for the unrest wrote scornfully about how black businesses would now have to "borrow money from the white banks for damage done in the name of police brutality" and warned that "the white power structure, when it tries to create Negro puppets, plays into the hands of Black Power." The student professed instead a new mentality: "we combine our class consciousness with black consciousness" to understand that the "present black leadership is out of date with our demands and grievances." While the assertion affirmed a fresh attitude associated with Black Power, fragmenting issues of race and class buried under this supposedly unifying consciousness would persist silently and latently throughout the 1960s and later.[29]

In truth, it was something in between, far from either riot or rebellion. In a broader sense, however, the disruption associated with Carmichael's lecture deepened and reinforced racial attitudes already held. Baxton Bryant, newly chosen to head the predominantly white Tennessee Council of Human Relations, was quoted as wanting "to pay my respect" to Stokely Carmichael, who "opened the window to let us see our own malignancy," as his audience responded with cheers. White student supporters of civil rights branded the weekend's events as "not coincidental, but the product of planned action" and indeed, "organized warfare by the Nashville police force, under the direction of the mayor." The group pointed especially to the "sensational headlines and the misdirected irrational accusations of the *Banner* and the *Tennessean*." A flier, circulated by anonymous sources, echoed this theme by lambasting the "lies that the white press tells us," saying instead that the riot "was a conspiracy of the white politicians to alienate us from the one leader for and of us. He is not a traitor to our cause as are many of our black 'leaders.'" Instead, "The riot was triggered by the beating of a black boy by white policemen. It was planned by white politicians so that we, the black community, would believe that Carmichael is only a troublemaker."[30]

Other white Nashvillians also reflected on what the Carmichael incident meant. The *Tennessean* defended Vanderbilt chancellor Heard for supporting Carmichael's right to speak and stressed that "it is absurd to say that Negroes . . . after listening to [Carmichael's] hate preaching for weeks—decided to riot Saturday night because Carmichael had made a formal speech in the Vanderbilt gymnasium." More to the point, the *Tennessean* noted that, "while Stokely Carmichael is a fit subject for blame, this community had better start asking how he could have had such an effect on so many hundreds of young people." In another editorial, the *Tennessean* remarked that "rather than fill the public's mind and eye with the endless number of social evils committed by the white community through the years, the city has chosen to speak only of one Big Bad Black Guy who spoke here one day." (The trend of scapegoating, it must be noted, was well-established in Nashville, despite some racial variation, with John Kasper in 1957 and James Lawson in 1960.) Similarly, national media across the nation spoke about the "bitter gospel of Black Power" and quoted blacks who warned that "there's not a young Negro in America that would not throw a rock at a policeman if you give him a chance." Contrasting the outbreak with past sit-ins in Nashville, a bystander commented that there was no deeper issue triggering this outbreak of violence: "they didn't seem to want to do anything but raise hell."[31]

Although the superficiality of this analysis was troubling, white conservatives bristled with more extreme conclusions.[32] As usual, a representative attitude came from Jimmy Stahlman, who continued airing his anger at a Vanderbilt Board of Trust meeting months later. He prefaced his remarks with a disclaimer that race had no influence on his views and that Carmichael's blackness was "of no consequence to me." As proof, the editor cited his efforts to help African Americans in Nashville—and yet his words revealed how he valued these relationships for his own benefit: "between many of them and me there exists a deep and abiding bond of personal warmth which I am privileged to enjoy." The singular issue of the Carmichael episode, to Stahlman, was the extent to which it showed the communist influence encroaching upon Nashville. With his signature colorful and rant-filled wording, Stahlman excoriated the "subversive deviltry [of] bearded beatniks who mouth cleverly designed sacrosanct shibboleths in the name of the freedoms which they are seeking to destroy." Despite taking umbrage with the widely held belief that he had backed the proposal to withdraw Carmichael's invitation, Stahlman was unable to disguise his contempt for the current Vanderbilt administration. He derided Chancellor Heard, who "debonairly approved the invitation to Carmichael and others on the rather dubious grounds of Vanderbilt's vaunted broad-mindedness." By giving Carmichael a forum, Stahlman argued, Vanderbilt had "thrown a cloak of respectability over the shoulders of this itinerant firebrand who admittedly had come to Nashville to raise hell, create trouble and preach his doctrine of 'kill and burn.'"[33]

Stahlman's ranting was consistent with the beliefs of many whites in this era. Reeking of willful ignorance and arrogance, he mingled condescension toward others and a protectiveness of Vanderbilt under a thin guise of color blindness. Although the trustees let Stahlman carry on, ultimately they ignored him. Chancellor Heard, who had the backing of the Vanderbilts and all but two of the trustees, reasserted his independence from the editor with an "implied threat of resigning."[34] Yet, in retrospect, the racial contempt and internal university politics remained almost secondary to chilling revelations about the extent to which Nashvillians lived in a virtual police state. During his military career in naval intelligence, Stahlman asserted that he had come "face to face with subversives in every category" and as such had worked hard to keep such influences out of Nashville, specifically referencing his ouster of James Dombrowski and John Kasper. But Stahlman warned that the danger was now far greater, explaining that leftists in the Southern Student Organizing Committee (SSOC), SDS, SNCC, and other groups "have successfully infiltrated several religious denominational student centers" and noted that at least one Vanderbilt professor was being watched by the authorities for similar views. Luckily, for Stahlman, the coordinated efforts of the FBI, Tennessee Bureau of Investigation, "the very excellent security division of Nashville's Metropolitan Police Department, directed by Captain John Sorace," as well as Briley, Governor Buford Ellington, the Tennessee Highway Patrol, and the navy ROTC at Vanderbilt formed an extensive network of informants and intelligence sharing.[35]

While fears about Communist influence, fervently held and argued, were undoubtedly important to Stahlman, private correspondence revealed a baser mentality. An individual had previously written the publisher with a number of wildly racist statements, including the belief that "a small segment of our American Negro is REVERTING TO HIS BARBARISTIC AND CANNABALISTIC [sic] background." Granted, the author allowed, this was "only a small percentage of our Negro population," but it served to silence other blacks that remained "fearful of expressing any condemnation of the small percentage who have gone berserk." The next day, Stahlman replied that he appreciated this "extremely sensible, truthful presentation," so much so that he "read [it] to several of the Banner's top news and editorial executives." Stahlman did temper the message slightly, writing that "what you say about the genetic and ethnic backgrounds of the Negro may have a strong basis in fact, but I would not be willing to blanket the entire Negro population by a general condemnation which would foreclose forever any hope." The blame, Stahlman believed, was with white politicians who "at every level have pandered to the Negro. They have catered to his basest instincts, they have bought his vote by relief, as they have the franchise of many whites," and Stahlman continued, "they have entrenched themselves, I am afraid forever, by the dastardly misuse of your money and mine, by the perpetual distribution of the handout to the indolent, worthless bastards." Ultimately, "the white people are going to have to live with [blacks], in their midst. . . . as best we can, in amity and accord." Yet, despite the disclaimer, Stahlman affirmed "you talk my language!"[36]

Well after the tear gas cleared, the Carmichael incident linked the political and police networks that Stahlman referenced with other perceived excesses. John Sorace helped this process, and triggered a national outcry, with bombshell testimony before the U.S. Senate's McClellan Committee, which was investigating the surge of riots across the country during the so-called "long hot summer." The policeman disclosed that Nashville SNCC activists had set up a Black Liberation school at St. Anselm's Episcopal Chapel on Fisk's campus where Reverend Woodruff pastored. The program was typical of many Freedom School curricula founded by civil rights activists across the South, which taught African American children lessons drawn from black history and culture and were taking on a nationalist flavor by this time. The schools were meant to equip youngsters with racial pride and basic learning skills in a more hospitable climate than what local schools provided. This particular liberation school had been born from the North Nashville Project, which rented a house in the middle of the Delk, one of the poorest neighborhoods in North Nashville. With support from citizens and community institutions, activists had begun to organize the area by establishing playgrounds, reading programs, and similar endeavors. They also planned to expand their work into nearby slums, including a nearby predominantly white one. As Reverend Woodruff told one journalist, "the purpose of the school is to eliminate in the minds of Negroes those structures that lead to negative thinking about themselves," by giving the children "access to their heritage and a vent for their despair."[37]

None of this mattered to panicked Nashvillians after Sorace's appearance before the McClellan Committee provided supposedly damning evidence to astonished senators. Testifying that both Leroy Wilson and Andrea Felder had worked in the Liberation School before becoming key figures in the April disturbance, he encouraged many to believe that racial turbulence and anti-American activities were being actively abetted and encouraged by the school. Sorace portrayed a web of subversives using St. Anselm's as a safe haven, citing specifically a March 23 meeting at which Diane Nash, now active in the peace movement, had shown a film supporting the anti–Vietnam War cause. Sorace's spying had also revealed links to members of the Revolutionary Action Movement, headed titularly by famed black self-defense advocate Robert F. Williams, and white leftist groups such as the Southern Conference Educational Fund (SCEF) and SSOC. The SCEF was particularly relevant because it had been associated with Communist links in decades past. The school, Sorace charged, taught "pure, unadulterated hatred" as part of a broader philosophy of "hate whitey." Equally incensing to many was Sorace's point that the Liberation School had received federal money from President Lyndon B. Johnson's Great Society programs. In private correspondence, Sorace noted that the media had misquoted him in running away with theories of conspiracy; for his part, although he allowed that the evidence was clearly circumstantial, he felt it very strong nonetheless.[38]

Revered as a national celebrity after this testimony, Sorace had a triumphant homecoming in Nashville. He received a standing ovation from the Rotary Club after delivering a speech that referenced the Liberation School as justification for increased police funding. The police department now introduced a new slogan, "support your local police," meant to rebrand the organization after April's events. Yet others who visited the Liberation School differed with Sorace's assessment, although these views gained little traction. One white Nashvillian tended to agree with the captain; aghast after his own visit to St. Anselm's, his conclusion was that the school "will inevitably lead to the children hating." His objections derived from a picture of Malcolm X displayed in the classroom, the use of lynching pictures in classroom lessons, and a teacher referring to police behavior as "Gestapo-like tactics." More rankling was the fact that all the teachers at the school were black; this, along with a recent quotation in the press that "no white child would be admitted," in his eyes violated federal law forbidding "discrimination on the basis of race." He believed that the school would only "undermine and destroy the responsible negro leadership of Nashville." But another witness, a writer for the *New Republic*, watched another class and came to more dispassionate conclusions. The curriculum included varied lessons that reenacted the Nat Turner slave rebellion, discussed armed self-defense groups including the Deacons for Defense and the California Black Panther chapters, and taught about lynchings and the 1963 Birmingham church bombing. When one child said aloud that it was "all right to have white slaves," the teacher, a Fisk student, replied that "slavery is wrong. Period. . . . Now, if you're going to learn to hate whites, then they're not wrong for hating you." When asked about possible responses to violence, one child responded with "shoot back" and another, "run and hide"; the teacher affirmed both answers as reasonable.[39] But it hardly mattered. After Sorace's public outing, the Liberation School was now a contested symbol of racial difference.

Helped by continued headlines, this symbolic importance had wider political implications after being connected to an issue that had been brewing for some time. Centered on the Metropolitan Action Commission (MAC), the controversy arose after Congress approved President Johnson's War on Poverty legislation on August 25, 1964. Nashville leaders, as always, moved eagerly in "a mad rush to get in on the 'Great Society' grab bag before the well ran dry," as one skeptic put it. That same night, the Metro Council passed an ordinance, signed by Mayor Briley a week later, readying the city for the application process. In February 1965, the first monies were released to MAC, the local agency charged with dispersing funds to appropriate programs. Over time, MAC oversaw some quiet successes, particularly institutions like the Matthew Walker Health Center and the Youth Opportunity Center in North Nashville. But publicly, the agency quickly drew complaints from all sides. As one scholarly account put it, "conflict had become the dominant characteristic" associated with MAC; it was "organizational chaos," another wrote. Despite early glowing reports from Briley, newspaper investigations in June 1965 reported instead on MAC's "duplication of services, overlapping of responsibilities, and bureaucratic inefficiency." The regional U.S. Office of Equal Opportunity (OEO) suggested that Nashville's MAC policies clashed with federal guidelines—a criticism that MAC's board voted to ignore. Others noted that this advisory board was composed mostly of affluent white Nashvillians supportive of the mayor and had an executive director who was a "political crony" of Briley's. Indeed, although MAC was supposedly an independent agency, Briley exerted a "strong informal control," particularly in having lone appointment powers. Briley insisted cleverly but disingenuously that this was the only way to keep MAC's million dollar budget "from the ward-heelers" who would "place it right in the middle of politics."[40]

Briley's power over MAC was one thing, but the question of MAC's effectiveness was equally worrisome. Kelly Miller Smith mentioned some troubling issues privately to a colleague: that blacks employed at all levels by MAC (from secretaries to assistant directors) were regularly discriminated against, that jobs intended for students in poor areas were instead being funneled to public school teachers, and that one administrator, who maintained a law practice, was being paid a full salary while working an estimated one hour per week for MAC. Smith also discussed one instance where he was notified about a meeting only after it had already started and that, when MAC head J. Paschall Davis had been accused of "paternalism" in his actions, his response was that "the child can't give directions to the parents." The combination of political intrigue and ingrained prejudice kept MAC from serving its intended audience and as a vehicle for African Americans to gain experience and clout working in city institutions. Moreover, Smith lamented the fundamental arrogance to the arrangement that was only partially racial: "when will we recognize that the poor know more about poverty than anyone else?"[41]

His critique pointed to a core issue: that Nashville's white paternalism continued to be class as well as racially based. Even two years before, citizens had complained about the War on Poverty leadership. One white liberal noted that "There is no actual involvement of the poor, and none planned. After all, the Chamber of Commerce representatives who are the Committee know what's good for people, and can't imagine why we question them." Another, Martha Ragland, saw MAC as being reduced to a "political arm of the mayor" who preferred to "defend its 'honor' against any 'federal blackjack'" than ensure that the money was used as intended. Instead, said Ragland, "the poor will continue to be poor—and if they don't like it, we will redouble the police force." The contradiction, of course, was that conservatives in Nashville readily took federal money even when insisting on local control of that money. Yet irregularities in outcomes from these federal programs were always blamed on the poor themselves. As one angry white house-wife wrote, "give-away monies never solved social ills—it adds comfort to the 'lazy bones.'"[42]

These beliefs meant that the fear conjured by Sorace's testimony about the Liberation School swept aside questions about MAC's political shenanigans. Those already inclined to skepticism about the Great Society's merits now had additional racially tinged reasons to oppose these measures. White Nashvillians were frantic about the idea that a federally funded program was breeding local leaders for racial upheaval. Nationally, too, headlines about the Liberation School wedged apart supporters and critics of the Great Society. MAC head J. Paschall Davis made the situation worse after backtracking on statements to Congress. After first saying that MAC funds had not supported the Liberation School, he later clarified that the school had been on the payroll, but that no funds had been dispersed. Then he admitted that some money had gone to the Liberation School for office supplies and routine expenses. Moreover, a bureaucratic screw-up had released the money from the regional office before Nashville had approved the expenditure. In fact, these activists had been independent of MAC; only after the students asked MAC for the use of a building did the agency invite them to apply for further funding. A local official disclosed that paying money to the school had been a "calculated risk" by agencies to "to help keep Nashville cool during the summer of 1967," but the backlash clearly proved this a political misstep.[43]

The storm of criticism meant that the school's funding was now cut, although it took up residence in a public park to continue its lessons. Nashville SNCC leader Fred Brooks, trying to clarify the school's objectives, only generated more head-lines when he argued that it was appropriate to teach children self-defense and that, "if a white man puts his hand on you, kill him before God gets the news." He also called Sorace "a white racist cracker cop." Later in November, when yanked before a Senate subcommittee hearing, Brooks continued to disavow connections between the Liberation School and the April disturbances. As senators interrogated him about SNCC's stance on violence, Brooks retorted that the Vietnam War was "not being fought on love and morality," which moved them not at all. In coming months, Brooks would be arrested for draft evasion after his suspension from TSU nullified his deferment.[44]

The national controversy forced Mayor Briley to disassociate himself from MAC as howls of outcry, particularly from James Stahlman from the pages of the *Banner*, increased. Privately, however, in a scorching letter to Briley, J. Paschall Davis chided the mayor for his subtle maneuvering, which included publicly supporting what Davis called Sorace's "certain misstatements and false impressions." Davis accused the mayor of slipping "misleading payroll information" to the *Banner* and coordinating with Senator James Eastland of Mississippi, a member of the McClellan Committee, as the Liberation School became a national political punching bag. Lamenting how he had been frozen out of Briley's confidences and referring to political "sniping behind closed doors," Briley had left Davis "holding the bag, which you also helped load, with someone else's laundry." He understood that he had committed a grave political sin: "I had turned against the man who appointed me." Ultimately, both Davis and MAC executive director William B. Davis Jr. were forced to resign from MAC as the designated fall guys after all the poor publicity. Likewise, Reverend Woodruff at St. Anselm's resigned after his bishop criticized him. More to the point, the controversy allowed Briley to publicly avow control over the program, a power that had always been his. Thus MAC persisted, even under this cloud. A later audit found that $540,000 had been misspent, prompting a rejoinder from the new MAC head that this money had been used "foolishly" but not "dishonestly." One neutral observer noted that dozens of handsome charts and figures were issued to create the appearance of effectiveness, but no money or protocol was set aside to self-evaluate MAC's programs. Fundamentally, the agency was an exercise in "public relations."[45]

The whole sordid situation concluded on an even more bizarre note after SNCC member George Washington Ware gave a talk at the Liberation School on August 21. That he had just returned from visiting communist Cuba did not endear him to the wider public, especially when he noted that "I saw a lot of good things I liked. Castro is doing a lot to try to bring his people out of oppression and build up Cuba." Dismayed by this, state representative Charles Galbreath, assisted by Jack Kershaw, the former vice chairman of the Tennessee Constitution for Federal Government, obtained a citizen's warrant and had Ware arrested for sedition. He spent a week in jail before a grand jury declined to indict him and rebuked the prosecutor for a lack of sincerity. The result prompted a long-winded missive from Kershaw about how the jurors had failed in their duties. Ware, for his part, continued calmly advocating his position, saying "nonviolence is effective only if it elicits a sympathetic response from the populace" and that "SNCC decided about 1963 it was not getting this kind of response. Then, we started changing." Ware further pointed out that "when a child dies in a Harlem hospital from malnutrition, that is violence just as real as when a kid throws a Molotov cocktail." He also stressed that "violence and nonviolence are not opposites" and that "As long as nobody bothers me, I am non-violent. But I'm certainly not going to allow myself to be beat on the head. If someone tries to attack me, I defend myself. Is that a violent action?"[46] But such nuances were lost amid the noxious climate of Nashville's racial politics.

Against these tides of white anger and black frustration, to say nothing of Black Power's separatist inclinations, white liberal organizations struggled to remain relevant in the aftermath of Carmichael's visit. Nowhere was this more apparent than in the Tennessee Council for Human Relations (TCHR). The group's story serves as an account for how social and political fracturing split interracial civil rights groups in this era as well. The TCHR had achieved some results by playing a supportive role, and occasionally a useful one, to black-led civil rights groups in the early 1960s. But internal debates had plagued the group since the mid-1960s, and there was ambivalence about how to move forward. As early as 1964, one member corresponding with national officials at the Southern Regional Council (SRC), the coordinating organization for human relations councils across the South, had bleak news. "The Nashville Council has fallen to pieces," wrote the member. There was "lots of talent it can use, if it can get some direction. And we need it worse now than in several years since all of our Negro top leadership has been stripped away, and it will take considerable time to grow up and sort some more." While some black Nashvillians had echoed this worry about the loss of black leadership as many left in previous years, some undercurrents of white paternalism may have remained in the supposed need to "grow" black leaders. This attitude would ill serve the group in a black separatist era. Moreover, the TCHR lacked its own representative leadership; the need for more members from all sectors of Nashville society was noted. Yet some also felt that not all of the existing members were "used fully." By 1967, the outlook was not much better. Although the group had "emerged somewhat from its previous apathy" due in part to the Stokely Carmichael situation, across the state younger whites and blacks preferred "more activist organizations" over the TCHR.[47]

Even before April 1967, the enormity of remaking a segregated society daunted the TCHR membership. The outgoing president, Martha Ragland, a deeply respected politico in Democratic Party circles and a sensitive appraiser of local events, confessed that "the more we get into the problem, the larger it gets." For example, "restaurants, formerly closed to Negroes, are now open. But very few Negroes can afford to eat in them." Pushing for better employment opportunities "revealed that Negroes widely lack the basic skills needed to get and hold jobs and to be promoted." And despite the Great Society's emphasis on "quality education," Ragland professed, "there are many who feel that by the time children start to school it is too late to overcome the blight caused by the deprivation of their environment," and "those who live in slums and ghettos, in the all-pervading, enervating culture of poverty simply will not have the motivation, the energy and health to take advantage of the schools, however good they might be." So the issue then became "housing and slums" which were "the toughest of all." Yet urban renewal programs yielded "cities that look better, but the poorest people to a very large extent are worse off than they were before" by being forced out of renewed and now unaffordable neighborhoods and being packed into "large complexes of barrack-type public housing that intensifies the concentration and the problems of the poor." Each symptom diagnosed missed the deeper disease of segregated legacies. It was time to "put or shut up," professed Ragland, even when working against the machinations of a "Far Right" who tried "to stop progress, economic, social, and political." She asked, "can this challenge be met?" and answered "at this point I am inclined to doubt it."[48]

Ragland's cynicism was perceptive about Nashville and more broadly, as events soon showed. She responded to a trend with long historical antecedents that was nonetheless snowballing by the late 1960s. This trend, usually rendered in shorthand as "the white backlash," comprised a number of demographic, economic, political, and social realities. In essence, the constant flood of whites to suburbs across the nation during the twentieth century had created new patterns of political and economic power in America. Expressing themselves with a rhetoric that espoused color blindness even as their actions remained color-conscious, these whites increasingly mobilized in defense of their suburbs, anxious to protect homes in white neighborhoods near white schools. With an ostensible belief in meritocracy, whites drew additional fortification for their values from counterexamples dominating the news of the day: blighted ghettos filled with the urban poor, riots in city streets, and governmental intrusiveness in a society supposedly permissive toward disgruntled and angry African Americans and insolent liberals. In this way, the white backlash fused together race- and class-conscious sentiments into an ingrained populism that responded enthusiastically to politicians who spoke to these values in promising a return to traditional values and support for "law and order." It was a unifying sentiment deeply hostile to movement endeavors.[49]

But internal bickering among liberal groups proved equally crippling. The TCHR soon found itself torn in two as a result of differences between activists like Martha Ragland and those supportive of the TCHR's executive director, Baxton

Bryant. A Methodist minister from Dallas, Texas, Bryant was a bit of a rapscallion; blustery, energetic, and outspoken, he had a special talent and penchant for championing—often loudly—the causes of "the poor and dispossessed," as he frequently referred to them. He had injected new and needed life into the moribund TCHR, which even in 1968 had a mixed bag of programs. Previous years had seen the TCHR working mostly to uphold civil rights bills through traditional methods of lobbying white leaders and back-channel diplomacy. Substantive programs included the West Tennessee Self-Help Development Corporation and "Operation Green Power," an effort to invest in black banks and businesses in Nashville. But less far-reaching ventures including circulating discussion materials on "White Racism" for community meetings and convening conferences to develop multiethnic textbooks for classroom use. While Bryant proved himself singularly able at gaining publicity—the latter not always favorable—he increasingly clashed with other TCHR members like Ragland. The problem was fundamentally how the TCHR should continue to work, and it was a pronounced difference of style between Bryant's charismatic activism and Ragland's preference for sustained organizational programming.[50]

Early indications of the problem surfaced at a meeting where Bryant asked for approval "to go to a community in the event of inaction so that the state council would be available to help organize local communities." Ragland dissented, arguing instead that the TCHR staff should try "to build, not take over" local chapters. The disagreement connected to wider debates about the TCHR's mission. The recent hiring of a consultant to increase fund-raising seemed to clash with the group's nonpartisan political stance but Ragland argued that, while the "political part could be hazardous," it was important to get people involved according to "their own level of understanding" to create more support for the TCHR. But others worried that fund-raising from white liberal elites would sacrifice the militancy needed to get things done in the current political climate. Two fundamentally different strategies for the TCHR's work were being articulated.[51]

The conflict continued as Ragland complained in correspondence with SRC officials about "state-wide complaints that Baxton is not interested in building up local chapters" and "that he 'under-cuts' local leadership." The problem, Ragland wrote, was that "he is a loner. He not only resents participation by others—he prevents it," and the result was "our city units are shambles." Higher-ups in the SRC, attuned to these rumblings from Nashville, found the problem "a quandary." While the recent annual state meeting showed Bryant's abilities, where "For the first time . . . there were more Negroes than white people there," proving both Bryant's ability to rally even the "the poorest and most militant" of blacks and the TCHR's overall strength, which was "better than it has ever been." But there was also reason for "grave misgivings about Baxton's lack of administrative concern (which Baxton openly admits)." Moreover, Bryant's "temperament" tended to see "what is at issue" as "much too important" and in response, "he takes over and bulls it through, pushing his potential constituency ahead or aside, as required." The reality, wrote an SRC official, was that both Bryant and Ragland "are so right" and both "sincerely dedicated in purpose, it bothers me greatly to have to predict that there is trouble ahead at best and that, at worst, the Tennessee Council may end in shambles."[52]

It was an astute analysis. Bryant's militancy and gung-ho approach were well-suited toward gaining vocal support but augured poorly for actually involving newly politicized individuals in activism. Ragland, for her part, was searching for new ways to influence the established political powers in a shifting climate. Neither could meet in the middle. Grateful that her misgivings had been heard, Ragland noted that she already had to "fend off alarmed board members" worried about Bryan but worried that "if I come forward with worries and warning they can easily be interpreted as 'personality clashes' with Baxton—or just plain crankiness." Still, Bryant continued his uncompromising ways. Although respectful of the TCHR's early years, he also asserted that "the passage of the civil rights bill revealed that though we were intellectually committed, emotionally some were still racists." Moreover, the new reality of racial activism meant that "the cutting edge was now action, not talk," and "only action speaks a truthful language today." This was especially true in Nashville, where, as Bryant put it, "it would be difficult to find a community that has promised more and delivered less." At best, "the official attitude of the normal community seems to be to keep promising, then evading, promising and evading in order that forces working for change can be fragmented, frustrated, [and finally] tire and go away." Referring to federal programs such as Model Cities just beginning in Nashville, Bryant charged that, even as "beautiful proposals are written with all the right social concepts for a new community" to gain federal funding and even "reactionary support," the result was the same: "the laws are implemented by racist concepts or not at all." Moreover, "the flagrant violation of the civil rights law by local, state and federal officials has bred contempt in the oppressed for all laws." The problem, Bryant wrote, was that by taking forthright action against racist practices, groups like the TCHR lost credibility with the wider white community that they were trying to reach. Similarly, militant sentiment required black leaders to avoid biracial groups lest they be branded as Uncle Toms. In the end, Bryant warned, "time may be running out on bi-racial groups." The TCHR's "efforts may have been too little and too late" as "the status quo has been changed a little, but in the meantime, the needs and demands for change have multiplied ten times."[53]

While details of what exactly happened within the TCHR during summer 1967 remain unclear, on August 5, Bryant's resignation was announced. This was followed by his rather grandiose farewell letter to the TCHR newsletter later that month suggesting that the council was less interested in "human dignity and aggressive action" and retained "loyalties to partisan factions" that threatened to keep the council as only "a public relations arm of the liberal-political establishment.[54] The broadside triggered a storm of recriminations that culminated in an October 28, 1967, board meeting that showed the schisms at full rupture. At issue was a motion, presented by Reverend Kelly Miller Smith, requesting that Bryant withdraw his resignation. The anti-Bryant faction, including Ragland, responded by lamenting that politics and personalities had become conjoined so unfortunately but accused Bryant of not incorporating local people into his TCHR work. It was also suggested that Bryant had alienated important political forces in Tennessee's cities and had feuded so much with his board of directors that a change was advisable. In Bryant's defense, supporters cited his successes in west Tennessee where he "got people to work together." Some also asserted that the conflict between Bryant was confined to Nashville, where he had "stepped on toes, maybe political toes," but that losing Bryant would not ensure the effectiveness of the next director. Nor would firing Bryant convey a positive impression to Tennesseans, argued Bryant's supporters. Although Bryant had alienated much of the political and business leadership across Tennessee, he still commanded a personal following among the grassroots.[55]

The real issue, as one member put it, was the question of "are we going to be an active group? Or just raise money and do nothing[?]" This prompted the board to debate the TCHR's mission. Immediately, Bryant's opponents lobbied in favor of the idea that the TCHR needed more participation and membership derived from "strong local councils." Said Nashvillian George Barrett, referring pointedly to Bryant: "we cannot have this kind of organization with a fire setter or stone thrower." Immediately, however, the anti-Bryant faction was attacked for its sacrifice of "principles"; as one person asked incredulously, "are we trying to raise money from the people who are putting down the Negroes?"[56]

The stormy meeting ended with the board voting decisively to ask Bryant to stay. Bryant promised to think the matter over; in the meantime, a rash of resignations from board members followed.[57] One, Martha Ragland, elaborated on her opposition to Bryant in subsequent correspondence to Leslie Dunbar, former director of the SRC and head of the Field Foundation that funded the SRC. Ragland detailed that Bryant's defenders had stressed that retaining Bryant would show African Americans that the TCHR was still a legitimate civil rights organization, which offended Ragland because it cast anyone against Bryant as inherently "anti-

Negro." Moreover, she stressed that Bryant's lone-wolf approach was dangerous. It was not only that Bryant had little "talent for involving our membership, no interest in programs, membership or broadening the financial base," but Ragland later "gradually learned that he actually opposed this kind of effort" because "his idea was that he, alone, should be 'on the cutting edge.'" She also referred to financial improprieties overseen by Bryant and gave anguished examples of how his leadership, to her, emphasized style over long-term network-building:

> When some issue came up they would call for Baxton and he would go. This pattern was reported over and over. . . . by people speaking in support of Baxton: "He came over to Knoxville and defended the Highlander School. This took real courage. This is the kind of man we need." I sat there wondering where the Knoxville CRC [Community Relations Committee] had been, why they had to call someone from Nashville and how much "courage" it took for Baxton to speak out. It just added to his impressive press clippings and re-enforced his position (and yours) that if Baxton weren't speaking out nobody would be. His loner approach keeps down participation from others. . . . he acts for people who are genuinely concerned and can feel good that 'something is really being done' (and they don't have to do it). . . . He preempts the field, charging in on every issue without consulting the local officers, calls press conferences, goes on TV, sets up meetings and then reports that he can't get the local people to do anything! He wins both ways.

She concluded that the "source of his power" was with Dunbar because of the foundation's money and "I feel dirtied because I was a party for so long trying to make it look like we were an active organization."[58]

Dunbar, in responses circulated to the aggrieved TCHR members, noted that, while Bryant was not "a saint, or even hero," the TCHR had clearly been revitalized under Bryant's leadership. Meetings now included "low-income Negroes plus a sizeable sprinkling of politicians," and Dunbar's sense of at least one member's assessment of Bryant was that, "though you still found Baxton hard to get along with, you thought he was doing a good job." More to the point, "we do not make grants to leaders, we make them to organizations."[59]

Thus fortified with his group's endorsement, Bryant opted to stay. He immediately asserted his desire to get a "'bloody nose' and "swing a few 'haymakers' once in a while." While continuing his work on behalf of the poor, Bryant also spent much of his time working for another misrepresented and persecuted group: hippies. An example was the extensive picketing campaign against the Pancake Pantry restaurant in Hillsboro Village near Vanderbilt, whose owner had refused service to patrons with long hair (saying, "We don't serve your kind. You're nothing but filth, garbage, and trash. We put stuff like you in the incinerator out back.")

Bryant's contribution included dressing up as Santa Claus and "giving candy to children entering the Pancake Pantry." When Santa also tried to enter, he was "refused admission in front of the children and cried each time he was turned away by a man who used to wait up nights as a boy for the long-haired Santa's appearance." Moreover, Bryant continued his goading by standing before the restaurant's windows to pick his nose as diners tried to ignore the crude Santa. Confrontations with the restaurant owner and police officers continued over several days and included some arrests. The ACLU declined to get involved on Bryant's behalf. News of such activities now filled the TCHR's newsletter, along with advertisements for the "Nashville Free University," which offered classes ranging from "joint rolling" and "methods of seduction" to "hunger in Tennessee" and "lead poisoning in ghetto children."[60]

For such activities, the Field Foundation both renewed and increased the TCHR's grant for 1970. Needless to say, however, Bryant continued to divide even those allied with his causes. Martha Ragland steadfastly maintained that there was "little or nothing of value" in the TCHR's activism; "everything depended entirely too much on Baxton's whims as well as his presence" and even the Pancake Pantry picket "accomplished very little." Kelly Miller Smith instead argued that, "prior to Baxton's arrival, the Council was mostly sponsoring tea parties, nice talk, and 'just responding,' usually belatedly and ineffectively, to problems after they had developed." Will D. Campbell noted that Bryant's outreach to students, "especially longhairs, at Vanderbilt," was often perceived as an "ego trip" but was "effective on crucial occasions." Even with the praise for his "flair for the dramatic," "fearlessness," and "political savvy," there were also questions about Bryant's "ability to exaggerate" and his penchant for "instant, controversial, ego-satisfying confrontations." An SRC official concluded on the basis of these opinions that Bryant was worthy of continued support but that he "should endeavor to build a broader-based constituency," and, in any event, that trying to control Bryant would be "futile and counter-productive." By March 1971, however, Bryant had resigned from his position, and a year and half later, the TCHR's funding from the Field Foundation was cut. The reasoning was that the "TCHR had become too dependent on Field."[61]

Despite Bryant's singular quirkiness, his Nashville career illustrates how the TCHR's internal dissension mirrored broader divisions in late 1960s America. The question of how to channel charismatic leadership into sustained grassroots activity was a problem that afflicted civil rights activity on both sides of the color line. Certainly Bryant's talent for influencing students and staging confrontations gave him a certain kind of cachet with younger and aggressive activists. But both Bryant and Black Power's penchant for exposing white hypocrisies, however powerfully, also obscured the nature of their own contradictions and did not always lead to rallying grassroots activity. Nor did Martha Ragland's attempts to stay connected to traditional avenues of political power while still trying to inspire participation from everyday people succeed; the TCHR could not completely divorce itself from its upper-class moderate heritage. Historian Kenneth Cmiel has remarked that the 1960s marked a shift from "civility" to "authenticity" in terms of the style that governed activism over the course of the decade. The bankruptcies of both strategies were on full display with the TCHR. So too did one leftist-inclined white citizen reflect in 1971 that his fellow white liberals had suffered not only from "apathy" but also "a sense of alienation from the processes, a sense of doubt about institutions and what they could accomplish" and that highlighted the fundamental issue.[62] That Ragland and Bryant responded to this issue in two diametrically opposed ways meant that neither path could succeed nor be reconciled, and that racial stagnation would continue.

The social conflicts drawn to the surface by Carmichael's lecture and roiled into visibility by subsequent developments also swirled around Nashville's black student population. Even among those who were often Carmichael's chief supporters, conflicted feelings remained. A few had chosen to attend predominantly white universities and, for them, race complicated the usual adjustment process that any new undergraduate experiences. The conservative climate at Vanderbilt was especially difficult for many African Americans. Because the Greek system dominated social life at the university, being excluded from fraternities and sororities meant there were few opportunities to feel socially welcomed. The situation was nominally rectified after the national black fraternity Omega Psi Phi founded a chapter at Vanderbilt in 1971. But the irony remained that, by that same year, and even with a substantial grant from the Ford Foundation to set up a black studies program, there remained only a single African American professor on campus. Some small victories occurred by the early 1970s: a Black Arts Festival was held on campus and African American students were elected as student association president and homecoming queen. But this was balanced against countless stings in a socially frigid atmosphere. As one black student put it in 1967, "White students are friendly to me in the dorm, but outside on the street it's a different thing: I cannot speak to them, they have to speak to me." The past lived on, according to the student: "Southern people look at me with the attitude that my forefathers were slaves—I can see it in their eyes."[63]

A poignant example is Vanderbilt basketball star Perry Wallace, a Nashville native who had been valedictorian at Pearl High School. There had been much rejoicing in 1968 after Wallace signed with Vanderbilt to become the first African American basketball player in the Southeastern Conference. Playing three seasons and named all-conference thanks to his aggressive rebounding, he won an appreciative five-minute standing ovation during his last game. It seemed supportive after years of brutal road games where fans chanted "We're going to lynch you" and opposing players sucker-punched him during games as fans cheered. Yet, at season's end, Wallace aired his feelings about his alma mater. He spoke publicly about being encouraged to leave University Church of Christ because his presence might harm donations to the collection plate. Despite the high-fives and nods he received across campus after basketball games, he described himself as "lonely" and had found no one willing to form substantial friendships with him. He was acutely conscious that his potential as a basketball player suffered from the low-grade constancy of stress. "It was not so much that I was treated badly," Perry concluded, "it was that I wasn't treated at all." It was, as another black student wrote, "a very subtle form of racism which results in one being simply ignored rather than the negative attention which is a part of overt racism. This subtle form entails the feeling that one's existence is not very important one way or the other to the life of the university community—that one is an active member of the community in name only."[64] Vanderbilt could and did point proudly to its black students. Embracing them as part of the university community remained a far harder effort and one not aggressively undertaken.

Many of Vanderbilt's African American students compensated by socializing at Fisk and Tennessee State functions. But this itself had its tensions. It was not unheard of for these students to feel some disdain from peers who had eschewed college or opted for Fisk or TSU. Indeed, a guide produced for Vanderbilt's incoming black freshmen by the current African American cohort warned that they would be viewed as "potential middle-class radicals who can expect either to be loved and respected by the [local] black community as true grass-roots workers and leaders" or instead "be dismissed as more high-falutin' class snobs and racial traitors." After one meeting at Fisk, Vanderbilt's African American students confided to a white sympathizer that they had criticized him sharply during the gathering so as to head off any criticism that they were "house niggers" by enrolling at Vanderbilt.[65]

The bubbling of political activism and civil disobedience in colleges and universities across the country was fermenting at Fisk and TSU in unique ways. At the former school, even as a different feel animated the campus, past legacies remained. Many saw changes in the color-conscious elitism that had characterized the school in decades past. A *New York Times* reporter visiting Fisk months after Carmichael's Vanderbilt lecture noted an "'intensified' student interest in the 'black consciousness' philosophy that is being promoted by black power-oriented civil rights organizations" and this was manifested especially in the belief that Malcolm X was "'must' reading" and that "soul music" is "most popular." Said one student, "Carl Sandburg, Bach and Beethoven are closed subjects among students now . . . we recognize that perhaps you ought to study them, but we don't really relate to them. There's no blackness there."[66]

Within this context, Nashville had been an important center for national attempts at unifying African American students, including hosting the Afro-American Student Conference on Black Nationalism meetings in 1964. Another national Black Power conference had occurred in March 1967—just weeks before Carmichael's visit. These conferences were important markers in the shift toward a Black Power consciousness. Similarly, Nashville's African American students enhanced the Black Arts Movement; Fisk alone produced author Julius Lester and poet Nikki Giovanni.[67] Yet political expression of this consciousness remained tempered. On December 8, 1969, student body president William Owen orchestrated a militant protest by overtaking a campus building and demanding that black department heads and administrators be hired. Fisk president James R. Lawson (no relation to the 1960 sit-ins leader) responded vigorously by suspending the participants, threatening force, and warning professors sympathetic to the endeavor that they could be fired. Some students retaliated against the president's actions by breaking library windows in protest; many more had little or no reaction. A similar outburst accompanied news of a massacre at Jackson State in Mississippi in May 1970 as students set fire to Livingstone Hall. Continued student outspokenness toward President Lawson continued for years.[68]

Despite these conflicts, that Owens's actions struck little chord with his peers was not entirely surprising. Nor was the fact that he criticized his peers as well as the administration. While the "mood" of black pride infused the campus, corresponding views on political consciousness and aggressiveness were much less vigorous. Fisk's SNCC chapter remained "small and doctrinaire," with only a handful of members, and for a time they were banned from campus and had to meet secretly in the chemistry building. The group's political fervency was a turn-off for many students; one student remembered being accused in public by a professor of being an "agent" for white Nashville, and her feeling, both frightened and discouraged, was that "something political on a large scale was going on that was getting really very dangerous." Yet, for all that, estimates identified only one or two dozen Fiskites as having been active in the April 1967 rebellion. Even two years later, a Fisk student wrote that the student body in general "basically supports the 'black program'" even as there were "many levels of involvement": perhaps "about ten per cent" as "the core of the revolutionaries" with "a peripheral group of about 20 percent." One Black Power advocate later recounted her frustration at a collective inability to challenge Fisk's white professors; "we were groping at the beginning . . . groping for a blackness," she concluded. Like earlier activism from the 1960s, there were "lulls . . . of apathy and non-apathy."[69]

Others saw the new consciousness as a facade. One student claimed that "they come in here black as freshmen ... but then they pledge to the sororities" and while "the Afro is in at Fisk," students "change their hair, but they don't change their minds." Another remarked on the void between "apathetic students" and "the self-righteous" black militants who "talk a hip language," noting that "if you are not hip, a black snob will not readily convert you." Some still saw Fisk as a finishing school where the latest fashion and the desire to find a marriageable partner absorbed student interest. Still others saw "apathy" and a rote routine where "dry and boring seminars" precluded creative thinking and self-growth—although this was a complaint among many university students, not only African Americans, during these years.[70]

These paradoxes at Fisk and TSU stemmed from tangled conflicts about being African American and middle-class in late 1960s Nashville. In the era of Black Power, Fisk students found themselves wrestling with old questions in new ways. Certainly their elders felt that Black Power rhetoric was just an updated version of longer black struggles. One TSU alumnus professed that his alma mater "taught black pride" in the 1950s, even though it was expressed differently; as he put it, earlier generations were more survivalist-minded and thus had to be more "subtle" in their actions. Black scholar C. Eric Lincoln noted the dilemmas of being an elite black college student in this era—of being African American in a world opening up and yet still frustrating black aspirations at every turn. He observed that the typical Fiskite "wants to make it in the world, but he does not like the kind of world that is offered to him." A local black politician affirmed the point by referring to "young Negroes in Nashville" who were "trying to find themselves in the history books, wanting to find their identity" instead of relying on old middle-class values. And a Fisk professor agreed, commenting on the tension of his students being "more aware, more community minded" and yet "security minded." Still another faculty member noted that such students were "not willing to play the same game their parents played." Another journalist, noting the contradiction of "nagging guilt" of race and class within Fisk students, quoted one as acknowledging "build[ing] up walls, imaginary and real." All told, the fading racial etiquette of the past was being replaced with new conflicts about negotiating race and class to survive in a world still shaped by race but where older strategies seemed inadequate.[71]

These social realities folded into broader arguments about Fisk, Tennessee State, American Baptist, and Meharry Medical College as powerful representations of community control. For some, historically black colleges were important as symbols of ownership and should be preserved as such, particularly since black-owned institutions were rare in Nashville (and, as time soon proved, about to become even rarer). For others, the very idea was laughable, since American Baptist for example depended wholly on the largesse of white Southern Baptists. Even Fisk's board of trustees was more than half white. Fisk students trying to articulate their identity frequently chafed under this reality. Students described the administration as "not open to new ideas," lacking "a black mentality," and "still trying to teach them to be white." The last assertion, given that the school had been established and largely sustained by white philanthropists since the Civil War, had some basis; Fisk had prided itself on its elitism and role in breeding African American leadership for decades. Yet some Fisk students were more fatalistic. One student argued that black revolution could only come from within the power structure and another noted that, with a school lacking resources, the idea was a "fantasy" for "we can't have Black Power without green power." (Similar echoes of this perspective were found with regard to Black Muslims, who were not prominent in heavily Protestant Nashville, and the first minister who arrived in mid-1969 felt some anti-Muslim sentiment. However, many local African Americans professed respect for the discipline and productivity of the Black Muslim community.)[72]

As at Fisk, tensions existed at TSU, where uncertainties racked the university at all levels and made for a conservative climate. TSU had fewer resources than Fisk or Meharry and was dependent on state funds for its survival, which meant that President W. S. Davis was in a perilous position. One observer noted that Davis was "dragging his feet out there in more ways than one, as far as racial integration is concerned," citing one white female student who enrolled at TSU for a chance to join TSU's nationally competitive track team but was "not welcomed nor encouraged." Further tension manifested itself over various hirings and firings at the school. One newly hired candidate received a letter warning him against working for "Super Tom President Davis," claiming that "we will not welcome you to Nashville to be a tool of the white man." The letter continued, "The entire town is upset about the way the politicians have controlled the affairs at [TSU] and they will treat you like 'dirt.'" Indeed, many felt that the Carmichael episode had helped the TSU administration oust more militant faculty members (often white) and replace them with more conservative teachers after quizzing prospective hires about their attitudes toward Black Power.[73]

Among the students, militant expressiveness actually predated the outbursts at Fisk. SNCC activists had some success in electing two student representatives shortly after Carmichael visited Nashville (although one would soon be expelled). But they had trouble rallying the wider campus, particularly in the spring of 1968, when James Montgomery used a shrewd parliamentary maneuver to win election as student body president over the militant candidate. The move earned the "personal plaudits" of state politicians passed on by President Davis, and Governor Buford Ellington even made Montgomery an honorary Tennessee Colonel.[74]

Militants kept up the drumbeat, however. On August 17, 1967, the TSU SNCC chapter had passed out a flier at the school's cafeteria calling for their peers to boycott course registration. In protesting the dismissal of TSU students involved in the April rebellion, SNCC saw warning signs in recent decisions to increase academic standards, out-of-state tuition costs, and dormitory fees. Along with the mandate that non-Nashvillians enrolled at TSU were required to live on campus, the author likened these events to a concentration camp patrolled by local law enforcement. "The puppet fools have taken this action to remove academic freedom and student dissent from university life," declared the SNCC flier. "The MAN initiated these moves so that he may 'morally' proceed to infiltrate our black university with his teachers and students who are more adept in perpetuating his culture than the puppets who are already here." Given that Tennessee Governor Buford Ellington had previously—and ominously—declared his unhappiness with "existing conditions" at TSU, it was understandable that SNCC would declare that "the great white fathers downtown have given the ultimatum to the administrators of this school. They've begun the conspiracy to seize total control of the puppet administrators and the entire student body."[75]

Time would suggest that these suspicions were well-founded. In 1968, a landmark court case known at the time as *Sanders v. Ellington* was filed. The lawsuit would undergo four name changes (as plaintiffs married, defendants changed, and coplaintiffs intervened) and last through six presidential administrations. Eventually known as *Geier v. Tennessee*, the case would elude resolution for thirty years.[76]

The *Geier* case addressed seemingly innocuous plans by the University of Tennessee to expand its modest branch campus in Nashville with a five million dollar building meant to be a night school for working students. This expansion, eagerly supported by the Tennessee General Assembly and the Nashville Chamber of Commerce, had by 1971 been fast-tracked through the legislative process and was poised for future growth. The problem was, as the lawsuit contended, that the expansion of UT-Nashville came in place of committing those resources to TSU, which despite its relative lack of finances was stronger academically than UT-Nashville at the time. By pumping money into UT-Nashville rather than black TSU, the lawsuit contended, higher education officials were perpetuating segregation in higher education. Of course, officials disavowed any such plans to restrict TSU's potential or retain segregation.[77]

Only the lawsuit halted these efforts for UT-Nashville to absorb TSU, but progress was still halting. Initially, the court had ruled that, while the expansion could go forward, it needed to accompany a plan to eliminate racial disparities in Tennessee universities. Attempts by the State of Tennessee to implement this decree were consistently deemed legally inadequate. As a result, a historic 1977 ruling ordered UT-Nashville to merge into TSU. It was the first time that such a post-secondary merger had been required and the first example of a predominantly white institution being ordered to incorporate into a historically black university.[78]

The *Geier* lawsuit successfully forestalled one encroachment upon a black community institution. As the 1960s gave way to the 1970s, however, other attempts to reshape the city according to white preferences would dominate the city's history, and with profound effect. But these processes were still only quietly coming to public attention by the late 1960s. More predominant was the reality that, despite the deep-rooted class and generational conflicts ever-present among black Nash-villians, white Nashville cared little for these distinctions. The Carmichael episode embodied the feeling instead that the constancy of police brutality on Nashville's streets now had a fuller and harsher manifestation. This point was confirmed in a particularly pointed insult to the black community when a plan for thousands of national guard troops to practice "riot maneuvers" on March 9, 1968, right by the Fisk campus gained publicity. In the context of recent police brutality as cops chased a murder suspect through black Nashville, and the shooting of Dan Massie, a SNCC activist left paralyzed by the event, African Americans saw the national guard plan as more of the same on a much bigger scale, and a storm of protest followed. Governor Ellington defended this decision by retorting that Martin Luther King was "training 3,000 people to start riots."[79]

Yet it was sadly portentous. On April 4, 1968, after Martin Luther King was murdered in Memphis, anger swelled in Nashville as it did across the nation. In response, "bands of students congregated on Centennial Boulevard and scattered incidents of rock and bottle throwing proceeded." This prompted four thousand national guardsmen to clamp down on the neighborhood, which, in turn, prompted sniper fire from TSU dorms. A "room-to-room search" followed, with "brutal treatment" from many who "reportedly were quite abusive in their search." There was a case of arson at TSU, but the fire department, in waiting for national guard protection, took forty-five minutes to respond. The *Meter* scolded the student body by asking, "have we avenged Dr. King's death by burning a building or rocking and sniping at law enforcers?" Aggressive watchfulness toward potential black violence continued and thus factored into triggering it. The hostile cycle of police repression and black retaliation continued to be reenacted—another reality exposing the myth of Nashville's moderation.[80]

Only three months after Stokely Carmichael spoke, the first legal interracial marriage in Tennessee took place in Nashville, a development that would have seemed unthinkable only years before.[81] But, as the 1960s closed, Nashville remained socially divided in powerful ways, and this reality included but was not confined to the color line. With Black Power a racially themed version of the generational dissent that swept through U.S. society in the 1960s, the new rebellious-ness was distasteful to many of both races. From taunts of "honky" to nose pick-ing, radicals challenged Nashville with potent political critiques and behavior that sneered at proper etiquette.

Still, Black Power's legacy in Nashville was mixed. It found itself confined mostly to black student campuses and mixed with other attitudes. Younger African Americans found themselves hungry for the fullest realization of their potential but aware of constraints imposed upon them, encumbered by less tangible racial obstacles but more conflicted about their place in a society that seemed harshly intolerant of black advancement. Indeed, for all of Black Power's rhetoric, one ac-tivist noted the pervasive reality that politically "complacency rules in Nashville," where in 1968 a grant for voter registration was returned unused, and "If any-thing the situation has worsened since then." As Black Power advocates reacted to earlier versions of the civil rights movement in attempting to reclaim some social distance, and potential political power, for African Americans, it marked a more assertive version of what blacks had done more subtly to survive Jim Crow. One account detailed how Reverend James Woodruff articulated the new dimen-sions of the age, that the past racial etiquette had consisted of "learning how to deal with the white man or manipulate so that the Negro could survive." But now everyday African Americans were rejecting their "so-called representatives" who "do not speak the true feelings of the grassroots people." Yet it was also noted that, as black Nashvillians found racial unity subsumed by issues of "race, gen-eration, and social class," it was as if they were speaking "different languages."[82] Black elites in Nashville preferred means of activism different from those of the student cohort, as they had throughout the 1960s. Black Power rhetoric sharpened the ongoing differences, both real and perceived, among different generations of Nashville's African American leaders. The psychological and personal appeal of speaking truth to power was immense; building a movement among diverse black constituencies in Nashville, each of whom viewed Black Power differently, was in-finitely harder.

A similar desire among white Nashvillians anxious to defend their institutions and power had much more of the negative and hostile views—and many more preemptive attacks—supposedly associated with Black Power. The white scorn for Black Power's separatist inclinations in a society that was already two separate worlds was just one contradiction in the white backlash, which would soon find even sharper grassroots expression. When interviewed about the ramifications of the Stokely Carmichael episode, Mayor Briley's summative point was that "they say I don't know them, but I know our niggers." It was a damning example of what had not changed.[83]

Above all, these social rifts seen in Nashville from the mid- to late-1960s were layered above more enduring changes that were about to become manifest. As whites continued to relentlessly claim racial privileges for themselves first, they drew further motivation from African Americans calling for that same control over black destinies and spaces. Born from and yet remaking Nashville's racial etiquette, the push and pull between the races continued anew. Over the next few years, such social realities would be reentrenched more firmly throughout Nashville with the forces of public policy, as socially divided Nashville found racial and class divisions reencoded in the urban landscape throughout the city.

Cruel Mockeries
Renewing a City

Just months after being assaulted with a rock to the head in North Nashville, Edwin Mitchell accepted an invitation to speak before the Nashville Chamber of Commerce in October 1967. It was a fraught moment in Nashville's racial history given changes slowly becoming visible across the city and, even at a formal event, Mitchell was not willing to mince words. He did carefully caution in his speech that he could not and would not be "speaking for the entire Negro community," nor would he "wish you to accept me as having those credentials," given the history of false communication between the races. With that disclaimer made, he proceeded to deliver a blistering lecture directly to some of the city's most powerful people about the current status of black Nashvillians.

Mitchell portrayed Nashville as a place where "super highways form concrete moats between Negro and white communities" and "huge jungles of compact housing" marked the homes of black people, whom he called "consumers of the slum rather than producers thereof." He lamented that many people looking at slum neighborhoods "see these thirty year old dilapidated and deteriorating buildings as the end result of those who reside therein, conspicuous in the man, because of their black skins, rather than as having resulted from the onslaught of time." He noted how African American elites were "driven to affluent black ghettoes" or "driven to second-hand, overpriced homes in transition neighborhoods" called "grey" but soon "all-black, with the help of certain enterprising realtors, that the term has never become popularized." He described a city tying itself to surrounding suburban Sumner and Wilson Counties with flowing expressways, labor, and tax dollars, instead of looking inward to black Nashvillians in the city center. And, in describing recent public policies that had helped shape these realities, Mitchell said: "Gentlemen, you of the Chamber, the city and state administrations endorsed this program, YOU DID NOT SPEAK FOR US!" The lack of communication embodied an immense divide, Mitchell warned "Tall buildings which allow you to gaze outward upon the green grass of suburbia cannot long shelter you from the despair, frustration and bitterness that continue to build around you. In a city that unites its governments but leaves its people divided, in a city that provides in the midst of want elegant show houses of luxuries, a cruel mockery is made. But sitting as they are in the midst of all this poverty, your businesses are just such a mockery to so many." He ended with caustic simplicity: "What brave and unthinking men you are!"[1]

One speech, no matter how emotionally searing and bleakly forthright, nor the resultant tension that hung over the ballroom as Mitchell spoke, does not carry the same inherent drama as sit-ins or demonstrations or race riots. But what he described was as fundamentally important to Nashville's racial history as the preceding events of the civil rights movement. This chapter examines how everyday Nashvillians, but particularly African Americans, found their lives and neighborhoods overturned by decisions made by bureaucrats, experts, and government officials. Although seemingly innocuous, these choices made in offices across the city, state, and nation converged to quite literally reshape Nashville's physical and social landscape. As Nashville's veteran white activist and minister William Barnes put it, speaking in 2001, "there is no way of understanding any of the problems of today when it comes to urban planning, schools, and race relations unless you know something about urban renewal . . . we are still writing checks to overcome the mistakes that were made then."[2]

Nashville's urban conditions were nothing short of grim. Well into the 1970s, city neighborhoods were mired in appalling, barely habitable squalor. Inhumane conditions persisted in houses little better than shacks, where a man froze to death during at least one frigid winter. Decades later, people recalled the wretched conditions, which included homes with "no running water, no heat, and unsafe wiring" or "leaky roofs and outdoor privies." One such house was cited for "harboring rats" and many others hosted illicit activities from "open prostitution to cockfighting to bootlegging." Some neighborhood sewers were so degraded that unknowing children played in the overflow that spilled onto city streets.[3]

In response, Nashville had witnessed a barrage of federal and local initiatives meant to alleviate lingering issues of urban decay. As early as 1959, the East Nashville urban renewal project had begun with an eye toward cleaning up the area but also linking new Ellington Parkway with the confluence of anticipated interstates that would crisscross the Upper South. A similar process had been more impactful in clearing out the slum areas around the Capitol downtown and relocating many residents to Edgehill. Then, only a few years later, the same effort began in Edgehill. By this point, wary of the urban renewal's encroaching consequences, civil rights groups had formed an initially promising coalition particularly centered on public housing. By fall 1966 the Edgehill committee was complaining about the placement of new housing projects that would aggravate residential displacement and thus reinforce segregation. The logic of the Nashville Housing Authority was that the chosen sites were cheaper than in other neighborhoods, although this attitude was criticized by a regional HUD administrator. Nonetheless, after the federal agency decided to compromise by locating some projects in the area but scattering other public housing to different areas, the effect was far less ambiguous: a net result of less housing and higher rents for those relocated as the Edgehill committee "faded out of existence" thanks to the contradiction that, as one activist put it, "HUD violated its own policies." Lawsuits tried to slow the process, but the housing authority continued its work largely unabated. As neighborhood groups pressured Metro government to enforce housing codes and deny commercial rezoning, they acknowledged that there was no court avenue open to them. It was all perfectly legal. It also meant that, as the effect multiplied across Edgehill and North Nashville, "an aspiring middle-class segment in the Negro population in Nashville is being destroyed."[4]

But this was one of many precedents adding up to a wider pattern. This chapter traces the construction of Interstate 40 through Nashville, the city's participation in the Model Cities program (a federal initiative that tried to forestall urban decay across the nation), and the ongoing dissension about local school desegregation. Taken together, these comprised distinct but interrelated issues that underscore how Nashville used local, state, and federal prerogatives to dictate how space throughout the city would be broken into distinct sectors segregated by race and class, thus setting the stage for new dimensions of political, economic, and social realities.

The story, at least in this phase of Nashville's history, began with a road. Since the 1950s, plans to place Interstate 40 diagonally across Tennessee had quietly proceeded through bureaucratic channels. Certainly the highway appealed to the city as an artery for shipping products in and out of Middle Tennessee, further enhancing Nashville's economic clout as a regional distribution center. It also would relieve local roads congested with suburbanites commuting to city jobs and pave the way to booming suburban areas already financed with attractive cultural and material incentives.

The sordid tale of how the interstate path was plotted, however, is as revealing as the effects. The initial consultation commissioned by the city recommended a path that ran eastward from Memphis along Route 70S, then hugged the Louisville & Nashville Railroad tracks for several miles before continuing directly downtown between Broadway and Charlotte Avenues (two major east–west corridors in the city). The idea was that, by widening an existing road and using the railroad path, engineers would minimize the destructive impact of constructing through Nashville's cityscape. However, this route skirted close to Belle Meade, the poshest suburb in Nashville and home to Nashville's white elite, and came precariously close to Vanderbilt, Baptist Hospital, and Centennial Park (which housed a replica of the Parthenon, a built reference to the "Athens of the South," which was a symbol of Nashville itself). As such, the State of Tennessee made a counterproposal that adjusted the interstate's route slightly north to follow Charlotte Pike, which becomes Charlotte Avenue as it nears the city. Tweaking the route in this way was sensible, as it generally followed Charlotte's path toward downtown but weaved north to avoid Centennial Park and Baptist Hospital. This path had the additional ramification of using the widened streets as physical dividers between white and black neighborhoods, a tactic frequently employed at the time in Nashville and elsewhere.[5]

During this ongoing debate, the city retained the prestigious New York planning firm of Clarke & Rapuano, which had done previous work in Nashville with the Capitol Hill redevelopment project and would soon be responsible for urban renewal endeavors in Edgehill and the now-famous Music Row, the center for Nashville's music industry. When Clarke & Rapuano entered the discussions, there was considerable urgency to select a route because all indications suggested that the federal highway legislation would soon pass. Whoever had a proposal ready would get first dibs on funding. As a result, the state proposal to build along Charlotte Pike was endorsed by Clarke & Rapuano and accepted by all. In subsequent years, however, many of the planners voiced doubt about their choice. Logistical concerns about engineering issues (including access points for local roads, interchanges, and railroad right of ways) were raised. The wisdom of threading the interstate directly downtown was also questioned, given that the interstate was meant to alleviate downtown traffic congestion although, to sweeten the deal, the state later offered to build an inner loop encircling the downtown. What happened next is murky, but somewhere between July 1955 and September 1956, a Metropolitan Planning Commission memorandum indicated that the "Memphis route" had been chosen. This new proposal was drastically different: it called for the interstate to parallel Charlotte, bend sharply north to cross 28th Avenue North and then twist again to trample over Jefferson Street, the major retail corridor in North Nashville.[6]

None of the plans nor their implications were discussed with local residents, even though the route would virtually disembowel North Nashville. This was not an exaggeration: the two-and-a-half-mile stretch of interstate would demolish a hundred square blocks, including sixteen blocks of stores along Jefferson Street that represented 80 percent of black-owned businesses in Nashville. These businesses were mostly sole-proprietor, mom-and-pop-type stores, not hugely lucra tive but stable and debt-free, if a bit "shabby," as a survey by a black businessmen's association later reported. Over a fourth had been rooted in the neighborhood for over twenty years. Certainly black businesses in Nashville had less purchasing power than white counterparts, due to their smaller size but also because of higher rents charged in black neighborhoods. Not being allowed into private clubs and trade associations because of race also constrained the professional expertise of black business owners. Despite these limits, these independent shops allowed the owners modest comfort. But that would change after the interstate carved a path that chopped many streets into dead ends and cut off access to clientele. Additionally, the demolition of approximately six hundred and fifty homes and twenty-seven apartment buildings would displace thousands of people, worsening an acute housing shortage. Even more ominously, the planned route veered squarely between TSU and the neighborhood around Fisk and Meharry Medical College. North Nashvillians now found themselves facing the prospect of being literally shepherded into segmented ghettos, "cut off on the south by the railroad, on the southeast by public housing, and on the north by the highway." It was, as one resident put it bitterly, "wretched, inhumane, illogical and an act of persecution" that "will emasculate the Negro community while leaving the white community intact." Another resident called the interstate a "visible and symbolic as well as a functional barrier" that cut off North Nashville in "physical as well as psychological" ways.[7]

Anecdotal evidence suggests that Rapuano himself, whose firm was now on the state payroll rather than the city's, formally suggested the route. The shift made sense to the planners; the logic was that the interstate's construction would usefully complement the city's desire for a new urban renewal project to rehabilitate North Nashville. At the time, using interstate construction in such a way was popular among highway advocates. One participant in Nashville's earlier urban renewal projects had posited that planners could "aim the interstate system 'like a gun, right at the heart of the slums.'" Indeed, a planning commission member reporting on the East Nashville project to the Chamber of Commerce in 1956 had said carefully that "urban renewal would make it possible to convert the highway construction into a great community asset if the construction were properly located and if the areas around the new highways were properly planned for new and better use." It was perfect in the abstract: in an act of creative destruction, Nashville could in a single stroke obtain an interstate as a blighted area was remade with new construction.[8]

The proposed urban renewal project, for reasons that remain lost to history, never occurred. (Only later a different project—the federal Model Cities initiative—revived the initiative to renew North Nashville; perversely, the disastrous effects of building the interstate helped North Nashville qualify.) City officials mulling over the plan realized that urban renewal programs required the city to pay one third of all costs, whereas the federal government paid 90 percent of interstate construction. That was easy math. But from the state's perspective, it was a bit more complicated. Routing I-40 through North Nashville was preferred because property values there were much lower than in white neighborhoods, so purchasing land for the interstate's construction would be considerably cheaper. Yet some worried that, by routing the interstate through a business district, the state faced the prospect of spending more money, because business-owners had to be reimbursed for the loss of income as well as property. Indeed, some accounts suggest that Rapuano (and perhaps the city as well) expected that black businesses would be fairly compensated as the interstate supplanted Jefferson Street. Instead, the state used an administrative sleight of hand once construction began by plotting the interstate's path just blocks north of Jefferson, gobbling up "all adjacent property right up to the rear of the businesses," as one report had it, but technically leaving them intact—albeit blocked off from the community and their customers. The interstate was being built to plow directly through the heart of North Nashville and leave the surrounding neighborhood to wither.[9]

This maneuver was doubly elegant from the state's perspective as it left the city with, as one scholar puts it, "the worst of all possible worlds." Designing the road's path in this way meant that additional costs associated with extra engineering work (such as condemning properties and widening access roads near Jefferson that would eventually connect with the interstate) now fell back on the city. Because the Jefferson Street businesses were not technically razed by the interstate construction, the state had no obligation to commit financially to any ameliorating urban renewal projects. Ultimately, the state highway department's grasp on purse strings and the ability to set the construction's "scheduling priorities" took precedence over any consideration for residents.[10]

In 1964, the state began buying land for I-40. Over the following years, some North Nashvillians voiced puzzlement about a curious influx of surveyors and real-estate people crawling over the area. Citizens' questions were met with conflicting information and outright disinformation. In later court hearings, black residents described the runaround they encountered. Bounced from office to office, sometimes shown unfamiliar maps and charts without explanation or help in deciphering these materials, the residents were frustrated in their attempts to understand the situation. One black councilman said that he had learned that the interstate would be somewhere near TSU "but could not find out exactly where." Another black citizen said that "the people who had charge of the maps, they seemed to be kind of vague themselves about it . . . they were indefinite just when it was to begin." Another likewise testified that "I was never able to find out anything" and "the real estate men who came out to buy their properties seemed to know much more than the homeowners of what was going on." Even the state highway department "refused to release information while insisting that the route was still in the process of being studied." One bureaucrat's response, as recounted by one North Nashvillian, was to say, "very indignantly . . . we can't give out any information. In fact, we don't know any of the designs, plans or what. Designs and plans are all done by out of town architects." Black citizens were not the only ones left clueless. The city editor and a reporter for the *Tennessean*, which had joined North Nashvillians in protest against the proposed path, "both testified that they never knew of any finalizing of plans on I-40's exact route." Although the plan had been formally filed with the state highway department on September 15, 1958, officials "consistently refused to admit" that a path had been chosen."[11]

Only in September 1967 did alarm spur more coordinated action. Reports that 18th Avenue North was being widened to accommodate future interstate traffic, and the announcement that bids would be accepted on October 1 for the highway's actual construction, finally exposed to the black community the threat before them. In response, a group predominately made up of Fisk and TSU professors formed the Interstate 40 Steering Committee. Issues of class were never far from the surface; said one observer, "the friction that did exist within the committee at the beginning tended to center around whether 'professionals' actually understood the needs and problems of the 'common man,'" but in overall, "cooperation was general." Digging desperately through archives, the commission had the unpleasant revelation that the original interstate route had been "somewhere near Vanderbilt," and anger only escalated in discovering the supreme insult: that a public hearing *had* been held, as required by law, on May 15, 1957. Yet publicity for the hearing had not been disseminated by news media; instead, fliers were posted in certain post offices, all in white neighborhoods, and each flier bore the wrong hearing date.[12]

The situation underscored some growing feelings of hopelessness and impotence. One black politician pointed out that his constituents "don't always feel free to ask the information because they don't feel like it would be given to them correctly" and moreover, "A little person don't feel like going into court fighting. He doesn't have money maybe to employ an attorney. So, consequently, he feels helpless and he gives up and many times he has to suffer." He also admitted that "I don't think any of us thought of how we could effectively protest." A later account of the controversy noted that "the established planning bureaucracy was too dispersed for direct confrontation" and a citizen echoed that "sometimes in this segregated community Negroes don't know who exactly makes the decisions." But it was easy enough to see who benefited. A letter to the *Tennessean* denounced the realtors who double-dipped in profiting from the interstate's construction: buying the property at "cut-rate" prices, then "collect[ing] from the government the value of the redevelopment as well as the property." Despite "vague platitudes concerning 'progress' and 'public interest,'" the writer warned that "the Negro citizen and Negro businessman should not be expected to take kindly to being corralled in a blighted urban area by Jim Crow real estate practices and bulldozed around by the high priests of the super-road cult." Pointing to riots in Newark and Watts, the author suggested that black frustration might easily erupt in similar ways: "it might give pause to those prone to say 'It won't happen here,' or 'It had better not happen here,' After all, it almost happened in April." The bitter conclusion was that "with tender loving care like this, North Nashville hardly needs Stokely."[13]

Working against the clock, the steering committee discovered that it had a window of opportunity before the construction contract was awarded because the state had failed to advertise the opening for bids properly. But others were equally determined to see construction begin immediately. Tennessee Governor Buford Ellington, for example, labored "behind the scenes" to "threaten the city with diversion of highway money elsewhere," a task undoubtedly helped by his close personal friendship with President Lyndon B. Johnson. Ellington had announced on July 21, 1967, a "crash program" to speed construction. The Chamber of Commerce likewise tried to keep the project's momentum moving forward "for business purposes" lest federal funding dry up.[14]

Mayor Beverly Briley was publicly sympathetic about North Nashville's situation, acknowledging frankly that the interstate formed "a barrier to the Fisk and Meharry area isolating it like a ghetto." But he noted that "planning for a Model Cities program had already begun, specifically to alleviate the problems created by the proposed highway." On August 31, he announced his inability to alter interstate planning and thereafter repeatedly stressed that everything was in the hands of federal and state engineers ("we are creatures of the state") and despite having "done all that [he] could to change it," his input was worth "about one-tenth of 1%." The mayor emphasized that he had warned everyone, "including 'people at the Belle Meade Country Club,' that if they 'stick their heads in the sand' the results will be disastrous in Nashville," but subsequent actions belied his words.[15]

The steering committee instead entreated federal Secretary of Transportation Allen Boyd for a ninety-day delay, which was denied despite widespread political support. As a result, Avon Williams Jr. was hired as legal counsel and filed a lawsuit with the U.S. District Court in Middle Tennessee claiming that the interstate planning discriminated against North Nashvillians. One of his experts testifying at the trial spoke of abundant evidence that "changes were suggested and made" because of the effect on any number of white businesses and institutions, but no such discussion took place regarding their black counterparts. Nor was there any explanation for the final changes in the plan, nor data collected to examine the impact on North Nashvillians. Defending the decision, one bureaucrat stated weakly that "I think it was considered to be a benefit to them."[16]

On November 2, Judge Frank Gray handed down his decision. He found that the public hearing had been entirely inadequate and filled with "irregularities," agreeing with the plaintiffs that the interstate would have an "adverse effect" on North Nashville, but nevertheless ruled against the steering committee. His reasoning was that "most of the evidence presented by the plaintiffs goes to the wisdom and not the legality of the highway department's decision." Despite "grave doubts," none of the evidence showed "discriminatory intent." The Sixth Circuit Court of Appeals sustained Gray's decision on December 8, and opportunities for further legal recourse were thwarted on January 29, 1968, when the U.S. Supreme Court refused to hear the case. A construction contract worth over six million dollars was awarded immediately with the news.[17]

With legal avenues closed, the steering committee turned instead to Lowell K. Bridwell, an official with the Federal Highway Administration and mediator between the committee and the city. Bridwell did not hide his desire to get the project rolling, citing the "ten million [dollars] already spent in public funds" and averring that he was "not responsible for people not knowing what's going on in their county." But he acknowledged that issues needed examining. The Chamber of Commerce similarly attempted a mediating role despite an avowed desire to get the road finished. Officials stressed their willingness to compromise on details such as access roads if it would move the project forward. Bridwell's energies instead turned toward a compromise potentially more equitable for both sides. The very first planners hired by the city had suggested that an elevated platform, known as an "air rights deck," could be built atop a section of the interstate to accommodate relocated businesses. Bridwell saw this deck as the best way to facilitate the interstate's completion while ameliorating the worst effects of lost business. Yet, even as a four-and-a-half-acre section bounded by Jefferson and Scovel Streets between 17th and 18th Avenues was identified as a prime spot, the steering committee remained wary, voting instead to take the matter directly to LBJ. Feelings still ran high. Some saw the committee as "not interested in attempting to make the present path more acceptable; only in getting the interstate rerouted." Internal correspondence from federal administrators suggested the view that the committee had "backed itself" into a corner by this hard-line stance. But these administrators also suggested that the highway issue and deeper racial conflicts in the city were "real but unconnected" issues. For his part, Avon Williams argued that "We're not saying that this should be the route. . . . What we are saying is that they did not consider the tremendous damage the road does going this way." Others noted that the steering committee acted as though it was "given the 'show' treatment" in their meetings with officials, which was "deeply resented." Moreover, "Mr. Bridwell was just as political as Governor Ellington and Mayor Briley even though Mr. Bridwell went through the motions of appearing sincere."[18]

Stymied by the Supreme Court ruling, the steering committee shifted to a strategy that might preserve some smaller victories. Even with the crushing blow that North Nashville was about to suffer, one observer noted, "they were haunted by various 'militant' voices that were saying, 'You can't work within the system' "; they had to keep a "united front" despite "deep personal divisions." Subsequent meetings between the steering committee and the city won some minor concessions modifying the interstate's effects on community streets with regard to planned overpasses, underpasses, and various access and feeder roads. Yet these had to be constructed anyway to trigger the release of continued federal money. Still more conversation about the air-rights deck took place, although the steering committee pointed out that it was a moot subject unless the federal government would be willing to finance the deck, as the committee requested.[19]

The plea proved fruitless. Although federal funds were made available to study the deck's feasibility, there was little or no follow-through. As Bridwell continued overseeing the Nashville dispute, he expressed agitation that planning for the deck had "not progressed." Blame for the inaction was spread around, with some "indirectly" targeting William Reinhart, Briley's aide in charge of the Model Cities program. Bridwell also came under fire from the steering committee for "playing games with us. First you promise us that the deck is a reality and now you are saying maybe." In the end, "almost every agency involved, although acknowledging the desirability of a deck, felt no responsibility to coordinate the planning." The ostensible excuse was the state's claim that drainage issues rendered the plan impossible because the targeted area sat in a geographic depression. Years later, however, it was acknowledged that such a problem "could have been handled," despite the costs. Similarly, Nashville's most prominent white businessmen had chipped in financing for relocated businesses and the proposed shopping center, and added a kitty of one million dollars for businesses affected by the interstate. Yet few black business owners took advantage of the windfall. Some attempted to form a stock company or negotiated to buy a small shopping center, but North Nashville's businesses had survived because of a close proximity to their customer base. The erosion of that customer base and the high rents in other areas were obstacles too great to overcome. With that reality, relocation monies were beside the point. Local black leader Flem B. Otey III, grandson of a grocer and son to a real estate and banking businessman, noted soberly that "No race or group has ever gotten out of the ghetto except by the entrepreneurial route . . . but now . . . they're closing off that route."[20]

And so the interstate came to Nashville. As Kelly Miller Smith said flatly, the road was "a bitter thing which tore the community apart. Destroyed it." The legal battle was the first of its kind in stalling highway construction on the grounds of racial discrimination, with the bittersweet outcome a new federal directive "that no highway or other public works shall be implemented on the basis of hearings more than five years old." As Mayor Briley said dismissively, "sometimes in relocation the operation is a success but the patient dies." The entire situation demonstrated literally how cheap the black community was in white eyes. Perhaps most wretchedly, black residents watched as "barbed-wire topped steel fences" were constructed near houses close to the highway exits, supposedly to "discourage commercial development in the area."[21] In large and small ways, North Nashville was being divided from the rest of the city. It may not have seemed that way to suburbanites surveying the scene at a glance as they drove past, but the interstate was a barrier that changed the human and economic geography of black Nashville decisively.

Superficially, the Model Cities legislation, part of LBJ's Great Society program, might have been viewed as a possible antidote for North Nashville's decline. Just as Mayor Ben West had anticipated federal financing for urban renewal and the Capitol Hill project, Mayor Briley was poised to replicate this success with Model Cities. He was fixated on North Nashville, having already sponsored a conference highlighting the area for realty interests, perhaps responding to a group of his supporters known as "the Real Estate Men." When the U.S. Congress passed the legislation in November 1966, Nashville had already laid the groundwork for an application. Briley coveted Model Cities money for a number of reasons. The program was designed to remake inner-city slums using a "comprehensive approach" that would target multiple but interrelated problems, including crime, housing, and poverty. Even better, the funds were "not all earmarked" for specific projects; there was significant leeway in how local politicians could dispense the money. As one partisan put it, the "block grant" money for mayors was "like the thirst of a man lost in the Sahara with no water." The tradeoff for this, however, was that the Model Cities program required active involvement from citizens in the designated neighborhood—what the writers of the bill called "maximum feasible participation of the residents."[22]

Mayor Briley, as a seasoned veteran of rough-and-tumble Nashville politics, was unsuited temperamentally and politically to share his power and the city's money. From the beginning of Nashville's Model Cities planning, his administration took steps to create a false appearance of "citizen participation." For example, early in the process, one meeting welcomed hundreds of North Nashville leaders for suggestions on what Model Cities should target. But two days previously the task force with the real authority had convened to decide these very same issues. Later, when the formal application went to the federal Department of Housing and Urban Development (HUD) charged with overseeing Model Cities, the list of North Nashville participants was supplied—without each individual's consent—as evidence that citizens were contributing to the program. After this inauspicious start, the Briley administration continued presenting a phony impression of substantial black citizen participation. Such subterfuge would mark the chief theme of Nashville's Model Cities story, even as federal officials were conscious of Briley's apparent willful misunderstanding of this issue.[23]

The application was submitted to HUD on May 1, 1967, just three weeks after Stokely Carmichael spoke at Vanderbilt, and only four months before the steering committee formed in response to the impending threat of Interstate 40. With Nashville's selection, a belabored bureaucratic process followed, as required by law, to refine Nashville's application and move from the first year of "planning" into a five year "action phase." Especially key was the establishment of the Citizens Coordinating Committee (CCC) as the group responsible for North Nashville's citizen participation. Although the relationship between the CCC and the mayor was unclear, the group's formation was sufficient for HUD and Nashville to sign a contract on February 28, 1968, for the first year of funding. The signing prompted a marked deceleration in getting the program moving in contrast to the frenzied energy that had accompanied the planning. A number of issues had to be dealt with and bureaucratic in-fighting now took precedence; the role and power of director William Reinhart and his access to the mayor threatened both the mayor's staff and other agencies of Metropolitan Nashville. When attention finally turned to defining exactly how the CCC should participate in Model Cities, the interstate situation and the April 4, 1968, murder of Martin Luther King had poisoned attitudes in the black community. After a lengthy and delayed process electing the CCC's members, which finally occurred on September 7, there was now a pressing January 1969 deadline for fleshing out details of how Model Cities money would be distributed to relevant programs. Meeting this deadline would net Nashville a healthy increase in its funding.[24]

By all accounts, the citizen groups functioned relatively smoothly. An exception was the task force dealing with planning issues, particularly urban renewal and housing, issues that had been downplayed by the city in the application process. The problem began when an urban-planning firm contracted by the city presented three options for North Nashville's redevelopment: remaking North Nashville into an industrial zone, upgrading and expanding the housing possibilities in North Nashville, or some combination of the two. The industrial option had some merit hypothetically: the cheap land and existing infrastructure (namely, sewers, railroad tracks, and soon, Interstate 40), combined with the area's proximity to the Cumberland River, would make for quick and comparatively affordable opportunities to redo the face of North Nashville. Moreover, this business could bring badly needed tax revenue to the city, especially in light of widespread agreement that Nashville needed to diversify economically. But that choice would obliterate the residential character of North Nashville.[25]

As one account puts it, the CCC reacted to the three proposals with "confusion coupled with defensiveness." The sheer scope and complicated technical nature of the plans made the CCC leery of committing to any option. The group's caution was understandable. While the CCC appreciated the possibilities of urban renewal, black Nashvillians had also watched as urban renewal pushed black residents from Capitol Hill into the Edgehill community, and then from Edgehill into North Nashville. Now that the latter neighborhood was "in a fluid and possibly dying state" thanks to I-40, the massive overhaul proposed made them justifiably wary. Some CCC members voiced support for the so-called "blended approach" mixing industry and housing. But others complained that the latter, the most pressing need in the neighborhood, was getting inadequate attention. Some also took issue with the lack of black representation in the local Model Cities bureaucracy. Others voiced suspicions about white businessmen with the financial and political means to exploit Model Cities and North Nashville for their own gain, about the city's use of a white consulting firm, and about secretive meetings that had accompanied the planning. Moreover, the interstate situation and Edgehill's redevelopment proved that merely giving fair market value for the property of those relocated was insufficient. The problem was critical for retirees, long-time residents who had already paid off their mortgages, and those not poor enough to qualify for public housing but without the means to finance a home. For these people, relocating to more expensive areas threatened to put them in worse economic straits. Moreover, some black businesses that rented rather than owned their property failed to qualify for any recompensation at all.[26]

The CCC decided not to select from the three choices and instead requested that Model Cities pay for an independent black consultant to help the citizens weigh their options. While this was granted, Briley continued steering other parts of the Model Cities program through the necessary bureaucratic hoops in order to meet another impending funding deadline from HUD. At the same time, the administration exhibited an almost pathological resistance to facilitating the black consultant's work: in one case, not allowing him office space to carry out his duties and, in another, refusing to provide him with copies of reports. Accordingly, the consultant advised the CCC that his work was secondary to the more important issue of clarifying exactly what role the CCC would play as part of "citizen participation." An April 18, 1969, meeting between the CCC and Mayor Briley did exactly that, as Briley declared that, as one contemporary puts it, "the role of the CCC was to recommend only, not to decide. The CCC had no veto power." Despite the legal requirement for citizen participation, the mayor "saw citizen involvement as a further jeopardy in a complex but essential planning task."[27]

Unwilling to suffer this condescension, the CCC voted to withhold its involvement in the Model Cities program and made its displeasure known in a formal letter of complaint to HUD. An op-ed by a black journalist in the *Tennessean* described the mix of "confusion and dissension" now rampant among Nashville's blacks. While acknowledging that "the side of town I live—North Nashville—has never looked as bad as it does now," the journalist also observed that "the real estate people—grapevine talk says—and a lot of people downtown know what's going to happen long before it ever comes to light," in contrast to the "half informed citizens on our side of town." Between urban renewal and the interstate, and with city agencies "doing little more than what Mayor Briley allows," North Nashville was "now being broken up into areas resembling little camps." He further warned that "the possibility of this city being a model one, over Atlanta or Miami or Louisville or any city in the nation, can only amount to a bunch of white dreams on white terms."[28]

Although HUD never responded to the CCC's letter, the agency made it clear to city officials that citizen participation must be enhanced for the program to proceed. As such, the mayor now sent the CCC a "surprisingly conciliatory" letter. Yet the situation remained deadlocked throughout the summer. Only through informal understandings between Reinhart and the CCC did a potential truce seem possible. The city needed to keep HUD happy to keep federal dollars flowing, and the CCC knew that its legal right to be active in the Model Cities programming was its trump card. Reinhart wrote up a compromise by which the CCC could get a more definitive outlining of its role in Model Cities if the group approved the current plans with a proviso allowing for future revision. When the mayor found out, he summarily fired Reinhart. The next letter to the CCC, rewritten by Briley's staff, was more elliptical, alluding to arrangements made with the CCC without detailing the terms, and was clearly written for HUD's eyes rather than as genuine dialogue.[29]

If Briley had been angered by Reinhart's perceived treason, he was even more enraged upon learning about the CCC's decision, also suggested by the group's consultant, to formally incorporate as the North Nashville Citizens Coordinating Committee (NNCCC). The idea was that incorporation would help the group qualify for matching funds from outside sources to complement Model Cities money. But it also meant that black consultants could be hired on the group's own terms—an important consideration for an organization anxious to assert its own voice. Briley, irate at a move potentially freeing the NNCCC from his control, argued "that a small group of 'troublemakers' and 'politicians' who wanted to 'handle the greenback' was trying to take over Model Cities." The mayor continued to offer NNCCC vague promises about involvement in the future as long as it would sign off on the paperwork for HUD. Avon Williams, serving as the NNCCC attorney, advised the group to decline and hold out for written assurance that the NNCCC's role would be that of an active participant, as HUD allowed, rather in a consultative oversight capacity.[30]

With the April 1 deadline for HUD past, the impasse remained. Only in September did negotiations between the mayor and the NNCCC resume, helped by urging from Dick Battle, a *Banner* journalist following the Model Cities story closely. With Edwin Mitchell as the new head of the NNCCC, a "working partnership" was formed, strengthened by what was called "concurrent approval"—an agreement that Mayor Briley had ultimate control over the Model Cities program but that the NNCCC could play a more direct role in replanning various programs before the final proposal was submitted to HUD. In revising the section of the formal application regarding housing, and in keeping with its desire to help North Nashville remain residential in character while improving the lot of current residents, the NNCCC devised an elegant solution: a corporation set up with Model Cities funding and serving as a "rolling investment plan." The corporation would purchase land for houses built by local black contractors, with mortgage payments from citizens reinvested in the corporation to finance future homes. The program would also have black contractors build the proposed air-rights deck for the black businesses crushed by Interstate 40 and called for a mortgage-free house given to any homeowner displaced by urban renewal. Above all else, the NNCCC made sure that the plan was "designed to displace the absolute minimum of homeowners" and that the Nashville Housing Authority would *not* be involved in the program—the NHA having long been viewed as an enemy because of its aggressiveness in urban renewal. The proposal received a unanimously favorable vote from the group's membership on February 25, 1970.[31]

The city had different ideas. Claiming that North Nashville was "deteriorating so rapidly" that extensive efforts to assist homeownership were doomed, the mayor's office wanted to address the housing shortage by relocating North Nashvillians into new units along the Cumberland River. This made Edwin Mitchell furious, as he pointed out that the proposed site lay precisely along the path that the steering committee had suggested as an alternate route for Interstate 40, but that idea had been rejected because the area was prone to flooding. "We insist that if the area was not adequate for the highway," said Mitchell, "it isn't adequate for people." The numbers, said Mitchell bluntly, were a "bunch of fairy tales," and "the theory of destroying any ghetto becomes but a myth." He likewise told the *Tennessean* that "voluminous material has been read to us; we have been listened out and herded away . . . someone else wrote the program."[32]

Even as Mitchell called out these contradictions, the behavior remained the same. After receiving the housing corporation proposal, the city overhauled the plan, removing all references to the NNCCC, as Mayor Briley still refused to recognize the incorporated version of the CCC. The revised version also cut all passages that contained "explicit recognition of CCC veto power," deleted projects that the NNCCC proposed to sponsor, and "virtually negated" the group's funding. Adding to the insult, the NNCCC was presented with a freshly inked-up copy of the new version. The city justified the drastic changes by reasoning that this would clean the document of everything not approved by HUD, but the city had also turned down an offer from HUD to do this editing. On March 10, 1970, the NNCCC, furious about the slight, rejected this version, but for naught. The next day, the Metropolitan Council approved the city's proposal by outvoting North Nashville's own representatives, despite NNCCC testimony against the plan and despite the fact that a deadline had left each member only twenty-four hours to digest a proposal numbering over seven hundred pages. Worried about the delay and the prospect of losing continued funding, the council rubber-stamped approval and sent the application to HUD. The NNCCC sent telegrams of protest to HUD offices in Atlanta and Washington, D.C., claiming that the plan "does not represent the desires of the citizens of the community nor afford them adequate involvement in its operation." An NNCCC meeting captured a worried citizenry, as North Nashville Councilman Harold Love "commented on how late it was when he and other Council men received their copies of the proposal. He fears there is trouble on the way and cautioned MNA [the Model Cities neighborhood] residents to be very careful." One participant noted succinctly that "the whole situation is 'political.'"[33]

By this point, the relationship between city and the NNCCC was marked by coldness. Edwin Mitchell continued butting heads with Buford Drake, Briley's new point man for the Model Cities program, who had been chosen without NNCCC input and was seen by the group as "the mayor's hatchet man." The "petty quarreling" worsened when Edwin Mitchell branded Drake "an Uncle Tom" and Drake, calling the group's leadership "obnoxious," "presumptuous," and "ridiculous," accused the doctor of refusing to speak to Drake's assistant. Further acrimony resulted after Drake fired staff people for "disloyalty," claiming that they were "spying for the CCC," amid charges that Drake was opening mail and delaying notice about meetings so as to keep the NNCCC in the dark. Drake retorted that communication was impossible, as in the case of decisions to end certain projects, because the struggling NNCCC "had voted to suspend all operations" and thus there was nobody to inform.[34]

The NNCCC's decision resulted from HUD's October 7, 1970, approval of Nashville's Model Cities application that released the next round of money for the action phase of the program. The definitive academic analysis of Nashville's Model Cities program had nothing but harsh words for the federal agency, seeing it as indifferent to citizen concerns and dodging any sort of responsibility for the program's oversight in Nashville. The citizens' group, looking for support from the courts and from HUD, found none and began to wither. The NNCCC quickly became a shadow of its former self, at most meetings struggling to meet a quorum. More importantly, the Model Cities program now served as the arm for a "stereotypical political machine," as one contemporary scholarly account called it, a federally funded tool for white political patronage that directed political wrangling and class issues so as to divide the NNCCC. Buford Drake derided the group's leadership, accusing it of saying, in effect, "don't do so-and-so, don't do nothing, leave those shacks right there. Leave the poor folk in them." Likewise, a flier drawn up by two black councilmen making the rounds in North Nashville read, "Watch Out North Nashville! Here comes the same group of self-appointed champions of the poor! These pseudo-leaders would have you believe their hearts bleed for the 47,000 people within the Model Cities area." Robert Lillard publicly accused the CCC of being "motivated by 'greed and desire for power.'" Drake even went to elaborate lengths to design neighborhood block meetings within North Nashville to undercut support for the NNCCC. Black political power remained split in being wedded to the two rival political machines in Nashville. Throughout the 1970s, the situation remained much the same, with the NNCCC stagnant and mired in political factionalism. In 1972, a Metro Council review of Model Cities found that "too much is being spent on administration" and too little on "programs of lasting impact." The program, branded by the *Banner*'s Dick Battle in a column as "Metro's muddled, sometimes misunderstood and occasionally misdirected Model Cities program," was soon mired in lawsuits that never went anywhere.[35]

In the end, the failure of Nashville's Model Cities program to provide any sort of meaningful change for black Nashville centered around two central questions, as contemporary accounts identified. The debates over what exactly constituted "citizen participation" and who should have the power over neighborhood planning were the critical issues. As with the Interstate 40, the black community learned that even having a voice in such decisions was secondary to other considerations. Citizen input was a facade. Model Cities became a funnel for federal dollars at the expense of North Nashville, just as Interstate 40 had brutalized black neighborhoods. It was little wonder that African Americans sneered that, as the saying went, "urban renewal" actually meant "nigger removal."[36]

In a much less pronounced way, white neighborhoods were not immune to urban renewal's destructive tendencies. In 1968, the Hillsboro neighborhood near Vanderbilt, an aging but solidly white middle-class neighborhood of elderly homeowners and student renters, was declared by HUD as qualified for urban renewal. The decision aggravated Hillsboro residents, who organized in protest to little avail. Accusations about collusion between the university and the NHA abounded. The favored tactic was "spotting"—the process of "systematically buying houses on different blocks, then tearing them down or allowing them to stand there and simply deteriorate," as a *Newsweek* story detailed. This technique's virtue was that it "drove down values in the area but scared away all other potential buyers except, of course, Vanderbilt and the authority." They were helped by HUD's elastic definition of what constituted a slum; the federal agency required only that 51 percent of the housing in the area be "substandard" in order to qualify. Residents recalled bitterly how housing inspectors used "technical violations" to condemn houses, one of which was declared "a blighting influence" because of "insufficient closet space." Said one homeowner, "This isn't a slum, never was a slum. . . . They're doing it for the sole benefit of Vanderbilt. It's nothing but a free land grab." Observers in North Nashville observed cynically that Nashville banks (frequently run by Vanderbilt graduates) also profited by bankrolling such urban renewal projects, which were nothing but "internal imperialism which is subsidized at the victim's expense through tax money converted into government grants." A federal lawsuit in spring 1970 accused Vanderbilt and the Nashville Housing Authority of "conspiring to create a slum district," but federal judge L. Clure Morton ruled that there was no indication that the defendants acted in ways "tainted with self-interest." Today, the former neighborhood lies beneath Blakemore Avenue.[37]

The curtailing of black economic and political activity by Interstate 40 and Model Cities were not isolated instances. Rather, they were dramatic examples of a consistent trend that fused personal racial attitudes with complex interrelated public policies in powerful ways. Nashville had countless examples of the former when it came to segregation in housing. It was an open secret that realty ads listing properties "for anyone" signaled that the housing was for black people. After twenty-four hours in their new home, one black couple watched FOR SALE signs take over their neighbors' lawns like crabgrass. Another black homeowner found trash thrown in her yard and feces put in her mailbox. And still another, a black professor, was the target of an arson attempt. African Americans found themselves dealing with inflated prices and sudden inabilities to obtain financing as "guidelines and court decisions" mandating fair housings were "flouted with impunity." One black newspaper described how white owners employed attorneys that could convince the city to rezone whole areas as commercial, thus driving up prices, and "subtle tactics that realtors are using to pressure white residents into selling their homes." Instead of "the days when a realtor might tell a white homeowner, 'You'd better sell because the niggers are moving in,'" the updated versions consisted of realtors in Edgehill making "guarded inquiries about whether the homeowner 'ever thought about' selling his house" and "casual references to the 'deteriorating' quality of Clemons School."[38] The difference, of course, was that African Americans had fewer options than whites for finding new housing.

Public policies on all levels reinforced racial divisions in housing and heightened socioeconomic disparities. Fisk economist Vivian Henderson had seen it as early as 1962. He observed that after 1959 the trend in North Nashville housing favored private multiunit rental buildings. These units were located in areas already marked by deterioration, "bound by junk yards, railroad tracks, manufacturing plants, and alleys cluttered with filth and trash" and often "several of the larger projects are located very close to the area of proposed super-highway construction." They were hurriedly constructed (in as quickly as two months) and ready to accept people relocated from the East Nashville urban renewal project. The minimum eighty-five-dollar monthly rent would have been lucrative, given that the units filled up rapidly with African Americans shut out of other neighborhoods. In sum, it meant that these houses, sited in specific isolated areas, were exacerbating local slums and blight, at a rate faster than urban renewals could clean them up, and all the while being subsidized by federal housing programs. As Henderson concluded, "It appears that Nashville has for some time been involved in a project to build a 'Negro ghetto' and more recently it appears that Nashville has embarked upon a project to build future slums and blighted areas to accompany its 'North Nashville Negro ghetto.'"[39] White Nashvillians were helping to create the depressed areas, then bidding for federal money to clean them up. And these realities, in turn, comprised the essential context for what seemed to be the angriest clashes about race in Nashville by the 1970s. As segregation continued to separate neighborhoods, it made another continuing saga, the ongoing battles over school desegregation, infinitely more difficult.

Like urban renewal and highway planning, developments in desegregating local schools continued quietly throughout the 1960s before reerupting in conflict. The 1957 Nashville Plan, approved despite reservations by the U.S. Supreme Court in 1959, had permitted school desegregation to proceed incrementally throughout the early 1960s. Davidson County had adopted the same plan in 1960. But Avon Williams and Z. Alexander Looby insisted on a quicker pace. Said Williams, "not only is 12 years too long . . . but the Nashville case gave carte blanche to every community in the South to sit back and say 'We won't move an inch unless we're sued, and if we are, we'll just start with the first grade.' It blocked progress completely, especially with the transfer provision." Indeed, the Nashville Plan had "enjoyed quite a vogue over the nation," as a *Tennessean* report noted, and had been "cited with approbation by many courts [as] the basis of various desegregation efforts in Virginia, North Carolina, Tennessee, Louisiana, and Texas." But Looby and Williams knew that the two local school boards were on shaky ground as grade-per-year desegregation strategies elsewhere had been overturned. As Looby and Williams persisted, federal courts required Davidson County to desegregate grades one through four all at once so that integration in the county and city schools would be in synchronicity. Regardless, the results continued to be mixed; there was some steady if meager integration in terms of numbers, but progress was less compelling when viewed in total.[40]

Two developments made 1963 an important year. First, in May, the U.S. Supreme Court overturned its earlier rulings and decided that grade-per-year integration strategies such as the Nashville Plan were unconstitutional. Second, the successful vote to merge Nashville and Davidson County into one metropolitan entity meant that, starting in 1964, desegregation matters would fold into the wider consolidation of the two school systems. By 1963, one citizen had asserted that "community acceptance [of school integration] has been more than many people expected" and "among white people, even those with rather strong pro-segregation tendencies, there is an attitude of *fait accompli.*" Yet the observer hastened to add that "the problem of social contact which intensifies in the high school grades has yet to be faced in Nashville." In subsequent years, the story remained much the same. By 1965, some stealthy desegregation had taken place, unknown to the general population, along with reports that school officials were now "planning to put a stop to further transfers." But, at the same time, attempts to desegregate Hume-Fogg, the white vocational-technical school, had been difficult, especially when "rebuffed by the school board." It was another way to suppress black employment prospects. Moreover, although administrative posts in the school system had been integrated, school faculties had not.[41]

Although the Metropolitan Nashville school board showed only occasional and grudging enthusiasm for desegregation throughout the mid-1960s, there was also a central question at stake about "how to define segregation" and thus integration.[42] In a school system 76 percent white and 24 percent black, but with concentrated pockets of residential segregation, what constituted integration? Put another way, what ratio of black and white children corresponded to successful integration? Statistically speaking, the 1960s had seen the number of all-black schools cut in half and all-white schools by three fourths. But such statistics derived from schools containing only a handful of the opposite race. Indeed, a closer look showed that, by 1969, 83 percent of whites attended a school that was at least 90 percent white, and 71 percent of black children attended schools at least 80 percent black. Ideally, most Metro schools would approximate the 76/24 black/white population split. But over time, driven by white flight, this proportion was impossible to reach: the more integrated schools were turning majority-black at a rate significantly faster than those schools with only a handful of blacks, and many schools remained all-white. All told, the reality was that "segregation in Nashville's schools decreased only slightly during the 1960s" and moreover "it seems clear that," rather than school board actions, "most of the school integration has occurred as a result of changing racial composition of residential areas." The situation demonstrated that integration was about more than mere numbers, and indeed, that numbers could mask white Nashville's evasions.[43]

By the late 1960s and early 1970s, even this glacial pace to school desegregation created molten anger from white communities in Nashville and across the nation in places like Denver, Charlotte, and Boston. The particular target was busing, a tool that judges were increasingly mandating for desegregating schools in recalcitrant school districts.[44] Yet white Nashville's intense bitterness toward busing conveniently ignored the salient reality that children had been bused across the county for years—including, by 1970, fully a third of Nashville's public-school pupils. As Avon Williams declared, "busing is opposed now because it is being used for desegregation rather than segregation," pointing out that when black students had been bused to Haynes High School, "no one said anything then about how unfair or how costly or how illogical it was to do that." Decades later, Nashville's school transportation director recalled that "there has always been transportation of students in the school system since early in the 1930s." At first, it bused black children to schools, which at the time was a relatively cost-effective way of maintaining segregation. "But when we started transporting white children in a different direction than they were used to, then the word 'busing' raised its head."[45]

In May 1969, distress escalated as the Nashville school board wrestled with how to zone new John Trotwood Moore Middle School. Zoning, of course, divided school districts so pupils could be assigned to specific schools. In establishing these zones, the key criteria was school capacity; zone lines had to drawn and redrawn to include students in numbers matching each school's enrollment size. But the additional requirement of desegregating complicated these considerations. Now zone lines had to crisscross the county in ways that also considered the racial demographics of each area, not just the number of students. This was problematic because neighborhood segregation was severe in Nashville. With whites and blacks living in mostly separate pockets across the county, school officials had to design zones covering fairly large swaths of land so as to include both blacks and whites. Since the schools in each of these large-area zones could not move, the students had to be moved, and that required buses. And given the size of Davidson County—533 square miles—that meant a lot of buses.

The school board's increasing preference for so-called comprehensive high schools complicated matters further. These were larger schools that accommodated more students and thus committed correspondingly larger resources and programs in one place. Such schools would theoretically help the desegregation process, assuming they were built on sites near both white and black neighborhoods, but the more numerous elementary and middle schools remained the problem. More schools meant smaller zones, which, in turn, restricted the possibilities for desegregating the schools racially. Moreover, each school's physical location and capacity were not always ideal for shifting neighborhood demographics. In the case of Moore School, parents anxious to insure that their children would be included in the new school's zone began organizing into citizens' groups to lobby the school board intensely; some wanted to make Moore into more of a "neighborhood" school (thus keeping it white) while others encouraged the board to err more on the side of racial balance. Ultimately, the board decided by a one-vote margin against its staff's recommendation and drew the zone deeper into the inner city to add, albeit slightly, to the school's potential black population. Yet even this modest gesture encountered deep resentment from white Nashvillians. "Moore was the first test," said school board chair C. R. Dorrier. "It was still only token integration, yet we had prominent people complain, not just red-necks."[46]

In September 1969, Judge William Miller ordered Nashville faculties integrated, and the school system responded by desegregating all but four of them—although it was acknowledged that in most cases this was done with a single teacher of the opposite race. Avon Williams derided the tokenism: "the only white teachers they assign to black schools are those who are really dedicated (in the field of integrated education) or somebody they want to get rid of." Moreover, continued Williams, "for the white schools, they pull out the best black teacher from the black schools, someone they really need in the ghetto school, and put this teacher in the white school. They only assign the black teacher who fits into the 'family.'" Indeed, desegregating faculties was a color-conscious exercise, as the key consideration was literally skin shade—lighter-skinned blacks being those chosen to teach at white schools. As one black teacher confirmed, "They came right down the color scale with those first transfers" and only later "started getting us a little browner and the shock had worn off by the time they had that great mass of transfers." The experience was met with "resistance of teachers of both races," which was not entirely a surprise. The Metropolitan Nashville Educational Association (MNEA) had previously surveyed teachers to gauge attitudes about faculty integration, and the results were "unbelievably disappointing" and "almost embarrassing." The mere shifting of numbers and statistics obscured how uncomfortable desegregation was on an individual level. DeLois Wilkinson, a black teacher and later school board representative, recalled how in 1962, when sent to a white school, she was alternately "welcomed warmly" and "snubbed." When she decided to skip faculty lunches so as to watch her weight, she was branded as "aloof" by her coworkers.[47]

On July 19, 1970, Judge Miller, disturbed by Nashville's zoning practices that clearly "were not drawn to maximize integration," ordered a new plan. Nationally, court rulings were becoming increasingly stringent, requiring rapider and fuller compliance while striking down machinations used by school systems to avoid implementing the *Brown* decision. With the new plan due to the court by August 19, emotions were becoming strained as alarmed citizens started rallying. One was Jack Kershaw, artist, attorney, and longtime Nashville eccentric who had served as vice chairman of the Tennessee Federation for Constitutional Government in 1957. Kershaw was a key leader in the local chapter of Save Our Schools (SOS), a nationwide group formed to oppose busing. The national group was sponsored by the right-wing Liberty Lobby, although Kershaw disavowed any connection with the broader organization. The attorney was critical of "moving people around like furniture to attain racial balance," and, while allowing that the 1954 *Brown* decision "outlawed state-imposed segregation," he nonetheless clung to the idea of voluntary association: "if the association is unwilling, it is not true association. Mere physical proximity of unwilling bodies creates neither community nor neighborhood; it creates a concentration camp." Kershaw represented a link to the bygone era of massive resistance, yet his cause would find ample support from white Nashvillians in the coming months.[48]

School officials continued trying to dampen white fears, soothingly telling the public that their proposed plan "assures the neighborhood school concept and minimizes busing" and that whatever busing was used would be for "in most cases small distances." But an astute observer noted that "until we get open integrated housing, this school problem is going to plague us." The *Tennessean* further stressed in a news analysis that there was "no way the board can satisfy" everyone. With faculty desegregation and new school construction proceeding, the issue was solely about rezoning: "the schools and students most affected are those near the boundaries of residential segregation," the places where "school zones can be drawn to include both white and black housing."[49]

The plan adopted by the board on August 18 discarded citizen recommendations for abandoning the simple and common tactic of "pairing," where one white school was matched with one black school and their pupils shifted accordingly to achieve the same racial ratio. Instead, the proposed plan opted for "somewhat less busing and somewhat less integration." The result was scorn from both sides, as Jack Kershaw complained that not filing an appeal to protest against the court order was irresponsible. Meanwhile, the NAACP criticized the plan's tendency to bus black children rather than white. Avon Williams noted that, under Nashville's veneer of compliance, the same patterns of injustice persisted. After 1957, he argued, "the school zones [the school board] adopted were substantially the same ones they had historically designed for segregation." Moreover, the placement of new schools, conjoined with the relocation of blacks due to urban renewal programs, served to "perpetuate and increase" segregation. "Of 4 additional new schools under construction last year [1970]," Williams said, "2 were destined to be 99% white and 2 85% white." Williams also observed that one of his plaintiffs had been fired from his job for being involved in the lawsuit and he took special aim at the "so-called white liberal parents (who gave lip service to the concept of racial equality until their own children seemed about to go to a black school)" who now "have all selfishly joined the forces of reaction seeking further delay." School officials responded with shrugs, saying that, although in principle the plan called for each school to be 15 to 35 percent black, "locations of present facilities and residential segregation have prevented the board from coming close to its ideal in many schools this fall." The administration now focused on readying the schools for students according to the new plan, even with the proposal still pending before the court.[50]

A dizzying sequence of legal rulings followed. Judge Miller interrupted his own order in anticipation of forthcoming legal clarification from the U.S. Supreme Court, a decision "greeted by cheers from about 250 parents attending the school board meeting to protest busing of their children." But only a few months later, the Sixth Circuit Court of Appeals, responding to an appeal by Avon Williams, reversed Miller's decision, requiring the school system "to proceed immediately with consideration of the board's integration plan." Said Mayor Briley, "the courts should stay out of education, and education should stay out of the courts." By this point, Judge Miller had ascended to the Sixth Circuit; the new judge for the Nashville case was Knoxville-born L. Clure Morton. As court proceedings resumed in early March 1971, the plaintiffs and defendants continued wrangling. School superintendent Elbert Brooks, defending the plan, said it meshed with the "long range planning" for the school system, which was more favorable than a "crash program" strictly for desegregation. But the board's lackluster efforts were apparent. One expert witness said flatly that, with the preponderance of predominantly black elementary schools, busing was the only solution: "I would see no way without transporting those children to schools that are predominately white." Further tension derived from Avon Williams's accusations of stalling after administrators claimed that they were awaiting a computer system that would track statistical information needed for more precise zoning. Williams observed that this implementation had stopped during the last summer's legal uncertainties and the revelation angered Judge Morton visibly. "Earlier in the afternoon, I made a statement that bygones were going to be bygones and I would not take umbrage at anything that was past," Morton announced. "I retract that statement and we will try this case on the basis of the record."[51]

The hearings took a dramatic turn when four hundred white parents staged an act of civil disobedience. Led by City Councilman Casey Jenkins and State Representative Earl C. "Buddy" Shacklet Jr., heads of the Concerned Parents Association (CPA), the citizens jammed the courthouse and "clapped their hands and shouted" to disrupt the proceedings. Jenkins had already filed a motion with Metro council claiming that "busing is definitely unconstitutional. It deprives a student of his constitutional rights as an American citizen. It's a direct form of discrimination." A week later, a similar demonstration with one thousand protesters forced Morton to recess the hearings and bring in U.S. marshals from across the country to bolster security. The white demonstrators blocked the courthouse entrance as two people were arrested for disorderly conduct, forcing Casey Jenkins to stand "upon the roof of the police car" as he "begged them to leave." Scoffed Avon Williams, "what would have happened if this was a black mob? They would have called out the National Guard."[52]

The protests culminated in an enormous rally at the War Memorial Auditorium on March 16, 1971. Casey Jenkins, as emcee of the event, continued his denunciations, saying "busing to create racial balance is an ugly creature. Busing is unconstitutional" and "busing is discrimination against all the people." He continued, "Nor do we intend to violate the law, but we shall not stop our protesting until the will of the majority is done." The crowd, estimated in the thousands, responded to state and local politicians by "interrupting the speakers with applause and frequently giving standing ovations." Signs waved by the audience read, "Judge Morton is Nixon's Southern Strategist," and "Voluntary Busing, yes, Government Slavery, no." One African American rose to tell his story of being bused as a child and mused aloud, "'I am wondering where all my people are.' This brought a thunderous ovation from the crowd as the people around him shook his hand and patted him on the back." A more pointed critique came from the Madison neighborhood, where white boycotts of schools took place. False rumors that pupils there would be subjected to a "test bus" program led to a 43 percent absentee rate.[53]

The black community watched aghast as local television news devoted ninety minutes of prime-time coverage to the protest. In response to this and to a U.S. attorney who had opined that busing was illegal according to the 1964 Civil Rights Act, Williams denounced the "apparent attempts to arouse emotionalism" that were "designed . . . to influence" the court's proceedings. Casey Jenkins, by contrast, said "we are very happy to hear about U.S. Atty. Anderson's comments, and I thank God for answering our prayers." Black leaders chimed in with a statement saying that "we recognize that 'busing' and 'neighborhood schools' are but evasive terms useful to bigoted politicians to conceal their bigotry and to promote division." Williams continued calling the Metro plan an "'insult' to the court and community." National news journalist Carl Rowan, a black Tennessee native who had attended TSU briefly before leaving the South for a tour of duty in World War II and education in the North, wrote a column about "this capital city agonizing in angry racial passions over busing," and using "surface statistics" to obscure its lack of integration, "gleefully seizing a new emotional issue that they think will enable them to turn back the clock." Rowan concluded that "the level of passion and unreason whipped up here are such that the children and educators of Nashville are bound to suffer. So will the institutions of law and order."[54]

The outcry had local and national implications. The *Banner*, for example, saw President Richard Nixon as someone who would "authenticate further" those "bitterly opposing as illegal and a monstrous imposition the busing proposal that would handicap and disrupt, if not destroy, the public school system." Yet Nixon was actually moving quite gingerly, giving a nationally televised address in which he condemned segregation but left ambiguous his plans to do anything about it. As the *Tennessean* observed the next day, the Nixon administration played both sides, allowing the federal courts to bear the burden of requiring desegregation while blunting the worst excesses of judicial orders. Thus Nixon's speech deliberately clouded an already uncertain climate. Despite pointed criticism of the U.S. Department of Health, Education, and Welfare (HEW) plan from Tennessee senators William Brock and Howard Baker, the Nixon administration, having allowed HEW to draw up a plan for Austin, Texas, now permitted the same for Nashville. The *Washington Post* asserted that these two cities were poised to be "likely precedents for most Southern cities, almost all of which now fall short of the new Supreme Court requirements."[55]

Locally, Briley's political career was threatened by the busing issue as he had to fight off a mayoral bid from Casey Jenkins. Briley's grasp on power had already been slipping. Certainly he had alienated much of the black community in Nashville with his handling of the I-40 and Model Cities situations. But he was also his own worst enemy. After losing some key political battles with the Metro Council, for example, Briley made matters by referring to them as "forty jealous whores." He also showed an alarming willingness to insult his constituents in public forums, a tendency no doubt exacerbated by his struggle with alcoholism. Yet, for all that, Briley was politically attuned to the white backlash. When he endorsed Richard Nixon in 1972, he alienated fellow Democrats already worried about Nashville's recent willingness to forsake its solidly Democratic affinities and support for George Wallace's 1968 presidential campaign. Briley's shift was consistent with what others saw as a growing Republicanism in Nashville. Attorney George Barrett reflected while driving through local suburban subdivisions that "it's socially very respectable for young people here to call themselves Republicans—a sign of breaking from the past, of a new cultural independence. . . . to be upwardly mobile here, you call yourself a Republican."[56]

Amid broader political pressures and the commotion caused by unruly white parents, Judge Morton remained in control of the courtroom, continually asking for new desegregation plans to consider. School officials, somewhat on the defensive after Avon Williams's fierce questioning, conceded that "more could have been done" in terms of desegregating schools and that their planning was not comprehensive. Observed the *Tennessean*, "witnesses have found themselves discussing not so much the defense of their plan as the best possible but why they could not do better." Williams went so far as to accuse the school administration of "using the 'hostility of the community attitude'" as an excuse for delay. Brooks instead argued that "there is more to bringing about integration in a community than drawing up a plan and putting it into effect." At one point, Morton, tired of the "nebulous figures and computations" given to him, resorted to handing a pencil to a witness and asking him to solve the problem "from scratch." The judge noted that "he was not sure what a unitary system was, but that he did know what a non-dual system was and that was what he wanted" and requested a map of the county's racial demographics to adequately weigh the plans before him and perhaps formulate his own as the court recessed.[57]

As Morton withdrew into his chambers to mull, he had plans before him from the school board, Avon Williams, and a team of HEW experts consulted at the judge's request. The plan authored by Williams was most radical in pairing each inner city school with a suburban counterpart and busing between the two to reach an integrated ratio, with especially heavy busing for elementary students. Unlike the school board, Williams preferred noncontiguous zones to better disperse inhabitants of segregated neighborhoods. HEW's proposal, more far-reaching than the board wanted, but less extensive than Williams's plan, disposed of all-black schools but kept some of the outermost schools all-white, although to a lesser extent than in the school board's plan. HEW experts argued that Williams's blueprint, although best in principle, was "more a model to follow than a detailed plan" because it failed to incorporate key details of pupil assignments. Yet the agency also argued that the board's plan, while effectively desegregating elementary schools, was less effective for the furthermost suburban schools and thus insufficiently broke up segregated neighborhoods.[58]

Naturally, none of the proposals pleased everyone. Williams and the HEW experts agreed that the board's plan was feeble at best—Williams dismissed it as one that "actually does nothing to increase integration" and added "there's no more time." But Williams was equally outspoken against HEW's plan, calling it "unconstitutional" in putting "the greater burden of desegregation upon black school children and their parents." He also resented the implication "that a majority white school is all right, but a majority black school is not." Yet a HEW expert had testified that, "from all the court decisions I've ever read about," recent federal rulings all led to that same conclusion. Williams noted that different zoning matched with HEW's plan would yield more integration—but would require more busing. School superintendent Brooks, for his part, registered displeasure with the HEW plan because it abolished neighborhood schools, while the board's attorney stressed fiscal considerations and the need to not "impinge on the educational system in order to accomplish universal mixing." Essentially, each plan valued desegregation and "neighborhood schools" differently and diverged over which priority should take precedence. Moreover, the same HEW expert observed, it was "up to the court to decide how much busing is too much."[59]

On June 29, 1971, Morton ordered a new busing plan for the coming school year, one that corresponded most closely to the HEW proposal. In explaining his reasoning, Morton scolded the board for its "mere tinkering with attendance zones," which "represents only a token effort." He likewise branded Williams's plan as "highly impractical," with "distance and transportation difficulties" that had some children riding a bus for over an hour each way. The judge instead ordered the district to drop the concept of neighborhood schools and to adopt a model of clustered or sectored schools for a more elaborate and inclusive busing pattern, adding 15,000 more students to the bus lines but excluding thirty-three schools on the outer rim of the district (considered to be too distant for efficient busing). Inner-city students bore a disproportional burden of busing, however. Morton's decision also jettisoned the planned Goodlettsville Comprehensive school, for "it clearly appears that erection of this school would tend to promote segregation," and further required that all future school construction be cleared by him to prevent new schools from serving as "escape valves" for whites fleeing desegregation. Morton also warned against future attempts at delay, saying sternly that "no stay will be granted by this court." The school board chair called the decision "pretty sweeping" and "difficult to understand"; Mayor Briley bluntly termed the ruling "inept" and said "we will resist it (the decision) to the nth degree." Indeed, Briley had gone so far as to consult with his legal officials to research "Who has the authority to control the opening of metro schools for the 71–72 year?" but was advised that Morton's order had precluded the sort of interference that Briley was considering. And the white business community remained "low profile" and "inactive" throughout the busing crisis.[60]

Unsurprisingly, many although not all African Americans viewed busing far differently. One Fisk professor wrote Mayor Briley to affirm that "busing, to date, has done more to persuade school administrators to take steps to improve predominately black, inner city schools than anything else in recent years. . . . an almost overnight improvement in the physical and educational countenance of the schools have been witnessed." Kelly Miller Smith also saw a "marked physical improvement" in inner-city schools, writing to Briley to say that he and his church "enthusiastically favor the busing of school children in our city in preference to the conditions to which they have been subjected in the past." The minister pointed out that "the problem is not busing. We do not need to find a remedy for the busing situation. Rather the problem is racism and we must find solutions to that problem."[61]

Yet the white perspective was altogether different and opposition to the ruling was intense. One citizen claimed that "I never thought there would come the day I could not adjust to the changing affairs of life and also make certain social adjustments with dignity. But," he continued, "this busing issue is something else. The federal judge's decision will ultimately break down all community's ties of a social and civic nature brought on by its association together on the local school level." Another asserted that, for whites, busing was a "violation of their civil rights," and further stated that "you can't legislate love and understanding and the more you try the more hate and misunderstanding you develop." This idea apparently resonated with many, as another wrote, "past injustice on the part of anyone cannot be corrected by present and future injustice inflicted on helpless children" and "equal opportunity is one thing, equality is another." Still others noted an alarming trend. One perceptive housewife asked, "if busing were the issue, would people be considering sending their children to 'private' schools some of which are thirty miles away?"[62]

She was right. In many ways, the most tangible effect of the busing order was the unparalleled growth of private schools in Davidson County. The trend of white flight in housing and neighborhoods now found similar expression in education. During the early 1960s, the desegregation of private schools had been at the same halting rate as for public schools. But, as the decade continued, "most of the private schools . . . adopted policies that will admit qualified Negro students but the schools have not recruited black students." In many cases, "substandard preparation in the lower grades" was sufficient pretext to block blacks from entering. Another issue was the "high tuition" that, it was noted, also blocked lower-class whites from being admitted.[63]

In many cases, whether private schools provided a better education remained unclear. Certainly in terms of facilities, any advantage was questionable. One journalist visiting Glencliff Academy wrote that the school was "like a mini-sized airplane hanger" and "basically a one room school house," where students on "concrete floors" were "forced to use portable outhouses since the bathrooms were not working" as the "air frosts their words." Another account noted that "portable classrooms abound, and some children have been served lunch in the hallways because the cafeteria has become a classroom." The director of admissions at Vanderbilt commented that, "oh, anybody can start a private school now. . . . Just find an old house, put a sign and a swing set out front and attach 'Christian' to your name . . . you're in business." The most glaring irony, and a painful one, was that in taking students from all across the county, many of these schools offered busing. But many whites instead harped on the fact that Avon Williams was sending his children to private schools even as he sued for desegregation in public schools.[64]

The most extensive contemporary study of Nashville's school situation found that over twenty-five hundred students were enrolled in private schools the year after Morton's busing order, whereas "normal growth for those districts, based on the trend in recent years, would have been about 1,000." This was reflected, in part, by an 8 percent loss in public school enrollment in that same year, as seven new private schools sprang into existence, spanning religious denominations from nonsectarian to Free Will Baptist, with Methodists, Church of Christ, and Baptist in between. Few of the schools were accredited, which mattered little because the State of Tennessee did not require such certification. Whites of course disclaimed any sort of racial motivations for opening what their opponents scorned as "segre-academies." In the case of Pioneer Christian Academy, opened in 1969, the whites-only entrance policy was said by a disingenuous school representative as "not to be misconstrued as a 'racist' approach but rather a means to keep 'colored' children from associating with white children and eventually, as he described it, 'inter-marrying.'" Another parent clarified that "they say we are prejudiced but we are not prejudiced. We are simply trying to preserve what little culture is left in this country."[65]

For those neither privileged nor desperate enough to pay for private schools, the first day of public schooling under court-ordered busing provided a grotesque echo of 1957. The newspapers tried hard to stay positive. The *Tennessean* had run a "special tabloid section" as a "public service" given the "anxiety and questions" in the community. Elliptical references to "one incident reported" of someone armed and "trying to run off the Negro students" were buried amid semiwhimsical stories of yawning children climbing on buses and saying, "I'm going to have to get to bed earlier." Only years later did the full extent of the disruption that day become apparent as "protestors picketed schools, rocks were thrown, and bomb threats called in to several schools." Even on the front lines, the bitterness and tension was thick. One police officer guarding the picket lines at Una School got into verbal altercations with teachers, calling blacks "inferior," "nigger," and "savages" and telling an educator "you should go live in the North" and "you're a fuzzy liberal." One school official remembers that over the first few days, white bus drivers picked up white students, and black drivers followed the same routes for black students. When one bus collided with an automobile, Mayor Briley blamed the court order. Anguished white parents told of the immense peer pressure they were experiencing; one claimed that a neighbor told her "you really don't love your child or you wouldn't send him to this school." That evening, fifteen thousand attended a CPA meeting at Fairgrounds Speedways, where Casey Jenkins (introduced as "General Casey Jenkins"), who had recently lost the mayoral run-off to Briley, exhorted his followers to stage a "parents protest" to boycott the schools. "We must protect our children," said Jenkins, "we have been sold out by politicians." Jack Kershaw also spoke at the meeting to "cite portions of the U.S. Constitution and laws of the State of Tennessee for [the] benefit of the audience."[66]

The CPA's efforts disrupted schools over the next several days by "blocking traffic" with pickets. Indeed, "in some instances over-zealous protestors came on school grounds and attempted to block driveways and walks to prevent pupil entrance." At one school, a crowd estimated at nearly six hundred chanted "ride the bus 50 miles a day" to the tune of "Row, Row, Row Your Boat." A week later there were still more than five hundred protesters, mostly women and children—Nashville's white mothers had mobilized against busing just as they had on the eve of public school desegregation fourteen years earlier.[67] The New York Times, a week and a half later, ran a photo of a white Nashville housewife in tears as she tried to drive through picketers to get her child to school. The Times journalist saw a contrast between the scene and the older era of massive resistance: "white mothers and children, walking up the hill, stared at the bus without expression. The days of New Orleans and Little Rock, when white mothers spat hatred at black children, seemed far away." But the contrast seemed unconvincing when compared to one white mother's profession that "'I don't mind her going to school with colored, long they don't mix, you know what I mean. . . . I just don't want them going across town to no nigger school with a nigger boy down the block.'"[68]

The busing crisis in Nashville marked a beginning more than an ending as the clash over busing continued for decades. It was an avoidance of history, really;

the evading of paying a toll long deferred due to Jim Crow practices. But there was also the unreality of the situation, as personal circumstances were interpreted without any reference to underlying problems that dictated racial matters in far more substantive ways than with a yellow school bus.

The reshaping of Nashville did not mean that the black freedom struggle had ended or even declined—what it meant was that once again the rules had changed. African Americans had gone from enslavement to Reconstruction-era restrictions, from plantation to city, from segregation to movement, but the struggle would continue. Certainly other examples of black activism and resistance occurred as black Nashvillians lobbied to assert their voices and for more chances to define their own destinies. Picketing against the Methodist publishing house for discrimination in hiring had occurred in 1969. The following year, a coalition of local black organizations protested against black-oriented radio station WVOL for not sufficiently supporting increased black employment opportunities or public service programming. Culturally speaking, black liberation theology took firm hold among the numerous black churches dotting Nashville.[69]

Politically, it was much the same story as before. The local black political scene continued to be comprised of "ward-based, weak organizations" where middle-class organizations and individual leaders had personal "prestige but no apparatus." There was the rivalry between the Davidson County Democratic League (DCDL), the declining remnants of Ben West's old city machine, versus the Davidson County Independent Political Council (DCIPC), which was itself an "outgrowth" of the local NAACP. The latter's links to local patronage and white liberals were criticized by many. The group was "reputed, by many Nashvillians, to be unwilling to share power and this unwillingness embraces the pathology of the white power structure" in not allowing an "average everyday guy to make meaningful input." This ineffectiveness was underlined by the 1970 mayoral election, in which the DCIPC declined to endorse a candidate and only marginalized its own influence. Edwin Mitchell, head of the group, argued that the point was that both candidates were unacceptable from a black perspective and that black votes were not to be "taken for granted." But rivals termed it "the most embarassing [sic] date in the [group's] nine year history." Regardless of the validity of such criticisms, no credible alternative ever emerged; above all else, said Edwin Mitchell, black politics continued to be "not really evolving."[70]

In 1971, a "buy black when possible" campaign for economic withdrawal focused on downtown and "suburban shopping centers." Some complained that "black officeholders have been badgered for seemingly avoiding any connection with the economic protest drive." And "many black activists had lamented the apparent apathy of the black community as a whole." But others saw promise in the campaign, particularly as the Chamber of Commerce made hushed overtures for negotiations through a state senator. Inexplicably, the economic withdrawal failed shortly after. One account reported the "chorus of 'Right-on's'" when a speaker called for blacks to use black-owned banks only, but "privately, one of the city's important freedom fighters confided to two friends a reluctance to 'take my money and put it in one of those nigger banks.'" Said one activist, "our people let us down in a very real sense."[71]

According to the racial etiquette of the Jim Crow South, African Americans used contradictions in race and class to survive and adapt individually, even as they tried to mount incremental changes against a wider system of oppression. In this new context, many complained about "too many blacks fighting blacks" and "strong opposition" by certain blacks created situations that some "exploit for personal gain." Many were bitter about how some black elites supported urban renewal to raise their own property values. Politically, it was less a question of rivalry as different people working to different ends with different means. Nor was it apathy, necessarily, just "not active" and "no great outpouring of money and support."[72] The black Nashville Way that had marked the 1960 sit-ins lay dormant among African Americans, leaving the struggle to be carried on in other ways.

The assault on black Nashville by the city's white political and economic elite, and the numbers of whites disgusted with busing's power to intrude upon white communities, showed how the black freedom struggle had only made partial progress toward freedom for African American aspirations and against the white tendency to see blacks as less than equal. Whites in Nashville—and across the nation—drew sustenance from framing their attitudes and anger in terms of reverse discrimination and color blindness, just as the myth of pleasant race relations had soothed them in the past. One parent wrote Mayor Briley to say that "now in 1971, my children are being discriminated against because their skin is white. Two wrongs do not make a right." Another writer branded busing as worse than slavery. At one point early in the 1971 school year, superintendent Brooks was asked to comment on the prevailing notion that "many parents of various economic and cultural levels think that classroom ratios of more Negroes than whites result in lower quality education in those classrooms." This pernicious myth about race and busing would be directly debunked years later by a study of Nashville schools commissioned by Brooks himself. But for now, "Dr. Brooks made no reply and turned to another subject."[73]

In such silences against unchallenged myths, the white Nashville Way would endure.

Achieving Justice

People are trapped in history and history is trapped in them.
—James Baldwin, "Stranger in a Village," 1953

A 1963 *New York Herald Tribune* article implicitly extolled the white Nashville Way as the reason why Nashville was the "most desegregated city in the South." The author observed that "one thing [Nashville] cannot abide is unpleasantness. It values peace and quiet as Birmingham, to the south, values separate water fountains and defiance." Indeed, the writer was quite taken with the difference: "a traveler from Birmingham is struck immediately by the contrasts of Nashville. It takes a day or so to adjust to it. Of course Nashville has had a long history of graciousness while Birmingham has no history at all." This meant that for African Americans, "'their battle is won here,'" according to Mayor Ben West, dubbed an "old friend of the Negro community." Black minister Metz Rollins responded to this characterization by snorting that "these people here got to believing their own press clippings about how progressive they were." But he qualified his instinctive derision: "the only difference between Nashville and Birmingham is one of degree. . . . of course I have to admit that difference is like night and day."[1]

Within the paradoxes of these comments lies the strange intersection of the black and white Nashville Ways, the interplay between whites and blacks trapped in segregated legacies. That opinion on Nashville's racial climate could agree and yet differ so sharply signals that something more complicated was at work. This book has tried to evoke how the lived realities of segregation were replicated in individual and collective ways as African Americans fought against and protected themselves from a system that every day tried to cheapen their lives and humanity. The elaborate facade that whites constructed in daily racial etiquette, creating a social world where interpretations of how individuals acted or reacted only perpetuated deeper fictions about race, conditioned responses that relentlessly maintained social distance. This was replicated on a broader scale with changing racial and urban patterns defending against black activism. Shifts in racial law and racial custom over time marked the protean character of white supremacy, even as African Americans continued and reinvented the struggle with each generation, balancing individual survival with a wide array of tactics on behalf of a broader bid for racial freedom.

That cultural myths about race and whiteness persisted in these years is perhaps best displayed by country music, which had been part of Nashville's identity since the early part of the twentieth century. Of course this genre had always blended elements of white and black musical traditions, even as its hillbilly roots had been superficially identified with whites. In 1979, venerable traditionalist and country music star Porter Waggoner facilitated a performance by James Brown, the famed Godfather of Soul, at the Grand Ole Opry. The concert was met with coolness from the audience (and hate mail, too, according to one account). Music star Del Wood said "I'm against James Brown's music on the stage of the Opry because I love the Opry and what it stands for." Such responses were not anomalies. As black country music star Cleve Francis relates, a meeting with record executives as he lobbied for increased representation of black music stars in the industry was met dismissively. Said one, "This may be the last thing that white people got." Indeed, the Grand Ole Opry mirrored broader trends when it relocated to suburban Nashville.[2]

Over the course of the 1970s, little changed as aspects of race relations continued echoing the past. Schools, as in the 1950s, often took the focus, and made for an uneasy racial environment. While relationships among children in the schools varied widely, there was a trend toward voluntary social segregation. Despite some newspaper articles glowing about a school's interracial cast in a production of *The Sound Of Music*, for example, there were far more muted admissions from students that a quiet truce prevailed in classrooms. "It's not hostility," said one student, "We don't like them and they don't like us." Said another, "There's still a lot of tension, even though people won't admit it." Yet there were also hints that the children's racial notions were not the only factor in play. Some people "didn't want poor white folks, let alone blacks," and class issues persisted because "in a lot of cases, the white kids have the money and the black kids don't."[3]

Even as public schools struggled to adjust, the increased numbers in private schooling persisted. An "all-time high" was recorded in 1972 as "more than 14,000 students" eschewed public schools and "most of the increase was in the new private and Protestant church-related schools." Enrollment at Church of Christ–affiliated Goodpasture Academy exploded from 148 to 800 in only six years. In 1973, across the county "total private school enrollment jumped 41% from the previous year."

Private schools now had "remarkable popularity" with filled rolls and waiting lists. Some noted that "parents see the private school as a status symbol," and prognosticators foresaw a three-tier schooling system in the future, with each tier catering to upper, middle, and lower classes. Explanations for the private-school trend varied; many argued that public and elite schools had reached "a saturation point," which created the demand for more private schools. Others said that, "we have no quarrel with the public schools. We just wanted to be able to teach the Bible every day" and "present academics in a high moral atmosphere," especially given the hot-button issues of sex education and evolution raging at the time. Some continued to "deny strongly" that busing fueled the private school boom, while others clarified that "busing, not integration" was the reason. Another estimate said that 50 to 75 percent of the students were there because of busing. The most dispassionate observer commented instead that, "while an unwillingness to desegregate is no doubt the main reason for white flight, it is not the only one," citing other factors as "elitism and class privilege," classroom discipline, college preparatory curricula, and the Bible.[4]

The busing issue remained touchy and ongoing for decades. The imposed zones could not keep up with rapidly shifting neighborhood demographics. In 1972, the court ordered the school system to buy more buses so as to continue the busing plan. When, in 1977, school officials tried to widen the plan to cover all schools in the county, the proposal "drowned in a storm of public protest." In the 1980s, when the thirty-three schools left untouched by the busing order were recognized as magnets for white flight, the school system had to draw up a new plan, setting up another round of legal battling. From 1969 to 1983, the school system lost 30,000 students, an overwhelming percentage of them white. Although one of several factors, busing was still the most potent symbol for demographic shifts as whites fled to suburbs. Not until September 28, 1998, was the Metropolitan School District declared "unitary," or free of any vestiges of segregation.[5]

Of course, much of the problem undergirding school desegregation was housing, and little on that front changed. In 1977, the *Tennessean* ran an exposé on interracial couples sent to find housing. The "combination of grossly inflated rental prices" and "subtle discriminatory practices" had led to a cynical definition of integration as "the length of time between the first black family's moving into the neighborhood and the last white family's moving out." The extent of "racial steering" was debated, but there was "zoned racial planning in terms of sections, areas of marketing, solicitation and advertising." This was done in ways "subtle rather than obvious," as prospective buyers were told that "there's not going to be any blacks in this subdivision, so your property value will remain constant and the community will be quiet." Realtors defended themselves as just supplying information for "making the wisest investment." Said one client, "They're very nice about the way they do it."[6]

The uncertainties of school desegregation rested uneasily with the more dedicated racial line dividing housing, but there were other ways in which the character of Nashville's segregation was reembedded in the city landscape. North Nashville was naturally confined on two sides by the Cumberland River, as only Clarksville Pike and the Jefferson Street Bridge linked the neighborhood to other areas. But, as part of the city's desire to diversify economically, the borders where North Nashville met both the river and the Central Business District was increasingly being occupied by wholesaling warehouses. This meant that the area was plum real estate for industrial development, particularly since this was the site where railroads, the river, and now the newly built interstate converged. As a result, African American residents and their homes were being squeezed out. Across the river in East Nashville, where urban renewal had specified industrial uses for the sliver of land between the river and Interstate 65, a parallel trend was developing.

Public housing also factored into city contours. The construction of Ellington Parkway parallel to Interstate 65 and ending near the Cumberland River isolated James Cayce Homes, the largest public housing project in the city, as if with pincers. This maneuver was replicated across the city, as all public housing projects were barricaded by major roads or interstates. To the south, urban renewal had remade a neighborhood near Vanderbilt University and Belmont College into what is now the famed "Music Row" housing Nashville's country music industry. Many music executives bought neighboring homes as a result, even with the predominantly African American neighborhood of Edgehill nearby, which had some black businesses and a thriving neighborhood center in the 1950s. As a result, 12th Avenue South was widened dramatically to become a major north–south corridor that also barricaded the Edgehill Homes public housing project nearby. In conjunction with Interstates 40 and 65, plus the connecter loop of Interstate 440, Edgehill was now confined on all sides by major traffic arteries. Street patterns now formed cul-de-sacs to buttress the spatial division between Music Row and nearby neighborhoods, and Wedgewood Avenue was expanded as a formidable line between Edgehill and Belmont College.[7]

By contrast, Bordeaux, across the river from North Nashville, had already experienced some growth as a black suburb for those African Americans who could afford to purchase homes there. Yet the retail space there had already been bought up by white merchants. And the later construction of Briley Parkway (also called State Route 155) arcing through northern and eastern Davidson County would essentially fence in both Bordeaux and East Nashville as both became increasingly

African American. Briley Parkway encircles essentially three fourths of the city, with I-440 completing the circle. Increasingly, Briley Parkway became the de facto border between city and suburbs and thus figured into school desegregation. By the 1970s, Nashville was trying to build comprehensive schools along Briley Parkway. By locating these large schools near Briley Parkway, school officials hoped to lessen the pressure of integrating schools because the schools would sit directly between the white suburbs and African Americans in the central city. As it turned out, these schools epitomized the loss of neighborhoods schools that rallied such intense opposition to busing throughout the decade.[8] In such a way did the built landscape replicate a different form of a segregated world than the one that had ruled Nashville under Jim Crow, as whites cloaked rhetoric and actions according to external abstract values, first in the guise of moderation and second in the supposedly color-blind procedures of politics and public policy. In 1955, Cecil Sims was mulling over how to build tokenism into legal compliance with school desegregation at about the same time that plans for Interstate 40 were being finalized to devastate black businesses. Both Evansville, Indiana, and a New York planning firm were points of reference as this southern city managed both these tasks effectively through "voluntary" or "legal" means. By the 1970s, the racial etiquette was not the color-conscious paternalism of midcentury, but one that tried to speak in terms of color blindness even as it codified white privilege. As one scholar had phrased it archly in 1961, "Progress in Nashville is essentially an attempt to maintain the old way of life as much as possible by giving it necessary transfusions." To local blacks, it felt eerily familiar. As Kelly Miller Smith noted in 1971, according to the new racial etiquette, "you don't say that Negroes are inferior, you just exclude them from any consideration. They don't exist. Invisible men." Or, as Robert Lillard put it in 1995: "Nashville is controlled by a different type of aristocratic people than other cities. . . . They are subtle people. They make (their prejudice) known by not letting things happen."[9] For all of their power, black activists could not overcome perhaps the strangest contradiction in the white Nashville Way: the need for whites to see themselves as better than they were, less race-conscious, more color blind, and thus ignore the repercussions of history.

This book has understood civil rights in Nashville as battles on two fronts simultaneously, the assault on southern racial etiquette and the fight over urban space. The struggle began in the false etiquette of race relations, where blacks were cast as second-class citizens for the material benefits of their labor and for the psychological benefits of whiteness. Cultural allegiance to a false memory of an Old South's noblesse oblige were updated in the rituals born from the necessities of Jim Crow life in an urban context. The public submission of racial etiquette, as social realities were acted out on Nashville streets, was imposed precisely to minimize the ugliness of segregation and to cast moral virtues upon individuals so as to ignore the broader system. So too was the paternalism the same, with power consolidated in separate worlds of business and politics that were inherently conservative, inclined to stability, anxious to control their respective terrain, and averse to change.[10]

African Americans fought back continually. The black elite used their diverse professional strengths to attack segregation through education, legal means, economic and sociological know-how, and more. Student energy at black schools put bodies on the line to signal their resistance to the segregated order. The exceptional moment occurred with the 1960 lunch-counter sit-ins and the devotion to principled nonviolence, where the range of black tactics converged with unity, shrewdly targeting the downtown where political and economic vulnerabilities of whites were manifest and compounding political and economic divisions among grassroots and elite segregationist resistance. This was precisely why the nonviolence of 1960 was so earth-shattering: now the political theater of everyday etiquette was altogether different. The sit-ins rewrote the script entirely, modeling a higher virtue and morality by capturing the initiative and redefining standards of etiquette and by twisting violence into a possibility for affirming rather than denying.

As the 1960s continued, this battle evolved in several ways. The first was whites ensuring that they would not be vulnerable to black pressure again. In struggling to find a new language and morality that would govern racial interaction, now that the moderation that had worked so well in the past was failing, whites tried to realign law and custom as interlocking elements. For African Americans, their evolution was in trying to sustain and broaden the struggle to other dimensions of segregation even in juggling multiple perspectives among themselves. Both these evolutions were tenuous because politics and economics were so disaggregated in Nashville society among blacks and whites alike. When the business and political elites from both races worked in harmony in being pushed and cajoled by black activists, as in 1960 and 1963, results happened. Otherwise, white indifference remained, with an emphasis on what had changed becoming an excuse for not changing further.

Similar internal divisions dictated black development, as multiple forms of activism did not always coalesce into a movement. Black student activists gathered themselves anew in the era of Black Power, itself a different attack on racial etiquette. But Black Power advocates could not make common cause with the black elite. And equally important, that uncertain relationship made Nashville's police suppression all the more effective. Even as blacks argued that they should adhere to their own racial standards rather than to those of whites, and claim social and political distance for themselves, it became easier for whites to stigmatize those terms and frames of thinking. The call for law and order was a state-sanctioned imposition of etiquette as African Americans expressed frustration at seeing their complaints go unheard. And having distanced themselves from Black Power activism, black elites now found themselves further cut off from economic and political power as urban renewal and interstate construction converged on their neighborhoods with devastating force. The combination of black activism and public policy ended with African Americans segmented into walled-off neighborhoods more closely bound to white businesses and landlords. The use of segregation to curtail economic growth became, with urban renewal, the excuse to create further black economic dependence in the name of economic growth for the city as a whole, but most disproportionately in support of white privilege.[11]

Whites created the world they wanted, even as they were pressured into doing so by African American activism, and their beliefs were replicated and perpetuated in multiple ways within the community and beyond. National media bought into the Nashville myth and thus fed it. Despite bombings, police violence, near-riots, civil rights clashes, and ongoing turmoil, the media compounded the pretenses of white Nashville in celebrating Nashville's supposed moderation despite a deeply troubling continuation of the past. Nashville's economic base of religious and educational institutions provided a black middle-class that white Nashvillians were compelled to at least pretend to flatter (politically and socially), which they could do so in ways that preserved white superiority but also use to cheerlead the city as a whole—thus presenting two faces within the city and to the wider nation. It was a massive whitewash on multiple levels. That such manners constituted an elaborate social fraud, and yet conditioned two distinct internalizations for blacks and whites, is eloquent testimony about the power of segregated legacies. The false sharing in the rituals of coexistence, in masking more profound divisions, speaks to central contradictions at the very heart of southernness and race.

That new versions of segregated realities continued in no way discredits the civil rights movement's legacy as a force in history, both on personal and societal levels. Indeed, the movement changed individuals as much as individuals changed the movement. The act of giving one's self to a cause, and discovering hidden individual talents and a collective power, transformed many of those who were graced with the chance to touch the spirit of this struggle. As Diane Nash observes, "if people understood the Movement, they wouldn't ask, 'When will we get another leader like that?' They would ask 'what can I do?'"[12] The movement made what was once unimaginable—the act of breaking bread with a person of another race, for example—now generally unremarkable, and thus began to erode away the visible top layer of white supremacy encrusted on the southern soil, the daily denigration of blackness that lurked on the most routine walk down a city street. The bedrock belief of supposed racial difference, however, persisted—if somewhat loosened by the movement, then repaved into the concrete path of an interstate that helped remake boundaries between the races. The dotted lines of roads now replaced the WHITE and COLORED signs of the past, recasting physical space to mirror the social space of the Jim Crow era. It is perhaps the ultimate testimony to how much the movement jarred the prevailing racial etiquette that an entire city was redrawn and reshaped in order to preserve the legacies of the past.

So both Nashville Ways were preserved. One was a daring exhortation for imagining a more just society; the other clung to the created fiction of a past and a history made utterly real. From one city came two separate legacies coinciding fitfully if at all, even as genuine, breathtaking change in the racial landscape coexisted with recapitulated patterns of the past. As Edwin Mitchell said in a speech, referring to Nashville's "Athens of the South" moniker and quoting the Greek scholar Thucydides, "We shall achieve justice in Athens when those who are not injured are as indignant as those who are."[13] Locked in an uncertain embrace, black and white Nashvillians shared in southernness while separated by race, always at arm's length and never in step or in time, continuing this odd dance as if to a country music song only the two of them could hear.

NOTES

Introduction

1. Josephine Taylor, Harry Walker, and Lewis W. Jones, "Forms of Segregation and Discrimination in Nashville, Tennessee," (no date), FUSC-CSJ, box 228, folder 10 (hereafter cited as "Forms of Segregation"), quotations on 40–41; see also 44. Mailroom detail from C. S. Johnson, *Patterns of Segregation*, 40.

2. "Patterns of Segregation in Nashville," pages 9–12, excerpting fuller information in "Institutions in Which Practice of Segregation Has a Legal Structure" (no author, no date), FUSC-CSJ, box 229, folder 7. Courtroom detail (32) and railway station and customs house details (40) in Johnson, *Patterns of Segregation*. See also Kelly Miller Smith, "The Shame and Glory," VUSC-KMS, box 28, folder 7, 15.

3. J. E. Windrow, "Nashville: Athens of the South," July 13, 1945, in RISL-MRR, box 13, folder 186, first quotations on 5, voter apathy quotation on 7, tuberculosis quotation on 9, final quotation on 6. See also D. Doyle, *Nashville Since the 1920s*, 185–86, and the *Globe*, July 20, 1945, NPL-NR.

4. E. L. Holland, July 17, 1962, letter in box 17, folder "correspondence April–Dec 1962"; Connelly, *Will Campbell and the Soul of the South*, 67. Kyriakoudes, *Social Origins of the Urban South*; D. Doyle, *Nashville in the New South, 1880–1930*, and introduction in D. Doyle, *Nashville Since the 1920s*. See also Egerton and Wood, ed., *Nashville: An American Self-Portrait*, 20–22, 94–95, 100; Egerton, *Nashville: The Face of Two Centuries*, 233–35, 237; Seigenthaler interview, UF-SPOHP; K. M. Smith, "Shame and Glory," 23.

5. West quoted in K. M. Smith, "Shame and the Glory," 3; Halberstam, *The Children*, 110; D. Doyle, *Nashville Since the 1920s*, 223. For Nashville highlighted as a place needing further scholarly examination, see Eagles, "Toward New Histories of the Civil Rights Era," 836.

6. Chafe, *Civilities and Civil Rights*, 8. See Chappell, *Inside Agitators*; Chappell, *A Stone of Hope*; Sosna, *In Search of the Silent South*; Egerton, *Speak Now Against the Day*; Badger, "Fatalism, Not Gradualism."

7. Frank D. Dorey, "Southtown and Christian Social Action," January 1, 1944, FUSC-CSJ, box 33, folder 7, 2:8 ("glory in the past"), 7:1 ("talk out of existence").

8. Lewis and Vivian quoted in D. Doyle, *Nashville Since the 1920s*, 223. For the Nashville influence on the wider Movement, see Branch, *Parting the Waters* and *Pillar of Fire*; Carson, *In Struggle*; Morris, *Origins of the Civil Rights Movement*; Arsenault, *Freedom Riders*; Hogan, *Many Minds, One Heart*.

9. This view is affirmed in Dorey, "Southtown and Christian Social Action," 14; Will D. Campbell interview, UF-SPOHP.

10. Cell, *Highest Stage of White Supremacy*, 134; Lamon; *Blacks in Tennessee, 1791–1970* and *Black Tennesseans, 1900–1930*; Lovett, *The African-American History of Nashville, Tennessee, 1780–1930*, and *Civil Rights Movement in Tennessee*.

11. Chafe, *Civilities and Civil Rights*; Green, *Battling the Plantation Mentality*; Moye, *Let the People Decide*; Crosbye, *Little Taste of Freedom*; Norrell, *Reaping the Whirlwind*; Colburn, *Racial Change and Community Crisis*; Payne, *I've Got the Light of Freedom*; Fairclough, *Race and Democracy*; Dittmer, *Local People*; Eskew, *But for Birmingham*; K'Meyer, *Civil Rights in the Gateway to the South*; Green, *Battling the Plantation Mentality*; Tuck, *Beyond Atlanta*; Thornton, *Dividing Lines*.

12. Litwack, *Trouble in Mind*; McMillen, *Dark Journey*; Hahn, *Nation under Our Feet*; M. Schultz, *Rural Face of White Supremacy*; Ritterhouse, *Growing Up Jim Crow*; Ownby, *Manners and Southern History*; J. D. Smith; *Managing White Supremacy*.

13. Kruse, *White Flight*; Lassiter, *Silent Majority*; Self, *American Babylon*; Crespino, *In Search of Another Country*.

Chapter 1. A Manner of Segregation

1. Gilmore, *Racial Disorganization in a Southern City*, 48–55.

2. "Most resistant" quotation in "Waiting Room Practices in 21 Southern Cities" report, GSU-SLA-EVP, box 3383, folder 3, July 17, 1959. There is a rich tradition of sociological literature examining the racial etiquette of the South, including B. Doyle, *Etiquette of Race Relations in the South*; Dollard, *Caste and Class in a Southern Town*; Powdermaker, *After Freedom*; A. Davis, B. Gardner, and M. Gardner, *Deep South*.

3. Frank D. Dorey, "Southtown and Christian Social Action," January 1, 1944, FUSC-CSJ, box 33, folder 7, 3:18–23 (quotations on 21, 22). Dorey's manuscript has irregular pagination; in my citations, the first number refers to the chapter and the number after the colon refers to the page number in that chapter. See also Josephine Taylor, Harry Walker, and Lewis W. Jones, "Forms of Segregation and Discrimination in Nashville, Tennessee" (no date), FUSC-CSJ, box 228, folder 10 (hereafter cited as "Forms of Segregation"), 11; "Institutions in Which Practice of Segregation Has a Legal Structure," (no author, no date), FUSC-CSJ, box 229, folder 7, 52; Spinney, *World War II in Nashville*, 58–59; On taxicabs, see C. S. Johnson, *Patterns of Segregation*, 52; for transportation clashes more generally, see C. S. Johnson, "Present Status of Race Relations in the South," Oct. 1944, FUSC-CSJ, box 171, folder 6. Fisk student anecdote from Antoinette S. Desmond, "On Sitting," *Crisis*, 62 (November 1955), 524. See also Hanson, *Report on Politics in Nashville*, 6:18, which documents segregation in some public places and "other private places by custom." For an example of the black response to streetcar segregation in 1905, see the letter to the *Banner* from influential leader R. H. Boyd in A. Meier, Rudwick, and Broderick, *Black Protest Thought in the Twentieth Century*, 28–31, and by A. Meier and Rudwick, "Negro Boycotts of Jim Crow Streetcars in Tennessee." On Fisk, see Lamon, "The Black Community in Nashville and the Fisk University Student Strike of 1924–1925"; see also Hale, *Making Whiteness*, 133–38.

4. "Forms of Segregation," 10–12; "Institutions in Which Practice of Segregation Has a Legal Structure," 68–93. Fisk student anecdote by Antoinette S. Desmond, "On Sitting,"

523–24. Note, however, that the *Globe*, November 9, 1945, talks about the ease with which credit was extended to blacks. See also Scruggs, *Claiming Kin*, 112–13.

5. C. S. Johnson, *Patterns of Segregation*; "Institutions in Which Practice of Segregation Has a Legal Structure," 26–32. On Meharry see C. W. Johnson, *Spirit of a Place Called Meharry*.

6. "Fine line of distinction" quotation in Nelson Fuson to Ralph and Marian Harlow, letter February 1, 1956, VUSC-NMFP, box 1, folder 1; white reporter in Kelly Miller Smith, "Shame and Glory," VUSC-KMS, box 28, folder 7, 18, see also 6; neighborhood stores quotations in "Forms of Segregation," 10, 12. See also interview with Prince Rivers and Dean W. T. Green, SCRBC-AMP, MG 340, box 70, folder 5 ("several places will serve mixed groups privately"); Van Til, *My Way of Looking at It*, 180. John Kasson particularly highlights dining as the particular fraught place where social distinctions threaten to be erased thanks to social fluidity, in *Rudeness and Civility*, 207–14; see also Quinn, "How to Behave Sensitively."

7. D. Doyle, *Nashville Since the 1920s*, 44; Hoss Allen in CMHOF-VF "WLAC"; Allen obituary in the *Tennessean*, February 26, 1997; Hoskyns, *Say It One Time for the Broken-hearted*, 51.

8. On Bailey, see *Nashville!* 1, no. 12 (March 1974): 54; Paul Broome interviewed by John W. Rumble, August 21, 1990, CMHOF-OH; *Nashville Scene*, November 3, 1997; *Nashville Globe*, April 27, 1956.

9. Kenneth Mack has discussed how "racial identity was defined by one's treatment in public spaces" in exploring how African American lawyers were able to "cut across the grain of normal racial interaction" by virtue of their profession ("Representing the Race," draft ms., in possession of the author). See also Pye, "Complex Relations."

10. Quoted in Day, "Flannery O'Connor and the Southern Code of Manners."

11. Dorey, "Southtown and Christian Social Action," 2:16, 2:4.

12. Quoted in Dorey, "Southtown and Christian Social Action," 3:24, see also 3:18; my following text condenses the material in "Forms of Segregation," 13–33.

13. "Forms of Segregation," 13–25—"we treat them" quotation on 15, the rest on 22–24; Johnson, *Patterns of Segregation*, 257.

14. Quotation in C. S. Johnson, "Crazy Quilt of Racial Segregation," FUSC-CSJ, box 159, folder 25, 7; "Forms of Segregation," 17 ("fur quotation"), 21.

15. "Forms of Segregation," 27.

16. Ibid., minister quotation, 28, housewife account, 29. Principal anecdote in Haynes, *Scars of Segregation*, 38. See also Dorey, "Southtown and Christian Social Action," 3:31; M. Schultz, *Rural Face of White Supremacy*, 85.

17. "Forms of Segregation," quotation on 35 ("hit me or shoot me"), see also 18; 36 (mechanics, "paying more" and "always polite" quotations); 54 ("adaptability"), later echoed in *Tennessean*, February 5, 1987.

18. The following is excerpted from Rhoda L. Goldstein, "A Study of Interracial Professional Practices and Attitudes of Negro Dentists in Nashville, Tennessee," June 1949, FUSC-CSJ, box 229, folder 5. Goldstein apparently was dark-complected enough to pass for black in some of the interviews she conducted, which she felt factored into some of the insights she gleaned from her interviewees.

19. Goldstein, "Study of Interracial Professional Practices and Attitudes of Negro Dentists in Nashville, Tennessee"; patients calling on 30, "crackers" quotation on 31, referrals

practice on 35, "dressing up" on 34, "accommodating negroes" on 42, "difficult living like this" on 27). For the *Globe*'s defense of "Uncle Tom," see the June 15, 1956, editorial.

20. Goldstein, "Study of Interracial Professional Practices and Attitudes of Negro Dentists in Nashville, Tennessee," 15–16 (both quotations) and on professional peer relationships, 36–37. On the latter see the *Tennessean*, September 15, 1954, and Summerville, *Educating Black Doctors*, 122.

21. "Forms of Segregation," with quotations coming from the sample interviews at the end, including Luther Martin (the teenage houseboy), June 17, 1939, and Martha L. Harris (describing the account of the white mother), June 22, 1939. These interviews are paged improperly according to the table of contents. For more on southerners learning racial etiquette, see Ritterhouse, "Reading, Intimacy, and the Role of Uncle Remus in White Southern Social Memory," and *Growing Up Jim Crow*.

22. Lamon, *Black Tennesseans, 1900–1930*, 283, and "Black Community in Nashville and the Fisk University Student Strike of 1924–1925," 236; S. Ramsey, *Reading, Writing, and Segregation*, 35; Berry, "Charles S. Johnson, Fisk University, and the Struggle for Civil Rights, 1945–1970," 9; Scruggs, *Claiming Kin*, 25; K. M. Smith, "Shame and Glory," 5 (but compare the *Tennessean*, August 31, 2005, which has a different account of events, even though the article quotes contemporary newspapers). A lynching of a Maury County citizen occurred near the Fisk campus in 1933, see O'Brien, *Color of the Law*, 78–86.

23. Teacher quotation in S. Ramsey, *Reading, Writing, and Segregation*, 40; medical student in "I Joined the Human Race," *Saturday Evening Post* clipping (ca. 1954), UNC-SHC-GPB, box 12, folder 1456. Bus line information in Halberstam, *The Children*, 106–7; Websdale, *Policing the Poor*, 53; Hall, "I-40's Route through North Nashville," 13.

24. D. Doyle, *Nashville Since the 1920s*, 42–45; Chavis, "Underworld of Nashville," 13, 26.

25. Chavis, "Underworld of Nashville," ch. 2 (prostitutes on 14).

26. Ibid., 5, 26, 41, 95–97.

27. Summerville, "The City and the Slum," 187–90; D. Doyle, *Nashville Since the 1920s*, 42–48.

28. D. Doyle, *Nashville Since the 1920s*, 96–99; see also "Preliminary Report on Special Housing Survey of Negro families, Nashville Tennessee" (August 1945), FUSC-RBJ, box 2, folder 2.

29. Summerville, "The City and the Slum," 185, 190–91; Gilmore, *Racial Disorganization in a Southern City*, 48–55, 60; Haynes, *Scars of Segregation*, 70–71, regarding reactions to a black church moving into Edgefield; Lovett, *Civil Rights Movement in Tennessee*, 32.

30. David Halberstam, "Nashville Was My Graduate School," in Egerton and Wood, *Nashville: An American Self-Portrait*, 38–39; K. M. Smith, "Shame and the Glory," 21 (where he also brands black businesses in Nashville as "small and unimpressive"); Hawkins, *Nashville Metro*, 19; Hanson, *Report on Politics*, 1:6; Dorey, "Southtown and Christian Social Action," 2:10.

31. Dorey, "Southtown and Christian Social Action," 2:9, 2:12, 3:18; Halberstam, *The Children*, 110; Rufus Jarman, "Nashville," *Saturday Evening Post* 224 (October 27, 1951): 22; George Barrett, UF-SPOHP; Hanson, *Report on Politics in Nashville*, 2:5; D. Doyle, *Nashville Since the 1920s*, 108, 110 (on Ford glass plant), 129, 132; Spinney, *World War II in Nashville*, 41–42. See also Egerton, *Nashville: The Face of Two Centuries*, 234–35. On Nashville gentility, see *New York Times*, June 12, 1964.

32. Dorey, "Southtown and Christian Social Action," 3:30; Summerville, *Educating Black Doctors*, xi, 135–36, 147; on American Baptist, see Spinney, *World War II in Nashville*, 2, 52–68; D. Doyle, *Nashville Since the 1920s*, 170; Robbins, *Sidelines Activist*, 65–67; C. S. Johnson, "Crazy Quilt of Racial Segregation," 5; Egerton, *Speak Now Against the Day*, 129–30, 234, on Fisk; Redd, "Educational Desegregation in Tennessee," 337; Lovett, *Civil Rights Movement in Tennessee*, 32.

33. Comments from Gloria Marshall (ca. May 1956), SCRBC-AMP, MG 340, box 5, folder 29; majorette anecdote from Catherine Burks Brook, BCRI-OHP; Miss Fisk anecdote in Berry, "Charles S. Johnson, Fisk University, and the Struggle for Civil Rights, 1945–1970," 46.

34. "Peasant class" quotation in Dorey, "Southtown and Christian Social Action," 3:30, see also 2:13, 3:18, 3:29; ganging places in Kyriakoudes, *Social Origins of the Urban South*, 120–21; Hanson, *Report on Politics*, 6:18, has employment statistics. On Vultee, see Spinney, *World War II in Nashville*, 56–58; S. Ramsey, *Reading, Writing, and Segregation*, 13, 40 on class distinctions and 56 on Vultee. The *Banner* ran a "Negro in Nashville" series in 1946 that marshaled an impressive array of statistics (if applying them to slanted conclusions); these articles are available in FUSC-CSJ, box 229, folder 16.

35. Statistic from Graham, "Desegregation in Nashville," 138. For more on the religious dynamics in Nashville, see Carty, *Nashville as a World Religious Center*; Dorey, "Southtown and Christian Social Action."

36. Catholic quotation in Lipman and Vorspan, *Tale of Ten Cities*, 146; ARC-TU-RRD box 23, folder 18, regarding the black parents and Catholic schools; scholar quoted is Spinney, "Jewish Community in Nashville, 1939–1949," and chapter 3 in his *World War II in Nashville* (quotation on 51). On southern Jews in general, see Webb, *Fight against Fear*; Dinnerstein and Palsson, *Jews in the South*; D. Schultz, *Going South*.

37. Lipman and Vorspan, *Tale of Ten Cities*, 139–65 and especially 144–45; Spinney, "Jewish Community in Nashville, 1939–1949," 229–30; Spinney, *World War II in Nashville*, 48–52. On Jews and Nashville's country clubs, see "Judaism and the Ecumenical Movement," a transcript from WLAC radio's *Focus*, in *Nashville Magazine* (January 1965): 20, 25. See also Dorey, "Southtown and Christian Social Action," 2:8, 2:9, 2:14, 2:15; D. Doyle, *Nashville Since the 1920s*, 174; Will D. Campbell, "Religion in Nashville, A.D. 2050," USM-WDC, box 10, folder 23; K. M. Smith, "We Seek a City," in Davies, *Pulpit Speaks on Race*, 180.

38. Spinney, "Municipal Government in Nashville, Tennessee, 1938–1951"; M. Scott, *Negro in Tennessee Politics and Governmental Affairs, 1865–1965*; Jones, "Black Community, Politics, and Race Relations in the 'Iris City,'" 319; *Globe*, January 12, 1940, August 11, 1944; Graham, *Crisis in Print*, 22; Spinney, *World War II in Nashville*, 6; VUSC-SPC; D. Doyle, *Nashville Since the 1920s*, 129–37.

39. Quotation in D. Doyle, *Nashville Since the 1920s*, 64, 180; Egerton, *Speak Now against the Day*, 224–25; Nat Caldwell sidebar in Egerton, *Nashville: The Face of Two Centuries*, 239.

40. Turn-of-the-century information in Elazar, "Case Study Of Failure in Attempted Metropolitan Integration," 64; Woody, "Natural History of a Slum Area," 97–99; Haynes, *Scars of Segregation*, 53, 130.

41. Jones, "Black Community, Politics, and Race Relations," 261, 271; Dorey, "Southtown and Christian Social Action," 2:12.

42. Spinney, "Municipal Government in Nashville, Tennessee, 1938–1951," 84–87.

43. D. Doyle, *Nashville Since the 1920s*, 96–97, 121, 126, 137–38, 230; Halberstam, *The Children*, 112; Ed Jones interview, UF-SPOHP; Dorey, "Southtown and Christian Social Action," 2:10.

44. Nat Caldwell sidebar in Egerton, *Nashville: The Face of Two Centuries*, 239, and 241 in the same source regarding Harvey; Parks, "Grasping at the Coattails of Progress," 128, 131, and ch. 3; D. Doyle, *Nashville Since the 1920s*, 121, 126, 129.

45. Quotation in Spinney, *World War II in Nashville*, 64. See also *Globe*, June 21, July 5, August 9, 1946; Summerville, *Educating Black Doctors*, 130; S. Ramsey, "More than the Three R's," 186. D. Doyle, *Nashville Since the 1920s*, 126.

46. "Wholly negative" quotation in *Nashville Sun*, October 7, 1950; recruiting trip quotations in May 21, 1951, memo, NAACP: part 26, series A, reel 20, starting on frame 185. See also Summerville, *Educating Black Doctors*, 130; TSU *Meter*, May 1954; *Globe*, May 19, 1944.

47. "Co-opted" quotation is in Spinney, *World War II in Nashville*, 53–54, 66–7. See also Jones, "Black Community, Politics, and Race Relations," 273–74, 309–12; Scott, *Negro in Tennessee Politics*, 94–95, 101, 107; *Nashville Sun*, October 7, 1950; *Tennessean*, April 22, 1951; *Globe*, December 6, 1946, October 24, 1947; interviews in VUSC-SPC.

48. Halberstam quoted in "'Good Jelly's' Last Stand," *Reporter*, January 19, 1961, 40–41; K. M. Smith, "Shame and Glory," 15; D. Doyle, *Nashville Since the 1920s*, 225; Egerton, *Nashville: The Face of Two Centuries*, 251; *Tennessean*, May 21, 1958; Halberstam, *The Children*, 111. See also Moody, "Effects of Metro on Negro Politics"—published in a Vanderbilt organ.

49. Quotation in *Block Bulletin*, January 1950; "Talk about voting" quotation in "Negro Participation in Civic Affairs (Government) in Nashville and Davidson County in 1958," in FUSC-CSJ, box 151, folder 15; VUSC-SPC; Summerville, *Educating Black Doctors*, 130; *Globe*, May 19, 1944, December 6, 1946; *Nashville Sun*, April 7, 1951; Scott, *Negro in Tennessee Politics*, 108; K. M. Smith, "Shame and Glory," 8, 15–17, 21; Hanson, *Report on Politics in Nashville*, 1:11; Egerton, *Nashville: The Face of Two Centuries*, 250.

50. S. Ramsey, *Reading, Writing, and Segregation*, 63, 65; interviews in VUSC-SPC; Woody, "Natural History of a Slum Area," 109–14.

51. West quotations in Hanson, *Report on Politics in Nashville*, 1:11, 2:4, 3:13, 3:14; Halberstam, *The Children*, 111–12; D. Doyle, *Nashville Since the 1920s*, 184–87, 190, 224–25; Scott, *Negro in Tennessee Politics*, 110; K. M. Smith, "Shame and Glory," 8–10, 16; Graham, "Desegregation in Nashville," 136–37; Hawkins, *Nashville Metro*, 21; Spinney, *World War II in Nashville*, 63, 68; *Banner*, July 23, 1953; Neill Brown, NMA-CMGOH; George Barrett, UF-SPOHP. On Ennix, see *Nashville Sun*, April 12, 1951. On Ben West's black appointees (H. H. Walker to the hospital board and E. A. Selby to the transportation committee), see the *Globe*, August 9, 1957; on West's Black cabinet, see the October 19, 1962, *780 Countdown*.

52. The teacher salary case was *Harold Thomas v. Louis H. Hibbits et al.*, 46 F. Supp. 368 (M.D. Tenn. 1942). Lawsuit quotations in *Globe*, March 22, 1957, and July 17, 1959; Halberstam, *The Children*, 112; D. Doyle, *Nashville Since the 1920s*, 228; Sarvis, "Leaders in the Court and the Community," 47–49; NAACP: part 15, series A, reel 6, beginning on frame 619; Jones, "Black Community, Politics, and Race Relations," 283; *Tennessean*, April 22, 1955, July 12, 1955, November 9, 1955; *Tennessean Magazine*, April 16 and 23, 1961; *Globe*, December 22, 1941, November 10, 1944; *Banner*, March 29, 1951, May 3, 1951, November 13, 1952, January 16, 1953, January 26, 1956, February 14, 1956. See also Laska, "History of Legal

Education in Tennessee, 1770–1970," 702; D. Doyle, *Nashville Since the 1920s*, 228. On the Columbia riot, see O'Brien, *Color of the Law*; Egerton, *Speak Now against the Day*, 363–65, 442–43. On teacher salaries see C. S. Johnson, *Patterns of Segregation*, 22; S. Ramsey, *Reading, Writing, and Segregation*, 48–55; *Nashville Sun*, October 7, 1950; *780 Countdown*, July 30, 1962; K. M. Smith, "Shame and Glory," 5–6.

53. Cross-burning bills in ARC-TU-RRD box 31, folder 19; K. M. Smith, "Shame and Glory," 12–14, 20; SCRBC-AMP, MG 340, box 70, folder 5, interview with Prince Rivers and W. T. Green on buses, as well as *Chattanooga Daily Times*, May 11, 1960.

54. K. M. Smith, "Shame and Glory," 7, 12–14.

55. Golf course materials in ARC-TU-RRD, box 117, folder 12; Moody, "Effects of Metro on Negro Politics," 47–48; restaurant irony in Halberstam, *The Children*, 112; George Barrett, UF-SPOHP; *Banner*, July 22, 1953; *Tennessean*, February 3 and 7, 1954.

56. First quotation in *Globe*, May 4, 1945; second in *Globe*, January 2, 1959. Rape cases discussed in Lee Lorch to Mrs. B. H. Netherland, letter May 13, 1953, ARC-TU-RRD, box 23, folder 18. See also S. Ramsey, *Reading, Writing, and Segregation*, 58; Jones, "Black Community, Politics, and Race Relations," 283; Dorey, "Southtown and Christian Social Action," 1:3, 2:16, 3:24; Spinney, *World War II in Nashville*, 58–60. See also the reference to a racial bombing, the antecedent to which is unclear, in *Block Bulletin*, January 1, 1950.

57. D. Doyle, *Nashville Since the 1920s*, 115; Halberstam, *The Children*, 116.

58. "Hyper-patriotism" quotation in Halberstam, *The Children*, 117–18; about Stahlman in Graham's *Crisis in Print*, 43; D. Doyle, *Nashville Since the 1920s*, 119. On Churchwell, see Halberstam, *The Children*, 180–86, 698–700, *Tennessean*, August 28, 2002 and EU-MARBL-RCP. See also Brown, "Black Press of Tennessee, 1865–1980," 148.

59. Halberstam, "Nashville Was My Graduate School," 38. Jennings Perry, an editor at the *Tennessean*, wrote the hyperbolic but engaging *Democracy Begins at Home*; Egerton, *Speak Now against the Day*, 136, 461; see also the *Globe*, July 7, 1944, on the poll tax. Graham, *Crisis in Print*, 155; Sumner, "Local Press and the Nashville Student Movement, 1960," 163, 190; D. Johnson, *Vanderbilt Divinity School*, 145–46. Quotation in *Globe* editorial, February 9, 1940. See also Graham, *Crisis in Print*, 252; Sarvis, "Leaders in the Court and the Community," 46; Lamon, *Black Tennesseans, 1900–1930*, 302; Brown, "Black Press of Tennessee, 1865–1980," 157, 110, and Spinney, *World War II in Nashville*, 164n32 on *Globe*.

60. Egerton, *Speak Now against the Day*, 250, 442–44; interviews in VUSC-SPC; and more generally, Sullivan, *Days of Hope*. Some early Nashville SCHW materials (ca. 1944) are in GSU-SLA-PCP, box 1897, folder 10.

61. Earlier, TCHR called itself the TCHOHR; I have adopted the first for consistency. See SRC, series 1: reel 66, folder 1996, quotations in order on frames 286, 289, 345. See also Egerton, *Speak Now against the Day*, 48, 210, 285, 311–16, and Van Til, *My Way of Looking at It*, 180.

62. Methodist quotation in Dorey, "Southtown and Christian Social Action," 2:15; see also 1:3, 2:14, 2:15, 4:3, 4:4. See also the letters to the editor in *Christian Century*, November 2 and 30, 1955, in conjunction with Roger L. Shinn to Ralph Harlow, letter February 7, 1956, VUSC-NMFP, box 1, folder 4, and the Fusons to Harlow, letter February 1, 1956, VUSC-NMFP, box 1, folder 4; Herman H. Long to Frederick Routh, letter February 13, 1958, ARC-TU-RRD, box 31, folder 19. On CORE, see Meier and Rudwick, *CORE*, 75.

63. Department store quotation in K. M. Smith, "Shame and Glory," 17, 22; "patronizing" quotation in Dorey, "Southtown and Christian Social Action," 4:2. See also the *Globe*,

February 9, 1940, September 13, 1946; "Negro Participation in Civic Affairs (Government) in Nashville and Davidson County in 1958," and Gertrude L. McCall, "Good News in Christian Social Relations, United Church Women of Nashville," both in FUSC-CSJ, box 151, folder 15; Ritterhouse, "Etiquette of Race Relations in the Jim Crow South" in Ownby, *Manners and Southern History*, 23. See also the anecdote in K. M. Smith, "We Seek a City," 177–83, especially 180, which recounts an undated interracial church service that many whites withdrew from at the last minute.

64. Glen, *Highlander*, 59–61, 186–87, 62, 93, 109, 143, 170, 185–87; Egerton, *Speak Now against the Day*, 158–62, 299; Cumming, "Facing Facts, Facing South," 166.

65. Glen, *Highlander*; Thrasher, "Fifty Years with Highlander"; Sanders, "Seeking Racial Tolerance," 119; Egerton, *Speak Now against the Day*, 161, 299.

66. Robbins, *Sidelines Activist*; Gilpin and Gasman, *Charles S. Johnson*; Sanders, "Building Racial Tolerance through Education," 44; Sanders, "Seeking Racial Tolerance"; Gilpin, "Charles S. Johnson and the Race Relations Institutes at Fisk University"; K. M. Smith, "Shame and Glory," 22–23; Spinney, *World War II in Nashville*, 61; D. Doyle, *Nashville Since the 1920s*, 166–68. The *New York Times* covered Johnson's induction as Fisk President; see November 8, 1947.

67. Quotation in D. Doyle, *Nashville Since the 1920s*, 237. See Winchell, *Where No Flag Flies*; Louise Davis profile in *Tennessean*, September 4, 1949; Egerton, *Speak Now against the Day*, 64–9, and specifically on Davidson, 66.

68. This point is most fully established in a racial context by Murphy, "Social Memory of the South"; see also Davidson, "Regionalism and Nationalism in American Literature," 61; Winchell, *Where No Flag Flies*, 109.

69. Davidson, "Preface to Decision," 395, 406, 409. A version of this ran in the *Banner*, September 7, 1945—see also Winchell, *Where No Flag Flies*, 283–89, and the lengthy rejoinder to the essay by the *Globe*, September 14, 1945. For elaboration on Davidson's views, see his "Gulliver with Hay Fever" and "Sociologist in Eden."

70. Spinney, *World War II in Nashville*, 62–65; Gilpin and Gasman, *Charles S. Johnson*, 239; Halberstam, *The Children*, 119, on Stahlman and the John Birch Society (see also the Seigenthaler interview on Stahlman and the Dixiecrats, NMA-CMGOH). Interviews in VUSC-SPC; "slapped down" quotation from *Chicago Defender* clipping (ca. 1945) in FUSC-RP, box 198, folder 3; Berry, "Charles S. Johnson, Fisk University, and the Struggle for Civil Rights, 1945–1970," 87–88.

71. Halberstam, *The Children*, 109; Jarman, "Nashville," 22; Board of Governor's minutes, November 2, 1951, TSLA-COC, reel 2 (no frame); Egerton, *Nashville: The Face of Two Centuries*, 245.

72. K. M. Smith, "Shame and Glory," 22.

Chapter 2. The Triumph of Tokenism

1. Anna Holden, "A First Step Toward School Integration," 3, 5, 8 (capitals added to the sign quotations in CORE, series 6, folder 12A, reel 49, frame 0270); *Time*, September 23, 1957, 15; *Tennessean*, May 15, 1979; D. Doyle, *Nashville Since the 1920s*, 239.

2. Graham, *Crisis in Print*, 37, 66–68, *Banner* quotations on 41–46; Graham, "Desegregation in Nashville," 146–47; Helen Fuller, "Nashville—First Steps Firmly Taken," *New Republic*, March 2, 1959, 12–16; TSLA-OAGR, record group 241, box 80, folder 10; transcript

of Clement in CBS's *Face the Nation*, September 15, 1957, TSLA-FGC, box 344, folder 24. See Clement's noncommittal response to a future TFCG member in TSLA-FGC, box 38, folder 14, and "The possible courses of action" memorandum, Harry Phillips and Val Sanford, no date, TSLA-FGC, box 257, folder 15. See Redd, "Educational Desegregation in Tennessee," 345, on the *Banner* and *Tennessean*'s responses to *Brown II*. For more on Clement, see Greene, *Lead Me On*; a profile in the *Chicago Sun Times*, June 19, 1955; a gushy *Saturday Evening Post* article, January 29, 1955; and the extended unpublished article in HUHL-DTMC, bMS Am 2090.1, box 8, folder 145.

3. Looby request referenced in *Tennessean*, January 24, 1996. See also the *Banner*, May 26, September 10, 1954, September 24, June 10, 1955; *Tennessean*, June 11, 1954, and June 17, 1955; Nashville School Board Minutes (hereafter NSBM), June 7, 1954; "Report on Nashville, Tennessee," SRC Special Report, SRC, series 16, reel 220, folder 2020, frame 0888; *Southern School News* (hereafter abbreviated as *SSN*), October 1955 and January 1956; Mauney, *Evolving Equality*. On Lorch, see S. Ramsey, *Reading, Writing, and Segregation*, 78; *Tennessean*, June 19, 1960, and ch. 18 in Gilpin and Gasman, *Charles S. Johnson*; *New York Times*, September 12, 1954, and the coverage in HUHL-DTMC, bMS Am 2090.1, November 23, 1954 (reel 163, folder 881), and December 8, 1955 (reel 179, folder 955); Redd, "Educational Desegregation," 340.

4. Shea's quotation in *Banner*, June 14, 1955; Newman, "Catholic Church and Desegregation, 1954–1973"; Redd, "Educational Desegregation in Tennessee" 406; Stritch, *Catholic Church in Tennessee*, 334–38; Campion interview, UF-SPOHP; *Tennessee Register*, September 24, 2004; Kelly Miller Smith, "Shame and Glory," VUSC-KMS, box 28, folder 7, 19; Katherine Jones to Paul Anthony, letter April 5, 1962, SRC, series 6, reel 147, folder 442, frame 1899; Sister Mary Felicia, R.S.M., "Cathedral High School Integration," *Social Digest* 8 (July–September, 1965), 242–44 (and note that the *Tennessean*, September 3, 1969, says Cathedral High School was desegregated prior to *Brown*); Sarratt, *Ordeal of Segregation*, 278. On Adrian, see J. Bass, *Blessed Are the Peacemakers*, 189–90.

5. *SSN*, June 8, 1955; Stritch, *Catholic Church in Tennessee*, 335, 337; Newman, "Catholic Church and Desegregation," 147–48; *Nashville Scene* retrospective, May 4, 1995.

6. Priest quoted in *Banner*, June 14, 1955; *SSN*, June 8, 1955; *New York Times*, September 22, 1957; see also the retrospective in the *Tennessee Register* Catholic newspaper, September 24, 2004, with "low-profile" quotation on 12; *Nashville Scene*, May 4, 1995.

7. McGarrity, "Testing Nashville's Progressivism," 32–33; TSU *Meter*, May 1954. The best treatment of SERS is Cumming, "Facing Facts, Facing South"—see 160, 203–12, regarding Valien. See also Gilpin, "Charles S. Johnson and the Southern Educational Reporting Service."

8. Coombs, "Search for Facts," 31–32; *New York Times*, September 1, 1957; Don Shoemaker to Virginius Dabney, letter July 25, 1955, UNC-SHC; TSU *Meter*, May 1954; Gilpin and Gasman, *Charles S. Johnson*, 158–68; correspondence in FUSC-CSJ, box 109.

9. Quotations from Stainback and Mayes in *SSN*, March 3, 1955, see also *SSN*, March 14 and April 7, 1955; *Banner*, March 15, 1955; Georgia quotation in James McBride Dabbs, "Ironies of '55, Southern Style," *Christian Century*, October 26, 1955, 1239. See also *Tennessean*, February 9, 1955; Graham, *Crisis in Print*, 68–72; Graham, "Desegregation in Nashville," 147. On the Stainback bill and other legislative efforts to maintain segregation, see HUHL-DTMC, bMS Am 2090.1 (reel 168, folder 903); Redd, "Educational Desegregation in Tennessee," 342. On the bill's effect on teachers, see ARC-TU-IAD, box 3, folder 5.

10. On massive resistance, see Wilhoit, *Politics of Massive Resistance*; Klarman, "How *Brown* Changed Race Relations"; McMillen, *Citizens' Councils*; McMillen, "Organized Resistance to School Desegregation in Tennessee"; Bartley, *Rise of Massive Resistance*.

11. Davidson to Russell Kirk, letter June 10, 1955, VUSC-DDP, box 3, folder 11, and to Jimmie Hicks, letter September 3, 1960, VUSC-DDP, box 3, file 22. See also Graham, *Crisis in Print*, 81, 91–93; McMillen, *Citizens' Councils*, 109, 120; McMillen, "Organized Resistance to School Desegregation in Tennessee," 323; Will D. Campbell, "Memorandum to All Human Relations Personnel in the South," August 20, 1957 (from Campbell's personal files; copy in possession of the author). On Kershaw and his art, see the *Tennessean Magazine*, April 16, 1950, 42–43, and Egerton and Wood, *Nashville: An American Self-Portrait*, 198–200. See also the *Chattanooga Times*, November 27, 1955; *Memphis Press-Scimitar*, February 10, 1956; *Banner*, July 12, 1955. On Davidson's attitude toward the Citizens' Councils, see his to "John," letter June 8, 1955, VUSC-DDP, box 3, folder 11. See also Chappell, "Divided Mind of Southern Segregationists," "Religious Ideas of the Segregationists," and *Inside Agitators*.

12. On the TFCG's founding, see *Banner* and *Tennessean*, July 12, 1955; Davidson extended quotation is in *Star Weekly Magazine*, November 9, 1957; TFCG quotation in *SSN*, July 6, 1955; the March 1956 issue has the TFCG's call for closing the public schools if need be. See also Conkin, *Southern Agrarians*, 155; *SSN*, August 1955.

13. McMillen, "Organized Resistance to School Desegregation in Tennessee," 325; Winchell, *Where No Flag Flies*, 288, 290–91; *Chattanooga News Free Press*, November 29, 1955.

14. NSBM, July 14 and August 11, 1955. See also *SSN*, July 6, 1955; *Tennessean*, June 28, 1955; *Banner*, June 20, 1955.

15. *Banner*, September 24, 1955; Mauney, *Evolving Equality*, 109; "How the Nashville Community Relations Conference Came About," SRC, series 1, reel 35, folder 1239, frame 2172; "Report on Nashville, Tennessee," SRC Special Report, SRC, series 16, reel 220, folder 2020, frame 0888; Gertrude L. McCall, "Good News in Christian Social Relations, United Church Women of Nashville," FUSC-CSJ, box 151, folder 15; *SSN*, June 8, 1955; timeline by Anna Holden in "Nashville School Desegregation" (September 23, 1955–April 14, 1958) in CORE, series 6, reel 49, folder 12, frame 0262; see also the chronology in the *Banner*, January 28, 1958; Peltason, *Fifty-Eight Lonely Men*, 31; Sarratt, *Ordeal of Segregation*, 90; S. Ramsey, *Reading, Writing, and Segregation*, 73, 79–80; D. Doyle, *Nashville Since the 1920s*, 235. The *Kelley* case is 139 F. Supp. 578.

16. Looby quotation in *SSN*, July 6, 1955.

17. *Banner*, June 21, 1955; *Tennessean*, June 17, 1955, and timeline in *Banner*, January 28, 1958; HUHL-DTMC, bMS Am 2090.1, March 28, 1956, box 1, folder 19; quotations in NSBM, July 14 and August 11, 1955. See also *SSN*, July 6, 1955; *Tennessean*, June 28, 1955; *Banner*, June 20, 1955; *Race Relations Law Reporter*, August 11, 1955, 1119.

18. Redd, "Educational Desegregation in Tennessee," 336–38; "Fisk University 1955," GSU-SLA-PCP, box 1926, folder 22; Long, "Status of Desegregated Higher Education in Tennessee."

19. On Peabody, see Conkin, *Peabody College*, 282; Dorn, "George Peabody College for Teachers, Race Relations and Education," 9; Van Til, *My Way of Looking at It*, 172.

20. Sarratt to "Jim," letter November 5, 1956; J. C. Foshee to Clyde Alley, letter October 24, 1956 (syphilis quotation); Sims Crownover to Vernon Sharp Jr., letter January 8, 1957 (broadminded quotation)—all in VUSC-CHP, box 21, "Administration—Integration

(Sarratt's File)" folder. Socialistic money quotation in Clyde Alley to Vanderbilt Alumni Association (with multiple CCs), letter October 7, 1956, VUSC-CHP, box 25, "Law School Integration" folder.

21. Long, "Status of Desegregated Higher Education in Tennessee," 315, HUHL-DTMC, bMS Am 2090.1, box 4, folder 63; "Fisk University 1955," GSU-SLA-PCP, box 1926, folder 22.

22. Cecil Sims, "Legal Implication of the Supreme Court Decision on Segregation," address to the Tennessee School Board Association, January 12, 1955, VUSC-CSP, box 20, folder 11 (see also draft in box 20, folder 7, and other drafted notes in box 20, folder 1), quotation on 5. The second quotation is in the draft version of this speech, box 20, folder 7, 9. The *Tennessean*, February 11, 1971, quotes Avon Williams's claim that Mayor Ben West hired attorneys to fight the school desegregation case.

23. Cecil Sims, "Legal Implication of the Supreme Court Decision on Segregation," address to the Tennessee School Board Association, January 12, 1955, VUSC-CSP, box 20, folder 11, quotation on 5. Delegation detail in ARC-TU-RRD, box 3, folder 11.

24. Cecil Sims, "Legal Implication of the Supreme Court Decision on Segregation," address to the Tennessee School Board Association, January 12, 1955, VUSC-CSP, box 20, folder 11, quotation on 6. See also *Tennessean*, June 16, 1954.

25. Grimmett in *SSN*, November, 1955; Clement's quotations in *New York Times*, January 24, 1956. See also *SSN*, October and November 1955, January, February, and April 1956; for more on the Pro-Southerners, see McMillen, "Organized Resistance to School Desegregation in Tennessee," 316; letter of support to Clement from Harvie Branscomb (Chancellor of Vanderbilt), January 26, 1956, TSLA-FGC, box 257, folder 13. The capital letter emphasis of the segregationists' signs is mine rather than in the sources.

26. This account is taken from HUHL-DTMC, bMS Am 2090.1, January 24, 1956, box 1, folder 4, which faults the *New York Times* article for missing much of the underlying symbolic actions in the confrontation.

27. "A Summary of the Findings of the Twelve Discussion Groups," FUSC-CSJ, box 90, folder 3 (another copy is in VUSC-NMFP, box 2, folder 16); NCRC in *Tennessean*, April 4, 1956. See also *Globe*, June 8, 1956, *Banner*, June 7, 1956; Campbell, "Memorandum to All Human Relations Personnel in the South"; *SSN*, March 1956; "Report on Nashville, Tennessee," SRC Special Report, SRC, series 16, reel 220, folder 2020, frame 0888; Holden timeline; William Van Til, "The Nashville Story," *Educational Leadership* (May 1958), reprint in FUSC-CSJ, box 90, folder 3.

28. NSBM, March 8, 1956.

29. Ibid.; see also *SSN*, April 1956.

30. Quotation in *SSN*, January 1956; TSLA-DEPCF, record group 92, reel 188, frame 1273; Van Til, "Nashville Story"; NSBM, March 21, 1956; *SSN*, March and April 1956; *Tennessean*, January 24, 1996.

31. Journalist and Clement quotation in *SSN*, July 1956; Kershaw speech in Lake City, Tennessee, October 6, 1956, in TSLA-FGC, box 258, folder 17; February 6, 1956, from Lambeth Mayes, TSLA-FGC, box 274, folder 18; Crownover in *SSN*, March 1956.

32. Quotations in *SSN*, July 1956; Graham, *Crisis in Print*, 91–92 on TFCG lawsuits; see also *SSN*, March, May, June, August, and November 1956; *Globe*, August 10, 1956.

33. On Oak Ridge, see Lovett, *Civil Rights Movement in Tennessee*, 38–41; *SSN*, February 3 and October 1955, and for Donald Davidson's take, "Tyranny at Oak Ridge," VUSC-DDP, box 39, folder 3. On Clinton, see Webb, *Rabble Rousers*, 44–49; Brake and

Baker, *Justice in the Valley*, 101–25; Holden, Valien, Valien, and Manis, *Clinton, Tennessee: A Tentative Description and Analysis of the School Desegregation Crisis* (New York: Anti-Defamation League of B'nai B'rith, 1957); McMillen, "Organized Resistance to School Desegregation in Tennessee," 317–23; Sarratt, *Ordeal of Segregation*, 156–57; Graham, *Crisis in Print*, 76–77, 91–113.

34. Extended quotation in Webb, "Outside Agitator," 178; Lovett, *Civil Rights Movement in Tennessee*, 44–50; "Crackers" quotation in *Newsweek*, March 18, 1957, 36.

35. *Commonweal*, May 24, 1957, 196; *Look*, February 19, 1957, 30; *Globe*, August 9, 1957; James Rorty, "Hate-Monger with Literary Trimmings: From Avant-Garde Poetry to Rear-Guard Politics," *Commentary*, December 1956, 533–42; March 18 (sensible person quotation) and March 25, 1957, report in EU-MARBL-NBF, box 7, "John Kasper" folder; Webb, *Rabble Rousers* 69.

36. *SSN*, September 1956, October and November 1956, January 1957; George McMillan, "The Ordeal of Bobby Cain," *Colliers*, November 23, 1956, 68–69; Wilma Dykeman and James Stokely, "Courage in Action in Clinton, Tennessee," *Nation*, December 22, 1956, 531–33; David Halberstam, "The Town that Became 'Everybody's Test Tube,'" *Reporter*, January 10, 1957, 32–36; McClelland, "Structural Analysis of Desegregation"; Adonsom, "Few Black Voices Heard"; Anderson, *Children of the South*; Muse, *Ten Years of Prelude*, 92–104; Greene, *Lead Me On*, 192–220; Bergeron, Ash, and Keith, *Tennesseans and Their History*, 294–95; Graham, *Crisis in Print*, 91–113; McMillen, "Organized Resistance to School Desegregation in Tennessee," 317–21; Brittain, "Case Study of the Problems of Racial Integration in the Clinton Tennessee High School"; "Clinton and the Law."

37. See Davidson's impressions of the events from afar based on TFCG member accounts in his September 1956 letters, VUSC-DDP, box 3, folders 15 and 16, which stress the TFCG's attempts to maintain order. See also Fuller, "Nashville—First Steps Firmly Taken," 14–15; transcript of Clement on CBS's "Face the Nation," September 15, 1957, TSLA-FGC, box 344, folder 24; Webb, *Rabble Rousers*, 72.

38. The plan's author remains unclear. Edwin Hunt and Reber Boalt were attorneys of record for the school board and represented the Plan in court. The *Tennessean*, August 31, 1969, claims the Plan was "dictated one night by [Superintendent] Bass in his living room." George Barrett, on the other hand, states definitively Cecil Sims wrote the plan (UF-SPOHP interview), which is certainly consistent with Sims's thinking and would explain Sims's relative popularity as a lecturer talking about the *Brown* decision. Halberstam also credits Sims (*The Children*, 54).

39. Sexual attractions quotation in Graham, "Desegregation in Nashville," 144; *SSN*, December 1956; NSBM, October 29, 1956; *Banner*, July 31, 1959; *Globe*, March 22, 1959; *Tennessean*, May 14, 1979; "Report on Nashville, Tennessee," SRC Special Report, SRC, series 16, reel 220, folder 2020, frame 0888; Eugene Wyatt, "A Report on School Desegregation," April 1963, SBHLA-CLC, AR 138-2 box 20, folder 17 (another copy is in FUSC-CSJ, box 151, folder 8); Fuller, "Nashville—First Steps Firmly Taken," 14; Peltason, *Fifty-Eight Lonely Men*, 183; Sarratt, *The Ordeal of Segregation*, 91; D. Doyle, *Nashville Since the 1920s*, 237; Campbell, "Memorandum to All Human Relations Personnel in the South."

40. Looby in *SSN*, December 1956; Edgar L. Jones, "City Limits: Segregation-Desegregation in the Cities," in Shoemaker, *With All Deliberate Speed*, 83–85; Graham, "Desegregation in Nashville," 145–46. Eugene Wyatt also recorded that the transfer provision came from Louisville—see "A Report on School Desegregation," April 1963, SBHLA-

CLC, AR 138-2, box 20, folder 17; TSLA-MEP, box 73, folder 2, has the proclamation and desegregation order of the Nashville Plan; GSU-SLA-SSP, box 676, folder 171, February 1, 1960, SRC report; Lovett, *Civil Rights Movement in Tennessee*, 54.

41. Donald Davidson, ed., *The Crisis in Tennessee*, VUSC-DDP, box 39, folder 3; see also Davidson to Thomas R. Waring, letter October 16, 1955, VUSC-DDP, box 3, folder 17; *Memphis Press-Scimitar*, November 21, 1956; *Banner*, November 20, 1956; *SSN*, December 1956. Davidson was optimistic about the legislature's support for his proposals; see Davidson to Thomas J. B. Walsh, letter, September 2, 1956, VUSC-DDP, box 3, folder 15.

42. "School Legislation—1957. What? Why?" in FUSC-CSJ, box 151, folder 8.

43. Graham, "Desegregation in Nashville," 147–49 (*Tennessean* quotation on 149); *Globe*, December 7, 1956. See also *Banner*, November 20, 1956; *New York Times*, January 6, 1957; Sarratt, *Ordeal of Segregation*, 91, 220; Fuller, "Nashville—First Steps Firmly Taken," 14; Muse, *Ten Years of Prelude*, 116–17; *SSN*, February, March, July (which has the TFCG criticizing the Tennessee Manifesto for its toothlessness), September, October, and November 1957; "Report on Nashville, Tennessee," SRC Special Report, SRC, series 16, reel 220, folder 2020, frame 0888; Shoemaker, *With All Deliberate Speed*, 137; Bergeron, Ash, and Keith, *Tennesseans and Their History*, 295–98. On Clement's shift in rhetoric, see UNC-SHC-DPP, box 10, folder 155.

44. Quotations in Van Til, "Nashville Story" and *My Way of Looking at It*, 176–77. See also *Tennessean*, April 3, 1957; Graham, *Crisis in Print*, 154–55. Sources differ about whether the PSPC was formed in late May 1957 or on June 23, 1957. See the *SSN*, February and July, 1957; Holden timeline; NSBM, April 15, 1957, July 11, 1957; *Tennessean*, April 3, 1957; *Globe*, May 31, 1957; *Banner*, July 12, 1957; November 1957 TFCG newsletter, VUSC-DDP, box 39, folder 3; Campbell, "Memorandum to All Human Relations Personnel in the South"; Muse, *Ten Years of Prelude*, 117; Sarratt, *Ordeal of Segregation*, 90, 214; D. Doyle, *Nashville Since the 1920s*, 237; Graham, "Desegregation in Nashville," 150–51.

45. Quotations about McCurrio in *Christian Century*, October 9, 1957, 1206–7; Alley in *Banner*, July 12, 1957. See the Holden timeline; Webb, *Rabble Rousers*, 63, 84–85, 90; Campbell, "Memorandum to All Human Relations Personnel in the South"; *New York Times*, August 24, 1957; Peltason, *Fifty-Eight Lonely Men*, 158, 161; Muse, *Ten Years of Prelude*, 118; D. Doyle, *Nashville Since the 1920s*, 238; Wayne Whitt, NMA-CMGOH; McGarrity, "Testing Nashville's Progressivism," 46, 48 (on Stroud and Kasper). See also the UF-SPOHP interview with Jack Kershaw, who said he was suspicious that Kasper was a "double-agent."

46. *Globe*, August 9, 1957; *SSN*, March 1957; Dykeman and Stokely, "Courage in Action in Clinton, Tennessee"; Muse, *Ten Years of Prelude*, 118; D. Doyle, *Nashville Since the 1920s*, 237–8; Webb, *"Outside Agitator,"* 182–84; Webb, *Rabble Rousers*, 55–56.

47. EU-MARBL-NBF, box 14, "Pre School Trouble Spots Aug '57" folder; *Globe*, May 10, May 3, June 28, July 12, August 2 (editorial; both quotations), and August 6, 1957. For the *Tennessean*'s campaign against the TFCG, especially pronounced during the Clinton crisis, see Graham, *Crisis in Print*, 102–6, 172, 174. For evidence that business issues played a very real role in diluting segregationist sentiment in Nashville and Tennessee, see Glen Robinson, "Man in No Man's Land: The School Administrator," in Shoemaker, *With All Deliberate Speed*, 195; *Newsweek*, October 22, 1962, 97, and more generally for the South, see Jacoway and Colburn, *Southern Businessmen and Desegregation*.

48. *Banner*, July 12 and September 27, 1957; *Tennessean*, September 6, 1957; NSBM, July 30, July 11, August 8, and August 10, 1957; *Globe*, June 28, August 16, August 23, and

August 30, 1957; *New York Times*, August 23, 1957; school board committee meeting and PSPC letter, August 21, 1957, TSLA-JEN, reel 5, frames 1032 and 1043; Peltason, *Fifty-Eight Lonely Men*, 158; Hugh Davis Graham claims that a rezoning took place due to segregationist pressure at this point that reduced desegregation, but did not eliminate it, but provides no citation, see *Crisis in Print*, 156; the *Race Relation Law Reporter* 2:859 reprints the July 16, 1957, letter from the school board attorneys advising them to stick with the Nashville Plan; *New York Times*, August 23, 1957, on PSPC asking school board to postpone.

49. Kasper in EU-MARBL-NBF, box 14, "Pre School Trouble Spots Aug. '57" folder; *New York Times*, August 29, 1957; threatening quotations in *Tennessean*, June 14, 1993; Bass quotation in *Time*, September 23, 1957, 14. See also *U.S. News and World Report*, September 6, 1957; *New York Times*, August 28 and 29, 1957; *Globe*, January 9, 1959; "Report on Nashville, Tennessee," SRC Special Report, SRC, series 16, reel 220, folder 2020, frame 0888; Mauney, *Evolving Equality*, 110.

50. Broadside in EU-MARBL-NBF, box 11, "Segregation Story—School Opening 1957" folder; HUHL-DTMC, bMS Am 2090.1, August 30, 1957, box 8, folder 143; Webb, *Rabble Rousers*, 82.

51. The section is drawn from the fantastic coverage in HUHL-DTMC, bMS Am 2090.1, box 8, folders 144 and 145.

52. K. M. Smith interview in MSRC-RJBOHC, 19; black parent quotation in S. Ramsey, *Reading, Writing, and Segregation*, 86.

53. Holden, "First Step," 6, quotation on 9–10. See also CORE, series 5, reel 42, folder 421, frame 1406; memorandum, "Report of Nashville Visit," November 6–16, 1957, CORE, series 5, reel 42, folder 421, frame 1386.

54. Rainstorm quotation in Halberstam, *The Children*, 54, and discussed in a June 11, 1984, interview with Will D. Campbell (notes in possession of author); Holden, "First Step," 12, 13; NSBM, April 15, 1957. See also Wyatt, "Report on School Desegregation," 7; Fuller, "Nashville—First Steps Firmly Taken," 15.

55. Mason quotation in TSLA-JEN, reel 5, frame 1031 (see also frame 1043). See also *New York Times*, August 24, 1957; *Tennessean*, August 23, 1957; *Globe*, August 30, 1957; Muse, *Ten Years of Prelude*, 117; "Report on Nashville, Tennessee," SRC Special Report, SRC, series 16, reel 220, folder 2020, frame 0888; Holden timeline; Graham, *Crisis in Print*, 156–7.

56. Many sources claim Miller's ruling was handed down on September 6; I follow instead the timeline in the *Banner*, January 28, 1958, and the Holden timeline. Judge Miller quoted in Graham, "Desegregation in Nashville," 151; PSPC letter to Clement, TSLA-FGC, box 259, folder 4; Bass quoted in *New York Times*, August 28, 1957. See the *Globe*, November 15, 1957, for Davidson's criticism of state leaders as well as the *Globe*'s perspective on Davidson, as well as November 1957 TFCG newsletter in VUSC-DDP, box 39, folder 3. See also Sarratt, *Ordeal of Segregation*, 91; *Tennessean*, June 14, 1993; *Race Relations Law Reporter*, September 6, 1957, 970.

57. HUHL-DTMC, bMS Am 2090.1, box 8, folder 147, September 14, 1957. See also some confusion on the transfer provisions in CORE, series 5, reel 42, folder 421, frame 1406. Note that there are discrepancies in terms of numbers when you factor in registration, enrollment, and actual attendance. John Egerton, "Walking into History," has documented the events in great detail, although my reading is that his appendix contradicts his text in discussion of enrollment numbers throughout the year.

58. Griffith quoted in Egerton, *Nashville: The Face of Two Centuries*, 251–53; *Tennessean*, May 14 and 15, 1979, February 1, 1987, June 14, 1993 (which has all other quotations); Holden timeline. See also *Tennessean*, September 10, 1957; S. Ramsey, *Reading, Writing and Segregation*, 83–85; *Christian Century*, October 9, 1957, 1206–7; timeline in *Banner*, January 28, 1958; D. Doyle, *Nashville Since the 1920s*, 239; Sarratt, *Ordeal of Segregation*, 160–61. See also the other retrospectives run by the *Tennessean*: January 24, 1996, February 1, 1987, February 11, 1971, and May 13, 1979.

59. All quotations from *U.S. News and World Report*, September 20, 1957, 125–57, see also November 21, 1958, 33; *Banner*, September 10, 1957; Holden timeline, *Tennessean*, August 31, 1969; Muse, *Ten Years of Prelude*, 119; D. Doyle, *Nashville Since the 1920s*, 239; TFCG newsletter, November 1957, VUSC-DDP, box 39, folder 3; PSPC petition to Clement, TSLA-OAGR, record group 241, box 80, folder 12 (or reel 65, frame 2181); *Christian Century*, October 9, 1957, 1206–7. See also Bob Holladay, "Bus Stop: Nashville Rethinks Desegregation," *Nashville Scene*, July 18, 1996, 19, 25.

60. Quotations in *Time*, September 23, 1957, 15; Stahlman's quotations in *Banner*, September 10, 1957; "godsend" quotation in *New York Post*, March 19, 1958. For more on Stahlman's perspective, see his interview in *U.S. News and World Report*, September 20, 1957, 125–26.

61. HUHL-DTMC, bMS Am 2090.1, box 8, folder 147; EU-MARBL-NBF, box 11, "Seg Story—School opening 1957" folder; *New York Times*, September 12, 1957.

62. HUHL-DTMC, bMS Am 2090.1, box 8, folder 147.

63. HUHL-DTMC, bMS Am 2090.1, box 8, folder 148, September 14, 1957; "Nigger justice" in Peltason, *Fifty-Eight Lonely Men*, 160.

64. *New York Times*, July 16, 1960; *Globe*, January 9, 1959, March 13 and May 8, 1959; "barbecue" quotation in *Tennessean*, February 14, 1960. See also *SSN*, October 1957; D. Doyle, *Nashville Since the 1920s*, 242; Muse, *Ten Years of Prelude*, 119–20; See also Holden timeline; *U.S. News and World Report*, September 20, 1957, 125–26; Fuller, "Nashville—First Steps Firmly Taken," 14; Graham, "Desegregation in Nashville," 151; Graham, *Crisis in Print*, 157; Michele P. Allen and Andrew White, MSRC-RJBOHC; Wayne Whitt, NMA-CMGOH. Regarding the church meeting, see HUHL-DTMC, bMS Am 2090.1, August 17 and 29, 1958, dispatches in box 13, folder 249; Webb, "Outside Agitator," 189.

65. Oliver quoted in *Banner*, September 27, 1957; *New York Times*, October 3 and 25 (scholastically and emotionally quotation), 1960; Holden timeline; HUHL-DTMC, bMS Am 2090.1, box 8, folder 157.

66. PSPC proposal, TSLA-JEN, box 36, folder 11. Holden timeline; timeline of events in *Banner*, January 28, 1958; NSBM, September 10 and 12, 1957, December 4, 1957; *SSN*, November 1957, January, February, March, April, and May 1958; *Tennessean*, December 6, 1957, and March 14, 1958; *Banner*, February 8, and March 11, 1958; *Globe*, January 24, March 21, and April 4, 1958, quotation in April 17, 1959; Graham, "Desegregation in Nashville," 152; Sarratt, *Ordeal of Desegregation*, 91; Muse, *Ten Years of Prelude*, 120; Graham, *Crisis in Print*, 172–77.

67. Note that the explosion happened only three days after civic groups requested that systemwide integration take place immediately—see CORE, series 5, folder 421, reel 42, frame 1391. *Tennessean* and *Banner*, March 17, 1958; *SSN*, April 1958, bomber quotation in Jackson Toby, "Bombing in Nashville: A Jewish Center and the Desegregation Struggle," *Commentary* 25 (May 1958), 385; ADL *Facts*, October–November 1958; *SSN*, April 1958; Sar-

ratt, *Ordeal of Desegregation*, 282, and the bio of Silverman in AJA biography files. For the role of Jews in the civil rights movement generally, see Webb, *Fight against Fear*. The *New York Times* had a story (March 17, 1958) and editorial (March 20, 1958) about the bombing.

68. Krause, "Southern Rabbi and Civil Rights"; Ruth Silberstein, "A Southern Rabbi Takes a Stand," *Congress Weekly*, January 20, 1958, AJA biography files (copy in JFA-JCC); Temple Israel newsletter, Dayton, Ohio, October 15, 1957, and *Intermountain Jewish News*, March 21, 1958, both in AJA, Small Collection 8799; D. Doyle, *Nashville Since the 1920s*, 243.

69. Capital letter emphasis in original: "We Will Not Yield," March 28, 1958, copies in AJA, excerpts reprinted in *Intermountain Jewish News*, April 18, 1958, file in AJA and JFA-JCC; see also his March 21, 1958, report to his congregation, copies in JFA-JCC files; TSLA-FGC, box 291, folder 10; Lipman and Vorspan, *Tale of Ten Cities*, 152–4; Webb, *Rabble Rousers*, 83, 92.

70. *New York Times* editorial, March 20, 1958; *Tennessean*, March 29, 1958; *Tennessean* editorial, March 18, 1958; quotation in Toby, "Bombing in Nashville," 389; Lipman and Vorspan, *Tale of Ten Cities*, 139–65. Toby, "Bombing in Nashville," 387; see also Professor Lou Silberman's correspondence with Toby in VUSC-LSP, box 1, folder 13; and Silberman to Eliot E. Cohen, letter May 26, 1958, JFA-JCC; *U.S. News and World Report*, October 24, 1958; Lou H. Silberman, "Report on Nashville: A Community Relations Committee in Action" (presentation to Southern Regional Board and Leadership Conference, Memphis, May 4, 1958), JFA-JCC.

71. Note that similar plans were both deemed insufficient by federal courts—see *SSN*, May 1958. *Banner*, August 15, 1958, June 17 and 18, July 31, October 16 and 23, 1959, September 1, 1965; *New York Times*, March 15, 1959; *Tennessean*, July 11, 1958; *Globe*, April 11, 1958, July 17, October 23, and December 18, 1959; "A Background Report on School Desegregation for 1959–1960," SRC report, August 10, 1959, SBHLA-CLC, AR 138-2, box 11, folder 13; Sarratt, *Ordeal of Segregation*, 214, 229; Mauney, *Evolving Equality*, 111–12; Graham, "Desegregation in Nashville," 152–53; Graham, *Crisis in Print*, 181, 185–86; D. Doyle, *Nashville Since the 1920s*, 243; residential segregation as involuntary in ARC-TU-IAP, box 3, folder 12. See also "Survey of School Desegregation in the Southern and Border States," United States Commission on Civil Rights (February 1966), TSLA-DEPCF, box 422, folder 10, 10, which argues that the court would later rule that "the original assignment was not based on race but the transfer right was."

72. Because the Nashville Plan would soon be overturned by the courts, North Carolina's pupil assignment plan would actually end up as the most gradualist of integration plans in linking similar transfer provisions as the Nashville Plan to a whole system rather than individual schools. See Sarratt, *Ordeal of Segregation*, 92, and Thurgood Marshall's interview with the *Tennessean*, July 8, 1959. *Globe*, March 21, 1958; April 3 and 17, 1959, August 21, 1959 (editorial); *Tennessean*, January 17, 1959, February 20, 1959; *Tennessean*, October 19, 1960, *Banner*, October 18 and December 12, 1960, regarding Davidson County employing the grade-per-year plan; Wyatt, "Report on School Desegregation in Nashville and Davidson County"; Fuller, "Nashville—First Steps Firmly Taken," 15. For details on state leadership and their tepid efforts on behalf of segregation, see Graham, *Crisis in Print*, 184; HUHL-DTMC, bMS Am 2090.1, box 15, folder 300; Bergeron, Ash, and Keith, *Tennesseans and Their History*, 302; *Tennessean*, February 20, 1959.

73. Oliver quoted in *Banner*, March 6, 1959; *Globe*, April 3 and 7, July 17, August 7, October 23, and December 18, 1959; *Tennessean*, May 14, 1979; Wyatt, "Report on School

Desegregation." For another black perspective on school integration, see M. G. Ferguson's remarks in "Negro Attitudes Today: Three Civic Leaders Show They Cannot Stereotyped," *Wall Street Journal*, October 3, 1960. In the same vein of Oliver's speech, see W. Bass, "In Nashville Schools"; note that Louisville, whose plan Nashville adapted, also did not integrate its faculties—*Tennessean*, July 9, 1958.

74. Henry H. Hill, "It Will Take Time," unknown periodical, clipping in SBHLA-CLC, box 21, folder 3; *Globe*, August 7, 1959; Weinstein's findings in Wyatt, "Report on School Desegregation"; Weinstein and Geisel, "Family Decision Making over Desegregation," 21–29; *Tennessean*, October 23, 1960. See "Enrollment of Negro Pupils in Desegregated Schools By Year," for enrollment statistics for each Nashville school through the 1962–63 school year, VUSC-NMFP, box 3, folder 13. See also the *Tennessean*, August 31, 1969; Muse, *Ten Years of Prelude*, 121, and for a comparative psychological study on Nashville students, see Powell, *Black Monday's Children*.

75. K. M. Smith quoted in Wyatt, "Report on School Desegregation in Nashville and Davidson County." See also the interviews with educators and parents in *SSN*, February 1958; *Banner*, October 16, 1959; white liberals quotation in unknown author, "Visit to Nashville, June 30–July 1 [1959]" SRC, series 1, reel 56, folder 1839, frame 1351.

76. Roger L. Shinn, "Symbolic Roles in Little Rock and Nashville," *Christianity and Crisis*, February 3, 1958, 5.

Chapter 3. The Shame and the Glory

1. Diane Nash, "Inside the Sit-ins and Freedom Rides," in Ahmann, *New Negro*, 47. For more on Nash, see Hampton and Fayer, *Voices of Freedom*, 57–58; Lewis with D'Orso, *Walking with the Wind*, 96.

2. Quotations in Halberstam, *The Children*, 52–56; Kelly Miller Smith, "The Shame and Glory," VUSC-KMS, box 28, folders 7 and 8; Andrew White interview, MSRC-RJBOHC; K. M. Smith interview, MSRC-RJBOHC; *This Is NCLC* (pamphlet), VUSC-NMFP, box 2, folder 9; "NCLC Purposes and Principles," SCRBC-AMP, MG 340, box 70, folder 5; L. Meier, "Different Kind of Prophet," 20; Lewis, *Walking with the Wind*, 73; D. Doyle, *Nashville Since the 1920s*, 244. For more on K. M. Smith, see DeGregory, "Kelly Miller Smith"; Walker, "Black Violence and Nonviolence in the Civil Rights and Black Power Eras," 76–80, 91; Ward, *Radio and the Struggle for Civil Rights in the South*, 102–6; *Wall Street Journal*, October 3, 1960.

3. Some feeble movement from predominantly white organizations also occurred at this time, spurred by the school desegregation crisis. See George Barrett to Louise Young, letter October 7, 1959, FUSC-CSJ, box 151, folder 7, and *Fisk Forum*, May 21, 1959.

4. K. M. Smith, "Shame and Glory," 6, 9 (emphasis in original); C. T. Vivian interview, UNC-SHC-TBP, box 131, folder 944, 28; C. T. Vivian interview, MSRC-RJBOHC; Will D. Campbell interview, MSRC-RJBOHC; Fleming, "C. T. Vivian," 51; *Race Relations Law Reporter*, March 11, 1957, 497; CORE, series 5, folder 421, reel 42, frame 1399; CORE, series 5, folder 418, reel 42, frame 1287; A. Meier and Rudwick, *CORE*, 76; D. Doyle, *Nashville Since the 1920s*, 244; Halberstam, *The Children*, 51–53; *Banner*, February 2, 1993. See also *Fisk Forum*, January 29, 1957, which announces the founding of a Social Action Committee under the auspices of the NAACP and CORE for boycotting segregated establishments. Note also that K. M. Smith said that he was invited to the SCLC meeting precisely because of his

NAACP connections, MSRC-RJBOHC. On Highlander, see McDuffie, "James Lawson," 50; interview with C. T. Vivian, UNC-SHC-TBP, box 131, folder 944, 32–34.

5. Halberstam, *The Children*, 22, 108, 122; K. M. Smith, liner notes in Guy Carawan, *Nashville Sit-in Story*, unpaginated; Will D. Campbell interview, FU-BOHC; K. M. Smith interview, MSRC-RJBOHC; *Banner*, September 14, 1986; *Banner*, February 2, 1993. See also Houston, "Aquinas of the Rednecks."

6. K. M. Smith interview; Ackerman and Duvall, *Force More Powerful*, 311; Carawan, *Nashville Sit-in Story*; Wynn, "Dawning of a New Day," 44; Hogan, *Many Minds, One Heart*, 14–16; Kapur, *Raising Up a Prophet*," 164; Walker, "Black Violence and Nonviolence in the Civil Rights and Black Power Eras," 11, 15, 18–48.

7. K. M. Smith interview, MSRC-RJBOHC; Hogan, *Many Minds, One Heart*, 13–18; D. Doyle, *Nashville Since the 1920s*, 244; Nat Hentoff, "A Peaceful Army," *Commonweal*, June 10, 1967, 277; Halberstam, *The Children*, 11–20, 27, 30–32, 35–50; Kapur, *Raising Up a Prophet*, 155–56; Ackerman and Duvall, *Force More Powerful*, 307–8; Fairclough, *To Redeem the Soul of America*, 59–60; Lovett, *Civil Rights Movement in Tennessee*, 121.

8. Quotations all in *Globe*, December 26, 1958. See also "The Purpose of the Nashville Christian Leadership Council," VUSC-NMFP, box 2, folder 9; *Banner*, September 14, 1986; Carawan, *Nashville Sit-in Story* (although it misidentifies the encounter as taking place in 1959).

9. L. Meier, "Different Kind of Prophet," 15–16; Wynn, "Dawning of a New Day," 44; K. M. Smith interview, MSRC-RJBOHC; "NCLC Purposes and Principles"; Carawan, *Nashville Sit-in Story*; Graham, *Crisis in Print*, 193; Wallace Westfeldt, "A Report on Nashville," 5, SRC, series 4, folder 88, reel 138, frame 1904. On the NCLC's successes in supporting black voting registration, see "Negro Participation in Civic Affairs (Government) in Nashville and Davidson County in 1958," FUSC-CSJ, box 151, folder 15.

10. Carawan, *Nashville Sit-in Story*; McDuffie, "James Lawson," 46; K. M. Smith interview, MSRC-RJBOHC; Westfeldt, "Report on Nashville," 7; *Tennessean*, June 28, 1960; quotation is from Halberstam, *The Children*, 90–91; Kowal, "Staging the Greensboro Sit-ins."

11. "The Sit-in Movement in Nashville, Tennessee," ARC-TU-BPVP, box 75, folder 15, suggests a boycott had already been used "to protest discriminatory practices in fitting rooms" at one of these department stores, ca. 1959. See also "Report on Nashville 1960: Its Problems and Possibilities," FUSC-CSJ, box 151, folder 8, 5 (with another copy in folder 15); *Banner*, March 9, 1959; *Globe*, January 1, 1960; Carawan, *Nashville Sit-in Story*; Randall, *Sit-in Story*, 1; Wynn, "Dawning of a New Day," 45; K. M. Smith interview; C. T. Vivian interview, MSRC-RJBOHC; *Fisk Forum*, April 24, 1957; Westfeldt, "Report on Nashville," 5.

12. Student interest in K. M. Smith interview, January 30, 1961, SCRBC-AMP, MG 340, box 70, folder 5; Lewis, *Walking with the Wind*, 76; Hogan, *Many Minds, One Heart*, 8–9, 17–26; Westfeldt, "Report on Nashville," 7; Beardslee, *This Way Out Must Lead In*, 1–5.

13. For general introductions to these leaders: on Lewis, *Walking with the Wind*; Sessions and Thrasher, "New Day Begun," 15, 17–8; Halberstam, *The Children*, 67–71, 237–48 ("pure of heart" quotation on 71). On Lafayette: Ackerman and Duvall, *Force More Powerful*, 314; Halberstam, *The Children*, 71–73. On Nash: D. Doyle, *Nashville Since the 1920s*, 244; Halberstam, *The Children*, 5–9, 59, 145–48; Olson, *Freedom's Daughters*, 151–212; Ackerman and Duvall, *Force More Powerful*, 307 (Tennessee State Fair quotation); "stifled" quotation in Ross, "Witnessing and Testifying," 168. On Bevel: Halberstam, *The Children*, 72, 94–102; Lewis, *Walking with the Wind*, 61, 62.

14. Halberstam, *The Children*, 4, 7, 63–66, 74–76, 79; Westfeldt, "Report on Nashville," 8; John R. Fry, "A New Nashville?" *Presbyterian Life*, June 15, 1960, 12; Ackerman and Duvall, *Force More Powerful*, 324; Beardslee, *This Way Out Must Lead In*, 8; "rolling" quotation in Troy Jones interview, FU-BOHC).

15. Hogan, *Many Minds, One Heart*, 20–26; Lewis quotation on Lawson in Lovett, *Civil Rights Movement in Tennessee*, 122; Nash, "Inside the Sit-ins and Freedom Rides," 44–47, 50; slavery quotation from author's notes from Nashville Public Library panel on the Nashville sit-ins, February 14–15, 2004. See also the interview with Nash, August 4, 1961, SCRBC-AMP, MG 340, box 70, folder 5, about the primacy of "self-respect."

16. Hogan, *Many Minds, One Heart*, 1–2, Lawson quotations on 22; Nash, "Inside the Sit-ins and Freedom Rides," 47–48.

17. Nash, "Inside the Sit-ins and Freedom Rides," 43–60; Lawson, "'Non-Violent Way,'" *Southern Patriot* (April 1960): 1, 4; Dykeman and Stokely, "'Sit Down Chillun, Sit Down!'" *Progressive*, June 1960, 11; *A Civil Rights Legacy*, videotape, FUSC; "The Nashville Sit-ins: Nonviolence Emerges," 32; Sessions and Thrasher, "New Day Begun," 21; "the ends you seek" quotation from author's notes from Nashville Public Library panel on the Nashville sit-ins, February 14–15, 2004; Halberstam, *The Children*, 78; Branch, *Parting the Waters*, 292; Carson, *In Struggle*, 17, 21, 24; Lewis, *Walking with the Wind*, 76.

18. *Christian Century* editorial, June 28, 1961, 787–88; quotation from *Civil Rights Legacy*; *Tennessean*, June 28, 1998; *Vanderbilt Register*, February 1, 1985; Halberstam, *The Children*, 78; Hogan, *Many Minds, One Heart*, 20–26.

19. Lewis, *Walking with the Wind*, 77–78, original emphasis; Halberstam, *The Children*, 79–80; Dykeman and Stokely, "'Sit Down Chillun, Sit Down!'" 11; *Civil Rights Legacy*.

20. Westfeldt, "Report on Nashville," 6–7; Ackerman and Duvall, *Force More Powerful*, 315; D. Doyle, *Nashville Since the 1920s*, 244–45; Sessions and Thrasher, "New Day Begun" (interview with John Lewis), 19; *Civil Rights Legacy*; Halberstam, *The Children*, 91–92; Beardslee, *This Way Out Must Lead In*, 6.

21. *Tennessean* and *Banner*, March 21, 1960; Lewis, *Walking with the Wind*, 91–92; Halberstam, *The Children*, 92–94; Ackerman and Duvall, *Force More Powerful*, 316; D. Doyle, *Nashville Since the 1920s*, 245; Hogan, *Many Minds, One Heart*, 27; Wynn, "Dawning of a New Day," 46; Westfeldt, "Report on Nashville," 8; Chafe, *Civilities and Civil Rights*, 70–101; Graham, *Crisis in Print*, 194; Halberstam, *The Children*, 93; Hampton and Fayer, *Voices of Freedom*, 53–71, and for this paragraph, 53, 56; Diane Nash interview, January 30, 1961, SCRBC-AMP, MG 340, box 70, folder 5; on wider student reactions to nonviolence, see interview with Angela Butler, ARC-TU-RRD, box 111, folder 5. See also Morris, "Black Southern Student Sit-in Movements," an excerpt from his *Origins of the Civil Rights Movement*. LaPrad was an exchange student from Manchester College in Indiana.

22. K. M. Smith, "Shame and Glory," 9.

23. Lewis, *Walking with the Wind*, 93; Wynn, "Dawning of a New Day," 46; Ackerman and Duvall, *Force More Powerful*, 316–18; S. Ramsey, *Reading, Writing, and Segregation*, 95–98; *Tennessean*, February 1, 1995; Beardslee, *This Way Out Must Lead In*, 7; Angela Butler interview, ARC-TU-RRD, box 111, folder 5.

24. Lewis, *Walking with the Wind*, 93 (clothing quotation); K. M. Smith, "Shame and Glory," 12–13; Hogan, *Many Minds, One Heart*, 47; Westfeldt, "Report on Nashville," 1, 3; Julia Moore, "From Jubilee Bell Tower" (column), *Fisk News* (spring 1960): 16–17 (this is the Fisk alumni magazine, not the student newspaper, and Moore dates the first two sit-

ins mistakenly; a copy of this is in VUSC-NMFP, box 3, folder 7); Halberstam, *The Children*, 103–4. See also an annotated chronology in TSU's *Meter*, February 1960.

25. Quotations in Lewis, *Walking with the Wind*, 95–96; *Tennessean*, February 14, 1960; Moore, "From Jubilee Bell Tower," 16; Halberstam, *The Children*, 103–6, 211; Ackerman and Duvall, *Force More Powerful*, 318; D. Doyle, *Nashville Since the 1920s*, 245; Olson, *Freedom's Daughters*, 156; Nash, "Inside the Sit-ins and Freedom Rides," 47. The numbers estimated in the first sit-in vary according to accounts, but both Halberstam and Lewis specify 124, so I have adopted that number.

26. On the second wave of sit-ins, see the *Tennessean*, February 19, 1960; quotation in Lewis, *Walking with the Wind*, 97. For the third wave, see *Tennessean*, February 21, 1960 (which has McClellan's and "officially ignored" quotation); *Business Week*, February 27, 1960; Westfeldt, "Report on Nashville," 2; Wynn, "Dawning of a New Day," 46; Halberstam, *The Children*, 10 (Nash quotation); Ackerman and Duvall, *Force More Powerful*, 318–19; D. Doyle, *Nashville Since the 1920s*, 245. For both, see Moore, "From Jubilee Bell Tower." On the United Church Women's support role, see Will Campbell's "Committees Playing a Supportive Role to the Sit-in Movement" (September 1960), SCRBC-EBP, MG 630, box 10, folder 9, and the interview with Prince Rivers and W. T. Green in SCRBC-AMP, MG 340, box 70, folder 5. In this same last citation, the interview with Diane Nash and Angela Butler discusses McClellan's and the increase in tension during the third demonstration. See also Inez Adams, Herman Long, Vivian Henderson, and R. Yokley, "Proposal—Continuing Outlines: The Nashville Story," ARC-TU-BPVP, box 76, folder 1.

27. Politician quotation in David Halberstam, "'A Good City Gone Ugly,'" *Reporter*, March 31, 1960, 19; D. Doyle, *Nashville Since the 1920s*, 190, 229; Westfeldt, "Report on Nashville," 3; Halberstam, *The Children*, 113–14, 126; Sumner, "Local Press and the Nashville Student Movement, 1960," 76–77; on Chattanooga, see *Southern School News*, March 1960 (hereafter, *SSN*), and briefly, *Time*, March 14, 1960, 21.

28. K. M. Smith, "Shame and Glory," 3, Hosse quoted on 4; K. M. Smith interview in SCRBC-AMP, MG 340, box 70, folder 5; Moore, "From Jubilee Bell Tower"; Westfeldt, "Report on Nashville," 3, which claims that the Hosse meeting took place on February 26; *Tennessean*, March 24, 1960. Will D. Campbell notes the confusion and indecision of the police in his interview with Don Doyle, June 11, 1984 (notes in possession of the author).

29. K. M. Smith, "Shame and Glory," 3–4; Will D. Campbell interview, FU-BOHC; Lovett, *Civil Rights Movement in Tennessee*, 128–29 on Stahlman; author's notes from Nashville Public Library panel on the Nashville sit-ins, February 14–15, 2004; Hampton and Fayer, *Voices of Freedom*, 58; Halberstam, *The Children*, 126–27; Ackerman and Duvall, *Force More Powerful*, 319; Beardslee, *This Way Out Must Lead In*, 7. In Campbell's MSRC-RJBOHC interview, he intimates that the New York office had requested that the police withdraw so the store could close. Also note that Lewis, *Walking with the Wind*, 99, says instead that Campbell said only that arrests would occur and "there might be violence," but compare it with Sessions and Thrasher, "New Day Begun," 20, and *Civil Rights Legacy* videotape.

30. Lewis, *Walking with the Wind*, quotation and flier on 98; Ackerman and Duvall, *Force More Powerful*, 321; Wynn, "Dawning of a New Day," 46; Sessions and Thrasher, "New Day Begun," 20; *Civil Rights Legacy*. On the discussion about Big Saturday, see the interview notes with Marian Fuson and Angela Butler in SCRBC-AMP, MG 340, box 70, folder 5.

31. As with all events, researchers must be attentive to compression in participants' memories, particularly as the first and the fourth sit-in tend to intertwine in later accounts. K. M. Smith, "Shame and Glory," 14–15 (all quotations); *Tennessean*, February 28, 1960; Moore, "From Jubilee Bell Tower"; Westfeldt, "Report on Nashville," 2; *SSN*, March 1960; Ackerman and Duvall, *Force More Powerful*, 321. Note also that Peggy Alexander in Carawan, *Nashville Sit-in Story*, claims that staggered seating was first used in later April sit-ins. "Proposal—Continuing Outlines," says there was a rumor that the hoods came from Chattanooga.

32. All quotations in K. M. Smith, "Shame and Glory," 14; *Tennessean*, February 28, 1960; Moore, "From Jubilee Bell Tower"; *SSN*, March 1960; Halberstam, *The Children*, 130–33. Lewis claimed that they only later learned of a nasty attack at the Arcade on a black teenager with no connection to the sit-ins. He may be conflating a later attack that I treat in due course. See Lewis, *Walking with the Wind*, 99.

33. K. M. Smith interview, MSRC-RJBOHC; black bystander quotation in report, FUSC-RBJ, box 2, folder 11, 3–4; police anecdotes in Phil Schrader, "A City Divided," *Ivory Tower*, April 25, 1960, 11, VUSC-NMFP, box 3, folder 8.

34. Will D. Campbell interviews, FU-BOHC and MSRC-RJBOHC. Campbell refers to a Doris Dennison in the latter interview, the phrasing is such that it is likely, but not entirely clear, that this is the poacher-buyer. Lewis, *Walking with the Wind*, 99–100; *Globe*, March 4, 1960; *Fisk Forum*, March 24, 1960; Ackerman and Duvall, *Force More Powerful*, 322; Halberstam, *The Children*, 129; D. Doyle, *Nashville Since the 1920s*, 245–46.

35. The fight account is furnished entirely from Will D. Campbell's memory, and thus should be treated carefully as a source; see his oral histories in FU-BOHC and MSRC-RJBOHC, quotation on 149. He also mentions the fight in my oral history with him (UF-SPOHP), specifying that he only heard, not saw, the knife, and adds additional details in his interview with Don Doyle, June 11, 1984 (notes in possession of the author). David Halberstam also makes a passing reference to the mysterious figure of Old Green Hat in his *Reporter* article, his quotations are on page 19. See also the *SSN*, March 1960, and McGarrity, "Testing Nashville's Progressivism," 143. According to the *Tennessean*, February 28, 1960, the fight upstairs involved an unnamed victim, who Kelly Miller Smith in another account identified as Maurice Davis, but Smith mentioned neither the knife nor the white interloper (K. M. Smith, "Shame and Glory," 15, which also refers to Old Green Hat). The newspaper article refers to another protester, Emory Irving, saying only that he "was rolled down a flight of stairs."

36. Ackerman and Duvall, *Force More Powerful*, 319–20; Hampton and Fayer, *Voices of Freedom*, 58; Lewis, *Walking with the Wind*, 101–2; Halberstam, *The Children*, 134–35, 139–40; John Seigenthaler interview, UF-SPOHP; Will D. Campbell interview, UF-SPOHP; CORE, series 5, folder 421, reel 42, frame 1398; Sessions and Thrasher, "New Day Begun," 20; Beardslee, *This Way Out Must Lead In*, 7; Wynn, "Dawning of a New Day," 47; John Lewis interview in UVA-JBP, box 74, "1/14/69" folder; on students "witnessing," see Prince Rivers and W. T. Green interview, SCRBC-AMP, MG 340, box 70, folder 5.

37. Peggy Alexander and E. Angeline Butler in Carawan, *Nashville Sit-in Story*; Lewis, *Walking with the Wind*, 101–2 (on jail without bail chant), 107 (regarding Marshall; see also *Tennessean* and *Banner*, April 7, 1960, on Marshall's speech); "Denison Exchange Student Arrested in Nashville, Tennessee," memorandum, VUSC-NMFP, box 3, folder 7; Moore, "From Jubilee Bell Tower"; Sessions and Thrasher, "New Day Begun" (interview with

John Lewis), 20; CORE quotation in CORE, series 5, folder 421, reel 42, frame 1398; *Banner*, March 2, 1960; *Tennessean*, March 3 and 4, 1960; *Time*, March 14, 1960, 21; "Nashville Sit-ins: Nonviolence Emerges," 31; interview with Diane Nash, August 4, 1961, SCRBC-AMP, MG 340, box 70, folder 5, about the beloved community and the jail without bail strategy, and for more on the latter see Ross, *Witnessing and Testifying*, 171.

38. K. M. Smith interview, MSRC-RJBOHC (undertaker quotation); C. T. Vivian, MSRC-RJBOHC; Flem B. Otey interview, FUSC-BOHC; CORE, series 5, folder 421, reel 42, frame 1398; "Nashville Sit-ins: Nonviolence Emerges," 30–31; Fry, "New Nashville?" 11–13; K. M. Smith's secretary quotation in *Banner*, September 14, 1986; *Tennessean*, February 20, 1990; *Time*, April 11, 1960, 64; Westfeldt, "Report on Nashville," 9; author's notes from Nashville Public Library panel on the Nashville sit-ins, February 14–15, 2004; Halberstam, *The Children*, 177. The cover of Fisk *News* (spring 1960) has a more extended version of Wright's remarks. See *Fisk Forum*, March 24, 1960, on Wright's displeasure at poor student attendance, as well as the *Tennessean*, May 1, 1960, on other professors' responses to students in their classes active in the sit-ins. On the mass arrests as the significant catalyst for the mass movement, see "Decision-making in the Southern Sit-in Movement," ARC-TU-BPVP, box 75, folder 15; Moody, "Effects of Metro on Negro Politics," 49; interview with John Hope II, March 2, 1961, SCRBC-AMP, MG 340, box 70, folder 5.

39. See the materials on W. S. Davis in ARC-TU-RRD, box 129, folder 7, and box 111, folder 5, plus the latter citation for interviews with Stephen J. Wright, Vivian Henderson, and Angela Butler, as well as a statement from Fisk to Vanderbilt faculty; K. M. Smith interview, SCRBC-AMP; Lewis interview in UVA-JBP, box 74, "1/14/69" folder; HUHL-DTMC, bMS Am 2090.1, box 21, folder 410; Lerone Bennett Jr., "The Plight of Negro College Presidents," *Ebony* (October 1960): 140.

40. Interviews with Rodney Powell, Marion Barry, Diane Nash, Prince Rivers and W. T. Green, Angela Butler, and Kelly Miller Smith, all in SCRBC-AMP, MG 340, box 70, folder 5; "Sit-in Movement in Nashville, Tennessee"; interview with Vivian Henderson in ARC-TU-RRD, box 111, folder 5.

41. *Civil Rights Legacy*; A. Meier, Rudwick, and Broderick, *Black Protest Thought in the Twentieth Century*, 24–29; Andrew White interview, MSRC-RJBOHC; Sessions and Thrasher, "New Day Begun," 21; Halberstam, *The Children*, 128, 141–42; Sumner, "Local Press and the Nashville Student Movement, 1960," 23, 30. Stephen J. Wright, in his MSRC-RJBOHC interview, claims that he received only one complaint from a parent about their child going to jail. On new forms of leadership and finding consensus, see interviews with Diane Nash, Angela Butler, and Rodney Powell ("trying thing" quotation) in SCRBC-AMP, MG 340, box 70, folder 5, and interview with Vivian Henderson in ARC-TU-RRD, box 111, folder 5. On student organization, see "decision making in the southern sit-in movement," ARC-TU-BPVP, box 75, folder 15; interviews with Angela Butler and John Hope II in SCRBC-AMP, MG 340, box 70, folder 5.

42. Interviews with K. M. Smith, Nash, Powell, Butler, and Marian Fuson, SCRBC-AMP, MG 340, box 70, folder 5; "Decision Making in the Southern Sit-in Movement," ARC-TU-BPVP, box 75, folder 15.

43. *Tennessean* and *Banner*, March 1, 1960; *Banner*, March 2 and 3, 1960; *Tennessean*, March 3 and 4, 1960; *Globe*, March 4 and 11, 1960; *Fisk Forum*, March 24, 1960; Westfeldt, "Report on Nashville," 3; Hentoff, "Peaceful Army," 275. See also *Concern* (newsletter of the National Conference of Methodist Youth), March 18, 1960, in TSLA-HFS, box 16, folder 17,

and John A. Smith's column in *Wesley Notes*, March 7, 1960, 2, in VUSC-CMSP, box 2, "Lawson case" folder (one of two folders so marked); Lewis, *Walking with the Wind*, 102–3.

44. Quotations in *Tennessean*, March 2, 1960; *Banner*, March 3, 1960; *Globe*, March 4, March 11, 1960; Moore, "From Jubilee Bell Tower"; Westfeldt, "Report on Nashville," 9; D. Doyle, *Nashville Since the 1920s*, 245–46.

45. *Banner*, March 1, March 2, and quotation in March 2 editorial, 1960; Lawson quoted in *Tennessean*, March 2, 1960; *New York Times*, March 2, 1960; Halberstam, "'Good City Gone Ugly,'" 19 ("no longer interested" quotation); Wynn, "Dawning of a New Day," 47; Sumner, "Local Press and the Nashville Student Movement, 1960," 77–79. The two students were Luther Harris and Earl Mays; see Lewis, *Walking with the Wind*, 86, and Halberstam, *The Children*, 142–43, on these two, plus *Tennessean*, March 2, 1960; *SSN*, March 1960; K. M. Smith, "Shame and Glory," 7–8. There is dissension over the start of the trial dates and the Ben West meeting. "In swing" quotations in Vivian Henderson interview, ARC-TU-RRD, box 111, folder 5, and see also the Angela Butler interview in SCRBC-AMP, MG 340, box 70, folder 5.

46. Halberstam, "'Good City Gone Ugly,'" 18; *Tennessean* and *Banner*, March 3, 1960; *Banner*, March 4, 1960; *Tennessean*, March 5 (which has Nichol's quotations), March 6 and May 12, 1960; Moore, "From Jubilee Bell Tower," 17; Westfeldt, "Report on Nashville," 3; Peggy Alexander in Carawan, *Nashville Sit-in Story* (which claims that Vanderbilt, Peabody, and Meharry students now joined); "Daily News Brief," March 8, 1960, VUSC-NMFP, box 3, folder 7; *Christian Century* editorial, March 30, 1960; Sumner, "Local Press and the Nashville Student Movement, 1960," 34; D. Doyle, *Nashville Since the 1920s*, 245–46. On the question of a city ordinance for segregation, see *Chattanooga Free Press*, May 11, 1960; interview with George Barrett, SCRBC-AMP, MG 340, box 70, folder 5.

47. Halberstam, *The Children*, 116, 188–91; *Banner* and *Tennessean*, March 1, 1960; *Banner* editorials, February 29 and March 1, 1960; compare the *Tennessean* editorial, March 1, 1960. See also Graham, *Crisis in Print*, 196, 199; Sumner, "Publisher and the Preacher," 34–43; D. Doyle, *Nashville Since the 1920s*, 246; Ackerman and Duvall, *Force More Powerful*, 323–24.

48. Leaver to John M. Flanigan Jr., letter March 15, 1960, VUSC-CHP, box 29, "Lawson/Stahlman" folder; *Banner*, March 1, 1960. For another reference to threats, see *Banner*, March 4, 1960. See also white reactions in Fry, "New Nashville?" 12.

49. The statement from the TFCG is in the *Banner*, April 2, 1960, with no editorial comment from Stahlman. L. V. DuBose to Madison Sarratt, letter March 18, 1960, VUSC-CMSP, box 2, "Lawson Case" folder (second of two), and the same for Thurman Sensing, "The Lunch Counter Sit-ins," March 13, 1960, press release from the Southern States Industrial Council. On legal confusion about whether the sit-ins broke the law, see *Tennessean*, May 12, 1960, and Westfeldt, "Report on Nashville," 4.

50. Benton McDaniel to Madison Sarratt, letter March 14, 1960, VUSC-CMSP, box 2, "Lawson Case" folder (second of two), same citation for "bludgeon" quotation in Thurman Sensing, "Lunch Counter Sit-ins"; TFCG in the *Banner*, April 2, 1960.

51. *Tennessean* and *Banner*, March 4, 1960; *Tennessean*, February 29, March 5 and 8, 1960; Kean, "'At a Most Uncomfortable Speed,'" 363–82; Conkin, *Gone with the Ivy*, 549–76; Halberstam, *The Children*, 191–207; *Globe*, March 11, 1960; *Banner* editorial, March 4, 1960, applauding Lawson's expulsion; Westfeldt, "Report on Nashville," 4; "Nashville Story" outline; Lovett, *Civil Rights Movement in Tennessee*, 130; Lomax, *Negro Revolt*, 138;

Wesley Notes in March 7, 1960, 3, 5, VUSC-CMSP, box 2, "Lawson case" folder (one of two); D. Doyle, *Nashville Since the 1920s*, 248.

52. Lewis, *Walking with the Wind*, 103–4; *Christian Century*, March 30, 1960, 380; *Tennessean* and *Banner*, March 10, 1960; TCHR newsletter (no date), FUSC-CSJ, box 151, folder 14, which also contains the TCHR's statement in reaction to Big Saturday; Wynn, "Dawning of a New Day," 49. Regarding displeasure over the black committee members, see *Tennessean*, March 31, 1960, and Halberstam, "'Good City Gone Ugly,'" 18; on the committee, see McGarrity. "Testing Nashville's Progressivism," 100–104; 113; 129–30; and the interview with George Barrett in SCRBC-AMP, MG 340, box 70, folder 5.

53. Nash and McDonald's statements, as well as "Summary of the Information and Impressions Given the Mayor's Committee by the Six Students Interviewed" (memorandum), are in VUSC-CMSP, box 2, "Lawson Case" folder (one of two). See also the *Tennessean*, March 9, 1960, for the after-quotations. See also, regarding divisions on how transgressing laws factored into the demonstrators' mentalities, the "Class on Nashville Sit-ins," by Myles Horton at Highlander, March 18–20, 1960, TSLA-HFS, box 4, folder 13.

54. *Banner*, March 9, 1960; *Banner* and *Tennessean*, March 12, 1960.

55. *Banner*, March 16, 17, and 24, 1960; *Tennessean*, March 16, 17, 18, and 22, 1960—contrast the newspaper coverage with Peggy Alexander in Randall, *Sit-in Story*, 2–3 (all quotations); *Christian Century*, April 27, 1960, 525–6; *Time*, March 14, 1960, 21; *Time*, March 28, 1960, 25; TSU *Meter*, March 1960; Lewis, *Walking with the Wind*, 104–5; D. Doyle, *Nashville Since the 1920s*, 248. There is some dissension on the dates for the two Post House servings—the *Meter*, to take one example, claims March 17 and 18, but they get other dates wrong too. For more on Edwin Randall, see Ward, *Radio and the Struggle for Civil Rights in the South*, 134–48.

56. See the interviews with Rodney Powell and Marian Fuson in SCRBC-AMP, MG 340, box 70, folder 5 ("Cloud 90" reference in latter); legal attitudes in "Proposal—Continuing Outlines."

57. Interviews with Marian Fuson, John Hope II, Diane Nash, Kelly Miller Smith, Rodney Powell, and "notes on mass meeting, January 29, 1961," SCRBC-AMP, MG 340, box 70, folder 5; Vivian Henderson interview, ARC-TU-RRD, box 111, folder 5; "Proposal—Continuing Outlines."

58. On student impatience, see *Tennessean*, March 18, 1960; on the biracial committee's procrastination, see *Tennessean*, March 22, 1960, and *Banner*, March 21, March 24, 1960; on the church encounters, see the *Banner* and *Tennessean*, March 21, 1960 (quotation in latter); *Christian Century*, April 27, 1960, 525; TSU *Meter*, March 1960. On the West vigil, see *Tennessean*, March 31, 1960; Randall, *Sit-in Story*, 3–4.

59. *Banner*, March 25 and 26, 1960; *Tennessean*, March 26, 1960 (all quotations); D. Doyle, *Nashville Since the 1920s*, 248; Halberstam, *The Children*, 211–12; Angela Butler interview in ARC-TU-RRD, box 111, folder 5; Sarratt quoted in Patrick J. McGarrity, "Testing Nashville's Progressivism," 116.

60. *Banner*, March 30 and 31, 1960; *Tennessean*, March 30 and April 3, 1960, (the former includes a fuller version of the statement and all quotations); TSU *Meter*, April 1960; Westfeldt, "Report on Nashville," 6.

61. *Banner*, April 7, 1960; *Tennessean*, March 28, 1960; Moore, "From Jubilee Bell Tower," *Fisk News* (summer 1961): 8; *SSN*, April 1960; TSU *Meter*, April 1960; *Christian Century*, April 27, 1960, 525; Seigenthaler interview, NMA-CMGOH; Lewis, *Walking with the Wind*,

105; D. Doyle, *Nashville Since the 1920s*, 248; Sumner, "Local Press and the Nashville Student Movement, 1960," 41, 94, 103–4. The program later ran, but affiliates in Nashville, Memphis and Chattanooga declined to air it, according to the *Tennessean*, April 23, 1960. On police surveillance, and for Hosse quotation, see Schrader, "City Divided," 11; Ellington quoted in the *Banner*, March 26, 1960.

62. This is Sumner's assertion, 114. But consider Lovett, *Civil Rights Movement in Tennessee*, 137, and the April 27, 1960, Chamber of Commerce minutes where, after a presentation from Greenfield Pitts from Harvey's, the executive committee agreed to "confer with both newspaper publishers — to seek a better understanding and more cohesive philosophy in the news presentation"—TSLA-COC, reel 2, no frame. Yet another merchant criticized the newspapers for their relative silence as contrasted to school desegregation: see Westfeldt, "Settling a Sit-in: A Report for the Nashville Community Relations Conference," Nashville: Nashville Community Relations Conference, 1960, 4. For more on Henderson, see *Wall Street Journal*, October 3, 1960.

63. *Tennessean* and *Banner*, April 5, 1960; *New York Times*, April 18, 1960; Westfeldt, "Report on Nashville," 5; Westfeldt, "Settling a Sit-in," 2–3; Moore, "From Jubilee Bell Tower," 17; *SSN*, May 1960; Lewis, *Walking with the Wind*, 105–7; Wynn, "Dawning of a New Day," 50; D. Doyle, *Nashville Since the 1920s*, 249; Lomax, *Negro Revolt*, 142–43; Hampton and Fayer, *Voices of Freedom*, 60; Southern Interagency Conference minutes from January 3–4, 1961, meeting, SBHLA-CLC, AR 138-2, box 5, folder 10. The *Tennessean*, March 3, 1960, further attested to the weather's effect. Henderson's figures can be compared with the SRC report "Negro Buying Power" from June 29, 1960, GSU-SLA-EVP, box 3372, folder 11.

64. This point is made especially strongly in "Sit-in Movement in Nashville, Tennessee." See also A. Meier, Rudwick, and Broderick, *Black Protest Thought in the Twentieth Century*, 19n; *Banner*, April 7, 1960; K. M. Smith and Vivian quoted in Westfeldt, "Settling a Sit-in," 2–3; Carawan, *Nashville Sit-in Story*; author's notes from Nashville Public Library panel on the Nashville sit-ins, February 14–15, 2004; *Banner*, September 30, 1960, September 14, 1986; *Tennessean*, February 20, 1990; Halberstam, *The Children*, 178; Ackerman and Duvall, *Force More Powerful*, 324. On the election, see *Tennessean*, April 3, 1960, and *New York Times*, April 18, 1960, and for Good Jelly's role, see David Halberstam, "'Good Jelly's' Last Stand," *Reporter*, January 19, 1961, 41. See also "Proposal—Continuing Outlines." Regarding the boycott, see SCRBC-AMP, MG 340, box 70, folder 5, interview with Vivian Henderson; "Sit-in Movement in Nashville, Tennessee"; and "Proposal—Continuing Outlines." Lovett, *Civil Rights Movement in Tennessee*, 136, claims Henderson asked for the boycott on April 5, but that is contradicted in ARC-TU-RRD, box 111, folder 5. Hawkins, *Nashville Metro*, 60, especially dates the sheriff defeat as the death knell for the West machine.

65. CORE, series 5, folder 421, reel 42, frame 1397; Lillard in Hampton and Fayer, *Voices of Freedom*, 60.

66. D. Doyle, *Nashville Since the 1920s*, 249; *Tennessean* and *Banner*, April 5 and 6, 1960; *Tennessean*, April 6 and 7 (editorial), 1960; *Banner*, April 7, 1960, on trial status; Westfeldt, "Settling a Sit-in," 1; the full committee report can be found in SRC, series 4, folder 88, reel 138, frame 1718.

67. April 6, 1960, meeting notes available in VUSC-KMS, box 76, folder 1 (all quotations); *Banner* and *Tennessean*, April 6, 1960; *Tennessean*, April 7, 1960; *Tennessean* and *Banner*,

April 8, 1960; *Tennessean*, April 9, 1960; Lewis, *Walking with Wind*, 106; K. M. Smith interview, SCRBC-AMP.

68. Quotations in *Tennessean*, April 10, 1960; dining rooms account in Westfeldt, "Settling a Sit-in," 1–2. See also *Christian Century*, April 27, 1960, 525; Moore, "From Jubilee Bell Tower," *Fisk News* (winter 1960): 7. The *Banner*, April 7, 1960, contains Kelly Miller Smith's reaction to the proposed permanent biracial committee. On white liberal groups see ARC-TU-BPVP, box 76, folder 1. Developments on this latter front were later helped by Davidson County head Judge Beverly Briley and West—see the executive committee minutes from May 12, 1960, 129, and board of governors minutes from the Nashville Chamber of Commerce, May 26, 1960, 134, in TSLA-COC, reel 2, no frame, but the Chamber of Commerce itself remained leery of helping, see executive committee minutes, from June 9, 1960, TSLA-COC, reel 2, no frame.

69. *Banner*, April 11, 1960; *Tennessean*, April 12 (all quotations), April 13, 1960; Moore, "From Jubilee Bell Tower," *Fisk News* (summer 1960): 8; *SSN*, May 1960; Wynn, "Dawning of a New Day," 50; D. Johnson, *Vanderbilt Divinity School*, 140.

70. *Tennessean*, April 12, 13 (all quotations except for editorial quotation, same day), and 14, 1960; *Banner*, April 15, 1960; Randall, *Sit-in Story*, 1. See also the interview with Jack Gunter, *Banner* reporter, in the *Banner*, January 16, 1989, where he refers to the Arcade incident but doesn't date it. See David Sumner, who notes that the *Tennessean* covered the 1960 sit-ins more aggressively in the reporting, but this did not equate to editorial support, in "Local Press and the Nashville Student Movement, 1960," 153, 163, and *Tennessean*, June 28, 1998.

71. *Banner*, April 19, 20, and 21, 1960; *Tennessean*, April 20 (all bombing quotations) and 22, 1960; Looby interview, MSRC-RJBOHC, 25; C. T. Vivian interview, MSRC-RJBOHC; Moore, "From Jubilee Bell Tower," *Fisk News* (summer 1960): 8; *SSN*, May 1960; Ackerman and Duvall, *Force More Powerful*, 325; D. Doyle, *Nashville Since the 1920s*, 249; Halberstam, *The Children*, 228–30; Hampton and Fayer, *Voices of Freedom*, 65. See also the *Tennessean*, April 24, 1960, regarding police protection at the homes of Ben West, Kelly Miller Smith, Looby, Robert Lillard, Fisk President Stephen J. Wright, and physician and NCLC official C. J. Walker, all prompted by bomb threats. James Summerville claims that it was only at this point that Meharry students joined the active front-ranks of the local movement, in *Educating Black Doctors*, 133–34.

72. Halberstam, *The Children*, 230–37, quotation on 232. Rodney Powell especially stresses the Looby bombing's influence on the movement, in SCRBC-AMP, MG 340, box 70, folder 5.

73. The quotations of this was reconstructed from both the *Banner* and *Tennessean*, April 20, 1960; *Tennessean*, May 12, 1985; *Banner*, February 2, 1993; C. T. Vivian interview, MSRC-RJBOHC; TSU *Meter*, April 1960; Moore, "From Jubilee Bell Tower," *Fisk News* (summer 1960): 8–9; Lewis, *Walking with the Wind*, 109–10; D. Doyle, *Nashville Since the 1920s*, 249; Ackerman and Duvall, *Force More Powerful*, 327; Olson, *Freedom's Daughters*, 159; Wynn, "Dawning of a New Day," 51; Hampton and Fayer, *Voices of Freedom*, 66–67.

74. Author's notes from Nashville Public Library panel on the Nashville sit-ins, February 14–15, 2004.

75. *Globe*, April 29, 1960 (all quotations); *Tennessean*, April 19, 1960; *Tennessean* and *Banner*, April 21, 1960; TSU *Meter*, April 1960; Wynn, "Dawning of a New Day," 52. A copy

of the evening's program is available in NPL-NR-ETS, along with the Vivian quotation. MLK theory is in "Sit-in Movement in Nashville, Tennessee."

76. All quotations in Westfeldt, "Settling a Sit-in," 4; Randall, *Sit-in Story*, 2; Lomax, *Negro Revolt*, 142–43; K. M. Smith interview, SCRBC-AMP; Halberstam, "'Good City Gone Ugly,'" 18; D. Doyle, *Nashville Since the 1920s*, 251. Regarding the two black college presidents, see Lewis, *Walking with The Wind*, 106.

77. All quotations in Westfeldt, "Settling a Sit-in," 4; Ackerman and Duvall, *Force More Powerful*, 324–25; Halberstam, "'Good City Gone Ugly,'" 18; D. Doyle, *Nashville Since the 1920s*, 251. For more on Chamber of Commerce reluctance, see the May 5, 1960, minutes from a joint meeting between executive committees of the NCLC and the NCRC in FUSC-CSJ, box 151, folder 8. Regarding the NCRC forum, see the announcement in the *Banner* and *Tennessean*, March 24, 1960; a copy of the panel discussion called "Report on Nashville 1960: Its Problems and Possibilities" is in FUSC-CSJ, box 151, folder 8 (second copy in folder 15). See Oppenheimer, *Sit-in Movement of 1960*, 129, on the boycott.

78. The idea that the agreement was a compromise for the students comes from Vivian Henderson in ARC-TU-BPVP, box 76, folder 1. See also the Fuson and Powell interviews in SCRBC-AMP, MG 340, box 70, folder 5.

79. *Tennessean*, May 11 and 12, 1960; *Reporter*, May 26, 1960; *Commonweal*, May 27, 1960. The most complete coverage is in the *Chattanooga Daily Times*, May 11, 12, and 13, 1960, which obviously owed no allegiance to Nashville advertising dollars, and Westfeldt, "Settling a Sit-in," 1, 6; see also Moore, "From Jubilee Bell Tower," *Fisk News* (Summer, 1960), 9; the TCHR May 1960 newsletter in NPL-NR-ETS (which includes a full list of the women's groups participating), the Unitarian story in the UCW 1960 annual report, in FUSC-CSJ, box 152, folder 7; *Tennessean*, February 20, 1990; Ackerman and Duvall, *Force More Powerful*, 327; Wynn, "Dawning of a New Day," 52–53; D. Doyle, *Nashville Since the 1920s*, 251. On Grant's recalcitrance, see *Globe*, June 17, 1960, and the various news clippings in CORE, series 5, folder 421, reel 42, frame 1401.

80. See "Proposal—Continuing Outlines"; interview with George Barrett in SCRBC-AMP, MG 340, box 70, folder 5, and SCRBC-AMP, box 150, folder 2; *Wall Street Journal*, July 15, 1963; Herman Long to Charles Steele, letter March 25, 1960, ARC-TU-RRD, box 130, folder 14. See also a white former Nashvillian's response from afar, a previously unpublished essay by Robert Penn Warren, "Episode in a Dime Store."

81. Interview with C. T. Vivian in UNC-SHC-TBP, box 131, folder 944; "Decision Making in the Southern Sit-in Movement," ARC-TU-BPVP, box 75, folder 15; interviews with Nash and Butler in SCRBC-AMP, MG 340, box 70, folder 5; see also Arsenault, *Freedom Riders*.

82. Report by R. B. Johnson, FUSC-RBJ, box 2, folder 11, 3; Fry, "New Nashville?" 12; K. M. Smith in *Banner*, September 14, 1986.

83. Lillard quoted in Hampton and Fayer, *Voices of Freedom*, 60; second Lillard quote, HUHL-DTMC, bMS Am 2090.1, box 21, folder 410; Nash, "Inside the Sit-ins and Freedom Rides," 47; Hentoff, "Peaceful Army," 275, 277; Lawson quoted in Walzer, "Politics of the New Negro," 240; Halberstam, *The Children*, 164–66, 177.

84. Westfeldt, "Report on Nashville," 9; Lawson, Nashville Public Library panel on the Nashville sit-ins, February 14–15, 2004 (author's notes); "Decision Making in the Southern Sit-in Movement" and "Sit-in Movement in Nashville, Tennessee"; *Chattanooga Free Press*,

May 11, 1960; James McBride Dabbs, "Dime Stores and Dignity," *Nation*, April 2, 1960, 289; Vivian Henderson interview in ARC-TU-RRD, box 111, folder 5.

Chapter 4. The Kingdom or Individual Desires?

1. This account is drawn from "It Happened in 1961," a typescript recounting the incident in VUSC-NMFP, box 3, folder 22, written by Nelson Fuson. In the essay, he calls the town where this incident occurred "Knoshville, Kennessina," but in another draft uses "Barton." I suppose the original pseudonym could translate to Knoxville as easily as Nashville, but given the detail about the seminary and the fact that Fuson lived in Nashville, I am presuming this took place in Nashville. More importantly, the essay included a note at the top reading "Authenticity of the incident, and of the 'note,' vouched for."

2. Inez Adams, "Decision Making in the Southern Sit-in Movement," ARC-TU-BPVP, box 75, folder 15; "The Nashville Story," ARC-TU-BPVP, box 76, folder 1; interviews with Kelly Miller Smith, Rodney Powell, and Marian Fuson in SCRBC-AMP, MG 340, box 70, folder 5. UNC-SHC-DPP, box 10, folder 156 has materials on sit-in students helping voter registration efforts.

3. Fumigator details in *Tennessean*, November 11, 1960; Lewis, *Walking with the Wind*, 121–22.

4. *Tennessean*, November 13, 23, and 24, and December 8, 1960; Julia Moore in *Fisk News* (winter 1960): 7; *Nashville News Star*, November 20, 1960; *Christian Century*, January 11, 1961, 61; D. Doyle, *Nashville Since the 1920s*, 251–52; Lewis, *Walking with the Wind*, 123.

5. *Tennessean*, February 2, 5, 8, and 10, 1961; "To the Citizens of Nashville" and untitled February 2, 1961, press release, both in NPL-NR; George Barrett to Harold Fleming, letter February 15, 1961, SRC: series 1, reel 35, folder 1239, frame 2180; Lewis, *Walking with the Wind*, 124–27.

6. Cheryl-Ann Jones, *Fisk News* (spring 1961): 8; TSU *Meter*, April 1–15, 1961; Kelly Miller Smith to "Dear Christian Friend," letter February 22, 1961, VUSC-KMS, box 1, folder 3; VUSC-NMFP, box 2, folder 3; Will D. Campbell interview, FUSC-BOHC; *Tennessean*, February 21, 1961—a copy of this article also ran in the TSU *Meter*, February 16–28, 1961, with additional information on the violent outbreaks, claiming that the violence became more pronounced on January 23, but February 23 makes more sense in this context. This article also confirms the reports of police assault, and the trial technicality. See also D. Doyle, *Nashville Since the 1920s*, 252; Lewis, *Walking with the Wind*, 125.

7. Flier in NPL-NR; K. M. Smith to David Moore, letter May 2, 1962, VUSC-KMS, box 1, folder 6; Cheryl-Ann Jones, *Fisk News* (summer 1961), 8; TCHR newsletter (March 1961), in USM-WDC, box 53, folder 15; *Voice of the Movement* (newsletter), May 20, 1961, CORE, series 5, reel 24, folder 101, frame 0526; "Nashville Tests Integration of Downtown Theatres," *New York Times*, April 30, 1961.

8. *Tennessean*, February 15, 1961; *Voice of the Movement* (newsletter), n.d., (ca. late March 1961), NPL-NR (copy in CORE, series 5, reel 24, folder 101, frame 0525).

9. *Tennessean*, July 19 and 21, 1961; *Banner*, July 21, 1961; *780 Countdown*, July 9, 1962. Note that the retrospective in the *Tennessean*, July 14, 2002, discusses a longer antecedent to this. See also *Voice of the Movement* (newsletter), July 27, 1961, VUSC-NMFP, box 2, folder 21, which has letters of protest regarding the "fictitious 'financial deficiency'" for the swim-

ming pools, as well as the Mansfield Douglas, Richard Fulton, and Jim Tuck interviews in NMA-CMGOH. The Hamlet parody is in the *Tennessean*, August 11, 1961, and reproduced in *Voice of the Movement*, August 11, 1961, SNCC, series 15, folder 245, reel 40, frame 0787.

10. Lewis, *Walking with the Wind*, 116; *Nashville News Star*, July 1960. See also the NCLC flier in support of the Hill's boycott in VUSC-NMFP, box 2, folder 5. On 1920s protests, see Flem B. Otey interview, FUSC-BOHC. For reference to worries about continuing demonstrations over the summer with a lack of students, see CORE, series 5, folder 421, reel 42, frame 1397.

11. August 10 and 11, 1961, reports in SNCC, series 15, folder 245, reel 40, starting on frame 0785; *Tennessean*, August 7 and 8, 1961; Lewis, *Walking with the Wind*, 175–76; D. Doyle, *Nashville Since the 1920s*, 252.

12. August 11, 1961, *Voice of the Movement* in SNCC, series 15, folder 245, reel 40, frame 0787; Lewis, *Walking with the Wind*, 175–78; Carmichael with Thelwell, *Ready for Revolution*, 235–40.

13. *Banner*, August 11, 1961; *Tennessean*, August 11, 1961. See also the September 12, 1961, NCLC minutes, VUSC-KMS, box 74, folder 12, which stressed that a commitment to nonviolent direct action was required to be on the student committee.

14. SNCC, series 15, reel 40, folder 245, starting on frame 0785. On Williams, see Tyson, *Radio Free Dixie*.

15. *Nashville News-Star*, March 24, August 14, and November 20, 1960; Kelly Miller Smith, "Shame and Glory," VUSC-KMS, box 28, folder 7, 21; Stephen J. Wright speech in *Charlottesville Tribune* (clipping), CORE, series 5, reel 42, folder 421, frame 1401; *Capitol City Defender*, May 7, 1963, WDC-USM, box 15, folder 18.

16. April 22–23, 1960, "Community Conference on Employment Opportunity," VUSC-NMFP, box 1, folder 24; an article in the *Banner*, April 23, 1960, gave rosy coverage on the keynote speaker rather than recounting Henderson's report. See also the report on black employment in Tennessee state government jobs, with similarly lackluster findings, in TSLA-BEP, box 51, folder 5, and the TSU *Meter*, November 1960, regarding a survey of 473 black businesses in Nashville to gather information. See also ARC-TU-RRD, box 115, folder 15; box 32, folder 9; and box 111, folder 5.

17. Nashville chapter NAACP report to Vice President Johnson, April 8, 1961, VUSC-NMFP, box 1, folder 27; *New York Times*, April 12, 1961; *Banner*, May 1, 1961; "Employment Progress in Nashville," Vivian Henderson statement, ARC-TU-RRD, box 32, folder 9.

18. "Conference with AVCO representatives on May 31, 1961," memorandum June 6, 1961, VUSC-NMFP, box 1, folder 25. See also the details of the Western Electric plant that, if the manager is to be believed, facilitated black employment, as well as the memorandum regarding the November 3, 1961, meeting in VUSC-NMFP, box 1, folder 26. See also the May 6, 1961, letter written to Henry Ford complaining about the lack of black employment at the local Ford plant in VUSC-NMFP, box 1, folder 25, as well as Kelly Miller Smith's account of dealing with a Ford manager in "Shame and Glory," 16; Herman Long, "confidential" memorandum, "AVCO Situation—Nashville, Tennessee as of November 15, 1961," ARC-TU-RRD box 115, folder 16 (hereafter Long, "confidential" Avco memo).

19. Herman Long, "The AVCO Situation," memorandum December 7, 1961, and Nelson Fuson, "Phone Call to Mr. B. L. Clark, AVCO," memorandum January 30, 1962, VUSC-NMFP, box 1, folder 26; Herman H. Long to Percy Williams, letter November 21, 1961;

Long, "confidential" AVCO memo; Long, "AVCO Situation" memorandum, all in ARC-TU-RRD box 115, folder 16; see also the ongoing correspondence and memos in ARC-TU-RRD, box 115, folder 17.

20. See the October 16, 1961, report in VUSC-NMFP, box 1, folder 26; Vivian Henderson interview, SCRBC-AMP, MG 340, box 70, folder 5. See Nashville labor statistics in TSLA-BEP, box 38, folder 4.

21. Quotations in TCHR newsletter (December 1961), USM-WDC, box 53, folder 15. See also the Coordinating Committee minutes from March 2, 1962, USM-WDC, box 53, folder 12; *Nashville News Star*, November 20, 1960; *City Examiner*, February 16, 1962; Vivan Henderson, "Employment Progress in Nashville," n.d., box 32, folder 9; Mahlon J. Griffith, "Report 1," August 1, 1962, 116/25; employment report, box 115, folder 26—all in ARC-TU-RRD, box 115, folder 17, 20 and 23.

22. The perspectives in the following paragraphs are drawn from the meeting transcript in ARC-TU-RRD, box 129, folder 7.

23. NCLC board minutes from December 5, 1962, VUSC-KMS, box 7, folder 13; Jim Lawson file, April 2, 1962, NPL-NBCF; *City Examiner*, February 16, 1962; "1st Joint Board meeting—NCLC-NAACP," minutes February 22, 1962, VUSC-KMS, box 74, folder 13; see also *Voice of the Movement*, April 7, 1962, VUSC-NMFP, box 2, folder 21.

24. Coordinating Committee minutes from the March 2, 1962, meeting in USM-WDC, box 53, folder 12; *780 Countdown*, July 16, 1962; "1st Joint Board Meeting—NCLC—NAACP," meeting minutes, February 22, 1962, VUSC-KMS, box 74, folder 13; K. M. Smith to Wiley Branton, letter March 11, 1963, VUSC-KMS, box 1, folder 8; *Voice of the Movement*," May 12, 1962, VUSC-NMFP, box 2, folder 9. On Hume-Fogg, see *City Examiner*, February 9, 1962; NCRC board minutes, January 30, 1963, FUSC-CSJ, box 151, folder 8; *Tennessean*, September 1 and October 11, 1963; USM-WDC, box 53, folder 12 (another copy in box 56, folder 18); report to Briley, November 14, 1963, NMA-MHRC, box 1, folder 3.

25. *Voice of the Movement*, February 28, 1962, VUSC-KMS, box 134, folder 7; K. M. Smith to Anne Braden, letter April 5, 1962, VUSC-KMS, box 1, folder 5; *Fisk Forum*, February 15, 1962; D. Doyle, *Nashville Since the 1920s*, 252.

26. Fisk *Forum*, February 15, 1962; *Tennessean*, February 15, 1962; *Voice of the Movement*, February 28, 1962, VUSC-KMS, box 134, folder 7.

27. Quotation in NCLC minutes, VUSC-KMS, box 74, folder 12; *Voice of the Movement*, February 28, 1962, VUSC-KMS, box 134, folder 7 (another copy is in VUSC-NMFP, box 2, folder 5); *Banner*, March 26, April 2, and May 22, 1962; Coordinating Committee minutes, March 2, 1962, USM-WDC, box 53, folder 12; memorandum from Fuson on a conference with Wilson-Quick representatives, March 2, 1962, VUSC-NMFP, box 1, folder 26. See also Wilson-Quick to Nelson Fuson, February 15, 1962, letter, VUSC-NMFP, box 1, folder 4, which claims that demonstrators "were not refused this service because of the color of their skin alone. There are many other factors involved and I feel sure that you are aware of many of them" and "everyone must do what they think best."

28. *Tennessean*, February, 16, 1962; *New York Times*, April 30, 1961; *Voice of the Movement*, April 7, 1962, VUSC-NMFP, box 2, folder 21; *Voice of the Movement*, May 12, 1962, VUSC-NMFP, box 2, folder 9; see the flier announcing King's appearance in VUSC-NMFP, box 2, folder 5; *780 Countdown*, July 16 and 30, 1962; *Voice of the Movement*, October 18, 1962, VUSC-NMFP, box 2, folder 21. Note that future mayor Beverly Briley was the no-show

politician. See also K. M. Smith to Campbell, letter March 11, 1964, USM-WDC, box 7, folder 22, about continuing patterns of black self-segregation.

29. The consolidation issue is amply discussed elsewhere, so I bypass many of the intricate issues involved: for elaboration, see the NMA-CMGOH interviews; D. Doyle, *Nashville Since the 1920s*, 179–221; Hawkins, "Public Opinion and Metropolitan Organization in Nashville"; Hanson, *Report on Politics in Nashville*; Elazar, *Case Study of Failure in Attempted Metropolitan Integration*; Booth, *Metropolitics*; D. Grant, "Urban and Suburban Nashville"; D. Grant, "Metropolitics and Professional Political Leadership." Daniel Grant was a political scientist in Nashville who worked on behalf of the proconsolidation forces.

30. Egerton, *Nashville: The Face of Two Centuries*, 260–65; Hawkins, *Nashville Metro*, 24, 56, 59–60, 62, 80, 101; D. Doyle, *Nashville Since the 1920s*, 198–214 but especially 204–6; Booth, *Metropolitics*, 78; Charlie Howell and Mansfield Douglas interviews, NMA-CMGOH. Hawkins, *Nashville Metro*, 90–91, has a useful list of the general constituencies for and against Metro. On Gene Jacobs's penchant for corruption, see *Time*, September 14, 1962, 73.

31. See D. Grant, "Urban and Suburban Nashville," for an overview of these issues, 86–92 (quotation on 83), as well as Hawkins, *Nashville Metro*, 85; D. Doyle, *Nashville Since the 1920s*, 193–98; Booth, *Metropolitics*, 11, 12–15, 44; Wayne Whitt interview, NMA-CMGOH.

32. Harry Lester interview, NMA-CMGOH; D. Doyle, *Nashville Since the 1920s*, 209; Booth, *Metropolitics*, 65, 86; Hawkins, *Nashville Metro*, 49, 53, 74, 96, 100–102, 132–33. Compare the Lester interview with the NMA-CMGOH interviews of John Seigenthaler, George Barrett, and George Cate.

33. Grubbs, "City-County Consolidation Attempts in Nashville and Knoxville, Tennessee," 100–102. On the relationship between Lillard and West, see the NMA-CMGOH interviews with George Cate and Tandy Wilson, as well as with Mansfield Douglas (quotations).

34. See the NMA-CMGOH interviews—particularly those with Charlie Warfield, Beverly Briley, Victor Johnson, Ferris Deep, Cecil Brandstetter, Mansfield Douglas, Neill Brown, George Cate, Fate Thomas, Wayne Whitt, Bob Horton, David Scobey (on the "dying city"), and Rebecca Thomas (which has Looby quotation).

35. D. Doyle, *Nashville Since the 1920s*, 211–14. For more on Briley, see his interview in NMA-CMGOH; Hanson, *Report on Politics in Nashville*, 3:32; Lovett, *Civil Rights Movement in Tennessee*, 284.

36. Herman Long to George Barrett, memorandum, n.d., ARC-TU-RRD, box 25, folder 7.

37. *Tennessean*, November 25, December 3, 9, and 10, 1962. Note also John Seigenthaler, the new editor of the *Tennessean*, claims that 1962 marked the only time that the Chamber of Commerce (and later Mayor Briley) tried to pressure him to downplay newspaper coverage of demonstrations, to which he and other media outlets refused—see his interview in NMA-CMGOH. On police and cooler heads, see USM-WDC, box 37, folder 13.

38. B&W pamphlet, ARC-TU-RRD, box 115, folder 28; also see the response in *780 Countdown*, December 14, 1962.

39. TCHR report, "Desegregation Progress in Tennessee," March 12, 1963, USM-WDC, box 53, folder 22. This can be cross-referenced with the March 14, 1963, report in VUSC-KMS, box 1, folder 8 (another copy is in VUSC-NMFP, box 2, folder 4), and the Open City Coordinating Committee minutes from March 16, 1963, in USM-WDC, box 53, folder 12. On Hill-

wood Country Club, see the January 30, 1963, NCRC minutes in FUSC-CSJ, box 151, folder 8, where, instead of the downtown, there was "much uncertainty about the outlying areas." On Briley and the swimming pools, see the *Tennessean*, February 26, 1963.

40. On the YMCA, see *Voice of the Movement*, October 18, 1962, VUSC-NMFP, box 2, folder 21; *Tennessean*, January 28, February 2, and March 5, 1963; *Banner*, September 20, 1963; TSU *Meter*, March 1–15, 1963; Fisk *Forum*, March 4, 1963, and later, *Capitol City Defender*, April 11 and November 15, 1963; *Voice of the Movement*, June 4, 1963, VUSC-KMS, box 134, folder 7; *Capitol City Defender*, March 15 and 30, 1964. On the YMCA, see Wills, *Brief History of the YMCA of Nashville and Middle Tennessee*, 17; Nelson Fuson to Allen M. Steele, letter March 26, 1963, ARC-TU-RRD, box 25, folder 7; Bucy, "Interracial Relations in the YWCA of Nashville."

41. *Banner*, March 11 and 13, 1963. The case was *McKinnie v. Tennessee*, 380 U.S. 449. See the *Banner*, December 5, 1964, and April 5, 1965; *Tennessean*, February 2 and September 11, 1963, and January 8 and 9, 1964; Fisk *Forum*, March 4, 1963; Open City Coordinating Committee minutes, March 16, 1963, USM-WDC, box 53, folder 12.

42. *Tennessean*, March 3, 5, 20, 24, and 27, 1963; K. M. Smith to Bernard Schweid, letter April 10, 1963, VUSC-KMS, box 1, folder 10; *Voice of the Movement*, March 29, 1963, VUSC-NMFP, box 2, folder 21; D. Doyle, *Nashville Since the 1920s*, 252.

43. The conversation is taken from the transcript in VUSC-KMS, box 75, folder 14—note that there is no date; I elected to write it in at this point of my narrative because the March 16, 1963, Open City coordinating committee minutes in USM-WDC, box 53, folder 12, indicate that Langford's, in contrast to B&W's and Morrison's, responded to overtures for dialogue from the committee. The wrestler bit is from Will D. Campbell interview, June 11, 1984, notes in possession of author. See also Lovett, *Civil Rights Movement in Tennessee*, 176–77. For more on Clifford Allen, see John Seigenthaler interview, NMA-CMGOH. On the chance for monopolies, see ARC-TU-RRD, box 129, folder 7.

44. K. M. Smith, letter March 29, 1962, VUSC-NMFP, box 2, folder 4; K. M. Smith speech to the NAACP, April 9, 1963, VUSC-KMS, box 23, folder 6. The boycott began on March 26, 1960.

45. Fisk *Forum*, April 29, 1963; K. M. Smith to Flem Otey, letter May 24, 1963, ,VUSC-KMS, box 1, folder 10.

46. K. M. Smith to Bernard Schweid, letter April 10, 1963, VUSC-KMS, box 1, folder 10.

47. "Chronology of Events Re: Nashville Racial Crisis," USM-WDC, box 56, folder 18; "Those Present at Interim Bi-Racial Committee, May 5, 1963," USM-WDC, box 54, folder 4; "List of Participants in May 6, 1963, Meeting with Briley," USM-WDC, box 56, folder 18.

48. "Chronology of Events Re"; *Tennessean*, May 7, 1963; Thomas H. Price to Beverly Briley, letter May 10, 1963, NMA-RFP, "General Correspondence 1963–4 P-S" (unprocessed); *Banner*, May 8, 1963; *Tennessean*, May 9, 1963; *Banner*, February 2, 1993.

49. *Tennessean*, May 11, 1963.

50. Kelly Miller Smith profile, *Tennessean*, June 2, 1963.

51. *Banner* editorial, May 11, 1963; Lewis, *Walking with the Wind*, 197; Michele Allen interview, MSRC-RJBOHC.

52. "Chronology of Events Re"; *Tennessean*, May 12, 13, and May 14, 1963.

53. *Tennessean*, May 15, 16, and 25, 1963; "Chronology of Events Re."

54. Allen Dobson, May 29, 1963, cover letter with transcript of Walter R. Courtenay, "Where the Desert Blooms," May 19, 1963, ARC-TU-RRD, box 25, folder 7.

55. D. Doyle, *Nashville Since the 1920s*, 252–54; *Tennessean*, May 16, 1963; *Tennessean*, May 17 (story and editorial), 1963; *New York Times*, May 16 and 17, 1963; Beverly Briley, memorandum May 15, 1963, USM-WDC, box 56, folder 18; documents on establishing the MHRC and its first appointees in USM-WDC, box 56, folder 18. See also *Nashville!* magazine's interview with Briley (August 1975): 36—Briley pinpoints these exchanges as coming "within three weeks after I took office in 1962," but I don't think his memory matches events and have placed it in 1963 instead. Note also that Briley mentioned Langford's as one of the hold-outs, along with usual suspects B&W, Cross-Keys, and Morrison's; "Nashville: A Preliminary Study of the Power Structure" by Dave Kotelchuck and Ronda Stilley, UVA-SSOC, 11192-f, box 1, folder 5, 5.

56. *Tennessean* editorial, June 11, 1963.

57. *Tennessean*, May 21, 1963; *Banner*, May 27, 1963. The list of founding members (also available in contemporary newspaper accounts), which included Will D. Campbell as secretary, is in USM-WDC, box 54, folder 4, and the minutes from the first meeting (not particularly informative) is in box 56, folder 18. The June 10 statement on hotel and motel desegregation is in USM-WDC, box 54, folder 4. See also the Chamber of Commerce's kudos for Briley in the Board of Governor's minutes from May 23, 1963, in TSLA-COC, reel 2, no frame; Will D. Campbell to Harold Fleming, April 7, 1964, memo, USM-WDC, box 3, folder 20; materials in ARC-TU-RRD, box 25, folder 4.

58. J. E. Naron to Fulton and Senators Gore and Kefauver, letter June 5, 1963; NMA-RF, "Civil Rights Correspondence" box (unprocessed).

59. Finner D. Whitman (a member of the Sons of Confederate Veterans) to Fulton, letter October 2, 1963, "Civil Rights Correspondence" box; T. Cecil Wray to Fulton, letter June 25, 1963 (emphasis in original), "Civil Rights Correspondence" box, both in NMA-RF, "Civil Rights Correspondence" box (unprocessed).

60. "Operation Benchmark" report, July 1, 1963, USM-WDC, box 53, folder 21.

61. Ibid., and the *Tennessean*'s summary coverage, October 13 and 27, 1963. See also the letters of thanks sent to those places that had integrated in USM-WDC, box 54, folder 4. Note also that six weeks later, the Nashville Retail Druggists Association opened local drugstores and lunch counters to African Americans: see the *Tennessean* and *Banner*, August 16, 1963.

62. *Tennessean*, September 1, 1963.

63. This paragraph condenses information from a wide variety of sources over time: see *Jet*, December 5, 1963; NCLC board meeting minutes, June 12, 1963, VUSC-KMS, box 74, folder 14; *Tennessean*, June 25, October 27 and November 16, 1963; NCRC to MHRC, memorandum June 18, 1963, USM-WDC, box 56, folder 18; J. E. Lowery to "my dear friends," October 11, 1963, USM-WDC, box 53, folder 6; report to Beverly Briley, November 14, 1963, NMA-MHRC, box 1, folder 3; TCHR report since October 1962, USM-WDC, box 53, folder 22; and *Tennessean*, December 13, 1963, with regard to Metro hiring. See also MSRC-RJBOHC, Michele Allen, which refers to resistance from some smaller establishments.

64. *Voice of the Movement*, June 4, 1963, in VUSC-KMS, box 134, folder 7.

65. *Capitol City Defender*, May 22, 1963; *Voice of the Movement*, June 4, 1963, VUSC-KMS, box 134, folder 7; President Andrew White remarks, November 5, 1963, VUSC-KMS, box 134, folder 7.

66. Michele Allen interview, MSRC-RJBOHC. For more on black apathy and "conservatism," see TSU *Meter*, February 1–15, 1962.

67. See *Capitol City Defender*, November 15, 1963, and January 16, March 15, and March 30, 1964; NCLC remarks by President Andrew White, November 5, 1963, VUSC-KMS, box 134, folder 7; K. M. Smith, "We Seek a City," 181, on children in school.

68. *Jet*, December 5, 1963, n.p.; *Banner*, December 2, 1963; *Capitol City Defender*, November 22, 1963 (the two churches were First Baptist and Mt. Zion Baptist); Kay Jones to Paul Anthony, letter December 5, 1963, SRC, series 4, reel 147, folder 442, frame 1995 (emphasis in original).

69. *Jet*, December 5, 1963, n.p. NCLC President Andrew White remarks, November 5, 1963, VUSC-KMS, box 134, folder 7; *Banner*, January 7, 1964.

70. NCRC Executive Committee minutes, January 7, 1964, VUSC-NMFP, box 2, folder 18; *Banner*, February 21, 1964; Marian Fuson's April 29, 1964, statement reproduced in the June 4, 1964, NCRC bulletin, FUSC-CSJ, box 151, folder 8. On Vanderbilt, see the *Capitol City Defender*, February 1, 1964; Vanderbilt *Hustler* editorial, February 14, 1964; TSU *Meter*, February 1–15, 1962, April 15–30, 1964.

71. *Banner*, April 27, 1964; *Tennessean*, April 28, 1964; April 27, 1964, news release, USM-WDC, box 56, folder 15; D. Doyle, *Nashville Since the 1920s*, 254.

72. *Banner*, April 28, 1964, which has excellent pictures; *Tennessean*, April 29, 1964.

73. *Tennessean*, April 30, 1964; *Banner*, April 29 and 30, 1964; *Tennessean* editorial, April 29, 1964. For more on black police officers, see the *Banner*, February 2, 1993.

74. *Banner*, April 30, 1964.

75. Ibid.; *Tennessean* and *Banner* editorials, April 30, 1964; May 14, 1964, document, USM-WDC, box 3, folder 20.

76. *Banner*, April 30 and May 1, 1964; *Tennessean*, May 1, 1964; TSLA-HRC, box 325, folder 4; Lewis interview, *Banner*, February 2, 1994.

77. *Tennessean*, May 1, 2, and 4, 1964; *Banner*, May 4, 1964.

78. *Tennessean*, April 30, May 1, 2, and 4, 1964. On Dodson, see the *Tennessean*, May 16, 1964; *Banner*, May 15, 1964; *Capitol City Defender*, June 15, 1964. See also the *Tennessean* editorial, May 1, 1964, applauding the four ministers. On Durick, see J. Bass, *Blessed Are the Peacemakers*, 187–98, and Newman, "Catholic Church and Desegregation, 1954–1973," 154.

79. *Banner*, May 4, 1964; *Tennessean*, May 5 and 6, 1964.

80. *Tennessean*, May 4, 7, and 8 (story and editorial), 1964; *Banner*, May 7 and 8, 1964; May 11, 1964, *U.S. News and World Report*, 64; Lovett, *Civil Rights Movement in Tennessee*, 181; NAACP statement, no title, n.d., VUSC-NMFP, box 2, folder 7; regarding the arrest of Looby and Williams, see also the interviews with Neill Brown and Beverly Briley, NMA-CMGOH; *Tennessean*, May 9 and 10, 1964. See also the May 7 telegram to Briley and Governor Clement from people from Buffalo State College complaining about Morrison's, in TSLA-FGC, box 525, folder 6, and the diary of a sixteen-year-old girl in jail after the May 7 demonstration at Morrison's, in VUSC-NMFP, box 2, folder 7.

81. *New York Times*, May 1, 1964 (reprinted *National Observer*, May 4, and *Tennessean*, May 6); *Tennessean* and *Banner* editorials, May 8, 1964.

82. *Capitol City Defender*, May 15 and June 15, 1964; Katherine Jones to Paul Anthony, letter May 22, 1964, SRC, series 4, reel 147, folder 442, frame 2010. Note also that at its May 12, 1964, meeting, the NCLC board voted NOT to become a member of coordinating council; see the minutes in VUSC-KMS, box 74, folder 15.

83. *Capitol City Defender*, June 15 and 2, 1964; appendix to the November 14, 1963, MHRC report to Beverly Briley, NMA-MHRC, box 1, folder 3.

84. *Tennessean*, July 4 and 1, 1964; "Business Serving *All* the Public" memorandum, no author, July 1, 1964, USM-WDC, box 53, folder 3.

85. Newman, "Tennessee Baptist Convention and Desegregation, 1954–1980," 245.

86. *New York Times*, July 1, 1954; *St. Thomas: A Century of Caring*, St. Thomas Archives, RG 1, "1960s" box 4a, "Integration 1960s" folder; Newman, "Catholic Church and Desegregation, 1954–1980."

87. Avon Williams to Briley, letter July 29, 1966, NMA-RFP, general correspondence, "R–V 65–66" folder; see also the June 4, 1963, July 19, 1964, and January 24, 1965, minutes in St. Thomas Archives, RG 1, "1960s" box 4a, "Integration 1960s" folder; and bylaws, approved March 20, 1966, in the same citation.

88. Laska, "History of African American Lawyers in Nashville," W. Ramsey, *Bench and Bar II*, 272; Lynch, *Service Above Self*, 164–70; on the chamber's desegregation, see *Banner*, December 25, 1964; on the bar association, see the TCHR newsletter, n.d. (ca. mid-June 1964), in FUSC-CSJ, box 151, folder 14, and a TCHR survey, 1965–66, in TSLA-BEP, box 38, folder 4.

89. Perry, "'The Very Best Influence'"; Creighton and Jackson, "Boys Will Be Men"; Marian Fuson to H. O. Forgy, letter January 20, 1965, VUSC-LSP, box 7, folder 14. For corroboration on the Boy Scouts, Bar Association, and regarding the Nashville Dental Society, see the NCRC's January 12, April 26, and May 27, 1965, minutes, all in VUSC-NMFP, box 2, folder 19.

90. Smith's letter in "Trek Toward the Dawn, *Katallagete* 2 (1965), in NPL-NR; K. M. Smith sidebar in Egerton, *Nashville: The Face of Two Centuries*, 257; Paschall to Aileen Henderson, letter May 31, 1968, SBHLA-HPP, box 14, folder 457.

91. K. M. Smith interview, MSRC-RJBOHC.

Chapter 5. Black Power/White Power

1. *Tennessean*, April 16, 1967.

2. On Black Power, see Ogbar, *Black Power*; Van Deburg, *New Day in Babylon*; Joseph, *Waiting 'til the Midnight Hour*; Woodard, *Nation within a Nation*; Street, *Culture War in the Civil Rights Movement*.

3. Kelly Miller Smith to Briley, letter May 16, 1964, VUSC-KMS, box 1, folder 14.

4. *Fisk Forum*, December 15, 1965; Silberman to Briley, letter February 5, 1965, VUSC-NMFP, box 2, folder 19; "African Students Arrested in Nashville," February 1965, VUSC-NMFP, box 2, folder 25; "Report on Staff Activities, October and November 1965," Tennessee Commission on Human Relations, TSLA-HRC, box 361, folder 2. NMA-AF also has an audio recording of a November 2, 1965, press conference held with regard to the latter situation. The *New York Times* also covered the Odour situation: November 3, 6, and 9, 1965.

5. For other episodes of police brutality, see the *Capitol City Defender*, February 1 and March 15, 1964; the accosting of a Fisk student from New Jersey on December 7, 1966, recounted in the *Fisk Forum*, January 13, 1966, and the case of white Vanderbilt graduate student Ramsay Hall, killed in January 1967 by Metro police officers: *New York Times*, January 27, April 11, and August 12, 1967. See Websdale, *Policing the Poor*, 8, 94 on jail elevator; regarding the rape, see "A Summary of Activities for 1969," SRC, series 1, folder 1996, reel 66, frame 0854, and the memo to the NCRC from Baxton Bryant, n.d. (ca. April/May 1969—from the personal files of William Barnes, copy in possession of the author). See

also the Mansfield Douglas and Charles Pruitt interviews in FUSC-BOHC; the reference to a 1971 incident in Cloud, "Working Together for Social Change," 68. Al Browning's *On The Run* is a nonfiction account of a long flight from justice after the shooting of a Nashville police officer, but for the context of wider trends of police brutality, see xv, 9, 29, 32, 35, 46, 57, 93, and 214. *Tennessean* editor John Seigenthaler claimed that much of the police department's excesses were curbed after corrupt cops left over from the West mayoral regime were indicted (in NMA-CMGOH).

6. Information about the three shootings in Browning, *On the Run*, 97–99; VUSC-KMS, box 53, folder 26; *Tennessean*, June 17 and 30, 1971; Briley quotation in Edwin Mitchell interview, FUSC-BOHC; one-third quotation in Baxton Bryant, MSRC-RJBOHC; *Fisk Forum*, March 29, 1968; Briley lecture in "A Study of Three Civil Disorders Associated with Negro Colleges in the South, Spring 1967," LBJ-NACCD-ES, box 68, 34. The mayor supposedly supported black demands for a police review board: see NMA-BBOF, box 6, "Misc. Letters of Mayor Briley 1968" folder.

7. *Tennessean*, October 15 and 1, 1965 (all quotations in latter). See also the *Tennessean*, November 3, 1965, as Briley discussed the Klan's attempt to form a second klavern through "several secret meetings" and alluded to the past arrest record of the local Klan leader.

8. *Tennessean*, April 6, 1962; quotations in *Tennessean*, November 26 and 27 (editorial), 1963, and June 20, 1965.

9. On Sorace, see EU-MARBL-NBF, box 14, "Nashville" folder; *Banner*, February 1, 1965; Pat Harris, "Sorace: Portrait of a Cop," in *Nashville Magazine* 6 (November 1968): 11–15, and the interview with Briley in *Nashville!* 3 (August 1975): 37, where Briley noted that Sorace "caused turmoil within the department. The men were afraid of him." On Hill, see *Banner*, August 22, 1967; on the police, see EU-MARBL-NBF, box 14, "Nashville" folder; Briley anecdote in John Seiganthaler, NMA-CMGOH; W. J. Prenzel to Baxton Bryant, letter February 23, 1968, in NMA-RF, "General Correspondence N-Q, 1967–8" box, "Legislative Correspondence 1968" folder; "Study of Three Civil Disorders Associated with Negro Colleges in the South, Spring 1967," 1, 30–32, 35.

10. Hendricks, "Stokely Carmichael and the 1967 IMPACT Symposium," 291–94; *New York Times*, April 11, 1967; Clayborne Carson, *In Struggle*, 246; *Banner* editorial, March 25, 1967; *Tennessean*, April 16, 1967. On the black community's watchfulness, see *Tennessean*, April 16, 1967. On the calls for Carmichael's deportation, see *Tennessean*, April 11 and 16, 1967; *New York Times*, April 11, 1967; Carson, *In Struggle*, 248; and Richard Fulton to Mrs. Robert Woodall, letter August 9, 1967, NMA-RF, "General Correspondence T-W, 1967–8" box, "General Correspondence w-1967" folder.

11. "Text of Stokely Carmichael's speech at Vanderbilt Impact—April 8, 1967," unpaginated copy in VUSC-JGS, box V-29, folder 2. For coverage of his pre-Vanderbilt speeches, see *Banner*, March 25 and 29, and April 1 and 8, 1967.

12. Carson, *In Struggle*, 245; *Banner*, March 25, 1967; Hendricks, "Stokely Carmichael and the 1967 IMPACT Symposium," 295–97. See also the *Vanderbilt Hustler*, April 11, 1967; D. Doyle, *Nashville Since the 1920s*, 254–55; Roy Blount Jr.'s account of the weekend in the *Vanderbilt Hustler*, April 28, 1967; Self, *American Babylon*, 226.

13. *Tennessean*, April 10, 1967, and editorial, April 11, 1967.

14. The account that follows is drawn variously from the *Banner*, November 22, 1967, which reprinted the testimony of Sorace and Hill to the Senate Investigating Subcommittee in its entirety; *Tennessean*, April 16 and June 1, 1967; "Press release" and "Nashville

Southern Student Organizing Committee, April 10, 1967," VUSC-JGS, box V-29, "Stokely Carmichael" folder 2; Mayor Beverly Briley, "Profile of Progress," April 16, 1967, on WSM-TV, available in NMA-CFCR; *Newsweek*, April 24, 1967, 28; "Nashville report 4/10/67," SNCC, series 15, folder 245, reel 40, frame 790; TSU *Meter*, May 9, 1967; Hendricks, "Stokely Carmichael and the 1967 IMPACT Symposium," 297; Carson, *In Struggle*, 245, 247; "Tennessee" in *New South* 22 (spring 1967): 103–4.

15. *Banner*, May 26, 1967.

16. Note that, regarding taunts toward African American policemen, 7 percent of the force was black at the time, or thirty-five officers, according to Sorace's Congressional testimony reprinted in the *Banner*, November 22, 1967.

17. *Tennessean*, April 16, 1967; testimony reprinted in *Banner*, November 22, 1967; TSU *Meter*, May 9, 1967; *Banner*, May 31, 1967; "Press release" and "Nashville Southern Student Organizing Committee, April 10, 1967." See also Sorace's later speech at Vanderbilt covered by the *Hustler*, May 2, 1967.

18. "Study of Three Civil Disorders associated with Negro Colleges in the South, Spring 1967," 6–7.

19. EU-MARBL-NBF, box 14, "Nashville" folder; see coverage of the court case *Frederick Brooks et al. v. Beverly Briley, Mayor, et al.,* 274 F. Supp 538 in the *Race Relations Law Reporter* 12:1784; *Tennessean*, April 16, 1967; police testimony reprinted in *Banner*, November 22, 1967; TSU *Meter*, May 9, 1967; *Newsweek*, April 24, 1967, 28; "Press release" and "Nashville Southern Student Organizing Committee, April 10, 1967," which claims that police "directed a bus to drive through the crowd of students"; Carson, *In Struggle*, 247, which notes that a later federal court found no example of "intentional firing on any students." Carmichael later claimed that Hill fired the shots in the air, in the transcript of a WSM newscast, May 30, 1967, in VUSC-JSP, box V-29, folder 2.

20. EU-MARBL-NBF, box 14, "Nashville" folder; *Banner*, May 31, 1967; *Newsweek*, April 24, 1967, 28; *Tennessean*, April 16 and June 1, 1967; "Press release" and "Nashville Southern Student Organizing Committee, April 10, 1967"; TSU *Meter*, May 9, 1967; "Nashville report 4/10/67," SNCC, series 15, folder 245, reel 40, frame 790; Stahlman's comments to Heard in Stahlman, "Original Text of Remarks . . ." Vanderbilt Board of Trust meeting, November 1, 1967, VUSC-CHP, box 27, "Impact 1967" folder; Kathy Alder, undated memorandum, LBJ-NACCD-ES, box 24, "Nashville General" folder.

21. *New York Times*, April 11, 1967; *Tennessean*, June 1, 1967; "Tennessee," *New South* 22 (spring 1967): 103–4; police testimony reprinted in *Banner*, November 22, 1967; LBJ NACCD-ES, box 24, "Nashville" folder, 2; "Study of Three Civil Disorders Associated with Negro Colleges in the South, Spring 1967," 1–11, 28; shotguns quotation in *Tennessean*, April 10, 1967.

22. *Tennessean*, April 11, 1967 (story and editorial), and April 12, 1967; *Banner* editorial, April 11 and 12, 1967; Stahlman, memorandum May 9, 1967, VUSC-JSP, box V-19, folder 16; Mayor Beverly Briley, "Profile of Progress," April 16, 1967, on WSM-TV in NMA-CFCR; *Tennessean*, April 16, 1967; *New York Times*, April 8, 11, 12, and 15, 1967, and April 9, 1968; SNCC April 10 press release in EU-MARBL-NBF, "Nashville" folder.

23. *New York Times*, April 11, 1967; Sorace quotation in *Tennessean*, May 31, 1967; Carson, *In Struggle*, 248. Regarding the check, see TSLA-BEP, box 11, folder 1; *Tennessean*, April 13, 1967; *Banner*, April 12, 1967; transcript of WSM newscast, May 30, 1967, in VUSC-JSP, box V-29, folder 2; and memorandum May 9, 1967, VUSC-JSP, box V-19, folder 16. On

Felder, see Carson, *In Struggle*, 246, she may have been the person in "Nashville report 4/10/67," SNCC, series 15: folder 245, reel 40, frame 790, about whom "Police said a Negro girl, who was with Carmichael at Vanderbilt, appeared to be calling the shots." "Study of Three Civil Disorders Associated with Negro Colleges in the South, Spring 1967," 1, 14; Carmichael with Thelwell, *Ready for Revolution*, 551–56.

24. "Press release" and "Nashville Southern Student Organizing Committee, April 10, 1967"; "Nashville report 4/10/67," SNCC, series 15, folder 245, reel 40, frame 790; *New York Times*, April 11, 1967; *Tennessean*, May 31 and June 1, 1967; *Newsweek*, April 24, 1967, 28; testimony reprinted in *Banner*, November 22, 1967; *Banner*, April 12, 1967; *Washington Post*, April 16, 1967. Regarding the controversy over Carmichael, see the coverage of the ensuing trial cited below; police testimony before a Senate subcommittee reprinted in the *Banner*, November 22, 1967; Stahlman, "Original Text of Remarks"; Carson, *In Struggle*, 248.

25. Press conference in NMA-AF; Carmichael quotations in the transcript of WSM newscast, May 30, 1967, VUSC-JSP, box V-29, folder 2, and the *Tennessean*, May 31, 1967. Note also that although Sorace denied police surveillance, Mayor Briley said that "we curtailed his activities by keeping him under constant surveillance and by arresting two of his aides" (*Tennessean*, April 11, 1967). For coverage of the lawsuit, see "Tennessee" in *New South* 22 (summer 1967): 102; Carson, *In Struggle*, 248; *Tennessean*, June 1, 1967; *New York Times*, August 4 and October 10, 1967. TSU students adopted the terminology of "rebellion" instead of "riot" in TSU *Meter*, May 9, 1967.

26. Quotation about Carmichael in *Tennessean*, August 18, 1967; Bevel quotation from *Banner*, May 9, 1968; Lawson quoted in *Tennessean*, July 1, 1969; Smith quoted in David Halberstam, "The End of a Populist," *Harper's* 242 (January 1971): 44–45.

27. Regarding Otey, see his oral history in MSRC-RJBOHC; regarding the Carmichael look-alike, see Bev Asbury in the periodical *Katallagete*, available in EU-MARBL-NBF, box 18, "Katallagete spring 1968" folder; quotations in *New York Times*, September 30, 1967; on insurance cancellations see "Study of Three Civil Disorders Associated with Negro Colleges in the South, Spring 1967," 37.

28. A contemporary estimate claimed 77 arrested and 26 injured (*Newsweek*, April 24, 1967, 28), but Carson, *In Struggle*, 248, cites instead 94 arrests. TSU *Meter*, May 9, 1967; Fisk student quotation in the *Washington Post*, April 16, 1967; see also the *Tennessean*, April 11, 1967. Coverage of the Black Power meeting is in the *Banner*, May 9, 1967—the leaflet attacked NAACP head Mansfield Douglas, Edwin Mitchell, and Inman Otey (whose beating is referenced in the *Tennessean*, April 16 and May 5, 1967). Otey also discusses the "smear sheet" in his MSRC-RJBOHC interview. James Stahlman cited Avon Williams and Meharry physician Dorothy Brown as being anti-Carmichael in "Original Text of Remarks." The *Tennessean* also praised the black community for criticizing white leadership even as they "repudiated" Carmichael: April 11, 1967 (editorial). See the *Tennessean*, April 12, 1967, for a reference to possible disciplinary action against a TSU administrator who voiced criticism of the handling of the situation. Mayor Briley credited older leaders in Nashville for restraining the militants in his NMA-CMGOH interview.

29. TSU and Avon Williams quotations in the TSU *Meter*, May 9, 1967; NAACP quotation in *New South* 22 (spring 1967): 104; Lillard quotation in *Banner*, May 8, 1967. Three button quotation in EU-MARBL-NBF, box 14, "Nashville" folder; Currier observation from his MSRC-RJBOHC interview; remark about Otey and the FBI in Sherri Myers's MSRC-RJBOHC interview; reference to the frightened black middle-class in EU-MARBL-NBF, box

14, "Nashville" folder. See also the "Nashville report 4/10/67" and the news ticker stories in SNCC, series 15, folder 245, reel 40, starting on frame 791. For more Fisk student reactions, see Hendricks, "Stokely Carmichael and the 1967 IMPACT Symposium," 298. See also coverage of the DCIPC (Davidson County Independent Political Council), NAACP, and NCLC's press conference protesting the "raw brutality" of the city government against blacks in *Tennessean*, April 20, 1967. On Otey, see memorandum May 2, 1967, LBJ-NACCD-ES, box 1, "Hearings—McClellan Investigation" folder, or LBJ-NACCD-ES, Box 34, "NACCD, Nashville" folder.

30. *Tennessean*, April 10, 1967; "Press release" and "Nashville Southern Student Organizing Committee, April 10, 1967," and also in VUSC-JGS, box V-29, "Stokely Carmichael," folder 2, see "STOKELY CARMICHAEL DID *NOT* START RIOT!!!!" (flyer).

31. *Tennessean* editorial, April 11, 1967; second *Tennessean* quotation in *Washington Post*, April 16, 1967; third *Tennessean* quotation in Hendricks, "Stokely Carmichael and the 1967 IMPACT Symposium," 297; *Newsweek*, April 24, 1967, 28; *Tennessean*, April 16, 1967.

32. See the "Straight Talk" column written by Tom Anderson, a member of the John Birch Society (in VUSC-JSP V-29, FF 4).

33. Stahlman, "Original Text of Remarks," and Stahlman, telegram to *Time*, both in VUSC-CHP, box 27, "Impact 1967" folder.

34. Stahlman later wrote bitterly of the board's "fear of offending Harold Vanderbilt in his senility and possibly jeopardizing the fifty million dollars which he is leave the University." See Stahlman to Fred B. Wachs, letter May 8, 1967, and Stahlman to Whiteford Mays, letter August 8, 1967, both in VUSC-CHP, box 27, "Impact 1967" folder.

35. Stahlman, "Original Text of Remarks." Note that Sorace had denied the use of police surveillance, *Tennessean*, June 1, 1967. In his senate testimony (reprinted in the *Banner*, November 22, 1967), he instead affirmed that intelligence operations had begun in early 1964 and combined surveillance with SNCC informants.

36. See J. Lawson Hutton to Stahlman, letter August 8, 1967, and Stahlman's August 9 response, VUSC-CHP, box 27, "Impact 1967" folder (emphasis in original).

37. The school was apparently an outgrowth of the North Nashville Project, explained in an August 15, 1966, newsletter in SRC, series 14, reel 215, folder 27, beginning on frame 682. See also "North Nashville Project: The Transition," Fred Brooks, *New South Student* 3 (December 1966): 12 (a copy is in SBHLA-CLC, box 21, folder 3); Woodruff quotation in "Tennessee" in *New South* 22 (summer 1967): 104; and the newsletters and information in SRC, series 14, reel 215, folder 37, starting on frames 1230, 1240, and 1242; and the materials in UNC-SHC-DPP, box 20, folder 280.

38. See the full testimony of Sorace and Hill reprinted in the *Banner*, November 22, 1967. See also *Banner*, August 21 and 22, 1967; *New York Times*, November 22, 1967; *Tennessean*, August 29, 1967; Carson, *In Struggle*, 246, on Nash's speech, and 258. See also Bev Asbury's take on Sorace's testimony in the pages of Katallagete, in EU-MARBL-NBF, box 18, "Katallagete spring 1968" folder. See Sorace's misquotation belief in UNC-SHC-AMP, box 18, folder 247. On the SSOC, see Michel, *Struggle for a Better South*.

39. T. Cecil Wray, statement August 11, 1967, VUSC-JSP, box V-29, folder 7; Livingston Jackson, "Tennessee Rebels," *New Republic* 157 (September 9, 1967): 9–10. See also the letter in *Fisk Forum*, November 17, 1967, and *Banner*, April 18, 1968.

40. Zuzak, McNeil, and Bergerson, "Beyond the Ballot," 251 (and 253 for the "organized chaos" quotation); Buell, "Uncertain Warriors," 66 and 69. For references to the dissension

over MAC, see Buell, 71–89 ("conflict" quotation on 71; 74 regarding the 1965 newspaper investigations; 75–76 regarding OEO criticisms). See also the *Tennessean*, April 29 and May 2, 1967; *New South* 22 (summer 1967): 103–4, and 22 (winter 1967): 80.

41. K. M. Smith to Samuel D. Proctor, letter March 16, 1966, VUSC-KMS, box 1, folder 19. This letter refers to an enclosed petition that is likely the undated "Statement of Concern" in VUSC-KMS, box 67, folder 12. See also Buell, "Uncertain Warriors," 74–75. The *Tennessean*, June 14, 1966, covers NCLC and NAACP charges of a "general climate of racism" within both MAC and the Nashville Housing Authority.

42. Kay Jones to Paul Anthony, letter May 14, 1965, SRC, series 4, reel 147, folder 442, frame 2004; Martha Ragland to the *Tennessean*, letter November 6, 1966, VUSC-NMFP, box 1, folder 8; Martha Ragland to (an apparently displeased) Briley, letter November 21, 1966, VUSC-NMFP, box 1, folder 8. See also *New South* 22 (winter 1967): 80, which references Ragland's *Tennessean* letter. The housewife letter, dated May 11, 1967, is in TSLA-BEP, box 38, folder 4.

43. Buell, "Uncertain Warriors," 89–91, 93; *New York Times*, August 9, 1967. Regarding the Nashville situation and national debates, see Carson, *In Struggle*, 258; Zuzak et al., "Beyond the Ballot," 252–53; and *New South* 22 (fall 1967): 105; regarding the bureaucratic screw-up and summer quotation, see the *Tennessean*, November 10, 1967. See also the *New York Times* coverage of the Liberation School, August 5, 12, 17, 19, and 22, 1967.

44. "Tennessee" in *New South* 22 (fall 1967): 105; Jackson, "Tennessee Rebels"; *Tennessean*, November 10, 1967; Carson, *In Struggle*, 246, 258–59. See also the excerpts from Sorace's August 21, 1967, speech before the Rotary Club in NPL-NR-NBCF, "Sorace." See also Mrs. Joey Ellis to Richard Fulton, letter August 7, 1967, NMA-RF, "General Correspondence E–F 1967-8" box, "General Correspondence E 1967" folder, and Fulton's response, August 10, 1967, in the same location. On Brooks, see Buell, "Uncertain Warriors," 93, with his quotation; *New York Times*, November 25 and 29, 1967, and January 9 and 19, 1968. Cracker cop quotation is in the *New York Times*, August 4, 1967.

45. Davis letter to Briley, November 1, 1967 (copy in possession of the author)—see also Buell, "Uncertain Warriors," 96–97. Regarding the resignations, see *New South* 22 (fall 1967): 105; *Banner*, *Tennessean*, and *New York Times*, August 22, 1967. For MAC's history after this episode, see Zuzak, McNeil, and Bergerson, "Beyond the Ballot," 254–66; Buell, "Uncertain Warriors," 97–99 (with foolish money quotation on 98–99). By October 1972, an OEO official called MAC "one of the most progressive and efficient community action programs in the Southeast"—in the October 1972 "Model Cities Responder" in the Nashville Metro Archives. On MAC's PR, see "Study of Three Civil Disorders Associated with Negro Colleges in the South, Spring 1967," E.9.

46. On Ware, see Jackson, "Tennessee Rebels." See also *Banner*, August 22, August 23, August 26, August 29, September 9, 1967; *Tennessean*, August 29, 1967; "Tennessee" in *New South* 22 (fall 1967): 105. See also the coverage in the *New York Times*, August 23, 24, 25, and 26, 1967.

47. The Nashville chapter of the TCHR was the old NCRC, which had formally affiliated with the SRC. Kay Jones to Paul Anthony, letter August 15, 1963, SRC, series 4, folder 442, reel 147, frame 1985; NCRC March 5, 1964, minutes of Executive Committee meeting, VUSC-NMFP, box 2, folder 18 (complaining about lacking labor and East Nashville representation); TCHR board minutes, August 19, 1964, in USM-WDC, box 53, folder 12; Bill Willis from Kay Jones, letter n.d. (ca. July 1964), USM-WDC, box 53, folder 14; minutes and rec-

ommendations of the Membership Committee meeting, April 22, 1967 (from the personal files of William Barnes, copy in possession of the author); TCHR Board of Directors meeting minutes, August 19, 1964, and May 13, 1967, USM-WDC, box 53, folder 12.

48. Martha Ragland's speech, given in early July 1967, is in RISL-MRR, box 13, folder 186. Newspaper coverage of the speech was in the *Tennessean*, January 29, 1967, copies of which can be found in SRC, series 3, reel 129, folder 753, frame 2050.

49. On the white backlash in this context, see Lassiter, *Silent Majority*; Kruse, *White Flight*; McGirr, *Suburban Warriors*; Sugrue, *Origins of the Urban Crisis*; Joseph Crespino, *In Search of Another Country*.

50. Quotations are in the TCHR "Director's Report," March 1972, which is an overview of the history of the group (from the personal files of William Barnes, copy in possession of the author). For accounts of these and more projects, see SRC, series 1, folder 1996, reel 66: for the TCHR report to the Field Foundation, October 23, 1968 (starting on frame 0776), the August 13, 1968, quarterly report (starting on frame 0738). See also the November 16, 1968, report of the executive director to the TCHR annual meeting in USM-WDC, box 53, folder 22. See also the interviews with William Barnes and Will D. Campbell in UF-SPOHP.

51. TCHR "Minutes of Ninth Annual Meeting," January 29, 1967; TCHR Executive Committee minutes, March 4, 1967 (both from the personal files of William Barnes; copies in possession of the author).

52. Moran's hiring was announced in a letter to TCHR members, n.d., in USM-WDC, box 53, folder 13; Ed Standfield (SRC's director of field activities) to Paul Anthony, memorandum February 1, 1967, RISL-MRR, box 11, folder 163; Ragland to Stanfield, letter February 2, 1967, RISL-MRR, box 11, folder 163; Stanfield to Ragland, letter February 6, 1967, RISL-MRR, box 11, folder 163.

53. Ragland to Ed Stanfield, letter February 23, 1967, SRC, series 4, reel 156, folder 795, frame 1515; "Analyses, Appraisals, Frustrations, and Dilemma," Report of the Executive Director to the TCHR Board of Directors, May 13, 1967 (from the personal files of William Barnes, copy in possession of the author).

54. TCHR Executive Committee meeting minutes, August 5, 1967, USM-WDC, box 53, folder 12; TCHR newsletter (August 1967), SRC, series 4, folder 786, reel 156, frame 1164.

55. TCHR Board of Directors meeting minutes, October 28, 1967, SRC, series 1, folder 1996, reel 66, frame 0811. See also *Banner*, April 18, 1968. Regarding Bryant and West Tennessee, see EU-MARBL-CCP, box 14, "Segregation Nashville" folder, which has a profile on Bryant from the *Tennessean* magazine, February 12, 1967.

56. TCHR Board of Directors meeting minutes, October 28, 1967, SRC, series 1, folder 1996, reel 66, frame 0811. See also *Banner*, April 18, 1968.

57. Letters of resignation, SRC, series 1, folder 1996, reel 66, frames 0658, 0663, 0665, 0681; *Banner*, November 11, 1967.

58. Martha Ragland to Leslie Dunbar, letter October 29, 1967, SRC, series 1, folder 1996, feel 66, from frame 0659; to Leslie Dunbar (regarding his letter to George Barrett), letter November 12, 1967, ibid., from frame 0676.

59. This correspondence is in SRC, series 1, folder 1996, reel 66, frame 0666 (Leslie Dunbar to George Barrett, November 6), and frame 0676 (Ragland to Dunbar, November 12).

60. Baxton Bryant, "From the Director's Desk," n.d., SRC, series 1, folder 1996, reel 66, frame 0804 (copy in USM-WDC, box 53, folder 22); memo on annual meeting, March 6–7, 1970 (from the personal files of William Barnes, copy in possession of the author); TCHR

newsletter (October 1970), from the personal files of William Barnes, copy in possession of the author; Bryant, "From the Director's Desk."

61. December 21, 1970, SRC, series 1, folder 1996, reel 66, frame 0859; all quotations except last in Horace Barker to Paul Anthony, memo December 28, 1970, SRC, series 1, folder 1996, reel 66, frame 0863; last quotation in TCHR "Director's Report," March 1972. Bryant resigned in March 1971, according to the meeting minutes of the executive committee, August 5, 1967, USM-WDC, box 53, folder 12.

62. Apathy quotation is from Halberstam, "End of a Populist," 44; Kenneth Cmiel, "The Politics of Civility," in David Farber, ed., *The Sixties: From Memory to History* (Chapel Hill: University of North Carolina Press, 1994), 263–90; see also the Baxton Bryant interview, MSRC-RJBOHC; profile on Bryant, *Tennessean Magazine*, February 12, 1967.

63. *Tennessean*, January 29 and February 21, 1971; *Hustler*, January 29, 1974. See also the June 9, 1967, memo regarding the black Rockefeller grant recipients in VUSC-CHP, box 27, "Students—Negro" folder; article on Vanderbilt and Black Studies in *Race Relations Reporter*, November 1, 1971.

64. Frye Gaillard, "Crumbling Segregation in the Southeastern Conference," *The Black Athlete—1970*, part 2, Race Relations Information Center, EU-MARBL-VHP, box 36, folder 10, 19–24, 38–39; *Tennessean*, February 21, 1971; "A Black Student at Vanderbilt" (from *Rap*, November 1972: 28–31), VUSC-CHP, box 27, "Students—Negro" folder; Carey, *Chancellors, Commodores and Coeds*, 293–97. See also the interview with Perry Wallace and others in "Heaven for Whites, Hell for Negroes?" in the *Baptist Student* (March 1969), in SBHLA-CLC, box 17, FF 3. A retrospective on Wallace is in the *Vanderbilt Hustler*, February 26, 2002, as well as a "perspectives on race" retrospective from March 1, 2002.

65. "Report on Negro Students to Arts and Sciences Faculty," January 16, 1968, VUSC-CHP, box 27, "Students—Negro" folder, 7–8; FUSC-BOHC interview, Frederick T. Work.

66. *New York Times*, September 30, 1967. On soul music and civil rights, see Ward, *Just My Soul Responding*.

67. See the Michele Allen interview, MSRC-RJBOHC, regarding the 1963 conference.

68. See memo January 6, 1970, EU-MARBL-VHP, box 33, folder 8, and the Black Power fliers in ARC-TU-AMAP, box 178, folder 18; C. Eric Lincoln in the *New York Times*, June 7, 1967. References to Lawson's contentious relationship with students are in EU-MARBL-NBF, box 14, "Nashville" folder,; MSRC-RJBOHC Currier interview; D. Doyle, *Nashville Since the 1920s*, 168.

69. Pamela Ice ("something political"), FUSC-BOHC; Michele Paul Allen ("groping") MSRC-RJBOHC—see also the Currier interview in the same collection.

70. TSU *Meter*, May 9, 1967; Outlaw quoted in Hendricks, "Stokely Carmichael and the 1967 IMPACT Symposium," 299; first Fisk student in *Newsweek*, February 10, 1969, 55, second Fisk student in the "The Void" guest editorial, *Fisk Forum*, February 16, 1968. Note also that the Fisk Student Council had previously given SNCC a "one year probation" as an on-campus organization, as "members left the room in disgust and anger"—*Fisk Forum*, November 18, 1966. With regard to Meharry, consider the *Fisk Forum* of March 29, 1968, which read, referring to a recent protest march: "never again can the Fiskites & Tenn. A&I students say the Meharryites are fraught with apathy, lethargy, and indifference; and are only concerned with the mansion they are to build or the Cadillac they are to drive." The "finishing school" quotation is from Pamela Ice, FUSC-BOHC, "dry and boring" from Adrian Capeheart, FUSC-BOHC.

71. See the Flem B. Otey III interview in FUSC-BOHC; C. Eric Lincoln and Cecil Eric Lincoln, "Voices of Fisk '70," *New York Times*, June 7, 1970; local black politician in Halberstam, "End of a Populist," 42. Game quotation in *New York Times*, September 30, 1967; see also *Fisk Forum*, March 1, 1968; final quotation in EU-MARBL-NBF, box 14, "Nashville" folder.

72. Regarding black schools and ownership, see the FUSC-BOHC interviews with Quincy Jackson, Edwin Mitchell, and Amos Jones. For color- and class-consciousness at Fisk, see the FUSC-BOHC interviews with Charles Pruitt and Pamela Ice and the MSRC-RJBOHC interview with Michele Paul Allen. See quotations and Fisk's links to in C. Eric Lincoln's article in the *New York Times*, June 7, 1967. Regarding Black Muslims, see FUSC-BOHC interviews with Minister Earl X, James Chandler, Amos Jones Jr.; Moody, "Effects of Metro on Negro Politics," 44–45; on militants being chased out, see "Study of Three Civil Disorders Associated with Negro Colleges in the South, Spring 1967," 32, 36.

73. *Tennessean*, April 21, 1967. On integrating TSU, see *Banner*, May 13, 1966, regarding a one-day conference on the subject. TSLA-DEPCF, record group 92, box 338, folder 6 (or reel 114, frame 1301, on the microfilm) has materials regarding a March 3, 1966, meeting, as well as the Black Power flier *The Word Has Been Given* in box 359, folder 6 (reel 122, frame 1333), with a note at the top: "This is the type of subversive materials being distributed on our campus by Black Power advocates." Regarding the track team incident, see TSLA-DEPCF, record group box 92, box 338, folder 6 (reel 114, frame 1303), for the student letter to Mrs. C. E. McGruder, head of Nashville's NAACP chapter. Regarding the new hiree, see the July 6, 1967, letter from "Your friend" to Arthur W. Danner, TSLA-DEPCF, record group 92, box 359, folder 6, (or reel 122, frames 1418–19), which presumably regards the situation alluded to in the May 31, 1967, letter from "Citizens for a better, university, community, state and country," to Richard Fulton, NMA-RF, "General Correspondence K 1967–8" box, which included a *Tennessean* editorial, n.d., regarding the controversy over the removal of the TSU business manager. See also the editorial defending President Davis against charges of Uncle Tomism in the TSU *Meter*, May 9, 1967.

74. See the article in the *Kappa Alpha Psi* journal included in Governor Ellington to Montgomery, letter March 13, 1968, inviting him to stop by and see the governor, in TSLA-BEP, box 11, folder 3. See also Montgomery's critique of the administration in *Tennessean*, May 10, 1967, as well as President Davis's report to the state board of education treated in the *Banner*, May 5, 1967.

75. TSLA-DEPCF, record group 92, box 359, folder 6 (reel 122, frame 1505). Michele Paul Allen, MSRC-RJBOHC, claimed that TSU students were more responsive to militancy due to generally being from more modest means. Charles Pruitt, FUSC-BOHC, charged that President Davis expelled students to scare others.

76. *Sanders v. Ellington* 288 F. Supp. 937 (M.D. Tenn. 1968); Lovett, *Civil Rights Movement in Tennessee*, 350–401; D. Doyle, *Nashville Since the 1920s*, 172–73.

77. *Banner*, August 20, 1968. Amos Jones, FUSC-BOHC, references the Chamber of Commerce's support for the *Sanders* case.

78. See the *Banner*, August 22, 1968; various materials in VUSC-JEP, box 25, folder 16; Egerton, "Tennessee's Long-Running Desegregation Drama"; Egerton, "Black Public Colleges, 9–14; Merger as a Remedy in Higher Education Desegregation," 511–38.

79. See *Fisk Forum*, March 1, 1968; *New York Times*, March 7, 1968; and correspondence in NMA-RF, "General Correspondence E–F 1967–8" box, "General Correspondence F, 1967–8" folder; "Nashville Protests Against Repression of Black Community (1968),"

http://www.hippy.com/modules.php?name=News&file=article&sid=349, accessed January 23, 2012.

80. TSU *Meter*, April 29, 1968; D. Doyle, *Nashville Since the 1920s*, 255; *New York Times*, March 3, 1968, references marches coordinated between Memphis and Nashville, part of a semisuccessful attempt to revive the "economic withdrawal" tactic. See also Briley's account in NMA-CMGOH.

81. *New York Times*, July 22, 1967.

82. Voter registration in UNC-SHC-DPP, box 11, folder 163; "different languages" in EU-MARBL-NBF, box 14, "Nashville" folder.

83. The contradiction was voiced by Paul Puryear in his MSRC-RJBOHC interview; Briley quotation in "Study of Three Civil Disorders Associated with Negro Colleges in the South, Spring 1967," 39.

Chapter 6. Cruel Mockeries

1. *Tennessean*, October 12, 1967 (some sources mistakenly say November 11); see also Pat Harris, "Dr. Edwin Mitchell: Gentleman from the Ghetto" *Nashville* 7, no. 3 (March 1969): 23, 26.

2. Quotations in Carey, "City Swept Clean," n.p.

3. Carey, "City Swept Clean," n.p.

4. On Edgehill, see the *Tennessean*, March 14, 1967; materials in UNC-SHC-DPP, box 20, folder 280; *Leveller* (newsletter), April 1969, NMA-CFCR; "Inner City Blight: Analysis-Proposals," Metro Planning Commission, September 1973, 32–33; TCHR newsletter, September–October 1966 in SRC, reel 215, series 14, folder 37, frame 1240; Holleman, "Evolution of Federal Housing Policy"; Hartmann, "Economic Analysis of Black Nashville," 243; Richard J. Whalen, "The American Highway: Do We Know Where We're Going?" *Saturday Evening Post*, December 14, 1968, 23.

5. Parks, "Grasping at the Coattails of Progress," 124; Zuzak, McNeil, and Bergerson, "Beyond the Ballot," n.p.; Hall, "I-40's Route through North Nashville," 17, 21.

6. Seley, "Spatial Bias," 6; Zuzak, McNeil, and Bergerson, "Beyond the Ballot," n.p.

7. R. Grann Lloyd, "A Survey of Negro-Owned and Operated Business Enterprises in Nashville Tennessee" (Nashville: Middle Tennessee Business Association, January 15, 1969), 3, 19–21; Hartmann, "Economic Analysis of Black Nashville," 2; *Banner*, November 2, 1967; Seley, "Spatial Bias," 7. See also the report (and final quotation) in "Model Cities Program Problem Analysis: Part I, Volume II," in *Air Rights Project—Interstate Highway 40—Nashville Tennessee*, 14 (available in NMA); *Fisk Forum*, March 3, 1967.

8. Seley, "Spatial Bias," 7; Zuzak, McNeil, and Bergerson, "Beyond the Ballot," n.p.; community asset quotation in Board of Governor's Minutes, July 24, 1956, TSLA-COC, reel 2, no frame.

9. Seley, "Spatial Bias," 6; Zuzak, McNeil, and Bergerson, "Beyond the Ballot," n.p.; "Model Cities Program Problem Analysis," 14.

10. Zuzak, McNeil, and Bergerson, "Beyond the Ballot," n.p.; Seley, "Spatial Bias," 3; *Tennessean*, February 13, 1968. Ford, "Interstate 40 through Nashville, Tennessee," 100–101; scheduling priorities quotation in Hall, "I-40's Route through North Nashville," 15, see also 19 and 21; Whalen, "American Highway," 57.

11. Seley, "Spatial Bias," 8, 12–13; Zuzak, McNeil, and Bergerson, "Beyond the Ballot," n.p.; "Model Cities Program Problem Analysis," 13.

12. Seley, "Spatial Bias," 3; Zuzak, McNeil, and Bergerson, "Beyond the Ballot," n.p.

13. Seley, "Spatial Bias," 10 (black politician quotation), 4 ("bureaucracy" quotation), and 11 ("segregated community" quotation); anonymous letter to editor, *Tennessean*, November 20, 1967.

14. Internal memorandum, September 27, 1967, and letter to Nelson Fuson, both in NMA-RFP, "General Correspondence E–F 1967–8" box, "F 1967" folder; *Banner*, November 9, 1967; Mohl, "Stop the Road," 680.

15. *Tennessean*, August 31, 1967; Zuzak, McNeil, and Bergerson, "Beyond the Ballot," n.p.

16. Seley, *Politics of Public-facility Planning*, 60–61.

17. See the entire issue titled "Nashville Model Cities: A Case Study," *Vanderbilt Law Review* 25 (May 1972): 729–844, and for this note, 745 (hereafter cited as *VLR*); Seley, "Spatial Bias," 8–9; *Tennessean*, October 25 and November 3, 1967; *Banner*, November 9 and 10, and December 9, 1967; *Banner*, January 31, 1968; Zuzak, McNeil, and Bergerson, "Beyond the Ballot," n.p.; *New York Times*, November 26, 1967; *Fisk Forum*, March 3, 1967.

18. The sequence of events can be reviewed through the *Banner*, November 9 and 10, 1967; *Banner*, December 9, 1967 (Williams quotation); January 31 and February 14, 1968; *Tennessean*, January 13 and 31, and February 13, 1968; *New York Times*, March 17, 1968. See the April 9, 1968, letter from Marian Fuson and April 16 Fulton response in NMA-RF, "General Correspondence, E–F 1967–8" box, "General Correspondence F 1967–8" folder. LBJ administration perspective in LBJ-WHCF (GEN) HI2/ST 42, box 5, folder HI2/ST 42.

19. *Tennessean*, May 10 and 14, 1968; Zuzak, McNeil, and Bergerson, "Beyond the Ballot," n.p.; *VLR*, 746.

20. *Banner* and *Tennessean*, August 21, 1968; Seley, "Spatial Bias," 9; Zuzak, McNeil, and Bergerson, "Beyond the Ballot," n.p.; *VLR*, 746; "Model Cities Program Problem Analysis," 15–16. On the white businessmen's financing, see *VLR*, 748; Seley, "Spatial Bias," 9, and Lloyd, "Survey of Negro-Owned and Operated Business Enterprises in Nashville, Tennessee," 32; Ford, "Interstate 40 through Nashville, Tennessee," 54; Otey quoted in Whalen, "American Highway," 22.

21. Zuzak, McNeil, and Bergerson, "Beyond the Ballot," n.p.; Smith quoted in David Halberstam, "The End of a Populist," *Harper's* 242 (January 1971): 45. The *Tennessean*, May 4, 1971, cited "234 businesses, 10 churches and hundreds of homes" as being destroyed by I-40. For more on the interstate's effects, see Lloyd, "Survey of Negro-Owned and Operated Business Enterprises in Nashville Tennessee"; Hartmann, "Economic Analysis of Black Nashville" and Kithcart, "Intra-Urban Travel Patterns of the North Nashville Tennessee Black Community"; "The Interstates and the Cities: Highways, Housing, and the Freeway Revolt," 31. Steel fences and commercial development quotations in Pamela Ice, FU-BOHC; White, "Nashville's Model Cities Program," 2, respectively.

22. White, "Nashville's Model Cities Program," 3–4, 30; Zuzak, McNeil, and Bergerson, "Beyond the Ballot," 173, 179 (the Model Cities section is paginated, unlike the Interstate 40 section); *VLR*, 763 n174, but see White, "Nashville's Model Cities Program," 23. Regarding the "Real Estate Men," see Ansley Erickson, "Siting Schools: Desegregation and the Built Environment in Nashville, Tennessee" (unpublished paper, copy in possession of the author), 30. See also the overview and summary of Model Cities in NMA-UPP, box 4,

"Model Cities Evaluations" folder. For a case study of Model Cities in New Haven, Connecticut, see Powledge, *Model City*.

23. *VLR*, 737–38, 740. Even years later, citizens complained about the Volunteer Citizens Advisory Committee as "a non-representative, do-nothing group originated solely to secure token accommodation to federal guidelines on housing"—in *Leveller*, March 1969, NMA-CFCR. For HUD's view on Briley, see LBJ-WHCF Confidential LG (3 of 4), box 64 (2 of 2), Donald Dodge to John McLean, memo November 28, 1967.

24. *VLR*, 749–51, 754, 757–59; White, "Nashville's Model Cities Program," 6–7. See Zuzak, McNeil, and Bergerson, "Beyond the Ballot," 187, regarding the first meeting of the CCC in early October 1968.

25. *VLR*, 764–65; Zuzak, McNeil, and Bergerson, "Beyond the Ballot," 174, 180–81; White, "Nashville's Model Cities Program," 7, 22.

26. Defensiveness quotation in *VLR*, 765. See also White, "Nashville's Model Cities Program," 2; Zuzak, McNeil, and Bergerson, "Beyond the Ballot," 174, 175, 181 (dying quotation), 183, 188. Regarding home relocation values, see Zuzak, McNeil, and Bergerson, "Beyond the Ballot," 183; *Leveller* (newsletter), November 1969, in NMA-CFCR). See also this same pattern in Edgehill, shown in the September–October 1966 TCHR letter in SRC, series 14, reel, 215, folder 37, frame 1240. See the *Banner*, December 26, 1966, citing urban renewal's positive qualities.

27. *VLR*, 767–68, 770–71; Zuzak, McNeil, and Bergerson, "Beyond the Ballot," 176, 186–89; White, "Nashville's Model Cities Program," 9, 12–13. See also the *Leveller*, November 1969, regarding some of the frustrations in dealing with city officials (in NMA-CFCR).

28. *VLR*, 771–74; *Tennessean*, March 29, 1969.

29. *VLR*, 775–77, esp. 776 n222; Zuzak, McNeil, and Bergerson, "Beyond the Ballot," 190. On Rienhart's firing, see the *Tennessean*, September 12 and October 5, 1969, and *VLR*, 777 n229.

30. White, "Nashville's Model Cities Program," 12–15; *VLR*, 778–79, 788; Zuzak, McNeil, and Bergerson, "Beyond the Ballot," 186, 190. See the CCC's claim that the planners preferred to get CCC approval rather than involve the group throughout the process in the *Leveller*, November 1969, in NMA-CFCR.

31. *Tennessean*, October 21, 1969; *VLR*, 779–83; White, "Nashville's Model Cities Program," 17–19; Zuzak, McNeil, and Bergerson, "Beyond the Ballot," 184, 189, and 195. For an example of Battle's coverage of Model Cities, see *Banner*, April 30, 1969. For an example of the suspicions of the CCC regarding the Nashville Housing Authority, see the *Leveller*, April 1969, in NMA-CFCR. For accusations on the "general climate of racism" in NHA, see *Tennessean*, June 14, 1966.

32. Zuzak, McNeil, and Bergerson, "Beyond the Ballot," 185; Mitchell quotations in the *Leveller*, November 1969, in NMA-CFCR; *Tennessean*, September 5, 1969.

33. Except for minor alterations in its bylaws, the NNCCC was exactly the same as the CCC. See also *VLR*, 784–87; Zuzak, McNeil, and Bergerson, "Beyond the Ballot," 195–96; White, "Nashville's Model Cities Program," 25, 28. Regarding the complaints to HUD, see *VLR*, 788 and 800, and the various correspondence and March 10, 1970, meeting minutes in NMA-UPP, box 5, "Minutes February 25–November 16" folder. Love's comment is in the March 16 meeting minutes in the same box and folder.

34. *VLR*, 798–99; White, "Nashville's Model Cities Program," 19, 21, 22, and 26; Zuzak, McNeil, and Bergerson, "Beyond the Ballot," 194. Drake had previously served in the

Metropolitan Action Commission—see White, "Nashville's Model Cities Program," 17 and 20, and Zuzak, McNeil, and Bergerson, "Beyond the Ballot," 192. See also Mitchell to Drake, letter January 2, 1970, NMA-UPP, box 4, "CCC" folder; and in the same citation, a same-day response. See *VLR*, 790, regarding the copy expense controversy and 799–80 on the firing. See also CCC meeting minutes, May 28, 1970, NMA-UPP, box 5, "Minutes February 25–March 16" folder.

35. The accusations of politics were due to Mitchell being head of the Davidson Independent Political Council in addition to the CCC; over time the latter would be seen as synonymous with the former—*VLR*, 821 n424. See White, "Nashville's Model Cities Program," 28–29; *VLR* 796 (esp. n327), 801–5, 809–10, 812, 813, 815, and 822. Drake quoted in White, "Nashville's Model Cities Program," 21 and flier on 26. On Lillard's accusation, see *Tennessean* and *Banner*, March 30, 1970. On the block meetings, see *VLR*, 817–18. See the June 6, 1972, report in NMA-UPP, box 12, 7.6 "June 1972" folder; councilman quoted from *Banner* story reprinted in *Model Cities Responder* (February 1972), in NMA; NMA-UPP, box 12, 7.8 "August 1972" folder; reprint of Dick Battle column in *Model Cities Responder* (July 1972), NMA.

36. White, "Nashville's Model Cities Program," 7, 8; Zuzak, McNeil, and Bergerson, "Beyond the Ballot," 176, 190; *Liberation Message* (newsletter) (September 1971), 36.

37. Carey, "City Swept Clean," n.p.; NMA-CFCR, *Leveller*, April and November 1969; *Newsweek*, October 11, 1971; Chamber of Commerce Board of Governor's Meeting minutes, November 18, 1965, TSLA-COC, reel 2, no frame. VU's complaints about "inaccuracies, omissions, and unjustified inferences" in the *Newsweek* article, as well as information on the federal lawsuit, is in *Versus* (the student magazine of Vanderbilt), October 8, 1971.

38. See the December 1970 Liberation Message in NMA-CFRC; *Tennessean*, April 3, 1968; *Tennessean*, September 5, 1968; Cole, "A Booby-trapped Magic Carpet Ride," *Nashville!* 2 (February 1975): 20, 26–27; Johnson and Sieveking, "Homeowners' Attitudes Toward Neighborhood Integration," NPL-NR, 1–2; "impunity" in RISL-MRR, box 11, folder 159; "Inner City Blight: Analysis-Proposals," Metro Planning Commission, September 1973, 32–33.

39. Vivian Henderson, "Housing Among Negroes in Nashville," February 28, 1962, ARC-TU-RDD, box 23, folder 17.

40. *Maxwell v. County Board of Education of Davidson County, Tennessee*, 203 F. Supp. 768 M.D. Tenn. 1960, filed September 19, 1960; D. Doyle, *Nashville Since the 1920s*, 257. See also Pride and Woodard, *Burden of Busing*; "Chronology of Major Events Related to Desegregation Case, Metropolitan Public Schools," in "Building Our Future: Metro Schools Plan for School Improvement" (February 1998), NMA, hereafter cited as "Chronology"; quotation on the Nashville Plan being in vogue in Wyatt, "A Report on School Desegregation in Nashville and Davidson County," April 1963, SBHLA-CLC, series AR 138-2, box 20, folder 17. On Davidson County integration, see the *Tennessean* and *Banner*, October 19, 1960. On black legal pressure, see *Banner*, October 22 and December 12, 1960, and August 23, 1961; *Tennessean*, December 13, 1960, and February 21, 1961. Williams quoted in *Tennessean*, July 20, 1960.

41. "Chronology"; Wyatt, "Report on School Desegregation in Nashville and Davidson County"; 1965 information in NCRC board of directors minutes, April 26, 1965, VUSC-NMFP, box 2, folder 19; teacher and administrator information is in *Jet*, December 5, 1963, and TSLA-HRC, box 362, folder 2. See also "Voice of the Movement," June 4, 1963, VUSC-KMS, box 134, folder 7; NAACP letter to school officials, letter May 4, 1964, VUSC-KMS, box

56, folder 2; "Enrollment of Negro Pupils in Desegregated Schools By Year," VUSC-NMFP, box 3, folder 13.

42. Leo C. Rigsby and John Boston, "Patterns of School Desegregation in Nashville, 1960–1969," NMA-UOM, box 2, folder 5, 2. See TSLA-BEP, box 107, folder 6, for the proposal for this study.

43. Rigsby and Boston, "Patterns of School Desegregation," 5, 7, 8, 10. See also the notes in VUSC-JEP, box 5, folder 3, where John Egerton notes the "arbitrary definitions" of "desegregation" and "racial balance" from federal courts; progress report, October 11, 1966, VUSC-JEP, box 5, folder 3. For more on neighborhood demographics pushing school integration, see the *Tennessean*, September 6, 1969, regarding North High School becoming all-black because of the "residential geographical zones." The article further noted that the natural solution would be to divide Nashville in "pie-shaped zones" so as to simultaneously incorporate inner-city and suburban schools, but that "the schools are in the wrong places" to do this. See also the case of Glendale Elementary School discussed in John Egerton's notes, VUSC-JEP, box 5, folder 3.

44. On busing generally, see Gary Orfield, *Must We Bus?*; Douglas, *Reading, Writing, and Race*; Graglia, *Disaster by Decree*; Wilkinson, *From Brown to Bakke*; Formisano, *Boston against Busing*.

45. Transportation director in *Tennessean*, June 14, 1993; one-third figure in Egerton notes, VUSC-JEP, box 5, folder 3; Williams quoted in *Tennessean*, September 6, 1969 (where Z. Alexander Looby, by contrast, argued that "busing is not going to help the situation . . . you have got to change people's hearts"); *Tennessean*, March 14, 1971; transportation director in *Banner*, February 21, 1997; John Egerton to Frank Grisham, letter November 19, 1968, VUSC-JEP, box 5, folder 4.

46. On the Moore situation, see the *Tennessean*, May 25 and September 2, 1969, and on the board's ultimate decision, see John Egerton's notes in VUSC-JEP, box 5, folder 3, and *Tennessean*, December 6, 1970. School board chair quoted in *Tennessean*, September 2, 1969. See also *Tennessean*, June 22, 1969, and Pride and Woodard, *Burden of Busing*, 64–65. On legal background, see H. Scott, "Desegregation in Nashville."

47. *Tennessean*, September 4, 1969, and February 12, 1971. Color scale recounted in *Tennessean*, May 23, 1979; Wilkinson in *Tennessean*, June 14, 1993. See also Pride and Woodard, *Burden of Busing*, 62.

48. On Miller's rulings, see "Chronology"; Dick Battle, "Nashville in the Summer of 1970," *Nashville Citizen Attitude Survey*, NPL-NR; *Tennessean*, September 7, 1969, and August 23 and 26, 1970. Regarding the resentment, see *Banner*, August 12, 1970; *Tennessean*, August 15 and 20, 1970; Kershaw quoted in "Visitors Corner," *Banner*, January 26, 1971.

49. Battle, "Nashville in the Summer of 1970"; *Banner*, August 13, 1970; *Tennessean*, August 15 and 16, 1970.

50. *Tennessean*, August 18, 20, and 23, 1970. The proposed zones are detailed in the *Tennessean*, August 22, 1970. Avon Williams, "Impact of the Recent Integration Efforts of Metropolitan Nashville Schools: A Panel Discussion—17 January 1971 speech by Avon Williams," VUSC-JEP, box 7, folder 8. See also the *Tennessean*, September 6, 1969, for the accusation that McGavock and Rose Park schools were built to perpetuate segregation.

51. *Tennessean*, August 26, December 19 and 20, 1970; *Tennessean*, February 28, 1971; Morton quoted in *Tennessean*, March 12, 1971; *Banner*, March 11, 1971. See also Pride and Woodard, *Burden of Busing*, 63, 69.

52. *Tennessean*, March 16 and 17, 1971. Jenkins would later link the unconstitutionality of busing to property values, saying that by driving house values down, busing violated white rights (*Banner*, June 29, 1971).

53. *Tennessean*, March 14, 1971; *Banner*, March 12, 1971; *Tennessean* editorial, March 13, 1971; Pride and Woodard, *Burden of Busing*, 71. On the meeting, see *Tennessean*, March 16, 1971, which noted an "obvious scarcity of blacks in the audience." Note also that a second smaller meeting at the American Legion, with an estimated nine hundred people attending, discussed legal appeals against busing. Despite having registered their disagreement with busing, Tennessee senators Howard Baker and William Brock declined to attend the rally, a fact not lost on the speakers.

54. *Tennessean*, March 20, 1971; *Banner*, March 18, 1971; Smith in the *Torch* (First Baptist newsletter), March 28, 1971, VUSC-KMS, box 38, folder 15; Carl Rowan in *Arkansas Gazette*, March 30, 1971.

55. *Banner* editorial, March 17, 1971; *Tennessean*, April 2, 1970. On Anderson, see *Tennessean*, March 20, 1971, and *Banner*, March 18, 1971. Carl Rowan noted that Anderson was a Nixon appointee in his column in the *Arkansas Gazette*, March 30, 1971, and strongly upbraided Anderson for his extralegal tactics to please Jenkins and "undermine" Judge Morton. There did seem to be some element of collusion or at least coordination between Jenkins and Anderson: see *Tennessean*, March 16 and 17, 1971; *Washington Post*, June 2, 1971. See *Tennessean*, March 20, 1971, for black leaders condemning Anderson's remarks.

56. On Briley, see D. Doyle, *Nashville Since the 1920s*, 218; Barrett quoted in Halberstam, "End of a Populist," 43. On Davidson County's support for Wallace, see Moody, "Effects of Metro on Negro Politics," 45; *Banner*, April 25, 1969; and *Beverly Briley and the Black Community*" (flier), undated, VUSC-JEP, box 7, folder 8; Halberstam, "End of a Populist," 41–42.

57. *Tennessean*, March 14 and 17, 1971; *Banner*, March 17, 1971.

58. This information is derived from the *Tennessean*, June 6, 1971, which compares the three plans. Note that Williams submitted two plans, the second one being more far-reaching than the one excerpted here. Note also that the article claimed that HEW's compromise plan was modeled after ones previously adopted by federal courts. See also the HEW plan explained in the *Tennessean*, June 8, 1971; *Banner*, March 17, 1971. Note also that the board presented last-minute amendments that borrowed from the other plans—see *Tennessean*, June 10, 1971.

59. *Tennessean*, June 7 and 10, 1971; *Banner*, June 8 and 9, 1971; HEW expert quoted in *Tennessean*, June 9, 1971.

60. *Tennessean*, June 29, 1971, which includes a full-text reprinting of the decision; *Banner*, June 29, 1971 (with a breakdown of the schools and their respective enrollments, as well as the Dorrier and Briley quotations); Frank Sutherland, "School Desegregation: A Report Card from the South," VUSC-JEP, box 24, folder 1. See also *Tennessean*, June 30, 1971, which clarifies that Morton chose HEW's plan for integrating elementary schools but changed the zones to decrease black percentages in North and Pearl High Schools, and used the board's proposal that clustered junior high schools to serve as "feeders" into Mc-Gavock Comprehensive High School. The term "escape valve" was used by Avon Williams in the same context in *Tennessean*, June 7, 1971. See also NSBM, June 30, 1971, where the decision to appeal was approved, although one board member worried about "false hope." See also the *Tennessean*, July 27, 1971; Briley's request for funding in NMA-BBBF, "School

Busing 1970–1" box, "Law Dept." folder; "School Desegregation in Nashville Davidson County" (Washington, D.C.: U.S. Commission on Civil Rights, 1977).

61. Rosentene B. Purnell (Fisk professor of English) to Beverly Briley, letter October 22, 1971; Kelly Miller Smith and Charles Walker to HEW, letter October 16, 1971, both in NMA-BBBF, "School Busing 1970–1" box, "Letters re: Busing (1971)" folder. See also the *Tennessean*, December 8, 1971, regarding the cleaning up of black schools.

62. Jack G. Stubblefield to Beverly Briley, letter June 30, 1971; James H. McCabe to *Banner*, letter July 1, 1971; Mrs. Wesley Stephens to Beverly Briley, letter August 11, 1971; Mrs. Frances Cunniff to Beverly Briley, letter July 27, 1971; Maxine Schoggen to Beverly Briley, letter August 26, 1971—all in NMA-BBBF, "School Busing, 1970–1" box, "Letters: Busing" folder.

63. *Tennessean*, September 3, 1969; Srouji, "Something Old, Something New, and Something Segregated," *Nashville!* 3 (April 1975), 30–35, 51–57, quotation on 32. See also Pride and Woodard, *Burden of Busing*, 85–106.

64. Srouji, "Something Old, Something New, and Something Segregated," 30, 31; Sutherland, "School Desegregation"; John Egerton, "Private Schools in Nashville-Davidson County, Tennessee," in Richard Fields, ed., *The Status of Private Segregated Academies in Eleven Southern States*, NAACP Legal Defense and Educational Fund, Division of Legal Information and Community Service report, September 1972, in VUSC-JEP, box 10, folder 1, 9; Bob Holladay, "Bus Stop: Nashville Rethinks Desegregation," *Nashville Scene*, July 18, 1996, 25, on Williams.

65. Fields, *Status of Private Segregated Academies in Eleven Southern States*, 33; Egerton, "Private Schools," 3, 5, 10; on page 7 he lists the new schools in academic year 1971–62. White parent quoted in Srouji, "Something Old, Something New, and Something Segregated," 34, 52.

66. *Tennessean*, September 6, 1971; *Banner*, September 7, 1971; *Tennessean*, October 4, 1998; *Banner*, February 21, 1997; *Banner*, September 8, 1971; Pride and Woodard, *Burden of Busing*, 73. Metro Nashville Education Association official to Robert Horton, letter October 11, 1971, and memo regarding busing incident, November 1, 1971, both in NMA-BBBF, "School Busing 1970–1" box, "Police Dept." folder; Ginger Carey to Briley, letter October 3, 1971, NMA-BBBF, "School Busing 1970–1" box, "Letters re: Busing (1971)" folder.

67. See Wrigley, "From Housewives to Activists."

68. *Banner*, September 15 and 17, 1971; *Tennessean*, September 18, 1971; *New York Times*, September 17, 1971. Regarding threats of violence, see the mayor's request for evidence against those "people who are calling the schools and others indicating bomb threats," September 10, 1971 (and another document from September 13, 1971), in NMA-BBBF, "Briley School Busing, 1970–1" box, "Mayor's Office" folder, and the September 13, 1971, Metro public schools news release in NMA-BBBF, "Briley School Busing, 1970–1" box, "Board of Ed Misc." folder. See also the September 15, 1971, police memo regarding threatening calls to a teacher: "they did not object to her being there as much as they did the students but wanted both out," NMA-BBBF, "Briley School Busing, 1970–1" box, "Police Dept." folder.

69. On the Methodist picketing, see *Tennessean*, April 10, 1969; on WVOL, see Ward, *Radio and the Struggle for Civil Rights in the South*, 281–82; on liberation theology in black Nashville churches, see *Tennessean*, February 10, 1971; on black politics, see Moody, "Effects of Metro on Negro Politics," 58; NMA-CFCR, "Liberation Message SPECIAL ISSUE," April 1971; TSU *Meter*, April 23, 1971.

70. Moody, "Effects of Metro on Negro Politics," 44 and 49; Harold Love, FUSC-BOHC (on black elites and urban renewal); Edwin Mitchell, FUSC-BOHC (not evolving). On the DCIPC, see NMA-CFCR, *Liberation Messenger*, September 1971.

71. NMA-CFCR, "SPECIAL ISSUE," *Liberation Messenger*, April 1971; Banks quoted in *Race Relations Reporter*, January 3, 1972, 7; Edwin Mitchell and Amos Jones ("let us down") both in FUSC-BOHC.

72. All quotations in Mansfield Douglas except "not active" in A. A. Birch; Charles Pruitt and Mansfield Douglas on black elites and urban renewal; see also Harold Love ("lack of identification"), all in FUSC-BOHC. See also *Tennessean*, May 4, 1971.

73. M. S. Boman to Beverly Briley, letter September 9, 1971; David M. Thompson to Beverly Briley, letter August 17, 1972, both in NMA-BBBF, "School Busing 1970–1" box, "Letters: Busing" letter; Brooks in *Banner*, September 20, 1971; on the study, see Pride and Woodard, *Burden of Busing*, 107–25.

Epilogue. Achieving Justice

1. *New York Herald Tribune* article reprinted in the *Tennessean*, May 21, 1963.

2. *Memphis Press Scimitar*, March 6, 1979; *New York Times*, October 29, 1995; Cleve Francis interviewed by John W. Rumble, December 29, 1995, CMHOF-OH.

3. Quoted in the *Tennessean*, May 21, 23, and 24, 1979.

4. *Banner*, September 2, 1972, includes figures on private school enrollments; see also the *Tennessean*, December 13 and 17, 1971. Quotes from the *Tennessean*, July 22, 1973, and *Banner*, August 25, 1976. See also *Tennessean*, July 29, 1973, about the educational ramifications of private schools, and John Egerton, "Private Schools in Nashville-Davidson County, Tennessee," in Richard Fields, ed., *The Status of Private Segregated Academies in Eleven Southern States*, September 1972, VUSC-JEP, box 10, folder 1, 11.

5. See the overview in Pride and Woodard, *Burden of Busing*; Goldring and Smrekar, *Shifting from Court-Ordered to Court-Ended Desegregation in Nashville*.

6. *Tennessean*, June 5, 8, and 14, 1977.

7. Websdale, *Policing the Poor*, xi; Kreyling, *Plan of Nashville*.

8. Hartmann, "Economic Analysis of Black Nashville," 13, 261; Parks, "Grasping at the Coattails of Progress," 135, 142, 248–49.

9. Smith quoted in David Halberstam, "The End of a Populist," *Harper's* 242 (January 1971): 44; Lillard quoted in *Banner*, January 27, 1995.

10. Litwack, *Trouble in Mind*, 11; Kasson, "Taking Manners Seriously."

11. For more on urban changes according to race, see especially Silver and Moeser, *Separate City*; Bayor, *Race and the Shaping of Twentieth-Century Atlanta*.

12. Nash paraphrased in Payne, *I've Got the Light of Freedom*, 419.

13. Mitchell speech, March 19, 1968, VUSC-NMFP, box 1, folder 10.

BIBLIOGRAPHY

Manuscript and Archival Sources in Nashville

CMHOF	Frist Library and Archive, Country Music Hall of Fame
OH	Oral Histories
VF	Vertical Files
FUSC	Fisk University, John Hope and Aurelia Elizabeth Franklin Library, Special Collections
CSJ	Charles S. Johnson Collection
GEH	George Edmund Haynes Collection
RBJ	Ralph B. Johnson Papers
RP	Rosenwald Papers
ZAL	Z. Alexander Looby Collection
JFA	Jewish Federation of Nashville, Annette Levy Ratkin Jewish Community Archives
JCC	Jewish Community Center Bombing File
NMA	Nashville Metropolitan Archives
AF	Audiotape Files
BBOF	Beverly Briley Office Files
BBBF	Beverly Briley Busing Files
CFCR	Clippings Files (Civil Rights)
MDC	Metropolitan Davidson County government records
MHRC	Metropolitan Human Relations Commission
RF	Richard Fulton Papers
UPP	Urban Policy Papers
NPL	Nashville Public Library
ETS	Everett Tilson Scrapbook
NBCF	Nashville Banner Clippings Files
NR	Nashville Room Collections
NSBM	Metropolitan Nashville School Board Minutes
SBHLA	Southern Baptist Historical Library and Archives
CLC	Christian Life Commission Papers
HFP	Henry Franklin Paschall Papers
TSLA	Tennessee State Library and Archives
BEP	Buford Ellington Papers

DEPCF	Department of Education: Commissioner's Files
FGC	Frank Goad Clement Papers
HFS	Highlander Folk School Papers
HRC	Human Relations Commission
JEN	James Emerick Nagy Nashville Public Schools Collection
MEP	Merl Eppse Papers
COC	Nashville Chamber of Commerce records
OAGR	State of Tennessee Office of the Attorney General and Reporter
VUSC	Vanderbilt University Special Collections
CHP	Centennial History Project
CMSP	Charles Madison Sarratt Papers
CSP	Cecil Sims Papers
DDP	Donald Davidson Papers
JEP	John Egerton Papers
JSP	James Stahlman Papers
KMS	Kelly Miller Smith Papers
LSP	Lou Silberman Papers
NMF	Nelson and Marian Fuson Papers
SPC	Southern Politics Collection

Manuscript and Archival Sources Outside Nashville

AJA	Jacob Rader Marcus Center of the American Jewish Archives, Cincinnati, Ohio
ARC-TU	Amistad Research Center, Tulane University
AMAP	American Missionary Association Papers
IAD	Inez Adams Papers
BPVP	Bonita and Preston Valien Papers
RRD	Race Relations Department
EU-MARBL	Emory University, Manuscript, Archives, and Rare Book Library
CCP	Connie Curry Papers
NBF	*Newsweek* Bureau Files
RCP	Robert Churchwell Papers
VHP	Vincent Harding Papers
GSU-SLA	Georgia State University, Southern Labor Archive
EVP	Emory Via Papers
PCP	Paul Christopher Papers
HUHL	Harvard University, Houghton Library
DTMC	Dispatches from *Time* magazine correspondents
LBJ	Lyndon B. Johnson Library and Museum, Austin, Tex.
NACCD-ES	National Advisory Committee on Civil Disorders—Embargoed Series
WHCF-C	White House Central File—Confidential
WHCF	White House Central Files
RISL	Radcliffe Institute, Arthur and Elizabeth Schlesinger Library, Harvard University
MRR	Martha Ragsdale Ragland Papers

SCRBC	Manuscripts, Archives, and Rare Books Division, Schomburg Center for Research in Black Culture, the New York Public Library, Astor, Lenox and Tilden Foundations
AMP	August Meier Papers
EBP	Ella Baker Papers
UNC-SHC	University of North Carolina, Wilson Library, Southern Historical Collection
AMP	Alan McSurely Papers
DPP	Dan Powell Papers
DSP	Don Shoemaker Papers
GJP	Guion Johnson Papers
TBP	Taylor Branch Papers
USM	University of Southern Mississippi, McCain Library and Archives
WDC	Will D. Campbell Papers
UVA	University of Virginia, Albert and Shirley Small Special Collections Library
JBP	Julian Bond Papers
SSOC	Southern Student Organizing Committee Papers

Oral History Collections

BCRI	Birmingham Civil Rights Institute
OHP	Oral History Project
FU-BOHC	Fisk University, Black Oral History Collection (various interviewers unknown)
	A. A. Birch, December 21, 1971
	Will D. Campbell, July 17, 1972
	Adrian Capehart, October 17, 1972
	James Chandler, February 6, 1973
	Mansfield Douglas, March 9, 1972
	Pamela Ice, April 6, 1972
	Quincy Jackson, June 28, 1972
	Amos Jones Jr., October 13, 1972
	Troy Jones, April 24, 1972
	Harold M. Love, November 21, 1972
	Edwin Mitchell, February 18, 1972
	Flem B. Otey III, January 16, 1973
	Charles Pruitt, March 31, 1972 and
	Frederick T. Work, May 27, 1972
	Minister Earl X (King), August 18, 1972
MSRC-RJBOHC	Howard University, Moorland-Spingarn Research Center Ralph J. Bunche Oral History Collection
	Michele Allen by Robert Wright, November 16, 1968
	Inman Otey by John Britton, November 30, 1967
	Paul Puryear by Stanley H. Smith, March 21, 1968
	Kelly Miller Smith by John Britton, December 22, 1967

C. T. Vivian by Vincent Browne, February 20, 1968

Andrew White by John Britton, November 28, 1967

Stephen J. Wright by Vincent Browne, [n.d.] 1973

NMA-CMGOH   Nashville Metropolitan Archives. Interviews compiled into Carole Bucy, *The Creation of Metropolitan Government, Nashville-Davidson County, Tennessee: An Oral History*. Nashville (Metropolitan Historical Commission, June 1995). All interviews by Carole Bucy, November 1994–June 1995 unless otherwise noted.

Neill Brown

Beverly Briley (by Paul Clements, 1980)

Mansfield Douglas

John Seigenthaler

UF-SPOHP   University of Florida, Samuel Proctor Oral History Program. All interviews by the author unless otherwise noted.

John Seigenthaler, June 16, 2003

Randall L. Falk, June 18, 2003

Ed Jones, July 2, 2003

Jack Kershaw, June 30, 2003

John Compton, June 11, 2003

William Barnes, June 26, 2003

Will D. Campbell, July 1, 2003

Will D. Campbell (by Susan Glisson), May 17, 2003

George Barrett, June 27 and 28, 2003

Everett Tilson, August 30, 2005

Microfilm Collections

SNCC   Student Non-violent Coordinating Committee Papers

CORE   Congress of Racial Equality Papers

SRC   Southern Regional Council Papers

NAACP   National Association for the Advancement of Colored People Papers

Court Cases and Government Documents

Frederick Brooks, et al., v. Beverly Briley, Mayor, etc., et al., 274 F. Supp. 538

Harold Thomas v. Louis H. Hibbits, 46 F. Supp 368 (M.D. Tenn. 1942)

Kelley et al. v. Board of Education of Nashville, 139 F. Supp. 578

Kelley v. Metro County Board of Education, 436 F. 2nd 856 (6th Cir. 1970)

Maxwell v. County Board of Education, 203 F. Supp. 768 (M.D. Tenn. 1960)

McKinnie v. Tennessee, 380 U.S. 449

McSwain v. County Board of Education of Anderson County, 104 F. Supp. (E.D. Tenn. 1952), rev'd 214 F. 2d. 131 (6th Cir. 1954)

Morrison Cafeteria Company of Nashville, Inc., v. Mitchell Lee Johnson, et al., 344 F. 2d 690 (6th Cir. 1965)

Nashville I-40 Steering Committee v. Ellington, 387 F.2d 179 (6th Cir. 1967) *cert. denied*, 390 U.S. 921 (1968)

Miscellaneous

Carawan, Guy. *The Nashville Sit-in Story.* New York: Folkways Records, FH 5590, 1960.

A Civil Rights Legacy. Civil rights presentation at Fisk University, n.d. (ca. 1980s). Available at Fisk University. John Hope and Aurelia Elizabeth Franklin Library. Videocassette.

"Clinton and the Law." *See It Now* CBS television news series, originally aired on January 6, 1957. Princeton, N.J.: Films for the Humanities and Sciences, videorecording number FFH 10809, 2000. Videocassette.

Randall, Edwin. *The Sit-in Story: The Story of the Lunch Room Sit-ins.* Album of radio broadcasts from the Friendly World Broadcasting Series. New York: Folkways Records, FH 5502, 1961.

Seley, John E. "Spatial Bias: The Kink in Nashville's I-40." Discussion Paper III (University of Pennsylvania: Regional Science Department, September 1970).

White, Jack E., Jr. "Nashville's Model Cities Program: An Unborn Partnership." Nashville: [Fisk University] Race Relations Information Center, February 1971.

Zuzak, Charles A., Kenneth E. McNeil, and Frederic Bergerson. "Beyond the Ballot: Citizen Participation in Metropolitan Nashville." A report from Urban Observatory of Metropolitan Nashville—University Centers. Knoxville: Bureau of Public Administration, University of Tennessee, 1971.

Books, Scholarly Articles, and Other Scholarly Works

Ackerman, Peter, and Jack Duvall. *A Force More Powerful: A Century of Nonviolent Conflict.* New York: St. Martin's, 2000.

Adonsom, June N. "Few Black Voices Heard: The Black Community and the Desegregation Crisis in Clinton, Tennessee, 1956." *Tennessee Historical Quarterly* 53 (spring 1994): 30–41.

Ahmann, Mathew H., ed. *The New Negro.* New York: Biblio and Tannen, 1969.

Alexander, Glenda Kate. "Dismantling Court Ordered School Desegregation: A Case Study of the Decision-making Process in Nashville, Tennessee." EdD dissertation, Peabody College of Vanderbilt University, 2001.

Anderson, Margaret. *The Children of the South.* New York: Farrar, Straus & Giroux, 1966.

Arsenault, Raymond. *Freedom Riders: 1961 and the Struggle for Racial Justice.* New York: Oxford University Press, 2005.

Badger, Tony. "Fatalism, Not Gradualism: Race and the Crisis of Southern Liberalism, 1945–1965." In *The Making of Martin Luther King and the Civil Rights Movement*, ed. Brian Ward and Tony Badger, 67–95. New York: New York University Press, 1996.

Bartley, Numan V. *The Rise of Massive Resistance.* Baton Rouge: Louisiana State University Press, 1969.

Bass, Jonathan S. *Blessed Are the Peacemakers: Martin Luther King, Jr., Eight White Religious Leaders, and the "Letter from Birmingham Jail."* Baton Rouge: Louisiana State University Press, 2002.

Bass, W. A. "In Nashville Schools." *National Education Association Journal* 52 (December 1963): 48–50.

Bayor, Ronald H. *Race and the Shaping of Twentieth-Century Atlanta*. Chapel Hill: University of North Carolina Press, 2000.

Beardslee, William R. *This Way Out Must Lead In: Life Histories in the Civil Rights Movement*. Westport, Conn.: Lawrence Hill and Co., 1983.

Bergeron, Paul H., Stephen V. Ash, and Jeanette Keith. *Tennesseans and Their History*. Knoxville: University of Tennessee Press, 1999.

Berry, Keith W. "Charles S. Johnson, Fisk University, and the Struggle for Civil Rights, 1945–1970." PhD dissertation, Florida State University, 2005.

Booth, David Albin. *Metropolitics: The Nashville Consolidation*. Lansing: Michigan State University, 1963.

Brake, Patricia E., and Howard H. Baker Jr. *Justice in the Valley: A Bicentennial Perspective of the U.S. District Court for the Eastern District of Tennessee*. Franklin, Tenn.: Hillsboro Press, 1998.

Branch, Taylor. *Parting the Waters: America in the King Years, 1954–1963*. New York: Simon & Schuster, 1988.

———. *Pillar of Fire: America in the King Years, 1963–1965*. New York: Simon & Schuster, 1998.

Brittain, David James. "A Case Study of the Problems of Racial Integration in the Clinton Tennessee High School." EdD dissertation, New York University, 1959.

Brown, Karen Fitzgerald. "The Black Press of Tennessee, 1865–1980." PhD dissertation, University of Tennessee, 1982.

Browning, Al. *On the Run*. Nashville: Rutledge Hill Press, 1989.

Bucy, Carole Stanford. "International Relations in the YWCA of Nashville: Limits and Dilemmas." *Tennessee Historical Quarterly* 61 (fall 2002): 190–92.

Buell, Emmett Harold, Jr. "Uncertain Warriors: The Political Roles of Members of an Antipoverty Agency Governing Board." PhD dissertation, Vanderbilt University, 1972.

Carey, Bill. *Chancellors, Commodores, and Coeds: A History of Vanderbilt University*. Knoxville, Tenn.: Clearbrook Press, 2003.

———. "A City Swept Clean: How Urban Renewal, for Better and for Worse, Created the City We Know Today." *Nashville Scene* (September 6, 2001), http://www.nashvillescene.com/Stories/News/2001/09/06/A_City_Swept_Clean/index.shtml, accessed November 15, 2006.

Carmichael, Stokely, with Ekwueme Michael Thelwell. *Ready for Revolution: The Life and Struggles of Stokely Carmichael*. New York: Scribner, 2003.

Carson, Clayborne. *In Struggle: SNCC and the Black Awakening of the 1960s*. Cambridge: Harvard University Press, 1981.

Carty, James W. *Nashville as a World Religious Center*. Nashville: Cullom & Ghertner, 1958.

Cell, John W. *The Highest Stage of White Supremacy: The Origins of Segregation in South Africa and the American South*. New York: Cambridge University Press, 1982.

Chafe, William. *Civilities and Civil Rights*. New York: Oxford University Press, 1980.

Chappell, David L. "The Divided Mind of Southern Segregationists." *Georgia Historical Quarterly* 82 (spring 1998): 45–72.

———. *Inside Agitators: White Southerners in the Civil Rights Movement*. Baltimore, Md.: Johns Hopkins University Press, 1998.

————. "Religious Ideas of the Segregationists." *Journal of American Studies* 32 (1998): 237–62.

————. *A Stone of Hope: Prophetic Religion and the Death of Jim Crow.* Chapel Hill: University of North Carolina Press, 2004.

Chavis, Douglas Carr. "The Underworld of Nashville: Its Character and Function as Based on Records of Personal Experiences of Prisoners in the Tennessee State Prison in Nashville." MA thesis, Fisk University, 1941.

Cloud, Fred. "Working Together for Social Change." In *Interracial Bonds*, ed. Rhoda Goldstein Blumberg and Wendell James Roye, 63–70. Bayside, N.Y.: General Hall, 1979.

Cmiel, Kenneth. "The Politics of Civility." In *The Sixties: From Memory to History*, ed. David Farber, 263–90. Chapel Hill: University of North Carolina Press, 1994.

Colburn, David R. *Racial Change and Community Crisis.* Gainesville: University of Florida Press, 1991.

Conkin, Paul K. *Gone with the Ivy: A Biography of Vanderbilt University.* Knoxville: University of Tennessee Press, 1985.

————. *Peabody College: From a Frontier Academy to the Frontiers of Teaching and Learning.* Nashville: Vanderbilt University Press, 2002.

————. *Southern Agrarians.* Nashville: Vanderbilt University Press, 1982.

Connelly, Thomas L. *Will Campbell and the Soul of the South.* New York: Continuum, 1982.

Coombs, Philip H. "The Search for Facts." *Annals of the American Academy* 304 (March 1956): 26–34.

Creighton, Wilbur F., Jr., and Leland R. Jackson. "Boys Will be Men—Middle Tennessee Scouting Since 1910." *Middle Tennessee Council Boy Scouts of America* (1983): 178.

Crespino, Joseph. *In Search of Another Country: Mississippi and the Conservative Counterrevolution.* Princeton, N.J.: Princeton University Press, 2007.

Crosbye, Emilye. *A Little Taste of Freedom: The Black Freedom Struggle in Claiborne County, Mississippi.* Chapel Hill: University of North Carolina Press, 2005.

Cumming, Douglas O. "Facing Facts, Facing South: The SERS and the Effort to Inform the South after *Brown v. Board*, 1954–1960." PhD dissertation, University of North Carolina, 2002.

Davidson, Donald. "Gulliver with Hay Fever." *American Review* 9 (summer 1937): 152–72.

————. "Preface to Decision." *Sewanee Review* 53 (summer 1945): 394–412.

————. "Regionalism and Nationalism in American Literature." *American Review* 5 (April 1935): 48–61.

————. "A Sociologist in Eden." *American Review* 8 (December 1936): 177–204.

Davies, Alfred T., ed. *The Pulpit Speaks on Race.* Nashville: Abingdon Press, 1956.

Davis, Allison, Burleigh Gardner, and Mary Gardner. *Deep South: A Social Anthropological Study of Caste and Class.* Chicago: University of Chicago, 1941.

Davis, Jack E. *Race against Time: Culture and Separation in Natchez Since 1930.* Baton Rouge: Louisiana State University Press, 2004.

Day, Matthew. "Flannery O'Connor and the Southern Code of Manners." *Journal of Southern Religion* 4 (2001), http://jsr.fsu.edu/2001/dayart.htm, accessed December 5, 2005.

DeGregory, Crystal A. "Kelly Miller Smith: The Roots of an Activist and the Nashville Movement." *A.M.E. Church Review*, 123 (spring 2008): 55–63.

Desmond, Antoinette S. "On Sitting." *Crisis* 62 (November 1955): 523–24.

Dinnerstein, Leonard, and Mary Dale Palsson, eds. *Jews in the South*. Baton Rouge: Louisiana State University Press, 1973.

Dittmer, John. *Local People: The Struggle for Civil Rights in Mississippi*. Urbana-Champaign: University of Illinois Press, 1994.

Dollard, John. *Caste and Class in a Southern Town*. New Haven, Conn.: Yale University Press, 1937.

Dorn, Sherman. "George Peabody College for Teachers, Race Relations and Education." Paper presented to the History of Education Society, 1997.

Douglas, Davison M. *Reading, Writing, and Race: The Desegregation of the Charlotte Schools*. Chapel Hill: University of North Carolina Press, 1995.

Doyle, Bertram. *The Etiquette of Race Relations in the South: A Study in Social Control*. Chicago: University of Chicago Press, 1937.

Doyle, Don H. *Nashville in the New South, 1880–1930*. Knoxville: University of Tennessee Press, 1985.

———. *Nashville Since the 1920s*. Knoxville: University of Tennessee Press, 1985.

Eagles, Charles W. "Towards New Histories of the Civil Rights Era." *Journal of Southern History* 76 (November 2000) 815–48.

Egerton, John. *Black Public Colleges: Integration and Disintegration*. Nashville: Race Relations Information Center, 1971.

———. *Nashville: The Face of Two Centuries: 1780–1980*. Nashville: Plus Media, 1979.

———. *Speak Now against the Day: The Generation Before the Civil Rights Movement in the South*. Chapel Hill: University of North Carolina Press, 1994.

———. "Tennessee's Long-Running Desegregation Drama." *Chronicle of Higher Education*, April 4, 1977, 6–7.

———. "Walking into History: The Beginning of School Desegregation in Nashville." *Southern Spaces*, 4 May 2009, http://southernspaces.org/2009/walking-history-beginning-school-desegregation-nashville, accessed 12 January 2012.

Egerton, John, and Thomas E. Wood, eds. *Nashville: An American Self-Portrait*. Nashville: Beaten Biscuit Press, 2001.

Elazar, Daniel J. *A Case Study of Failure in Attempted Metropolitan Integration: Nashville and Davidson County*. Chicago: University of Chicago, 1961.

Eskew, Glenn T. *But for Birmingham: The Local and National Movements in the Civil Rights Struggle*. Chapel Hill: University of North Carolina Press, 1997.

Fairclough, Adam. *Race and Democracy: The Civil Rights Struggle in Louisiana, 1915–1972*. Athens: University of Georgia Press, 1995.

———. *To Redeem the Soul of America: The Southern Christian Leadership Conference and Martin Luther King Jr.* Athens: University of Georgia Press, 1987.

Fleming, Cynthia Griggs. "C. T. Vivian: Disciple of Assertive Nonviolence." *AME Church Review* 118, no. 387 (July–September 2002): 26–54.

Ford, Hubert James, Jr. "Interstate 40 through Nashville, Tennessee: A Case Study in Highway Location Decision-making." MS thesis, University of Tennessee, 1970.

Formisano, Ronald P. *Boston against Busing: Race, Class, and Ethnicity in the 1960s and 1970s*. Chapel Hill: University of North Carolina Press, 1991.

Gilmore, Harlan W. *Racial Disorganization in a Southern City*. Nashville: McQuiddy Press, 1931.

Gilpin, Patrick J. "Charles S. Johnson and the Race Relations Institutes at Fisk University." *Phylon* 41 (3rd quarter, 1980): 300–311.

———. "Charles S. Johnson and the Southern Educational Reporting Service." *Journal of Negro History* 63 (July 1978): 197–208.

Gilpin, Patrick J., and Marybeth Gasman, *Charles S. Johnson: Leadership Beyond the Veil in the Age of Jim Crow.* Albany: State University of New York Press, 2003.

Glen, John M. *Highlander: No Ordinary School.* Lexington: University of Kentucky Press, 1988.

Goldring, Ellen B., and Claire Smrekar. *Shifting from Court-Ordered to Court-Ended Desegregation in Nashville.* University of North Carolina at Chapel Hill: UNC Center for Civil Rights, 2002.

Graglia, Lino A. *Disaster by Decree: The Supreme Court Decisions on Race and The Schools.* Ithaca, N.Y.: Cornell University Press, 1976.

Graham, Hugh Davis. *Crisis in Print: Desegregation and the Press in Tennessee.* Nashville: Vanderbilt University Press, 1967.

———. "Desegregation in Nashville: The Dynamics of Compliance." *Tennessee Historical Quarterly* 25 (summer 1966): 135–54.

Grant, Daniel R. "Metropolitics and Professional Political Leadership: The Case of Nashville." *Annals of the American Academy of Political and Social Science* 353 (May 1964): 72–83.

———. "Urban and Suburban Nashville: A Case Study in Metropolitanism." *Journal of Politics* 17 (February 1955): 82–99.

Green, Laurie Beth. *Battling the Plantation Mentality: Memphis and the Black Freedom Struggle.* Chapel Hill: University of North Carolina, 2007.

Greene, Lee Seifert. *Lead Me On: Frank Goad Clement and Tennessee Politics.* Knoxville: University of Tennessee Press, 1982.

Grubbs, David. "City-County Consolidation Attempts in Nashville and Knoxville, Tennessee." PhD dissertation, University of Pennsylvania, 1961.

Hahn, Steven. *A Nation under Our Feet: Black Political Struggles in the Rural South, From Slavery to the Great Migration.* Cambridge, Mass.: Belknap Press of Harvard University Press, 2003.

Halberstam. David. *The Children.* New York: Random House, 1998.

Hale, Grace Elizabeth. *Making Whiteness: The Culture of Segregation in the South, 1890–1940.* New York: Vintage Books, 1998.

Hall, Christopher Dean. "I-40's Route through North Nashville: The Path of Least Resistance." MS thesis, University of Texas—Austin, 1996.

Hampton, Henry, and Steve Fayer. *Voices of Freedom: An Oral History of the Civil Rights Movement from the 1950s through the 1980s.* New York: Bantam Books, 1990.

Hanson, Bertil L. *A Report on Politics in Nashville.* Cambridge, Mass.: Joint Center for Urban Studies of the Massachusetts Institute of Technology and Harvard University, 1960.

Hartmann, G. Bruce, "An Economic Analysis of Black Nashville." PhD dissertation, State University of New York at Albany, 1974.

Hawkins, Brett W. *Nashville Metro: The Politics of City-County Consolidation.* Nashville: Vanderbilt University Press, 1966.

————. "Public Opinion and Metropolitan Reorganization in Nashville." *Journal of Politics* 28 (May 1966): 408–14.

Haynes, Arthur Vetrease. *Scars of Segregation.* New York: Vantage Press 1974.

Hendricks, Jennifer. "Stokely Carmichael and the 1967 IMPACT Symposium: Black Power, White Fear, and the Conservative South." *Tennessee Historical Quarterly* 63 (winter 2004): 285–302.

Hogan, Wesley C. *Many Minds, One Heart: SNCC's Dream for a New America.* Chapel Hill: University of North Carolina Press, 2007.

Holleman, Margaret Martin. "The Evolution of Federal Housing Policy From 1892 to 1974 in Nashville, Tennessee." http://www.civicdesigncenter.org/policy-federalhousing.html, accessed December 13, 2005.

Hoskyns, Barney. *Say It One Time for the Brokenhearted: Country Soul in the American South.* New York: Bloomsbury Press, 1998.

Houston, Benjamin. "The Aquinas of the Rednecks: Reconciliation, the Southern Character, and the Bootleg Ministry of Will D. Campbell." *Sixties: A Journal of History, Politics, and Culture* 4, no. 2 (December 2011): 135–50.

————. "Donald Davidson and the Segregationist Intellect." In *Southern Character: Essays in Honor of Bertram Wyatt-Brown,* ed. Lisa Tendrich Frank and Daniel Kilbride, 160–77. Gainesville: University Press of Florida, 2011.

Jacoway, Elizabeth, and David R. Colburn. *Southern Businessmen and Desegregation.* Baton Rouge: Louisiana State University Press, 1982.

Johnson, Charles S. *Patterns of Segregation.* New York: Harper & Brothers, 1943.

Johnson, Charles W. *The Spirit of a Place Called Meharry: The Strength of Its Past to Share the Future.* Franklin, Tenn.: Hillsboro Press, 2000.

Johnson, Dale A., ed. *Vanderbilt Divinity School: Education, Contest, and Change.* Nashville: Vanderbilt University Press, 2001.

Jones, Yollette Trigg. "The Black Community, Politics, and Race Relations in the 'Iris City': Nashville, Tennessee, 1870–1954." PhD dissertation, Duke University, 1985.

Joseph, Peniel E. *Waiting 'til the Midnight Hour: A Narrative History of Black Power in America.* New York: Henry Holt, 2006.

Kapur, Sudarshan. *Raising Up a Prophet: The African American Encounter with Gandhi.* Boston: Beacon Press, 1992.

Kasson, John F. *Rudeness and Civility: Manners in Nineteenth-Century Urban America.* New York: Hill & Wang, 1990.

————. "Taking Manners Seriously." In *Manners in Southern History,* ed. Ted Ownby, 152–62. Jackson: University Press of Mississippi, 2007.

Kean, Melissa Fitzsimons. "'At a Most Uncomfortable Speed': The Desegregation of the South's Private Universities, 1945–1964." PhD dissertation, Rice University, 2000.

Kithcart, Phillip Eugene. "Intra-Urban Travel Patterns of the North Nashville Tennessee Black Community, 1969 and 1975." PhD dissertation, University of Cincinnati, 1981.

Klarman, Michael J. "How Brown Changed Race Relations: The Backlash Thesis." *Journal of American History* 81 (June 1994): 81–118.

K'Meyer, Tracy E. *Civil Rights in the Gateway to the South: Louisville, Kentucky, 1945–1980.* Lexington: University Press of Kentucky, 2009.

Kowal, Rebekah J. "Staging the Greensboro Sit-ins." *TDR: The Drama Review* 48 (winter 2004): 135–54.

Krause, Allen. "The Southern Rabbi and Civil Rights." MA thesis, Hebrew Union College, 1967.

Kruse, Kevin M. *White Flight: Atlanta and the Making of Modern Conservatism.* Princeton, N.J.: Princeton University Press, 2005.

Kreyling, Christine. *The Plan of Nashville: Avenues to a Great City.* Nashville: Vanderbilt University Press, 2005.

Kyriakoudes, Louis M. *The Social Origins of the Urban South: Race, Gender, and Migration in Nashville and Middle Tennessee, 1890–1930.* Chapel Hill: University of North Carolina Press, 2002.

Lamon, Lester C. "The Black Community in Nashville and the Fisk University Student Strike of 1924–1925." *Journal of Southern History* 40 (May 1974): 225–44.

———. *Blacks in Tennessee, 1791–1970.* Knoxville: University of Tennessee Press, 1981.

———. *Black Tennesseans, 1900–1930.* Knoxville: University of Tennessee Press, 1977.

Laska, Lewis L. "A History of Legal Education in Tennessee, 1770–1970." PhD dissertation, George Peabody College for Teachers, 1978.

Lassiter, Matthew D. *The Silent Majority: Suburban Politics in the Sunbelt South.* Princeton, N.J.: Princeton University Press, 2005.

Lewis, John, with Michael D'Orso. *Walking with the Wind—A Memoir of the Movement.* New York: Simon & Schuster, 1998.

Lipman, Eugene J., and Albert Vorspan, eds. *A Tale of Ten Cities: The Triple Ghetto in American Religious Life.* New York: Union of American Hebrew Congregations, 1962.

Litwack, Leon F. *Trouble in Mind: Black Southerners in the Age of Jim Crow.* New York: Knopf, 1998.

Lomax, Louis E. *The Negro Revolt.* New York: Signet, 1963.

Long, Herman H. "The Status of Desegregated Higher Education in Tennessee." *Journal of Negro Education* 27 (summer 1958): 311–17.

Lovett, Bobby L. *The African-American History of Nashville, Tennessee, 1780–1930: Elites and Dilemmas.* Fayetteville: University of Arkansas Press, 1999.

———. *The Civil Rights Movement in Tennessee: A Narrative History.* Knoxville: University of Tennessee Press, 2005.

Lynch, Amy. *Service Above Self: A History of Nashville Rotary.* Nashville: Rotary Club of Nashville, 1995.

Mauney, Connie Pat. *Evolving Equality: The Courts and Desegregation in Tennessee.* Knoxville: University of Tennessee Press, 1979.

McClelland, Janice M. "A Structural Analysis of Desegregation: Clinton High School 1954–1958." *Tennessee Historical Quarterly* 56 (winter 1997): 294–309.

McDuffie, Scott Patterson. "James Lawson: Leading Architect and Educator of Nonviolence and Nonviolent Direct Action Protest Strategies During the Student Sit-in Movement of 1960." MA thesis, North Carolina State University, 2007.

McGarrity, Patrick J. "Testing Nashville's Progressivism: The Sit-ins of 1960." MA thesis, Murray State University, 1993.

McGirr, Lisa. *Suburban Warriors: The Origins of the New American Right.* Princeton, N.J.: Princeton University Press, 2002.

McMillen, Neil R. *The Citizens' Councils.* Urbana: University of Illinois Press, 1971.

———. *Dark Journey: Black Mississippians in the Age of Jim Crow.* Urbana: University of Illinois Press, 1989.

————. "Organized Resistance to School Desegregation in Tennessee." *Tennessee Historical Quarterly* 30 (fall 1971): 315–28.

Meier, August, and Elliott Rudwick. *CORE: A Study in the Civil Rights Movement, 1942–1968*. New York: Oxford University Press, 1973.

————. "Negro Boycotts of Jim Crow Streetcars in Tennessee." *American Quarterly* 21, no. 4 (winter 1969): 755–63.

Meier, August, Elliott Rudwick, and Francis L. Broderick, eds. *Black Protest Thought in the Twentieth Century*. 2nd ed. Indianapolis: Bobbs-Merrill, 1971.

Meier, Leila A. "A Different Kind of Prophet: The Role of Kelly Miller Smith in the Nashville Civil Rights Movement, 1955–1960." MA thesis, Vanderbilt University, 1991.

Michel, Gregg L. *Struggle for a Better South: The Southern Student Organizing Committee, 1964–1969*. New York: Palgrave Macmillan, 2004.

Mohl, Raymond A. *The Interstates and the Cities: Highways, Housing, and the Freeway Revolt*. Washington, D.C.: Research Report Poverty and Race Research Action Council, 2002.

————. "Stop the Road: Freeway Revolts in American Cities." *Journal of Urban History* 30, no. 5 (July 2004).

Moody, Peter. "The Effects of Metro on Negro Politics." *Spectrum* 4 (fall 1965): 43–60.

Morris, Aldon. "Black Southern Student Sit-in Movements: An Analysis of Internal Organization." *American Sociological Review* 46 (December 1981): 744–67.

————. *The Origins of the Civil Rights Movement: Black Communities Organizing for Change*. New York: Free Press, 1984.

Moye, Todd J. *Let the People Decide: Black Freedom and White Resistance Movements in Sunflower County, Mississippi, 1945–1986*. Chapel Hill: University of North Carolina Press, 2004.

Murphy, Paul V. "The Social Memory of the South: Donald Davidson and the Tennessee Past." *Tennessee Historical Quarterly* 55 (fall 1996): 257–69.

Muse, Benjamin. *Ten Years of Prelude: The Story of Integration Since the Supreme Court's 1954 Decision*. New York: Viking Press, 1964.

"The Nashville Sit-ins: Nonviolence Emerges: Interviews with Marion Barry and John Lewis." *Southern Exposure* 9 (spring 1981): 30–32.

Newman, Mark. "The Catholic Church and Desegregation, 1954–1973." *Tennessee Historical Quarterly* 66 (summer 2007): 144–65.

————. "The Tennessee Baptist Convention and Desegregation, 1954–1980." *Tennessee Historical Quarterly* 57 (winter 1998): 236–57.

Norrell, Robert J. *Reaping the Whirlwind: The Civil Rights Movement in Tuskegee*. New York: Knopf, 1985.

O'Brien, Gail Williams. *The Color of the Law: Race, Violence, and Justice in the Post–World War II South*. Chapel Hill: University of North Carolina Press, 1999.

Ogbar, Jeffrey. *Black Power: Radical Politics and African American Identity*. Baltimore: Johns Hopkins University Press, 2005.

Olson, Lynne. *Freedom's Daughters: The Unsung Heroines of the Civil Rights Movement from 1830 to 1970*. New York: Scribner, 2002.

Oppenheimer, Martin. *The Sit-in Movement of 1960*. Brooklyn, N.Y.: Carlson, 1989.

Orfield, Gary. *Must We Bus? Segregated Schools and National Policy*. Washington, D.C.: Brookings Institute, 1978.

Ownby, Ted, ed. *Manners and Southern History.* Jackson: University Press of Mississippi, 2007.

Parks, Robert James. "Grasping at the Coattails of Progress: City Planning in Nashville, Tennessee 1932–1962." Master's thesis, Vanderbilt University, 1971.

Payne, Charles. *I've Got the Light of Freedom: The Organizing Tradition and the Mississippi Freedom Struggle.* Berkeley: University of California Press, 1995.

Peltason, J. W. *Fifty-Eight Lonely Men: Southern Federal Judges and School Desegregation.* New York: Harcourt, Brace & World, 1961.

Perry, Elisabeth Israels. "'The Very Best Influence': Josephine Holloway and Girl Scouting in Nashville's African American Community." *Tennessee Historical Quarterly* 52 (summer 1993): 73–85.

Perry, Jennings. *Democracy Begins at Home: The Tennessee Fight against the Poll Tax.* Philadelphia: Lippincott, 1944.

Powdermaker, Hortense. *After Freedom: A Cultural Study in the Deep South.* New York: Viking Press, 1939.

Powell, Gloria J. *Black Monday's Children: A Study of the Effects of School Desegregation on Self-concepts of Southern Children.* New York: Appleton-Century-Crofts, 1973.

Powledge, Fred. *Model City: A Test of American Liberalism—One Town's Efforts to Rebuild Itself.* New York: Simon & Schuster, 1970.

Pride, Richard A., and J. David Woodard. *The Burden of Busing: The Politics of Desegregation in Nashville, Tennessee.* Knoxville: University of Tennessee Press, 1985.

Pye, David Kenneth. "Complex Relations: An African-American Attorney Navigates Jim Crow Atlanta." *Georgia Historical Quarterly* 91, no. 4 (winter 2007): 453–77.

Quinn, Elizabeth Lasch. "How to Behave Sensitively: Prescriptions for Interracial Conduct from the 1960s to the 1990s." *Journal of Social History* 33 (winter 1999): 421–22.

Ramsey, Sonya. "More than the Three R's: The Educational, Economic, and Cultural Experiences of African American Female Public School Teachers in Nashville, Tennessee, 1869–1893." PhD dissertation, University of North Carolina at Chapel Hill, 2000.

———. *Reading, Writing, and Segregation: A Century of Black Women Teachers in Nashville.* Urbana-Champaign: University of Illinois Press, 2008.

———. "We Will Be Ready Whenever They Are: African American Teachers' Responses to the *Brown* Decision and Public School Integration in Nashville, Tennessee, 1954–66." *Journal of African American History* 90, no. 1–2 (winter 2005): 29–51.

Ramsey, William T., ed. *Bench and Bar II.* Nashville: Nashville Bar Foundation, 2003.

Redd, George N. "Educational Desegregation in Tennessee—One Year Afterward." *Journal of Negro Education* (summer 1955): 333–47.

Ritterhouse, Jennifer. *Growing Up Jim Crow: How Black and White Southern Children Learned about Race.* Chapel Hill: University of North Carolina Press, 2006.

———. "Reading, Intimacy, and the Role of Uncle Remus in White Southern Social Memory." *Journal of Southern History* 69 (August 2003): 585–622.

Robbins, Richard. *Sidelines Activist: Charles S. Johnson and the Struggle for Civil Rights.* Jackson: University Press of Mississippi, 1996.

Ross, Rosetta E. *Witnessing and Testifying: Black Women, Religion, and Civil Rights.* Minneapolis, Minn.: Augsberg Fortress Press, 2003.

Sanders, Katrina Marie. "Building Racial Tolerance through Education: The Fisk University Race Relations Institute, 1944–1969." PhD dissertation, University of Illinois Urbana-Champaign, 1997.

———. "Seeking Racial Tolerance: The Fisk University Race Relations Institute." *Journal of the Midwest History of Education Society* 25, no. 1 (1998): 116–19.

Sarratt, Reed. *The Ordeal of Segregation: The First Decade.* New York: Harper & Row, 1966.

Sarvis, Will. "Leaders in the Court and the Community: Z. Alexander Looby, Avon Williams, Jr., and the Legal Fight for Civil Rights in Tennessee, 1940–1970." *Journal of African American History* 88 (winter 2003): 42–58.

Scott, Hugh J. "Desegregation in Nashville: Conflicts and Contradictions in Preserving Schools in Black Communities." *Education and Urban Society* 15 (February 1983): 235–44.

Scott, Mingo, Jr. *The Negro in Tennessee Politics and Governmental Affairs, 1865–1965: The Hundred Years Story.* Nashville: Rich Printing, 1964.

Schultz, Debra L. *Going South: Jewish Women in the Civil Rights Movement.* New York: New York University Press, 2001.

Schultz, Mark. *The Rural Face of White Supremacy: Beyond Jim Crow.* Urbana: University of Illinois Press, 2005.

Scruggs, Afi-Odelia E. *Claiming Kin: Confronting the History of an American Family.* New York: St. Martin's Press, 2002.

Seley, John E. *The Politics of Public-facility Planning.* Lexington, Mass.: D. C. Heath & Co., 1983.

Self, Robert O. *American Babylon: Race and the Struggle for Postwar Oakland.* Princeton, N.J.: Princeton University Press, 2003.

Sessions, Jim, and Sue Thrasher. "A New Day Begun" (interview with John Lewis). *Southern Exposure* 4 (fall 1976): 37–48.

Shimeall, Kent M. "Merger as a Remedy in Higher Education Desegregation: *Geier v. University of Tennessee.*" *University of Toledo Law Review* 11, no. 3 (spring 1980): 511–38.

Shoemaker, Don, ed. *With All Deliberate Speed: Segregation-Desegregation in Southern Schools.* New York: Harper & Bros., 1957.

Silver, Christopher, and John V. Moeser. *The Separate City: Black Communities in the Urban South, 1940–1968.* Lexington: University Press of Kentucky, 1995.

Smith, J. Douglas. *Managing White Supremacy: Race Politics and Citizenship in Jim Crow Virginia.* Chapel Hill: University of North Carolina Press, 2002.

Smith, Kelly Miller. "We Seek a City." In *The Pulpit Speaks on Race*, ed. Alfred T. Davies, 177–83. New York and Nashville: Abingdon Press, 1956.

Sosna, Morton. *In Search of the Silent South: Southern Liberals and the Race Issue.* New York: Columbia University Press, 1977.

Spinney, Robert G. "The Jewish Community in Nashville, 1939–1949." *Tennessee Historical Quarterly* 52 (winter 1993): 225–41.

———. "Municipal Government in Nashville, Tennessee, 1938–1951: World War II and the Growth of the Public Sector." *Journal of Southern History* 61 (February 1995): 77–112.

———. *World War II in Nashville: Transformation of the Homefront.* Knoxville: University of Tennessee Press, 1998.

Street, Joe. *The Culture War in the Civil Rights Movement.* Gainesville: University of Florida Press, 2007.

Stritch, Thomas. *The Catholic Church in Tennessee: The Sesquicentennial Story.* Nashville: Catholic Center, 1987.

Sugrue, Thomas J. *The Origins of the Urban Crisis: Race and Inequality in Postwar Detroit.* Princeton, N.J.: Princeton University Press, 1996.

Sullivan, Patricia. *Days of Hope: Race and Democracy in the New Deal Era.* Chapel Hill: University of North Carolina Press, 1996.

Summerville, James. "The City and the Slum: 'Black Bottom' in the Development of South Nashville." *Tennessee Historical Quarterly* 40, no. 2 (1981): 182–92.

———. *Educating Black Doctors: A History of Meharry Medical College.* Tuscaloosa: University of Alabama Press, 1983.

Sumner, David E. "The Local Press and the Nashville Student Movement, 1960." PhD dissertation, University of Tennessee, 1989.

———. "The Publisher and the Preacher: Racial Conflict at Vanderbilt University." *Tennessee Historical Quarterly* 56 (spring 1997): 34–43.

Thornton, Mills J. *Dividing Lines: Municipal Politics and the Struggle for Civil Rights in Montgomery, Birmingham, and Selma.* Tuscaloosa: University of Alabama Press, 2002.

Thrasher, Sue. "Fifty Years with Highlander." *Southern Changes* 4, no. 6 (1982): 4–9.

Tuck, Stephen G. N. *Beyond Atlanta: The Struggle for Racial Equality in Georgia, 1940–1980.* Athens: University of Georgia Press, 2001.

Tyson, Timothy B. *Radio Free Dixie: Robert F. Williams and the Roots of Black Power.* Chapel Hill: University of North Carolina Press, 2001.

Van Deburg, William L. *New Day in Babylon: The Black Power Movement and American Culture, 1965–1975.* Chicago: University of Chicago Press, 1992.

Van Til, William. *My Way of Looking at It: An Autobiography.* San Francisco, Calif.: Caddo Gap Press, 1996.

Walker, Jenny Louise. "Black Violence and Nonviolence in the Civil Rights and Black Power Eras." PhD dissertation, University of Newcastle-upon-Tyne, 2000.

Walzer, Michael. "The Politics of the New Negro." *Dissent* (summer 1960): 235–43.

Ward, Brian. *Just My Soul Responding: Rhythm and Blues, Black Consciousness, and Race Relations.* Berkeley: University of California Press, 1998.

———. *Radio and the Struggle for Civil Rights in the South.* Gainesville: University Press of Florida, 2004.

———, ed. *Media, Culture, and the Modern African American Freedom Struggle.* Gainesville: University Press of Florida, 2001.

Ward, Brian, and Anthony J. Badger, eds. *The Making of Martin Luther King and the Civil Rights Movement.* New York: New York University Press, 1996.

Warren, Robert Penn. "Episode in a Dime Store." *Southern Review* 30 (autumn 1994): 650–57.

Webb, Clive. *Fight against Fear: Southern Jews and Black Civil Rights.* Athens: University of Georgia Press, 2001.

———. "Outside Agitator: John Kasper and the Desegregation Crisis in Clinton, Tennessee." In *Making a New South: Race, Leadership, and Community After the Civil War*, ed. Paul A. Cimbala and Barton C. Shaw, 171–90. Gainesville: University of Florida Press, 2007.

———. *Rabble Rousers: The American Far Right in the Civil Rights Era.* Athens: University of Georgia Press, 2010.

Websdale, Neil. *Policing the Poor: From Slave Plantation to Public Housing.* Boston: Northeastern University Press, 2001.

Weinstein, Eugene A., and Paul N. Geisel. "Family Decision Making over Desegregation." *Sociometry* 25 (March 1962): 21–29.

Wilhoit, Francis M. *The Politics of Massive Resistance.* New York: G. Braziller, 1973.

Wilkinson, Harvie J., III. *From* Brown *to* Bakke: *The Supreme Court and School Integration: 1954–1978.* New York: Oxford University Press, 1979.

Wills, Ridley, II. *A Brief History of the YMCA of Nashville and Middle Tennessee.* Nashville: YMCA of Nashville and Middle Tennessee, 1996.

Winchell, Mark Royden. *Where No Flag Flies: Donald Davidson and the Southern Resistance.* Columbia: University of Missouri Press, 2000.

Woodard, Komozi. *Nation within a Nation: Amiri Baraka and Black Power Politics.* Chapel Hill: University of North Carolina Press, 1999.

Woody, George Washington, Jr. "The Natural History of a Slum Area and Some of Its Inherent Characteristics." MA thesis, Fisk University, 1940.

Wrigley, Julia. "From Housewives to Activists: Women and the Division of Political Labor in the Boston Antibusing Movement." In *No Middle Ground: Women and Radical Protest,* ed. Kathleen M. Blee, 251–88. New York: New York University Press, 1998.

Wynn, Linda. "The Dawning of a New Day: The Nashville Sit-ins, February 13–May 10, 1960." *Tennessee Historical Quarterly* 50 (spring 1991): 42–54.

INDEX

Nashville General Hospital, 15, 157, 160
Nashville Globe, 33, 40, 102; on black
    teachers, 37, 79–80; on Clement, 65–66;
    on Kasper, 76; on school desegregation,
    54, 68, 77, 81
Nashville Housing Authority (NHA), 203,
    216, 219
Nashville Plan (for public school
    desegregation), 8, 66–68, 71–72, 83, 225;
    adopted by Davidson County, 220; as
    attractive to other school systems, 79;
    contested by NAACP attorneys, 220–
    21; gaining legal sanction, 78–79; and
    Nashville school board, 63–64
Nashville Tennessean, 39–40, 48, 104; on
    Brown, 48, 65, 68, 72, 224; on demon-
    strations, 110, 114, 128, 134, 147, 150,
    155–56, 159; on housing, 237; and Metro,
    135, 137; on Nashville's national image,
    147, 158; on North Nashville, 173, 178,
    208, 209, 215; on pool closings, 127; and
    Southern School News, 50–51; on Stokely
    Carmichael, 179
National Association for the Advancement
    of Colored People (NAACP): activist style
    of Nashville chapter, 111, 132, 157; and
    DCIPC, 233; and Hume-Fogg vocational
    school, 133; Lawson critique of, 121;
    Looby lawsuits, 37; Nashville chapter, 33,
    51, 54–55, 58, 83; reaction of Nashville
    chapter to Nashville Plan, 71, 80; rivalries
    of Nashville chapter with NCLC, 83,
    108–9, 151, 156
New York Herald Tribune, 235
Nichol, Harry, 103, 104
Nixon, Richard, 226–28
Nobles, Gene, 16
nonviolence, 6, 8, 120, 240; aggressive,
    162–63; as identified with Nashville, 5; in
    lunch-counter campaign (1960), 83–84,
    88–92, 104, 117; reservations about, 91–
    92, 120–21, 139, 155, 176, 185–86; struggles
    with in 1960s, 143–44. *See also* civil
    rights activism
North Nashville, 164, 174; ghettoization of,
    220, 238; heart of black Nashville, 13, 23,

25, 32; Interstate 40 and, 205–12; Model
    Cities and, 212–18; redevelopment of,
    204, 213

O'Connor, Flannery, 17
Odour, Ralph, 166
Oliver, William H., 68, 76, 79, 154
Operation Open City, 124, 133, 151, 153,
    162
Otey, Flem B., 99, 142, 153, 211–12
Otey, Inman, 176–78
Owen, William, 195

Pancake Pantry, 191
Parents School Preference Committee, 66,
    68, 70, 72, 74, 76–77
Parent-Teacher Association, 66, 80–81;
    black chapter in Davidson County, 53
Parthenon, 205
Paschall, H. Franklin, 162
Peabody College for Teachers, 25, 153;
    integration in, 55–56; as interracial
    venue, 41
peace movement, 181
Pearl High School, 15, 143, 156
Pioneer Christian Academy, 231
Pitts, Greenfield, 86, 107, 110, 117
Plan of Progress, 130
police brutality: in Black Power era, 166,
    171, 175–78, 199; against civil rights
    demonstrators, 128, 154–55, 165–66; in
    Jim Crow era, 20, 22, 38; against whites,
    74, 166
police collusion with criminals, 96, 125–27,
    138; and Z. Alexander Looby bombing,
    115
police spying, 164, 168, 179, 181, 184
politics, Nashville, 30–32; city council race
    (1947), 35; and corruption, 30; culture
    of, 30; local elections (1938), 31; mayoral
    power enhanced, 32; patronage, 36;
    political apathy, 199; political machines,
    30, 137, 169, 183, 218, 233; politicized
    interstate debate, 210; public policy, 6;
    redistricting (1949), 36
poll tax, 40

pool closings, 133, 149–50
Post House restaurant, 107
Powell, Rodney, 108
public accommodation, 6, 8; bill to desegregate, 133, 156, 157, 163
public housing, 25, 32, 238

racial etiquette: Black Power and, 169, 196, 199–200; falseness in, 239; food and, 15–16, 138–39; forbidden space, 82; manners and white identity, 17–18; and "naming," 19, 20, 22; nonviolence and, 82, 89–90, 98, 103, 105–6, 121; politeness, 162; shifts during 1960s, 147, 163, 196, 234, 240; and urban segregation, 6–9, 11, 14–15, 19–20, 22–24, 26, 235, 239. *See also* African Americans; civil rights activism; segregated patterns; whites
Ragland, Martha, 184, 186, 190, 192–93; clashes with Baxton Bryant, 187–88; speech on white power, 186–87
Reinhart, William, 211, 213, 215
religion (in Nashville): and conflict, 80; groups as paternalistic, 41–42; institutions, 28; and "John Barnett," 123; and Oral Roberts, 85–86; and private schools, 230; and race, 109, 126, 150, 152–53, 157, 162; religiosity of Nashville, 28
Rempfer, Robert W., 48–49, 54
Richbourg, "John R," 16
riots, 168, 199, 209; aftermath of Stokely Carmichael's visit, 174–79; and Stokely Carmichael visit, 170–74
Rollins, Metz, 83, 143–45, 152, 235
Roman Catholicism, 24, 29, 109
Rotary Club, 146, 161; Sorace speech to, 182
Rowan, Carl, 227

Sarratt, Madison, 107, 109
Save Our Schools, 224
Scarritt College, 28, 41, 55
segregated patterns: on buses and trains, 13–14; color blindness, 234; cultural realm of segregation, 16; dentists and patterns of, 21; downtown, 1; economic

considerations of, 20, 141, 147, 238; erosion in, 7; in hospitals, 150–51, 160–61; interracialism and, 15–16, 31, 59, 64, 199; in music realms, 17; in neighborhoods, 2, 6, 23, 223; in physical space, 23, 241; racial superstition, 146; and swimming pools, 127, 150; and tokenism, 79, 131, 149, 151, 223; and voluntary association, 150, 224, 239; water fountains, 15; and women, 41. *See also* African Americans; civil rights activism; racial etiquette; whites
segregation in education: Davidson County schools, 53; desegregating faculties, 221, 223–24; desegregating Tennessee universities, 54; first day of desegregated public schools, 47; locating schools as escape valves, 229; and neighborhood schools, 223, 229, 239; 1963 as pivotal year, 221; and pairing schools, 223–24; school placement, 225; voluntary preference plan, 72, 76–77. See also *Brown v. Board of Education*; busing; Nashville Plan
segregation in employment, 6, 8–9, 36, 221, 233; early focus of NCLC (1960), 86; focus during 1960s civil rights activism, 124, 128–30, 132, 150–51, 160, 163
segregation in housing: and Interstate 40, 206; and Model Cities, 212–17; in Nashville, 3, 23, 25, 32, 64, 237–38; realtors, 209, 212, 215, 220; and school desegregation, 73, 79, 224; slums, 25, 32, 202–3, 212, 219–20; and urban renewal, 202, 204, 219–20
segregationists, 105, 167; lack of organization, 117–18; rally before Clement, 58–59; resistance to *Brown* decision, 51, 53, 55, 58, 60–61, 65, 68, 70; response to sit-ins, 105–6; and Vanderbilt, 56. *See also* whites
Shacklet, Earl C., Jr., "Buddy," 226
Shea, Ed, 143
Shinn, Roger L., 81
Silverman, William B., 77, 78
Simple Simon, 138, 143

Sims, Cecil, 57, 68, 238–39; and *Brown* ruling, 58; similarities with Donald Davidson, 58

sip-in, 157–58

sit-ins (1960 lunch-counter campaign), 82; aftermath, 124, 129, 132; and "Big Saturday," 94, 99, 100–102; and biracial committee, 106–7, 109–10, 112–13; embodying segregated hypocrisies, 86; financial support, 99; legacy of, 5, 8, 121; media, 100–101; merchants, 107, 117; merchants and whites, 118; negotiations over, 112–13; and "ol' Green Hat," 97–98; questionable legality of, 119; resolution, 119; segregationist response to, 105–6; unifying black community, 99; white gangs at, 95–96

sleep-in, 134

Sloan, John, 86, 106, 107, 110

Smith, Kelly Miller: on Baxton Bryant and TCHR, 190, 192; on busing, 230; and civil rights activism during the 1960s, 124, 126, 128, 133, 140–42, 145; fears for safety, 165; founding NCLC, 82–84; on Great Society, 183; on Interstate 40, 212; on Lawson, 85; on Lewis, 87; on Lillard, 37; and lunch-counter campaign (1960), 85, 87, 92, 94, 109, 111, 117, 121; move to Cleveland, 152; on Nashville etiquette, 239; on nonviolence, 176; and school desegregation, 70, 80

Solid Block, 34–35

Sorace, John, 167–68, 171–72, 174, 179, 181–82, 184; testimony before McClellan Committee, 181–82

Southern Baptist Convention, 162

Southern Christian Education Fund (SCEF), 182

Southern Christian Leadership Conference (SCLC), 82

Southern Conference for Human Welfare (SCHW), 40

Southern Education Reporting Service (SERS), 50

Southern Regional Council, 40, 125, 186, 190

Southern School News, 50–51, 80; and Bonita Valien, 50–51

Southern Student Organizing Committee, 179, 182

South Nashville, 23–25

Stahlman, James: ability to hound enemies, 40, 41, 45; background of, 38–39, 44, 61; and James Lawson, 104, 106; and John Kasper, 74; and lunch counter sit-ins (1960), 94–95; racist views of, 180–81; and Stokely Carmichael, 168, 173, 179–81

Stainback, Charles A., 51; and Stainback bill, 61

stand-ins, 125

St. Anselm's Episcopal Church, 172, 181–82

Stephens, Earnest, 174

Stroud, Fred, 69, 73, 75

St. Thomas, 160–61

St. Thomas Catholic Hospital, 150

Student Nonviolent Coordinating Committee (SNCC), 5, 114, 195, 199; and Stokely Carmichael visit, 171, 173, 174, 175

Students for a Democratic Society (SDS), 179

suburbs, 6, 10, 202, 204, 212; Grand Ole Opry, move to, 236; and Sun Belt, 10

Tennessee Council on Human Relations (TCHR), 40–41, 149; internal debates in, 187–91; symbolic of liberal rifts, 193

Tennessee Federation for Constitutional Government (TFCG), 52–53, 63–64, 72, 105, 167, 185, 224; and Citizens' Councils, 52; and civil disobedience, 53; and interposition, 65; and Kasper, 66; and race and Constitutional questions, 52–53; and rejected political candidates, 61–62

Tennessee General Assembly, 62, 64–65, 79, 84, 198

Tennessee State Capitol, 13

Tennessee State University, 27, 50, 57, 88, 114; color consciousness in, 28; rivalries with Fisk, 100; SNCC chapter, 198; student rebelliousness in, 197, 199

Thurmond, Strom, 61, 168, 170

Tic Toc restaurant, 125, 138, 154, 156–58, 160

Todd, Molly, 95

Trailways bus terminal, 125, 126
Tripp's restaurant, 160
12th Avenue South, 238

Una School, 232
Uncle Tom (stereotype), 38, 126, 171, 189, 217
Union Station, 134
Unitarian church, 109
United Church Women, 53, 94, 119

Valien, Bonita H., 50–51
Vanderbilt, Harold S., 169
violence: and Black Power era, 125, 151,
    168, 175–79, 182, 185–86; and lunch-
    counter sit-in campaign (1960), 94,
    103, 106, 111, 113–14, 117; lynchings, 22;
    in Nashville, 9, 10, 22, 195, 199, 240–41;
    during 1960s civil rights demonstrations,
    106, 108, 126–27, 138–39, 144–47, 156, 158;
    relationship to nonviolence, 89–90; and
    school desegregation, 53, 63, 66, 74
Vivian, C. T., 83, 108, 111, 115–16, 158
Vultee aircraft plant, 28

Waggoner, Porter, 236
Walker, Claude, 152
Walker, Matthew, 108
Walker, Maxine, 96
Wallace, George, 62, 147–48, 228
Wallace, Perry, 193–94
Ware, George Washington, 174, 185–86
War Memorial Auditorium, 116, 226
War on Poverty, 184
Watauga Club, 30
Wedgewood Avenue, 238
Weinstein, Eugene, 80
West, Ben, 4, 11, 109, 233, 235; courthouse
    meeting with (1960), 115–16; handling of
    sit-ins (1960), 94, 102, 104, 106, 112; and
    Metro, 135–37; and pool closings, 127;
    and proposed public accommodations
    ordinance, 133; rise to power, 35–37; and
    school desegregation, 67, 70; and urban
    renewal, 212
West End Avenue, 25, 154–55
Whip restaurant, the, 160

White, Andrew, 151–53, 160
whites (in Nashville): attitudes to black
    voting, 35; backlash, 187; banks, 15;
    boycotts, 130, 226, 232; businesses,
    214, 230; changing attitudes to blacks
    (1960s), 148–49; civil rights supporters,
    178; connections to black underworld,
    31; conservatism of, 239; delusions, 234;
    dentists and professional groups, 21;
    liberal divisions, 192–93; liberals, 4, 38,
    43, 59, 113, 169, 225; moderates, 4, 8, 10,
    48, 51, 74, 80–81, 145, 164–65, 193, 241;
    networks of conservatives, 38; networks
    of progressives and segregationists, 8;
    political and business elite, 3, 5–6, 18, 135,
    144, 151, 200; reactions to busing, 226,
    230; school officials, 71; and segregation,
    89–90; white flight, 6, 25, 79, 135, 136;
    white Nashville Way, 4–5, 234, 235, 239;
    whiteness, 239; white resistance, 8–10.
    See also segregationists
Wilkinson, DeLois, 224
Williams, Avon: and busing lawsuit,
    225–28; and CCC, 216; and hospital
    employment, 161; and Interstate 40, 209–
    10; and jail, 158; on James Lawson, 108;
    and Nashville Plan, 220–23; and private
    schools, 231; on Stokely Carmichael, 176
Williams, Robert F., 128, 181
Wilson, Leroy, 172, 181
Wilson-Quick Pharmacy, 134, 138–40, 142–
    43, 148
Windrow, J. E., speech, 2–3
WLAC, 16
Wood, Del, 236
Woodmont Country Club, 29
Woodruff, James, 174, 181, 185, 200
Woolworth's, 93, 95–97, 107, 113
Wright, Stephen J., 99, 106, 157; harassment
    of, 100
WVOL, 233

YWCA, 139

zoning, 64, 79, 137, 222–24. See also
    Nashville Plan

POLITICS AND CULTURE IN THE TWENTIETH-CENTURY SOUTH